6

VOICES AGAINST DEATH

VOICES AGAINST DEATH

American Opposition to
Capital Punishment, 1787-1975

Edited by
PHILIP ENGLISH MACKEY

Preface by Hugo Adam Bedau

BURT FRANKLIN & CO., Inc.
NEW YORK

364.6
V889

© 1976 Burt Franklin & Co., Inc.
New York

All rights reserved.
No part of this book may be reproduced
in whole or in part by any means,
including any photographic, mechanical,
or electrical reproduction, recording, or information
storage and retrieval systems,
without the prior written consent of the publisher,
except for brief quotations for
the purposes of review.

Library of Congress Cataloging in Publication Data
Main entry under title:

Voices against death.

Bibliography: p.
Includes index.
1. Capital punishment—United States—Addresses,
essays, lectures. I. Mackey, Philip English.
HV8699.U5.V64   364.6'6'0973   75-33199
ISBN 0-89102-062-4
ISBN 0-89102-038-1 lib. bdg.

This book has been printed on
Warren 66 Antique Offset,
chosen for its high
degree of permanency, good quality,
and acid-free characteristics.

CONTENTS

PREFACE

In the twenty-six selections Philip Mackey has assembled, we are presented with the first opportunity to examine nearly two hundred years of argument by critics of the death penalty in America. And what an impressive range and variety that argument has! The diversity of the texts themselves—essays, reports, letters, poems, debates, briefs—reflects the many different kinds of audiences before whom death penalty abolitionists have pled their cause. Likewise, reflected in the pages that follow, the abolition movement in this country has had spokesmen of every vocation: lawyers, doctors, legislators, journalists, editors, poets, feminists, social scientists, clergymen, prison wardens, condemned convicts, executioners. Ideologically, the diversity has been no less great: religious and secular, conservative and radical, utilitarian and contractarian, egoist and altruist—both sides of these familiar dichotomies have their representatives in the two centuries of opposition to punishment by death.

In the polemics, exposés, tracts, testimonials, petitions, and scholarly studies that make up these position papers by American abolitionists, one can amply document both continuities and discontinuities in the themes and arguments. In reading them over myself, I have been struck with several features of the abolitionist cause that are readily apparent only when viewed historically. An historical perspective is especially valuable if, as will be true of many readers of this book, one's knowledge of the current death penalty controversy is based mainly on televised debates, news reports, and occasional essays weighing the increase of violent crime, the deterrent effect of severe sanctions, the de facto and de jure moratorium on executions in this country, and the failures of our prison system. For such readers, at least four features of the style and substance of the attacks over the past two centuries deserve notice.

First, the confidence with which our predecessors asserted empirical generalizations in support of their abolitionist convictions is little short of amazing, and even somewhat embarrassing. A century and more ago there were no reliable criminal, judicial, or penal statistics (some would complain that we have yet to obtain such data today, at least on a national scale). Yet without such statistics it is impossible to confirm, much less verify, many of the empirical claims on which rest the most familiar assertions of abolitionists. The ineffectiveness of the death penalty as a deterrent, the deterrent superiority of certainty over severity, the costs of administering a judicial system built around capital punishment, the racial and class bias of our society revealed in the administration of criminal justice where the death penalty is involved, the way mandatory capital statutes tend to result in jury nullification through acquittals or convictions for lesser crimes, the neglected role of capital punishment as a cause of homicide and suicide among the mentally unbalanced—none of these and many more equally crucial claims familiar in abolitionist literature throughout this and previous centuries are fit objects for rational belief without considerable empirical evidence.

Today such evidence is readily available in several books and monographs,[1] so much so that the main question still remaining is the academic one of whether these hypotheses are the best confirmed empirical beliefs in modern criminal science.[2] A century and more ago, however, none of them was more than conjecture. No abolitionist, from Dr. Benjamin Rush writing in the late 1700s to Newton M. Curtis speaking to his fellow Congressmen in 1892, had anything like the evidence in his possession needed to make such assertions with confidence.

The argument against the death penalty, of course, does not consist of a series of empirical hypotheses; consequently, the abolitionist position cannot be impeached or destroyed by exposing the weakness in the evidence for such empirical beliefs. For there are profound moral questions, relatively immune to any conceivable array of facts, which are raised by the practice of killing as punishment. Most of the selections that follow amply illustrate how difficult it is to answer these moral questions in a fashion supportive of the death penalty. Nevertheless, opponents of the death penalty have always relied upon a wide variety of empirical generalizations, especially in regard to the whole issue of deterrence; so much so that shock waves could at any time fracture and perhaps destroy the abolition movement if it could be convincingly shown that the death penalty were really necessary as a social defense and deterrent to violent crime.

The debate over these empirical questions continues down to the present. One can sample the kind of evidence that has had great impact on uncommitted observers by a careful study of selection 22, one of many essays by Thorsten Sellin in which the fruits of his empirical investigations on capital punishment in America have been reported to the general public. It is scholars like Sellin in this century who have transformed the abolitionist argument from one in which empirical beliefs were advanced to one in which empirical evidence is presented. As one reads through the selections that precede Sellin's, one occasionally feels as if the repeated assertion by one writer after another of such beliefs somehow made up for, even as it tends to disguise, the lack of evidence offered on their behalf. This is no longer true, and the abolitionist argument is much the stronger for it.

Second, like fashions in everything else, fashions in the dominant mode of argument against the death penalty have changed. Today few argue, as Edmund Clarence Stedman did a century ago or William Dean Howells did in 1900, that the wretched mess of bungled executions is a ghastly horror and can be avoided only by abolishing the death penalty altogether. Electrocution and gas have long since superceded hanging in most American jurisdictions as the only legal modes of execution. The relative reliability and cleanliness of these modes (along with the privacy and secrecy with which executions have been conducted since the 1930s) have blunted the Stedman-Howells argument and one never hears it any more, although it is true that only thirty years ago the State of Louisiana tried to electrocute Willie Francis and failed in the first attempt.[3] (Similar cases of bungled attempts to execute by lethal gas may exist, though I know of none.) But such ineptitude is rare, or anyway the reports of it are.

Similarly, the risk of executing an innocent man, not perhaps as prominently asserted in the selections below as one might have expected it to be (it is mentioned in the essays by Edward Livingston and Charles C. Burleigh), has all but vanished from the arguments of contemporary abolitionists. When this argument is advanced, it is transformed into a sophisticated reflection on the unfairness endemic to the plea bargaining structure of modern American criminal jurisprudence.[4]

The most obvious, not to say profound, change is in the all-but-complete disappearance of learned argument over the true meaning of Genesis 9:6 ("Whosoever sheddeth man's blood, by man shall his blood be shed"). As the following selections show, this text and the indisputable biblical record of capital punishment among the ancient Hebrews was a continuing topic of concern for abolitionists until well after the turn of this century. Textual scrutiny and interpretive analysis such as that found in selection 6 by Reverend Charles Spear in the 1840s by no means sufficed in its day to quell support for the death penalty among good Christian clergymen and laymen. The disappearance of this entire issue as a major preoccupation of the abolitionist argument can be dated from the time, half a century ago, when Clarence Darrow (represented in selection 16), an avowed secularist, became America's leading spokesman for abolition. Today, with most Jewish and Protestant and some Catholic religious organizations on record against the death penalty,[5] the dispute between abolitionists and retentionists revolves almost entirely on empirical and moral issues with no theological overtones like those that marked, and perhaps marred, the debates of a century ago.

Third, during recent years one issue more than others has tended to emerge as the central controversial question. Is the death penalty consistent with, or is it implicitly ruled out by, the United States Constitution? No one denies that when Rush and Livingston first voiced their opposition to capital punish-

ment in this country, few, if any, leading thinkers supposed that
the death penalty was incompatible with the Bill of Rights. A
century ago—even a generation ago—few responsible thinkers
thought differently. In the past decade or so, however, as Philip
Mackey explains in his Introduction, a growing number of lawyers, judges, attorneys general, senators, governors, and others
with legal training and juridical responsibilities have concluded
that capital punishment today is, indeed, forbidden by federal
Constitutional protections.[6] Today this controversy is far from
concluded, and another chapter will be written sometime during
1976 when the Supreme Court resolves the issues disputed in
Fowler v. North Carolina.

This profound change in attitude, which focusses on constitutional issues before our highest judicial tribunal, appears to
have been anticipated more than a century ago in the remarks
of one of America's most influential abolitionists. In the still-
interesting philosophical argument advanced by Robert Rantoul
to the Massachusetts legislature in the 1830s (selection 3), much
is made of every person's natural right to life, a right that Rantoul believed cannot be alienated, waived, or forfeited. (On this
last point, however, other rights theorists such as Locke and
Blackstone thoroughly disagreed; they supported the death
penalty with equanimity.) Rantoul joined to this line of reasoning the explicit protections of his state and the federal Constitutions. Then, with stunning prescience, he remarked:

> The whipping-post and the pillory survived, for a period, the consti-
> tutional prohibition of cruel and unusual punishments. They have
> disappeared, and the gallows, which is more unusual than either of
> those barbarities had been, and infinitely more cruel and revolting,
> must soon follow in their train. After the reformation shall have
> been accomplished, mankind will look back with astonishment at its
> tardy progress. They will be unable to comprehend how or why it
> was delayed so long.

Were Rantoul alive today, he could not but be gratified by the
1972 decision of the United States Supreme Court in *Furman v.
Georgia,* and by the interest taken since 1973 by the Massachusetts Supreme Judicial Court in several death penalty cases.[7]

It is a pity that Rantoul's constitutional reflections seem to have had little or no subsequent influence, and have been largely overlooked until resurrected by Professor Mackey in his diligent researches. The antepenultimate selection in this volume, the brief written in the *Furman* case by the Legal Defense Fund attorneys, shows the kind of ingenuity needed to transform Rantoul's insight into a persuasive legal attack on the death penalty. It is little wonder, perhaps, that it took well more than a century before lawyers were ready to present the Supreme Court with a sober attempt to overthrow the hoary practice of capital punishment on constitutional grounds. As the LDF brief shows, it takes a remarkable adaption of constitutional law, principles of justice, empirical generalizations, and social science research evidence to mount such an argument. Now, with the wisdom of hindsight, we can truly say that all the rest was prologue, and that two centuries of argument in this country against capital punishment have culminated in the series of legal briefs prepared in recent years by the LDF and presented to the Supreme Court.

Finally, the abolitionist cause has always been a single-issue movement, and its argument has always been a negative one. Opponents of the death penalty have never been united except on one point: the death penalty is not a justifiable and necessary mode of punishment. Whether the death penalty is legitimate in extreme or unusual circumstances—under martial law, for example, or in dealing with a Quisling or an Eichmann—is not something on which abolitionists have ever had a fixed position.

Neither have they had a uniform position on one far more important and immediate matter: the preferred alternative to the death penalty. Uncertainty and disagreement over the alternative to capital punishment stems partly from the very different views abolitionists have had on the proper nature and purpose of punishment in general. Obviously, Christian pacifists such as Spear are not likely to share the same general theory of punishment held by determinist humanists such as Darrow, even though they can make common cause against hangings. As the selections show, abolitionists have often been silent on the alternative they would substitute for the death penalty, or they have embraced the somewhat ambiguous idea of "life imprison- ment." As everyone with any knowledge of the criminal justice system realizes, "life imprisonment" covers a multitude of alter- natives: Is it a fixed or an indeterminate term of years? Does it involve solitary or communal confinement? Can parole eligibil- ity be achieved after serving a fixed minimum sentence? Is pa- role ever appropriate? It is neither sensible nor serious to advo- cate abolition of the death penalty without reasonably precise answers to these and other questions.

The following selections do not reveal disagreement over the answers as clearly as they might simply because most of the abolitionists recorded here either have kept their answers to themselves or have had no answers at all. Here, as elsewhere, politics—especially single-issue negative politics—tends to make uncomfortable bedfellows. Today, if not in earlier decades, op- ponents of the death penalty increasingly tend to be opponents also of the entire prison system, and their opposition to the one is likely to be based on substantial familiarity with the workings of the other. Accordingly, they are much more careful than were their predecessors not to attack executions only to end up defending "life imprisonment" without any possibility of pa- role. But discussion and documentation of the merger between the traditional abolitionist movement and the current move- ment to overthrow the prison system would take us well be- yond the confines of this book.

Similarly, just as current opponents of the death penalty in- creasingly tend to criticize all forms of punitive cruelty as well, so the old single-issue abolitionist organizations (chief among which has been the American League to Abolish Capital Punish- ment, founded in the 1920s by Darrow, Lawes, and others) have disappeared in the face of the adoption of anti-death penalty policies by multi-issue civil liberties and civil rights or- ganizations (notably, the American Civil Liberties Union and the Legal Defense Fund, whose abolitionism dates back roughly a decade). Here, again, a study of the social and political forces at work would take us far beyond the topic of the present volume.

Professional historians still owe us detailed intellectual, social, and legal studies of the history of capital punishment, and of the opposition to it, in the United States (students of English history have been much better served by scholars during the past decade than we have[8]). Meanwhile, thanks to Philip Mackey's careful winnowing of the vast and varied abolitionist literature, now at least we have the materials before us for a close look at the abolitionist cause, its several arguments, and its leading spokesmen, and that is no small contribution.

Hugo Adam Bedau

1. The most complete recent volume of social science research on capital punishment is William J. Bowers, *Executions in America* (Lexington, Mass.: D. C. Heath & Company, 1974). A volume of essays containing subsequent research, co-edited by H. A. Bedau and Chester M. Pierce, is scheduled to be published by AMS Press sometime in 1976.

2. See, e.g., the discussion of capital punishment as a deterrent in Franklin E. Zimring and Gordon J. Hawkins, *Deterrence: The Legal Threat in Crime Control* (Chicago: University of Chicago Press, 1973).

3. *Louisiana ex. rel. Francis v. Resweber,* 329 U.S. 459 (1947), discussed in detail in Barrett Prettyman, Jr., *Death and the Supreme Court* (New York: Harcourt, Brace & World, 1961), pp. 90-128.

4. See Charles L. Black, Jr., *Capital Punishment: The Inevitability of Caprice and Mistake* (New York: W. W. Norton & Company, 1974).

5. Evidence, and in several cases policy statements, of opposition to the death penalty from various sects, denominations, and religious bodies may be found in the three volumes of hearings published by Congress, as follows: "Abolition of Capital Punishment " Hearing Before Subcommittee No. 2, Committee on the Judiciary, H. R., 86th Congress, Second Session, 1960; "To Abolish the Death Penalty," Hearings before the Subcommittee on Criminal Laws and Procedures, Committee on the Judiciary, Senate, 90th Congress, 2nd Session, 1968; "Capital Punishment," Hearings before Subcommittee No. 3, Committee on the Judiciary, H. R., 92nd Congress, 2nd Session, 1972.

6. The modern constitutional argument against the death penalty originates with Gerald H. Gottlieb, "Testing the Death Penalty," *Southern California Law Review* 34 (Spring 1961), pp. 268-281, reprinted in H. A. Bedau, ed., *The Death Penalty in America* (Chicago:Aldine Publishing Co., 1967).

7. See *Commonwealth v. A Juvenile,* 300 N.E. 2nd 439 (1973), and *Commonwealth v. O'Neal,* argued in 1975.

8. The latest study is David D. Cooper, *The Lesson of the Scaffold: The Public Execution Controversy in Victorian England* (Athens: Ohio University Press, 1974).

INTRODUCTION

An Historical Perspective

THE COLONIAL BACKGROUND

The capital statutes of seventeenth-century America reflected British tradition transplanted to a number of heterogeneous colonies. Of consequence, they were harsh and varied.

New York was typical of the mid-seventeenth-century colonies: there, eleven crimes were capital. The so-called Duke's Laws of 1665 mandated death for denial of the true God; premeditated murder, slaying someone who had no weapon of defense, slaying by lying in wait or by poisoning; sodomy, buggery; kidnapping; perjury in a capital trial; traitorous denial of the king's rights or raising arms to resist his authority; conspiracy to invade towns or forts in the province; and striking one's mother or father (but only upon complaint of both).

Massachusetts' *Book of the General Lawes and Libertyes* of 1647 contained a similar list of capital crimes, but added witchcraft, adultery, cursing one's parents, and the crime of being a rebellious son. On the other hand, Massachusetts law made death discretionary for rape, permitting judges or the legislature to inflict "some other greivous punishment" if circumstances warranted.[1]

Rhode Island's original legal code of 1647 was somewhat more lenient. It directed death for arson, robbery, and burglary, it is true, but Roger Williams' more libertarian colony declined to kill blasphemers, idolators, adulterers, and fractious children. Moreover, in an enlightened feature, the Rhode Island law code excused "Fools" and those who "Steale for Hunger" from its capital provisions against burglary.[2]

To the south, the earliest settlers of Virginia were ruled for a time by an extremely harsh code. The "Divine, Moral and Martial Laws" of 1612 ordered death for a host of crimes including perjury, trading with Indians, stealing grapes, and unauthorized killing of horses, chickens, or dogs. The code was no empty threat, for Governor Sir Thomas Dale enforced many of its provisions with savage zeal. Yet such severity was likely to discourage colonists from settling in Virginia and the "Martial Laws" were abandoned during the reorganization of the Virginia Company in 1619. For the rest of the century, Virginia relied upon criminal laws roughly similar to those of New York.[3]

Pennsylvania and West Jersey were the sole exceptions to the rule of harsh penal policy in seventeenth-century America. The original Quaker settlers of these provinces, scorning the example of mother country and sister colonies, established but two capital crimes, treason and willful murder.[4]

During the course of their history, most of the American colonies added new capital crimes to their already broad criminal statutes. In this they followed the example of the mother country, where the number of capital offenses increased from about fifty in 1688 to over two hundred in the early nineteenth century. New York, for example, between 1665 and 1776 ordered capital punishment for such additional crimes as rape, burglary, grand larceny, mutiny, counterfeiting, and, in the case of slaves, for conspiracy, mutilation, attempted murder, attempted rape, and arson of any kind. Pennsylvania, so lenient in its early laws, authorized three new capital crimes for blacks in 1700 and twelve more, for blacks and whites alike, between 1718 and 1756. Rhode Island may have been the only colony to decrease the number of its capital crimes in the eighteenth century, omitting arson, rape, and witchcraft in successive revisions of its criminal code.[5]

All the American colonies, then, had severe criminal codes at the time of the American Revolution. All except Rhode Island threatened capital punishment for ten or more crimes. The means of execution, moreover, were such as to make the modern reader recoil. Felons were either hanged, often so clumsily that they died in slow agony, or burned at the stake (a method usually reserved for blacks and Indians). In either event, the execution took place in public, with rowdy onlookers jockeying for the best view. In some cases, the publicity of the punishment did not end with the criminal's death. The authorities sometimes ordered the corpse exhibited in a public place—in rare instances for periods exceeding a year—for the edification of potential wrongdoers.[6]

But, despite the severity of colonial criminal laws and practices, there is evidence of an underlying leniency toward criminals in American society of the mid-eighteenth century. No state actually carried out executions for each type of capital offense—in some cases because there were no offenders, perhaps, but in others because officials chose to ignore the laws. Even when prosecutors actively sought capital punishment, they often met resistance during the judicial process. Jurors might circumvent the mandatory capital punishment laws by ignoring the evidence and refusing to convict or by convicting for a lesser included offense. Judges might ignore the law and send a convicted felon to the whipping-post instead of the gallows. In certain cases, convicted felons themselves might invoke the so-called benefit of clergy, by which first offenders were branded and released. Other condemned men were saved by governors' pardons. All in all, there must have been a significant percentage of cases in which felons did not receive the capital punishment prescribed for their crimes. This undercurrent of leniency, this seeming reluctance to kill, probably resulted from America's low crime rate and chronic labor shortage. The colonies had undeniably harsh laws (though far milder than those of Europe), but the criminal justice system was more lenient in practice than it was in print.[7]

THE FIRST REFORMS, 1776-1800

The American Revolution produced no revolutionary changes in the criminal laws of the former colonies. The newly independent states, in fact, retained virtually all their old capital statutes and in some cases added to them. Virginia came closest to a "revolutionary" approach, perhaps, when the legislature, in November 1776, authorized Thomas Jefferson and four other men to undertake a complete revision of its laws. When the revisors met in early 1777, they agreed that capital punishment should be abolished for all crimes except treason and murder and wrote a bill incorporating this change. The legislature did not consider the bill until 1785, however, and then defeated it by a one-vote margin in the House of Delegates. Virginia, almost ten years after the break with England, was unwilling to break with English penal practices. [8]

In the 1770s and 1780s no other state considered similar revision of its colonial capital code. Yet most of the former colonies did repeal a few of their more truculent capital statutes. North Carolina, for example, in 1786, reduced its penalty for horse-theft from death to whipping, ear-cropping, and branding. Massachusetts, in 1784, abolished the death penalty for polygamy, larceny, and concealment of the death of a bastard child. New York repealed a number of colonial slave-conspiracy laws in 1788. [9]

Essentially untouched by such minor alterations, the capital laws of most states in 1790 exhibited much of their colonial severity. Capital punishment was commonly authorized for treason, murder, rape, arson, buggery, burglary, robbery, and counterfeiting. In a few states, it was also directed for such crimes as mayhem, horse-theft, and stealing from a church. Executions were actually carried out for the crimes of murder, arson, rape, burglary, robbery, forgery, counterfeiting, and unpremeditated killing. [10]

In a few states, however, most notably Pennsylvania, some Americans in the 1780s, imbued with revolutionary ideology and republican pride, began to question the morality and expediency of such harsh penal laws and cruel waste of life. The reformers' inspiration, like virtually all the intellectual currents of the new nation, came from Europe, where a number of Enlightenment philosophers and humanitarians had recently begun to suggest alternatives to draconian punishment. Most influential of the Europeans was the Italian jurist Cesare Beccaria

(1738-1794), whose *On Crimes and Punishment*, published in English in 1767, soon became popular among America's intellectuals. Montesquieu, Voltaire, and Bentham also provided stimulating ideas for concerned Americans. Pennsylvania proved especially receptive, too, to the writings and example of English Quaker prison reformers John Bellers and John Howard.[11]

As early as 1776 Philadelphians had organized a Society for Relieving Distressed Prisoners, but revolutionary turmoil had crippled its efforts. Interest in penal reform remained high in the state, though, and after the war a movement was quickly organized to advocate revision of the criminal code. The reform bore fruit in 1786, when the legislature abandoned many corporal punishments and abolished the death penalty for robbery, burglary, and unnatural crimes. Spurred in part by this success, reformers, many of them Quakers, in 1787 made another attempt to found a prison society. This organization, the Philadelphia Society for Alleviating the Miseries of Public Prisons, was considerably more successful than its short-lived predecessor. It inspired a number of significant reforms in its early years, improving the lot of prisoners and altering criminal law, and continues its work almost two centuries later as the Pennsylvania Prison Society.[12]

Inside and outside their new society, Philadelphia reformers advocated further reductions in the number of capital crimes. One renowned citizen, Dr. Benjamin Rush, went further when, in March 1787, he first proposed the complete abolition of capital punishment (see selection 1). Rush believed that capital punishment was contrary to both reason and divine revelation and he published several carefully argued defenses of this position.[13]

Rush's arguments for total abolition were too radical for most Americans, even most Pennsylvanians, of the day but he unquestionably accelerated the drive for reform of the statutes. Of greater importance to immediate reform interests was a pamphlet written by another prominent Pennsylvanian William Bradford. Bradford, attorney general of the state, undertook an investigation of capital punishment at the behest of the governor and, in 1793, produced *An Enquiry How Far the Punish-*

ment of Death is Necessary in Pennsylvania. Far from advocating complete abolition of the death penalty, Bradford was strong in his insistence upon its retention for murder, but he argued that capital punishment was useless in preventing some crimes. It was worse than useless, in fact, because it sometimes made convictions harder to obtain. A system of laws which encourages the acquittal of felons, Bradford reasoned, must be altered.[14]

The Pennsylvania legislature was quick to respond to such arguments from an official source, especially when they were buttressed by the humanitarian pleas of a powerful minority of citizens. In an act of April 22, 1794, the lawmakers abolished capital punishment for all crimes except first-degree murder. Pennsylvania, in eight years, had firmly rejected the penology of its colonial past in favor of a system which, at least with respect to capital punishment, would be the most lenient in America for half a century.[15]

The Pennsylvania reform was quick to arouse reformers in other states. In New York, the few citizens who had been advocating that fewer crimes be capitally punishable greeted the new statute as a model for their state. New York City Quaker Thomas Eddy rose to leadership of the reform group partly because he was a native Philadelphian with close friends among reformers there. In 1794, Eddy distributed copies of Bradford's pamphlet to the New York legislature. In 1795, he visited Philadelphia's Walnut Street Prison to inspect records and interview inmates. Convinced that a similar edifice in New York would provide secure and humane keeping for criminals then punishable by death, Eddy vowed to win reform in the 1796 session of the legislature.[16]

Eddy enlisted two powerful allies, state Senators Philip Schuyler and Ambrose Spencer, and the three men drafted a reform bill. Assisted by a call to reform in Governor John Jay's annual message of 1796 and by the support of ex-Governor George Clinton, Schuyler and Spencer won legislative approval on March 26, 1796. New York's new law authorized construction of the state's first penitentiary, abolished whipping, and reduced the number of capital crimes from thirteen to two

—treason and murder. New York did not follow Pennsylvania's lead in creating degrees of murder.[17]

The Pennsylvania reform did not have so immediate or so strong an impact on other states, but, in the next several decades, its influence was felt throughout much of the Union. In Virginia, George Keith Taylor, impressed by the Pennsylvania experiment, cited it frequently as he guided a similar reform bill through the legislature in December 1796. Kentucky Assemblyman John Breckenridge, who had been arguing for reform since 1793, pointed to the success of the Pennsylvania law in convincing his colleagues to approve a related measure in early 1798. Elsewhere, Vermont reduced its capital crimes to three in 1797; Maryland to four in 1810; New Hampshire to two in 1812; and Ohio to two in 1815. In all these states, as in Pennsylvania, the reform was accompanied by the construction of prisons adequate to house criminals who formerly would have been executed.[18]

Some states, of course, resisted the movement for reform. South Carolina was unimpressed by Robert J. Turnbull's accounts of Pennsylvania's success and spurned his arguments for modification of the state's stern criminal laws. Rhode Island increased the severity of its criminal code in 1798 by restoring death for rape and arson, a penalty which the colonial legislature had found too harsh eighty years before. The early decades of the nineteenth century would still find northern states like Massachusetts, Connecticut, and New Jersey mandating death for six to ten offenses, including sodomy, maiming, forgery, and robbery. Most southern states continued to list even more, though many of the crimes were capital only when committed by slaves.[19]

Pennsylvania had provided proof, in 1794 and after, that there was a reasonable alternative to harsh criminal codes. Some states were quick, some slow, to make similar changes. Meanwhile, the most ambitious reformers turned to a goal suggested by the Pennsylvania success. If society could exist as well with one or two capital offenses as with twelve, could it not survive the complete abolition of the death penalty? Benjamin Rush's ideas of 1787 no longer seemed so preposterous.

FIRST PROPOSALS FOR ABOLITION, 1800-1833

During the 1790s only a handful of Americans had gone so far as to oppose the death penalty for murder as well as for lesser crimes. During the first third of the nineteenth century, this once radical idea became more popular. By 1833, some eminent Americans were campaigning for complete abolition, many politicians and religious leaders were familiar with reform arguments, and some state legislatures had already considered enacting this proposal.

Not surprisingly, the first legislative consideration of complete abolition came in Pennsylvania. Governor Simon Snyder, in his annual message of 1809, urged an experiment to ascertain how far abolition "would be attended with . . . beneficial consequences to society." A Senate committee supported the idea, but the full Senate voted to postpone the question. Snyder continued to advocate the reform throughout his tenure as governor, but with the same lack of success.[20]

In New York, too, abolition found a gubernatorial champion in Daniel D. Tompkins. In his annual message of 1812, Tompkins proposed that the legislature efface "that vestige of barbarism" from the laws of the state. Few of New York's legislators were receptive to such a suggestion, but Tompkins continued to urge abolition and with considerable eloquence.[21]

Americans who did not hear of Snyder's or Tompkins' suggestions had many other opportunities to discover and consider the novel idea that the state should not kill its citizens. Some might have read the pseudonymous appeals of "Tyro" in the *Evening Fire-Side* of 1805, of "Philanthropos" (probably the Connecticut pacifist William Ladd) in one of several newspapers in 1809, or of "Philo Humanitas" in a pamphlet published in Philadelphia in 1816. Others might have perused articles, pamphlets, or books like those of New York Quaker John Edwards in 1811, New York clergyman Caleb Whelpley in 1816, Ohio editor Elisha Bates in 1821-1824 or Maryland physician G. F. H. Crockett in 1823. Those who could not read might have encountered reform arguments at a debate like that excerpted in Roland Diller's *Discourse on Capital Punishment* of

1825. Churchgoers might have heard abolition appeals from such sympathetic clergymen as New York's Whelpley, Philadelphia's Abel Charles Thomas, or Massachusetts' Charles Spear. Reform arguments in a less sophisticated form were also likely to be encountered in hundreds of towns and cities in the days just before an execution.[22]

One name stands out, however, among all the Americans who were advocating abolition in this period. It is that of Edward Livingston, whose intelligence, eloquence, and energy in behalf of reform made him one of the most influential opponents of capital punishment in the nation's history (see selection 2). After decades of interest in penal reform, Livingston wrote his historic first attack on the death penalty as part of a report to the Louisiana legislature in 1822. A later report, in 1825, amplifying and extending these arguments, accompanied the "Code of Crimes and Punishments," which the legislature had commissioned him to draft. Livingston also drafted proposed codes for the national government which, if enacted, would have abolished capital punishment for all federal offenses.[23]

Livingston's reform ideas were too advanced for legislators in Louisiana or Washington. But, published in a variety of editions and actively circulated by Livingston and others, they soon became influential among a large number of prominent Americans. Not surprisingly, Livingston's arguments began to appear in the speeches and writings of other reformers throughout the country. The New York and Tennessee legislatures received their first anti-gallows committee reports in 1832; both documents quoted Livingston extensively. Livingston's influence was also apparent in the first anti-gallows committee report in Massachusetts in 1831 and in the renewed activity against the death penalty in Pennsylvania after 1827.[24]

THE FIRST GREAT REFORM ERA, 1833-1853

When Edward Livingston died in New York in 1836, no American jurisdiction had come close to abolishing capital punishment. But, armed with his arguments, reformers of the next twenty years would lead one of the most widespread and popular campaigns ever directed against the death penalty. Their efforts would be facilitated by a climate of reform which permeated the non-slave states in the second quarter of the century. European immigration, the declining power of conservative elites, religious revivalism, economic growth, burgeoning nationalistic pride, and the lure of the frontier all helped create a society in which every institution was challenged, every convention probed.

To many Americans in the 1820s and 1830s, the most obvious flaw in the institution of capital punishment was public execution, which, intended as a sobering and edifying ceremony, had too often turned into a disgraceful scene of commercialism, riot, and bloodlust. A scheduled hanging could be expected to draw thousands, sometimes tens of thousands, of eager viewers. Exploited by local merchants, plied with drink and excited by the prospect of a bloodcurdling event, witnesses often became unruly. Pushing and fighting were not uncommon as the victim was led to the scaffold or as the crowd surged to view the corpse. Cursing onlookers might revile the widow or tear at the scaffold and rope for souvenirs. Drunkenness and violence at times ruled the town far into the night after such a display of public justice.[25]

Appalled by such scenes, legislators in northern states, beginning with Rhode Island in 1833, Pennsylvania in 1834, and New York, Massachusetts, and New Jersey in 1835, enacted laws calling for private hangings. It would be going too far to call this a reform triumph, however. Many opponents of capital punishment did not want to end public hanging without abolishing hanging itself. As one New York reformer put it, if there were to be any executions at all, he wanted them to be public "that their consequences and enormity might be more vividly impressed on the public mind." Another reformer was confident that "public executions would be ultimately instrumental in abolishing capital punishments." The anti-gallows legislators tended to oppose bills abolishing public executions, but in state after state they eventually saw the law changed. By 1849, fifteen states were holding executions in the relative privacy of the prison or the enclosed prison yard.[26]

The end of public executions aided the reformers indirectly, for it undermined claims of the deterrent value of the death penalty. On the other hand, it is clear that in some states the end of public executions slowed the abolition movement in subsequent years. In New York, for example, Horace Greeley remarked in 1836 that the previous year's abolition of public hangings had "subtracted much of the force" from the anti-gallows campaign.[27]

Retentionists in Maine must have regretted that their state had not abolished public hangings before 1837. For in that year, largely as a result of a riotous public execution in 1835, Maine became the first state in the Union to enact what was, in effect, a moratorium on capital punishment. Maine had execu-ted only one felon in its fifteen-year history as a state before Joseph Sager was convicted of murder and sentenced to hang in 1835. The ten or twelve thousand people who jammed into Augusta's streets on the appointed January day soon became unruly and the police had to intervene to stop some brawling. Within ten days the legislature was receiving petitions complain-ing about the violence and pressing for complete abolition of the death penalty.[28]

There were constitutional questions involved, and the legisla-ture did not act on capital punishment until 1837. In the in-terim, Maine's reformers published two influential attacks on the death penalty: Bowdoin College philosophy professor Tho-mas C. Upham's *The Manual of Peace* (1836) and state Senator Tobias Purrington's *Report on Capital Punishment,* submitted to the legislature early in the same year. Quaker and Universalist groups also began to agitate for the reform. On the other hand, an unusual rash of killings just after the Sager execution con-vinced some legislators that this was no time for leniency to-ward criminals. Of consequence, in the 1837 session of the legis-lature, there was enough opposition to outright abolition to force a compromise. Instead of ending the punishment altogeth-er, Maine's new law purportedly altered only the procedures for carrying out executions. Felons convicted of capital crimes, it read, would be sentenced to solitary confinement and hard la-bor at the state prison until infliction of the death penalty. No such felon could be executed until at least one year after sentencing and then only by specific order of the governor. The reformers calculated that no executive would take affirmative action and issue such an order, especially after a year's demonstration that the criminal could safely be left alive. The law of 1837, or the "Maine Law" as it was called, had just this effect for twenty-seven years.[29]

Although no other state went so far as Maine, the mid-1830s saw a flurry of anti-gallows activity in a number of legislatures. In some states, like Vermont and Pennsylvania, the subject was broached but not seriously debated. In Massachusetts, the reform, though failing to make much of an impression on the legislature, produced reform writings, the reports of Robert Rantoul, Jr. (see selection 3), destined to play an important role in future battles. In a few states—Rhode Island, New Jersey, and Ohio—and in Michigan Territory, abolition measures came close to success in at least one of the legislative houses; in New Jersey, the Assembly actually voted for abolition in 1837, but the Senate refused to concur.[30]

The activity of the mid- and late 1830s was only a prelude to a storm of anti-gallows campaigning in the 1840s. Now reformers came forward by the thousands, agitating the issue in almost all the northern and in a few southern states. Of great importance were those who controlled influential newspapers and journals of the day, such men as John L. O'Sullivan (see selection 4) of the *United States Magazine and Democratic Review,* William Cullen Bryant, editor of the *New York Post,* and Horace Greeley (see selection 9) of the *New York Tribune.*

Other prominent reformers included writers like John Greenleaf Whittier (see selection 5), Lydia Maria Child, and Walt Whitman (see selection 8); jurists like New York's Chancellor William T. McCoun and Iowa's Chief Justice Charles Mason; doctors like Philadelphia's Henry S. Patterson and Boston's Walter Channing; legislators like Ohio's Clement Vallandigham, Alabama's Benjamin F. Porter, and Pennsylvania's Thaddeus Stevens; and those who might be called professional reformers— William Lloyd Garrison, Wendell Phillips, and Charles C. Burleigh (see selection 7). National politicians like John Quincy

Adams, Vice-President George M. Dallas, and former Vice-President Richard M. Johnson also lent their names to the reform, though they do not appear to have taken a very active role.

Perhaps the most influential group of reformers was the clergy. Certainly no profession contributed more able workers to the cause. Charles Spear (see selection 6), Adin Ballou, and Theodore Parker helped spread reform notions in their sermons and in the religious press in Massachusetts, as did Sylvester Judd in Maine, William Henry Channing and Samuel Joseph May in New York, Edward B. Hall in Rhode Island, Abel Charles Thomas in Pennsylvania, and C. F. Le Fevre in Wisconsin, to name only a few. The ministers' effect was diminished by the fact that virtually all of them belonged to two unorthodox denominations, Universalism and Unitarianism. Still, their efforts won many others to the reform movement.

Arrayed against this army of reformers was a small but immensely powerful and prestigious band of men dedicated to the retention of capital punishment. Almost without exception, they were members of the orthodox Calvinist clergy—especially Congregationalists and Presbyterians—those who might be termed the religious establishment of nineteenth-century America. George B. Cheever of New York was unquestionably the most active and influential of the group, a man whom Charles Spear called "the champion of the gallows in America." But he had ministerial allies everywhere—Albert Baldwin Dod in New Jersey, William T. Dwight in Maine, Samuel Lee in New Hampshire, Timothy Alden Taylor in Rhode Island, Lyman Beecher in Connecticut, Joseph F. Berg in Pennsylvania, Jared D. Waterbury in Massachusetts, George Duffield in Michigan, and many more. These men defended capital punishment in sermons, articles, and books. They circulated petitions and distributed tracts. They traveled to state capitols to lobby against reform bills. In all, their efforts lent credence to a reformer's claim that *"the Church of America alone upholds the Gallows."* [31]

The ministers' arguments in behalf of capital punishment were best expressed by George Cheever in his *Punishment by Death* (1842), the most famous and influential defense of the gallows in American history. Cheever's primary argument was an appeal to divine authority. God had commanded death for murderers, he said, in Genesis 9:6 ("Whosoever sheddeth a man's blood, so shall his blood be shed") and had never amended or abrogated this directive. Therefore, it would be defying Jehovah and risking divine wrath to abolish capital punishment for murder. For Cheever, this argument alone was sufficient to end discussion of the matter, but the minister also discussed the expediency of capital punishment for those who still required convincing. The death penalty, he insisted, was uniquely terrifying and thus uniquely able to deter murderers. It protected prison guards, who otherwise would be wantonly slain by felons serving life terms. Moreover, it hastened the conversion of sinners. In a third argument, Cheever appealed to an abstract sense of justice. "There is such a thing as justice, separate from the other aims of penalty," he wrote, and all societies and ages have recognized the fact. Hence, all people knew at some level that the inherently just punishment for murder was nothing less than the death of the murderer.[32]

The reformers knew that it would take vigorous action to overcome such arguments from anti-reform spokesmen like Cheever and his allies, and most shared the same basic strategy about how to do so. First, Americans would have to be informed and aroused about the evils of the death penalty and the safety of incarcerating even the most vicious criminals. Then the reform-minded citizenry would bring pressure to bear on state legislators to force passage of more humane laws.

Reformers carried out the first part of their mission with a high degree of success. Most Americans outside the South certainly had the opportunity to hear the reform message in the 1840s. In addition to the two great New York newspapers already named, hundreds of other daily and weekly papers frequently printed articles on the reform. Hundreds of books and pamphlets attacking the death penalty were produced in the 1840s. Some, especially those of Livingston, O'Sullivan, and Spear, sold briskly. Many periodicals, particularly those staffed by the reformers, were generous with their columns. Two, Charles Spear's *The Hangman* (later renamed *The Prisoner's*

Friend) and New York shopkeeper George Baker's *The Spirit of the Age,* were devoted exclusively to anti-gallows and prison reform.

While some reformers furthered the cause through written appeals, others delivered speeches, called open meetings, and arranged debates. The most likely vehicles for this sort of activity were voluntary anti-gallows societies, and many such groups were formed between 1842 and 1846. There were organizations like Philadelphia's Committee of Twenty-Five on Capital Punishment, founded in 1842 with the purpose of responding to a specific pro-gallows sermon, but still active three years later. There were state organizations like the Massachusetts and the New York Societies for the Abolition of Capital Punishment, both formed in 1844. These, in turn, helped organize local and county societies like those in Brooklyn, New York, Roxbury, Massachusetts, Erie County, Pennsylvania, and Granville, Ohio. The New York State Society, by far the most powerful and active, was also instrumental in founding a national organization intended to coordinate the various state campaigns. An initial meeting in New York City in April 1844 produced limited results, but a second gathering in Philadelphia in November 1845 was well attended. Here, delegates from at least five states heard addresses by Horace Greeley and Vice-President George M. Dallas and established the American Society for the Abolition of Capital Punishment, with Dallas as president.[33]

With this plethora of books, pamphlets, articles, speeches, and organizations, anti-gallows advocates of the 1840s were decidedly successful in their efforts to broadcast their beliefs to the public. They seem to have been far less successful with the other half of their program, translating citizen support into political pressure on the legislatures. Indeed, to the modern observer, they do not appear to have tried very hard. The New York State Society was the most aggressive of all the anti-gallows organizations, yet even it was severely limited in its dealings with the legislature. Its officers mailed pamphlets to every member of the state Assembly and Senate, circulated petitions and forwarded them to Albany, and then waited for results. Not surprisingly, they waited in vain. The mailings to individual

legislators probably altered very few, if any, votes and the petition signatures, even when they outnumbered anti-reform signatures by a ratio of seventy to one, failed to affect most lawmakers. The New York Society and similar organizations elsewhere do not seem to have considered sending lobbyists to the
state capitals or supporting the election of friends and the
defeat of enemies of the cause. Like many other contemporary
organizations, the anti-gallows societies placed virtually all their
hopes in the power of moral suasion. That was not enough.[34]

At least partly because of faulty tactics, the reformers did
not win many victories in the 1840s. Pennsylvania, New York,
and Massachusetts saw the greatest reform activity, but none
came close to ending hangings. In a few other states, reformers
won skirmishes, but lost the war. In Vermont, the legislature
enacted a Maine Law in 1842, but abandoned it two years later.
In Connecticut, a reform bill of 1841 won approval in the
House but failed in the Senate. The New Hampshire legislature,
in 1844, agreed to submit the question of abolition to the
voters, who rejected it by a vote of 21,544 to 11,241.[35]

The sole unqualified success for the reform in the 1840s
came from a state where renowned reformers and a network of
societies had played no role. Michigan, in 1846, became the first
state in the Union to abolish capital punishment (except for the
unlikely crime of treason against the state). The primary factor
in the Michigan success was peculiar to that frontier state and
was not exportable to the East: Michigan simply had no long
tradition of capital punishment. The last of the few criminals
executed in that state was hanged by the territorial government
in 1830. Thus, it was not necessary for reformers in Michigan to
convince the legislature to end executions, but only to bring the
laws into conformity with established practice in the state. It is
significant, too, that frontier Michigan lacked the religious establishment which had crippled the reform in many eastern
states.[36]

Eastern reformers reacted with joy to the news of Michigan's
abolition and talked glibly of the new state's leading the entire
nation into an era of enlightened penology. The future, in fact,
was far less bright. In most states, the reform reached an acme

of activity in 1846 or 1847, then slowly dwindled. Reform leaders lost interest, anti-gallows societies shriveled, and newspapers no longer devoted much space to the cause. The reasons were many, but the paramount problem was the Mexican War and the factionalism and sectionalism it fostered. In the fifteen years after Zachary Taylor's troops entered Mexico in 1846, the United States weathered foreign war and domestic riot, antislavery crusades and frontier terrorism, shifting political alignments and threats of secession. It is not remarkable that the anti-gallows movement and most other reforms drowned in this sea of troubles.

The reform did not collapse completely in a year or two, of course, and a few victories were scored before anti-gallows activity virtually ceased. Most of the triumphs were hollow. Only one house of the legislature passed abolition bills in Ohio in 1850, Iowa in 1851, and Connecticut in 1853. New Hampshire passed a modified Maine Law in 1849 and Massachusetts in 1852, but neither stopped hangings as the original statute had in Maine. More significant was Massachusetts' abolition of capital punishment for the crimes of treason, rape, and arson in 1852. The Bay State, at last, had followed Pennsylvania's half-century-old example and limited the death penalty to first-degree murder.[37]

Two major victories came in states where there had not been especially strong reform agitation in the 1840s. In both, local circumstances led to the reform success. Rhode Island, in 1852, was ripe for the sort of reform effort absent during that state's turbulent 1840s. She had both a tradition of relative leniency toward criminals reaching back to the colonial period and a heritage of unorthodoxy in religion as old as the colony itself. The state's influential communities of Unitarians, Universalists, and especially Quakers were sympathetic to reform goals. When Quaker reformer Thomas H. Hazard and state Senator Ariel Ballou coordinated their abolition efforts in early 1852, they were met with surprisingly little opposition: within a month, their abolition bill became law.[38]

Wisconsin followed suit in the next year, but apparently more as a result of local murder cases, than Rhode Island's example. Public opposition to hanging was aroused in that state in 1851 when word circulated of the gruesome hanging of John McCaffary in Kenosha. McCaffary continued to struggle for five minutes after he was jerked into the air and it was eighteen minutes before his heart stopped beating. Hangings had been rare in Wisconsin, and many citizens were appalled to learn what they were like. Another problem with capital punishment was demonstrated in Milwaukee the following year when a jury refused to convict a man whom many thought guilty of murder. Presumably, the jurors, aware of the McCaffary execution, rebelled at sending another felon to a similar fate. In 1853, reformers, angered by executions, joined others concerned about the lack of convictions and supported an abolition bill. Under the leadership of Marvin H. Bovee and James T. Lewis in the Senate and C. Latham Sholes in the Assembly, the reformers overwhelmed their opposition and ended the death penalty in Wisconsin.[39]

Thus, all the reformers' efforts in support of the cause in the 1830s and 1840s had led to abolition in but three states, de facto abolition in a fourth. In terms of their success in eradicating capital punishment, Rantoul, O'Sullivan, Spear, and their allies had failed. Still, Walt Whitman thought that anti-gallows efforts had succeeded in subtler, but perhaps more significant, ways. The reformers, he wrote, had been effective in "diffusing more benevolence and sympathy through the public mind [and] elevating the range of temper and feeling." They had improved "popular taste . . . criminal law, the doings of Courts and Juries, and the management of Prisons."[40] It seems reasonable to suggest that the reformers of the antebellum period had built a foundation for victories which lay decades, even a century, in the future.

HARD TIMES, 1854-1895

Already in 1846 some reform leaders had ceased their efforts to abolish the death penalty and had turned to anti-slavery reform, party politics, or personal affairs. In the 1850s, the decline of the movement quickened, and by the middle of that decade, there were virtually no activists left. The anti-gallows organizations were defunct, newspapers printed few reform articles, legislatures debated few abolition bills.

Of the old reformers, some could be persuaded to rehearse their familiar arguments at a day or two of legislative hearings— as in Massachusetts in 1854 [41] —but only Charles Spear continued to devote a major portion of his time to the problem. In 1857, even he reluctantly became less active when failing health and financial troubles forced him to cease publication of *The Prisoner's Friend*. Only the rise of a passionate and energetic new reformer kept the cause alive around the time of the Civil War.

Marvin H. Bovee (see selection 11), after helping to secure the Wisconsin victory in 1853, had resolved to devote his life to "relentless warfare against the cruel laws and cruel practices of government." Over the next thirty years he was active in more states than any reformer before him. In 1858, he campaigned against the gallows in Illinois. In the winter of 1859-1860, he spent over three months urging support of an abolition bill in New York. There his work was rewarded when the legislature, greatly affected by the plight of a beautiful young woman awaiting execution, passed a short-lived Maine Law. The Civil War slowed Bovee's efforts, but 1866 found him back in Wisconsin helping to prevent restoration of capital punishment. In 1867, he aided Illinois reformers and in the following year toured New Jersey and Minnesota in behalf of the cause. His movements are not well recorded thereafter, but it is certain that he continued to work for abolition in Massachusetts, New York, Kansas, Missouri, and Nebraska. His book *Christ and the Gallows* (1869), containing anti-gallows comments by such famous Americans as Henry Wadsworth Longfellow, Gerrit Smith, and Elizabeth Cady Stanton (see selection 10), helped the movement in states he did not reach. [42]

The America of the 1860s and 1870s, with its massive violence and cries for revenge, did not welcome Bovee's efforts, and he was never able to duplicate his Wisconsin success. With time, he lowered his sights and, while continuing to call for outright abolition, actually aimed at a less ambitious reform which he believed would amount to the same thing: substitution of discretionary for mandatory capital punishment.

Virtually all capital laws in colonial and early nineteenth-century America had been mandatory; a death sentence automatically followed a guilty verdict. But the opinion became widespread, especially in the 1830s and after, that such laws prevented convictions. Jurors sometimes resisted condemning a criminal to death, even if this meant acquitting someone plainly guilty of murder. The obvious solution was a law allowing jurors an alternative to mandatory capital punishment. Tennessee, in 1838, was the first state to pass such legislation for the crime of murder. Alabama, in 1841, and Louisiana, in 1846, soon followed suit. But under the urging of Bovee and others, eighteen more states shifted from mandatory to discretionary capital punishment in the period 1860-1895. In each, either judge or jury was authorized to decide whether a convicted murderer would die or be imprisoned. Bovee at first naively believed that discretionary sentencing would mean the virtual end of executions. He was wrong, of course. The legislators of the eighteen states were in no mood to abolish capital punishment. They had approved discretionary sentencing not to save lives, but to increase the rate of convictions. To Bovee's dismay, executions continued unabated.[43]

That capital punishment tended to prevent convictions had been an abolitionist argument of long standing, but one that was now destroyed. Even if it were proved true, retentionists could now argue, the solution was not to abolish capital punishment but to make it discretionary. Thus, abandonment of mandatory capital punishment may have hurt the reform in the post-Civil War period just as the end of public executions did in the late 1830s.

The loss of one of their strongest arguments, in addition to the inauspicious climate for reform, meant that anti-gallows advocates would win only rare victories in the period 1854-1895. The first came in Iowa in 1872, when that state, which had seen only one execution since 1838, enacted an abolition law. In a pattern that other states would repeat in the twentieth century, however, subsequent crimes were automatically attributed to

the lack of capital punishment, and a restoration campaign succeeded in 1878. Nearby Kansas was also in a reform mood in
1872. There the legislature passed a Maine Law, which unlike
those of Vermont and Massachusetts operated as a de facto
abolition as its proponents intended.[44]

Maine itself experienced a complicated series of events when,
between 1876 and 1887, the state legislature abolished the
death penalty, restored it, and then abolished it again. The
Maine Law of 1837 had operated to prevent executions until
1864, when the murder of a prison warden prompted Governor
Samuel Cony to order the death of the offender. The legislature
abandoned the Maine Law provision in 1875, but due in part to
the emotions aroused by a tragically bungled hanging in June of
that year, abolished capital punishment completely in the 1876
session. As in Iowa, opponents of abolition began blaming every
murder, and, oddly enough, some non-capital crimes as well, on
the lack of capital punishment. The 1883 legislature accepted
this specious reasoning and restored the death penalty. The abolitionists could count too, however, and soon were able to
demonstrate that there was a higher murder rate since restoration than before. Convinced that restoration had been a mistake, the legislature banned the death penalty again in 1887 and
Maine, always uneasy about capital punishment, joined the abolition ranks to stay.[45]

Iowa, Kansas, and Maine, then, were the only states to see
reform success in these years, and Iowa for only a six-year
period. It seemed as though New York might join the abolition
states in the early 1890s, but the cause of the activity there was
unusual and transient. New York's Governor David B. Hill, in
1886, had appointed a commission to study alternatives to
hanging as the mode of execution. That such action had not
come earlier is surprising in view of Edmund C. Stedman's (see
selection 12) and other reformers' assaults on bungled hangings.
Hill's commission considered the guillotine and the garrote, but
felt that electric shock was the ideal replacement for the noose.
Electric companies opposed the idea, arguing that the killings
would make the public fear and avoid electricity. But the New
York legislature approved the change, and at Auburn Prison, on

August 6, 1890, William Kemmler became the world's first victim of legal electrocution.[46]

The result, according to some, was far more repulsive than a hanging. George Westinghouse himself thought that the job could have been "done better with an axe." The entire episode was a boon to reformers. Before Kemmler's execution, friends of the electric companies helped abolitionists in the New York Assembly win an amazing seventy-five to twenty-nine vote against capital punishment. After the first electrocution, reformers found new allies, including workers' groups and medical societies whose members were disturbed at this new means of taking life. It still seemed possible in 1892 that the legislature would react by banning the death penalty, but a series of better-performed electrocutions gradually erased the memory of Kemmler and the impetus his execution had lent the reform.[47]

THE SECOND GREAT REFORM ERA,
1895-1917

The anti-capital punishment movement, relatively inactive and unsuccessful in the period following the Civil War, revived in the last few years of the nineteenth century and enjoyed two decades of considerable success. Among the factors producing this new reform era were the general reform milieu of the Populist and Progressive periods, the rise of social concerns among Christian denominations, a growing rejection of determinism and acceptance of pragmatism, and, more directly relevant to capital punishment, the rise of a more scientific view of criminals and prisons.

The new reform period had no national focus, no national leaders, and no really national organizations. It was characterized by hundreds of small campaigns and modest successes, adding up to a great deal of progress toward the goal of general abolition. At first there was evidence of new interest in ending capital punishment, but little to show for it. The United States House of Representatives rejected Congressman Newton M. Curtis' (see selection 13) arguments for abolition, but in 1897 approved his bill greatly reducing the number of federal capital crimes. The Senate concurred and the bill became law. In the state of Washington, in the same year, the House passed an abolition bill. In Colorado, also in 1897, reformers won a fight for abolition, but only temporarily. Opponents of the new law argued that several lynchings which occurred in 1900 were the result of abolition. The legislature restored the death penalty in the following year.[48]

Elsewhere, Massachusetts prison reformer Florence G. Spooner organized the Anti-Death Penalty League in 1897 and for the next several years led a campaign in the state legislature against capital punishment. In 1900, her efforts brought Massachusetts closer to abolition than ever before. In 1900, Newton M. Curtis formed a similar organization and, in 1901, allied with the Society of Friends in an effort to end the penalty in New York. In 1905, Pennsylvania reformers succeeded in persuading the state Senate to pass an abolition bill, but it was badly defeated in the House. In the same year, there seemed to be a real possibility that New Jersey would abandon executions. In 1906, the Illinois House passed an abolition measure by a surprising eighty to forty-three vote, and in Ohio, Progressive Mayor Brand Whitlock of Toledo helped to win Senate passage of a similar proposal. The anti-reform *New York Times* regretfully admitted that there was a tendency abroad in the land "heading straight to the abolition of the executioner."[49]

The *Times* editor was correct. In 1907 Kansas, where a Maine Law had prevented hangings since 1872, made abolition official. In 1911, Minnesota ended its executions partly as the result of the wide publicity accorded a scandalously inept hanging five years before. Then, over the next six years came a steady stream of abolitions: Washington in 1913 and four states, North and South Dakota, Oregon, and Tennessee (the latter, ending capital punishment for murder, but not for rape) in 1915. Arizona, as a result of a popular referendum vote of 18,936 to 18,784, abandoned capital punishment in 1916. In March of the following year, Missouri swelled the abolitionist ranks to twelve, one-quarter of the states in the Union.[50]

But a mere list of abolition states cannot communicate the

intensity of the reform in the period 1907-1917. While nine states ended capital punishment, six more and one territory won abolition votes in at least one house of their legislatures. An Ohio constitutional convention in 1912 submitted an abolition amendment to the voters, who rejected it by only eight percent of the vote.[51] Hundreds of magazine and newspaper articles were devoted to the reform.

Not since the 1840s had so many prominent Americans campaigned for the cause. Governors were especially active. Hiram Johnson in California, George W. P. Hunt in Arizona, and Samuel W. McCall in Massachusetts worked for the reform in their respective states. So many other state executives shared their sentiments that annual governors' conferences of the decade sometimes resembled reform meetings. The young science of penology contributed a number of respected abolition advocates. George W. Kirchwey and Thomas Mott Osborne, the past and present wardens of Sing Sing, aided the fight in New York; penologist Maynard Shipley played a similar role in California and throughout the country. Other prominent reformers of the period included novelist William Dean Howells (see selection 14), Jane Addams, Samuel Gompers, muckraking journalist Charles Edward Russell, New York Rabbi Stephen S. Wise, humorist and social critic Finley Peter Dunne (see selection 15), financier Jacob H. Schiff, and U.S. Vice-President Thomas R. Marshall.[52]

There were also more reform organizations in the 1910s than at any time since the 1840s. Arizona's Governor George W. P. Hunt headed the Anti-Capital Punishment Society of America, headquartered in Chicago; manufacturer Charles H. Ingersoll of New York served as president of the Anti-Capital Punishment League; and George Foster Peabody, New York banker and philanthropist, chaired the Committee on Capital Punishment of the National Committee on Prisons. Two other New York organizations dedicated to several reforms concentrated their efforts in 1916-1917 on the death penalty. The People's Campaign League, led by attorney Grace Humiston, sought to arouse support for abolition bills in the New York legislature. Mischa Appelbaum's Humanitarian Cult published reform articles in its journal and utilized a new medium to aid the cause: the society's feature film "The People vs. John Doe," played the Broadway Theatre in 1916, earning praise from the *New York Times'* critic as "the most effective propaganda in film form ever seen here." [53]

The defenders of capital punishment who rose to meet these new challenges were of a different sort from the ministerial antagonists of Rantoul and O'Sullivan. The grip of orthodox Calvinist ministers upon their congregations and upon the society at large had weakened considerably since Cheever's time. Although many clergymen opposed abolition, their pronouncements were no longer so crucial to the fate of the reform. Instead, other guardians of society—judges, district attorneys, policemen—and their legislative allies formed the front rank of the retentionist brigade.

Anti-reform arguments differed correspondingly. Genesis 9:6 was occasionally bruited about, but it usually was only an afterthought to a series of arguments about the expediency of the death penalty. The new retentionists relied most heavily on the supposedly unique deterrent effect of capital punishment. Common sense, public opinion, and such revered authorities as Supreme Court Justice John M. Harlan, they said, all affirmed that the death penalty was indispensable in preventing murder. But when the retentionists sought statistical support for the same proposition, they frequently overreached themselves. They were wont to point out that crime rose in a state after abolition, but neglected to add that it continued to rise after restoration. Or they showed that there were far more murders in Michigan in the 1880s than just before abolition in the 1840s, but failed to take into account the octupling of the state's population in that period. Other retentionist arguments were that abolition would cause an increase in lynching, as presumably happened in Colorado after 1897, and that the United States was too violent a country to permit any relaxation of legal severity. The latter claim took on racist and nativist overtones when retentionists insisted that capital punishment was necessary so long as the American population was "composed so largely of foreigners and Negroes." [54]

Such retentionist arguments as these would function best in an atmosphere of racism, nativism, suspicion, and fear. American entry into World War I fostered precisely this atmosphere. Consequently, there was an abrupt turnabout in the fortunes of the abolitionist cause. Tennessee, which had abolished capital punishment for murder only two years before, reenacted the death penalty in 1917, and the reform was suddenly crippled in other states where success had appeared likely. In at least two states, the war was the direct cause of the reversal. In Illinois, an abolition bill passed both houses of the legislature, but the governor vetoed it at least partly because he felt the action inappropriate while the country was at war. In Pennsylvania, where the *Philadelphia Public Ledger* had led an active campaign for reform, the Senate passed an abolition bill by the remarkable vote of thirty-two to twelve, and the House seemed sure to follow suit. Several days before the House vote, however, an explosion at a munitions factory near Philadelphia killed one hundred fifty workers. Amid rumors of sabotage, the House on April 17 defeated the abolition bill ninety-seven to eighty-three. War psychology unquestionably contributed to defeats in other states as well. As in the 1860s, the reform had again become a war casualty.[55]

NO GAINS AND SOME LOSSES,
1917-1955

For a long period after American entry into World War I, there was virtually no progress toward the abolitionist goal of ridding the American states of their capital laws. At first the reform was hurt by the brutality and callousness bred by war, then by the post-war belief that America was being engulfed by a crime wave. Later, the worst depression in the country's history would shift attention to other concerns. Not long thereafter, another war would inure the public to killing and dreaded ideologies would seem to merit the harshest response. Only in the late 1950s would the reform make any significant advance.

The reform climate could hardly have been worse than in the period 1918-1920. War psychology and anticipation of a crime

wave combined with hatred of immigrants and fear of radical-
ism to produce a virtual hysteria among the American people.
In this atmosphere, four abolition states reenacted capital punishment statutes—Washington, Arizona, and Missouri in 1919
and Oregon, after another referendum, in 1920. A few sensational crimes prompted the reinstatement of the death penalty
in all four states. Fear of the radical International Workers of
the World was a contributing factor in Oregon. In other states,
the reform made no headway. The new mood of the legislators
could be gauged by the 171-20 defeat of an abolition bill in the
Massachusetts House in 1920.[56]

It took the reformers several years to regroup after these
stunning defeats. There was very little reform activity in the
years 1919-1920. In 1921 and 1922, Ohio's Governor Harry L.
Davis and former Sing Sing wardens George W. Kirchwey and
Thomas Mott Osborne resumed their attacks on the death penalty, but they had little support. A third Sing Sing warden,
Lewis E. Lawes (see selection 18), enlisted in the reform in
1923, began to arouse considerable attention. He soon became
one of the most active abolitionists in the nation. As the current
officer in charge of one of the country's most famous prisons,
Lawes gained wide notice and he seems to have planned a continual flow of speeches, books, articles, and news stories for the
education of the public. In 1923, he addressed New York's
Government Club and the congress of the American Prison
Association, of which he was president. In an interview in *Outlook* magazine, Lawes stressed his knowledge of the criminal
mind, his experience with executions, and how his work had
turned him against capital punishment. In 1924, he testified for
the first of many times in behalf of an abolition bill in Albany
and won a radio debate on capital punishment with state Senator William Love of New York.[57]

While Lawes concentrated his efforts in New York, an already famous Chicago lawyer won a victory which excited reformers everywhere. Clarence Darrow (see selection 16) had
been a vigorous and passionate opponent of capital punishment
for over thirty years. In 1924, he combined this with his pen-
chant for seemingly hopeless causes when he agreed to defend

Nathan Leopold and Richard Loeb, two wealthy Chicago youths charged with kidnapping and murder. Darrow waived a jury trail, had his clients plead guilty, and, in a moving address, argued that to hang them would be useless and immoral. When Judge John R. Caverly agreed and sentenced the felons to life imprisonment, reformers throughout the country were amazed and encouraged. Their activity expanded rapidly in the following year.

Further encouragement came from an unlikely source, the anti-reform *New York Times*. The *Times'* editors were becoming increasingly convinced in late 1924 that capital punishment was unworkable. "Jurors use almost any excuse to escape the abhorrent task of rendering a verdict that means death," the paper editorialized, "and nobody minds particularly...." The end of executions would inevitably mean more convictions, the editors concluded. "While the abolition of capital punishment might not be wise, it would be less unwise than leaving the matter as it is, with death the penalty for murder only in instances when juries think it has been earned by what they consider special atrocity." [58]

Emboldened by Darrow's success and the *New York Times'* despair, reformers stepped up their activities in 1925. Probably their most significant achievement was the founding in July of the American League to Abolish Capital Punishment. A national body, with offices in New York City, the American League sought to organize and coordinate abolition attempts in state legislatures. Darrow, Osborne, and Lawes were among the organizers of the League and they saw to it that its officers included some of the most active abolitionists of the day. The group's executive committee included academics Franz Boas of Columbia University, Raymond Bye of the University of Pennsylvania, and Louis M. Robinson of Swarthmore College; psychiatrist and criminologist Herman Adler of the University of Illinois; Hastings Hart of New York's Russell Sage Foundation; William F. Beckert, chairman of the Christian Science Committee of New York; Unitarian minister and civil libertarian John Haynes Holmes; New York attorneys Dudley Field Malone, Amos Pinchot, Samuel Untermyer, and Frank P. Walsh; statistician Frederick L. Hoffman; economist and feminist Doris Stevens; penologist Katherine Bement Davis; philanthropist Adolph Lewisohn; and pre-war reformer Governor George W. P. Hunt of Arizona.[59]

In the first year of its existence, the American League enrolled over a thousand members in thirty-three states and helped organize state affiliates in New York, California, North Carolina, and Minnesota. New bursts of membership came with some of the sensational executions of the 1920s, especially those of Sacco and Vanzetti in Massachusetts in 1927 and Ruth Snyder and Judd Gray in New York in 1928.

In the late 1920s, the League was a motivating force for most of New York's and much of the rest of the country's abolitionist activity. The League sponsored speeches by Lawes, Darrow, English reformer E. Roy Calvert, and New York feminist and novelist Kathleen Norris (see selection 17). It petitioned and sent representatives to testify at hearings of the New York and New Jersey legislatures. It served as a clearinghouse for pamphlets on the death penalty, receiving materials from sources as diverse as William Randolph Hearst and the Philadelphia Yearly Meeting of Friends and distributing them wherever they might do some good. The League also began its own publishing program, printing pamphlets by Will Durant and Charles Edward Russell.[60]

There was other abolitionist activity in New York and elsewhere, of course, which was unassociated with the League. The late 1920s saw attacks on capital punishment by Detroit Judge (later Supreme Court Justice) Frank Murphy, popular New York columnist Heywood Broun, and industrialist Henry Ford, to name only a few. Sing Sing prison, where Warden Lawes, prison doctor Amos O. Squire, and executioner Robert Elliott (see selection 19) were all bitter opponents of the punishment they had to supervise, had become a center for abolitionist activity. Lawes arranged for showings of anti-capital punishment films to the inmates and assigned prison personnel to collect data supporting reform arguments. In Massachusetts, the executions of Sacco and Vanzetti stimulated the formation of the Massachusetts Council for the Abolition of the Death Penalty and also brought Sara Ehrmann and her husband, Herbert B. Ehrmann (see selection 20), an attorney for the condemned men, into the ranks of active reformers. Newspapers and magazines opposing capital punishment included periodicals with a relatively low circulation—*Survey, Outlook, New Republic, Nation,* and *Christian Science Monitor*—but also others with a vast readership—*Collier's* and the entire Hearst newspaper chain.[61]

That reformers continued so active in the late 1920s and the 1930s is surprising in view of the poor reception their efforts received in state legislatures. The American League supported abolition legislation in New York, Pennsylvania, New Jersey, Massachusetts, Vermont, Colorado, and California. Other reformers contributed to campaigns in these and other states. Yet, at no time in the two decades did any state come close to passing an abolition bill.[62] In fact, abolitionists were forced to spend some of their time and resources fighting restoration attempts in states where the reform had previously triumphed. Restoration efforts were defeated in South Dakota in 1927, when the governor vetoed a new capital punishment law. A series of brutal murders in the late 1930s, however, persuaded Governor Harlan Bushfield to propose restoration and, in 1939, the legislature quickly complied. The first abolition state proved more steadfast. The Michigan legislature's attempt to restore capital punishment was forestalled by a gubernatorial veto in 1929, but proponents of the death penalty won the next governor's signature for a similar bill in 1931. This measure called for a referendum, however, and Michigan voters, satisfied with eighty years of abolition, rejected capital punishment by a comfortable margin. Kansas, agitated like South Dakota by some widely publicized murders, also found restoration attractive. Here, too, gubernatorial vetoes killed restoration bills in 1931 and 1933, but the legislature passed another in 1935 and found Governor Alf Landon willing to sign it into law.[63]

Reformers were also forced onto the defensive in states that had never outlawed the death penalty, for the 1930s saw numerous attempts to make kidnapping a new capital crime. In 1932, only Missouri classified kidnapping as a capital offense. The kidnapping and murder of the Lindburgh baby that year, however, prompted hasty action in many state legislatures. Abolitionists opposed the new capital statutes, but could not prevent over twenty states from passing such laws during the remainder of the decade.[64]

The American League, unable to advance the cause of abolition or even to protect previous gains, continued to function in the late 1930s and early 1940s, but at a lower level of activity than ten years earlier. Clarence Darrow, then president of the group, and other officers tried a new tack in 1936, when they began concentrating on abolishing capital punishment for minors. They may have felt they could win general support for this modest reform and then argue that it made no more sense to kill adults than teenagers. The new campaign gained publicity, but had little effect on state legislatures. Dr. Miriam Van Waters, head of the Massachusetts Reformatory for Women, succeeded Darrow as president of the League in 1938. Under her direction in the early 1940s, the League renewed its publication program, printing pamphlets by Lawes, Pennsylvania Judge Michael A. Musmanno, and psychiatrist Karl Menninger.[65] World War II soon removed any remaining chances for abolition, however, and the League weakened. In later decades, it would be led by such able reformers as Sara Ehrmann, criminologist Donal E. J. MacNamara, and philosopher Hugo A. Bedau, but it would never again play the leading role in the abolition movement.

The reform itself was quiescent throughout the 1940s and into the mid-1950s. The pending executions of Julius and Ethel Rosenberg, 1951-1953, stirred up stormy protests, but only against *their* deaths, not against the death penalty in general. At another time, this ordinary-looking couple, whom some thought entirely innocent and many saw as persecuted, might have provided the focus for a great national campaign against capital punishment. In a period of anti-Communist hysteria, however, indeed at a time when Texas Governor Allan Shivers could seriously propose the death penalty for membership in the Communist Party, accused Soviet spies inspired no outpouring of sympathy.[66] A campaign of this sort would have to await the end of the witch-hunting mentality of the McCarthy era and a more sympathetic object of compassion.

GROWTH AND TRIUMPH, 1955-1972

In the mid-1950s, the movement against capital punishment began to revive slowly. With McCarthyism and the Korean War behind them, Americans were once again able to devote their energies to social reforms like abolition of the death penalty. Though there had been virtually no organized anti-capital punishment activity in the previous fifteen years, there were signs that Americans were finding the penalty increasingly repulsive. Opinion polls continued to show that some sixty-eight per cent of Americans supported capital punishment, it is true, but judges and juries were sending fewer and fewer felons to their deaths. In 1930, 155 Americans had died at the direction of state and federal authorities, 199 in 1935; but the post-war years showed a decline in executions. In 1950, 82 men and women were executed and in 1955, only 76, less than half the figure of twenty-five years before. World War II, with its executions of millions, had given preventable death a bad name, perhaps. At any rate, Americans, despite a growing population, urban stresses, racial and ethnic bitterness, and one of the highest homicide rates in the world, were condemning a very small number of criminals to death, only a tiny fraction of those convicted of capital crimes.[67]

There were more specific factors, too, in the new reform interest. England and Canada had just completed exhaustive investigations, largely critical, of capital punishment, and books and articles about their findings were plentiful. One such book was Arthur Koestler's *Reflections on Hanging*, which saw wide circulation in the United States. In the preface to the American edition, New York University law professor Edmond Cahn exhorted his countrymen to abolish executions. Many rose to the challenge. American reformers also gained inspiration from the November 1952 issue of the prestigious *Annals of the American Academy of Political and Social Science,* in which a score of social scientists reported the results of their research on capital punishment: some reviewed experiments with abolition; others examined deterrence and surveyed errors of justice; all indicted capital punishment as inefficacious and unwise.[68]

The impending or actual execution of criminals with whom the public sympathized, for one reason or another, had always stimulated abolition activity in the United States. Two such cases, both in California, piqued reform interest in the mid-1950s. Convicted kidnapper Caryl Chessman rose to fame as early as 1954, with the publication of his *Cell 2455 Death Row*; his *Trial by Ordeal* followed in 1955. Many readers felt that this man must not be killed. Barbara Graham attracted similar concern and sympathy, but most of it came after her execution for murder in 1955. *I Want to Live!* , an account of her life, her claims of innocence, and her death, reached millions as a book and, after 1958, as a film.

The subject of capital punishment became acceptable, if infrequent, fare for television in the late 1950s. Programs called "Thou Shalt Not Kill" and "The Sacco-Vanzetti Case" were telecast for Los Angeles and New York viewers in 1958. A nationwide audience watched a devastating attack on capital punishment on the season's premier of "Omnibus" in the same year. Boston attorney Joseph Welch, who had won millions of admirers during the televised McCarthy hearings four years before, narrated the "terrifyingly real documentary," which the *New York Times'* critic thought succeeded "brilliantly." [59]

The new reform activity produced scores of abolition bills in state legislatures, but it scored victories in only one state and in two territories on the verge of statehood. Hawaii and Alaska, neither of which had seen an execution for over twenty-five years, ended the death penalty in 1957, as did Delaware in 1958. Delaware's action seemed most significant because her abolition campaign might prove exportable to nearby states where the reform had always been most active. In Delaware, Herbert L. Cobin, president of the Prisoners Aid Society and former deputy attorney general of the state, assumed leadership of the abolition effort in 1957 and compiled the so-called Cobin Report. This 198-page document, the product of several months' intensive labor, made a powerful case for the reform, and Cobin mailed hundreds of copies to state and city officials, religious leaders, mental health experts, and newspapermen. His report and his personal efforts won wide support—even the police agreed not to oppose him—and the legislature, after a public hearing on the subject, passed an abolition bill in March 1958. Governor J. Caleb Boggs signed the bill into law in April, making Delaware the first state to abolish capital punishment in forty years.[70]

The Delaware victory was an exception, however. In other states reformers fought for abolition, but in vain. In California, San Quentin Warden Clinton T. Duffy, San Francisco attorney George T. Davis, the state chapter of the American Civil Liberties Union, and the Friends Committee on Legislation were active in support of reform bills, including several proposals for a moratorium on executions. One moratorium bill won the support of the Assembly in 1957, but no legislation resulted. In New Jersey, in 1958, philosophy professor Hugo A. Bedau began his long and seemingly tireless quest for abolition. Aided by a Princeton Citizens Committee, the Americans for Democratic Action, the Women's International League for Peace and Freedom, and especially the Society of Friends' Social Order Committee, headed by Edmund Goerke, Jr., Bedau sought passage of several reform bills. Police opposition, however, helped kill the measures in committee. In Oregon, in 1957, Governor Robert Holmes and the Oregon Prison Association helped secure an abolition bill and, in 1958, campaigned for voter approval in the required referendum. The state's citizens narrowly rejected the proposal, 278,000 to 264,000 votes. Ohio Governor Michael V. DiSalle led the abolition forces in his state. He made a novel appeal for reform in 1959, when he testified before a legislative committee that nine of the ten members of the governor's household staff were convicted murderers. "Do you think my family is less dear to me than yours?" he asked. The legislators ignored DiSalle's cogent point and the reform bill never passed the committee stage.[71]

Such defeats were to be expected and they failed to daunt the new abolitionists. Delaware had given them hope; now the impending execution of Caryl Chessman would help win the support of thousands and the attention of millions. Chessman, an intelligent and sensitive, if calculating, man, had been sentenced to death for kidnapping in 1948. The books and articles he had written during his twelve years on death row had built his reputation as a literary lion about to be thrown to the Christians. Reprieved an agonizing eight times, Chessman was finally executed on May 2, 1960 (see selection 21), but only after the loudest and most widespread outcry against capital punishment in over thirty years. In California, Governor Edmund G. Brown championed abolition and called a special session of the legislature to consider passage of a bill that would end executions and spare Chessman. When the legislature defeated the bill, Brown reluctantly announced that the state constitution forbade his granting clemency and he steadfastly refused to do so.[72]

Around the nation hundreds of groups asked that Chessman be spared or called for an end to executions in general. State legislators took advantage of the excitement and vainly attempted to push reform bills through to passage. Presidential aspirants were unable to avoid questions on the issue; Nixon announced support for capital punishment, Humphrey opposition, Rockefeller that he would be unable to reply at the present time. The American public could read hundreds of articles about Chessman or capital punishment in general, or watch the documentary film "Justice and Caryl Chessman," or listen to a folk song called "The Ballad of Caryl Chessman." Internationally "the world's most famous prisoner" provoked editorials, petition campaigns, and demonstrations throughout Europe and Latin America. The outcry failed to save Chessman, but it made the American public more conscious of capital punishment and its victims, more aware of some of the arguments for abolition.[73]

Encouraged in part by the Chessman controversy and the moral and practical questions it raised, previously silent individuals and groups in the late 1950s and early 1960s began to register disapproval of the death penalty. By 1960, important conventions or organizations representing large numbers of Baptitsts, Episcopalians, Jews, Methodists, Disciples of Christ, Ethical Culturists, Unitarians, Universalists, and Presbyterians had gone on record in opposition to the death penalty. A large number of local and state religious bodies had taken similar stands. Among elected officials now willing to announce their support of abolition were state executives LeRoy Collins of Florida, Frank Clements of Tennessee, Orville Freeman of Minnesota, G. Mennen Williams of Michigan, Edmund Muskie of Maine, and Endicott Peabody of Massachusetts. Governors Holmes, Brown, Boggs, and DiSalle, of course, had already made their position clear.[74]

Some prominent congressmen, too, shed their customary reticence on the subject. Senator Philip Hart of Michigan and Representative Emmanuel Celler of New York were the chief sponsors of abolition bills in the 1960s. Among their supporters were Senators Morse and Hatfield of Oregon, Javits of New York, Nelson and Proxmire of Wisconsin, Williams of New Jersey, Douglas of Illinois, Mondale and McCarthy of Minnesota, and Kennedy of Massachusetts. Other prominent figures to declare their opposition to the death penalty ranged from Supreme Court Justices Felix Frankfurter and Attorney General Ramsey Clark, to influential popular writers like Truman Capote and William Styron (see selection 23).[75]

Bolstered by such support, reformers created a number of new organizations in the late 1950s and the 1960s. Many were state societies affiliated with the still functioning American League to Abolish Capital Punishment, headed since 1958 by criminologist Donal E. J. MacNamara of New York. Others, independent of the national group, included the California-based People Against Capital Punishment, the New York Committee to Abolish Capital Punishment, and the National Committee to Abolish the Federal Death Penalty.[76]

All of this reform activity did not proceed unopposed. Law enforcement organizations and officials from J. Edgar Hoover to local sheriffs formed the bulwark of the anti-reform camp, and they were able to shore up their position by citing appalling figures about increases in violent crime. Mass murders, urban riots, radical terrorism, and drug-related crimes also were cited in police arguments that only harsh punishments—especially the death penalty—could save the country from anarchy inspired by ubiquitous outside agitators. Abolitionists might produce criminologists and legal scholars of the highest integrity to discount the role of capital punishment in deterring violent crimes and to suggest that it might even encourage them. Federal or state legislators might listen in rapt attention to scholars like Yale's Louis Pollack, Harvard's Sheldon Glueck, Columbia's Herbert Wechsler, and the University of Pennsylvania's Thorsten Sellin (see selection 22). But the legislators' constituents, afraid to walk the streets at night and increasingly uneasy in broad daylight, generally favored the simplistic police position. Most of the legislators voted accordingly.

This was almost precisely the pattern in Delaware, where capital punishment was restored in December 1961. Some murders of elderly whites by young blacks aroused a white population already embittered by the civil rights movement. Law enforcement officials argued that only the death penalty could stop such outrages. Scholars and Governor Elbert N. Carvel pointed out that Delaware's homicide rate had, in fact, dropped in the three years since enactment of abolition. But a few sensational crimes weighed more heavily than sober statistics in the public mind. Legislators, voting for their political futures, passed a restoration bill and, two weeks later, voted to override Governor Carvel's veto. [77]

Other legislators also demonstrated that there was no room for abolition in their practical politics. Vermont and California rejected abolition measures by margins of at least two to one in 1961. Congress held hearings on capital punishment in 1960, but few Congressmen expressed interest in reform. Indeed, in 1961, both houses, in unseemly haste, authorized the death penalty for the new federal crime of air piracy, and President Kennedy signed the act without demurral. Congress added yet another federal capital crime in 1964, when, in response to the Kennedy murder, it authorized death for assassination of the president or vice-president. [78]

Yet the reform made progress in some states. The New York legislature closed the book on an era in 1963, when it became the last American jurisdiction to abandon mandatory capital punishment for first-degree murder. It had taken one hundred twenty-five years for all the states to come to Tennessee's realization of 1838 that mandatory death sanctions inhibited convictions. In 1963, Michigan abolished capital punishment for treason, the only capital crime to survive that state's general abolition law of 1846. Treason against a state was the unlikeliest of crimes—no one had been executed for it in all of American history—and the Michigan action was more a cleansing gesture than a meaningful reform.[79]

Oregon, in 1964, demonstrated that a careful abolition campaign could still overcome fear and unreason. Oregon reformers, led by Hugo Bedau, who in 1962 had moved to that state from New Jersey, won legislative approval of an abolition bill in 1963. The Oregon constitution directed that the voters must approve such a change before enactment, however, and it was to the referendum of November 1964 that the reformers bent most of their efforts. In late 1963, Bedau and his allies organized the Oregon Council to Abolish the Death Penalty, which directed a superbly planned and coordinated campaign. The Council solicited funds nationally (with the assistance of the American League to Abolish Capital Punishment), enlisted sponsors and supporters from Oregon notables of every description, convened a National Conference on Capital Punishment in Portland, and flooded the media with news stories and advertisements. Governor Mark Hatfield and United States Senators Wayne Morse and Maurine Neuberger lent their support, as did several law enforcement officials.

The exhaustive work of the Council and allied organizations, especially the state ACLU affiliate and the Oregon Council of Churches, paid off handsomely. Voters in November 1964 abolished capital punishment by a margin of 455,000 to 302,000, the greatest majority ever obtained for the reform in America. As in Delaware in 1958, the keys to abolition seem to have been detailed planning and the support, or at least acquiescence, of law enforcement officials.[80]

Five other states abolished or strictly limited capital punishment in the middle and late 1960s. Iowa, New York, Vermont, and West Virginia ended executions in 1965; New Mexico became the thirteenth abolition state, in 1969. The abolition victories were a product of gubernatorial leadership, the presence of new legislators carried into office in 1964 on Lyndon Johnson's coattails, and, in at least one state, a bizarre criminal case.[81]

New York was the most significant triumph for the reformers—the Empire State had executed 329 men and women since 1930. Yet the victory, there, was the result of events beyond the reformers' control. George Whitmore, Jr., a nineteen-year-old black man, had confessed to the widely publicized murders of two white women in 1963, and police announced that the crime was solved. By early 1965, however, Whitmore's confession had been exposed as the product of police pressure and Whitmore's weakened frame of mind. The evidence of his guilt, it turned out, was completely concocted by the police, who had believed too much and overlooked too much in their scramble to avoid the adverse publicity attending unsolved murders. The case was shocking to say the least. Whitmore might eventually have died for a crime he did not commit. The carelessness the police had shown in questioning and charging the black man also lent credence to accusations by civil rights leaders that America's criminal justice system discriminated against minorities. Revulsion over the Whitmore case heated the formerly tepid New York abolition campaign to the boiling point and the legislature passed a partial abolition bill by slim majorities.[82]

Victories like that in New York were impossible to duplicate. Oregon's referendum triumph in the year of the Johnson landslide could not be repeated in Colorado in 1966 or in Massachusetts in 1968, where voters upheld capital punishment by wide margins. West Virginia, Iowa, Vermont, and New Mexico proved exceptions to the rule of legislative conservatism elsewhere in the country. Although popular opinion about capital punishment, as recorded by Gallup polls, was almost evenly split between those favoring and opposing the sanction for murder, most of the remaining thirty-seven states seemed destined to preserve their hoary death penalty traditions.[83] If capital punishment was to be ended throughout the United States, reformers would have to devise new strategies, radically different from those of the past one hundred thirty years.

Such a plan was born in 1963, when civil rights attorneys in

New York began to consider the implications of a suggestion by Supreme Court Justice Arthur Goldberg that the death penalty for rape might be unconstitutional. The attorneys were Leroy Clark, Frank Heffron, and Michael Meltsner, all of the NAACP Legal Defense and Educational Fund; their interest in abolition would eventually lead to the greatest single victory ever scored against the executioner in America. With the support of Fund Director Jack Greenberg, staff lawyers began to investigate racial discrimination in capital sentences in southern rape cases. Eventually a summer-long project directed by University of Pennsylvania sociologist Marvin Wolfgang and Fund consultant Anthony G. Amsterdam, then a professor at the University of Pennsylvania Law School, gathered enough data to document this deadly form of racism. [84]

But appeals courts resisted arguments based solely on such statistics, and in 1965 the Fund lawyers agreed on a new moratorium strategy. Henceforth, they would widen their interest from southern black rapists in an effort to block every execution in the United States. In this way, they hoped to create a capital punishment crisis in which death rows would become crowded with inmates. Thus a resumption of executions would necessitate a sudden bloodbath of unprecedented proportions, revolting, it was hoped, to judges and governors alike. Meanwhile, the Fund's lawyers, led by Amsterdam, would undertake a series of test cases in an attempt to restrict or abolish capital punishment. [85]

In 1967, the Fund hired twenty-six-year-old lawyer Jack Himmelstein to coordinate the moratorium efforts; he and Amsterdam cooperated closely over the next five years. One of their first accomplishments was to prepare a so-called "Last Aid Kit," a collection of briefs and forms which would give any attorney with a client on death row the tools to stave off execution. Himmelstein and Amsterdam also established contacts with a large number of experts in related fields, including scholars like Hans Ziesel and Hugo Bedau and psychiatrists like Bernard Diamond and Louis J. West (see selection 25). [86]

In 1970 the Fund also hired Douglas Lyons as a part-time staff member. Lyons was a young law student who had crammed more abolitionist activity into his twenty-two years than some reformers had contributed in a lifetime. His most effective efforts were accomplished through an organization called Citizens Against Legalized Murder, which he had founded in college and had run, sometimes almost single-handedly, ever since. Lyons' chief contribution to the moratorium campaign was to organize a "death watch" to determine when executions were scheduled so that the Fund's attorneys or their allies could head them off. In most states, the reformers won stays of execution for individual criminals. First in Florida, and then in California, unprecedented class action suits won stays for the entire death row population. The result was gratifying. There were seven executions in the United States in 1965, one in 1966, one more in early 1967. Then, on June 2, 1967, Luis José Monge died in Colorado's gas chamber; thereafter, executions ceased entirely.[87]

With the moratorium campaign working, it now devolved upon Amsterdam to devise legal strategies to prevent the resumption of executions. Amsterdam, only thirty years old in 1965, had enjoyed a brief but brilliant legal career. A man of genius and compassion, he had thrown himself into hundreds of civil rights cases in the early 1960s, but gradually came to concentrate on abolishing capital punishment. In the period 1965-1972, no man in America was more important to the achievement of this goal. There were many setbacks before the final victory. Amsterdam and the Fund's attorneys refined the argument that capital punishment was cruel and unusual, in violation of the Eighth Amendment, and presented it to the Supreme Court in *Boykin* v. *Alabama,* a case involving the death sentence for simple robbery. The Court reversed Boykin's conviction, but avoided the Eighth Amendment question. Next the Fund's lawyers shifted to an attack on two common practices, standardless capital sentencing and simultaneous jury determination of guilt and sentence. Both, they argued, violated the Due Process Clause of the Fourteenth Amendment. In *Maxwell* v. *Bishop* (1970), the Supreme Court again spared the petitioner on the narrowest possible grounds and declined to rule on the crucial constitutional issues. In two other cases, *McGautha* v.

California (1971) and *Crampton* v. *Ohio* (1971), Amsterdam and the Fund did not represent the petitioners, but filed an *amicus* brief repeating the arguments of *Maxwell* v. *Bishop*. This time the Court met the arguments, but coldly dismissed them.[88]

The abolition campaign now seemed to be in deep trouble, and Legal Defense Fund attorneys and friends talked forlornly about possible next moves. In June, however, the Supreme Court announced that it would review four cases involving the cruel and unusual punishment question. Hopeful again, the Fund's attorneys began to prepare briefs, the most elaborate for the lead case, *Aikens* v. *California* (see selection 24). Amsterdam and his colleagues presented oral argument on January 17, 1972, then, worriedly, awaited the Court's decision.[89]

It was more than five months before the Supreme Court announced the results of its deliberations. An intervening California Supreme Court decision on February 18, 1972, buoyed the attorneys' hopes. In the California case, *People* v. *Anderson*, Amsterdam had argued that the death penalty violated the state constitution's prohibition of cruel or unusual punishments. The California court agreed in a six-to-one decision and banned capital punishment in the state.[90]

The United States Supreme Court was not as forthright, but its decision on June 29, 1972, in *Furman* v. *Georgia*, which had replaced *Aikens* v. *California* as the lead case, was even more important. There were nine separate opinions, but a bare majority of the Court ruled that capital punishment was cruel and unusual and therefore violative of the Eighth Amendment in the cases under review. Justices Marshall and Brennan indicated in their opinions that they thought capital punishment was cruel and unusual per se. Justices Douglas, Stewart, and White suggested that it was unconstitutional because of its arbitrary and discriminatory operation. The concurrence of the five on the basic issue meant, by extension, that all of the six hundred thirty-one men and women on death rows were spared and that capital punishment, insofar as it was imposed by judges and juries with untrammeled sentencing discretion, was abolished in the United States. The goal of Rush, Livingston, Bovee, and Lawes had at last been won or was at least within reach.[91]

AFTER *FURMAN,* 1972—

The advocates of capital punishment, of course, did not simply give up after the *Furman* decision. Instead, they began proposing new death penalty statutes which they believed would end discrimination in capital sentencing and thus satisfy a majority of the Supreme Court. By January 1975, thirty states had reenacted capital punishment, and almost two hundred prisoners inhabited death row.[92]

The new laws—enacted or proposed—took two forms. Some sought to erect standards which would permit rational, nondiscriminatory means for the courts to decide which convicted criminals should live and which should die. Others attempted to solve the problem by directing a return to mandatory capital punishment for certain narrowly defined crimes.

The state legislators who voted for the new capital punishment statutes were representing the wishes of their constituents as they understood them—and there were indications that they understood them very well. A June 1973 Harris poll found fifty-nine per cent of the American public in favor of capital punishment and only thirty-nine per cent against it. Californians, voting on a referendum question in November 1972, approved four new capital punishment provisions by a two-to-one margin. Colorado voters expressed their clear support for the death penalty in November 1974.[93]

The fight against capital punishment is far from won. A major new Supreme Court decision is inevitable, and reformers—Anthony Amsterdam, Hugo Bedau (see selection 26), and Marvin Wolfgang at their head—are preparing their case for complete abolition. Their new arguments against the death penalty will stress that discrimination in criminal procedure is ineluctable and, thus, that all capital punishment is unconstitutional. There are many imponderables: the makeup of the Supreme Court, the crime rate, the occurrence or non-occurrence of a few especially vicious crimes. The skill and dedication of the reformers are beyond question, however, and it seems a reasonable expectation that the United States will never see another execution.   *Philip English Mackey*

Acknowledgements

The editor would like to thank the many friends and associates who aided in the making of this book. Hugo A. Bedau, Douglas Lyons, Ann Mahoney Mackey and Charles D. Mackey, Jr., provided valuable editorial advice. Generous assistance was also given by the Rutgers University Research Council, Ms. Eve Henry's secretarial staff and the reference librarians of Rutgers University—Camden and the University of Pennsylvania.

A Note On the Selections

Thousands of arguments against capital punishment have been written in the United States over the past two centuries. The twenty-six selections on the following pages represent what I consider the most eloquent, the best argued, or the most characteristic appeals of the periods in which they were written. Some of the arguments are presented in their entirety; others have been edited extensively in order to feature the most appropriate passages. I have indicated alterations in the originals (except for my corrections of typographical errors) by the conventional symbols.

1 BENJAMIN RUSH

The first prominent American to publish an appeal for the complete abolition of capital punishment was Dr. Benjamin Rush (1745-1813). Rush, born near Philadelphia, studied medicine in Edinburgh and returned to Pennsylvania in 1769 to become one of the leading physicians in America. Rush was interested in treating society as well as its individual members, however, and, to use his language, was "engaged in combatting vulgar errors or popular prejudices" for most of his life. In the 1770s, he wrote tracts on temperance and the abolition of slavery. At the same time, he took a lead in the patriot cause and was a signer of the Declaration of Independence. After the Revolution, Rush added penal reform to the causes he championed. He was, in fact, a founder of the Philadelphia Society for Alleviating the Miseries of Public Prisons, which became a fountainhead of reform progress from its creation in 1787.

It is not clear just when Rush came to the conclusion that capital punishment was a "vulgar error" or what influenced this decision. His first public pronouncement of this view came in an essay he read to acquaintances at the home of Benjamin Franklin on March 9, 1787. In this essay, published shortly thereafter as *An Enquiry into the Effects of Public Punishments Upon Criminals and Upon Society*, Rush discussed the death penalty only peripherally. Yet he soon produced another paper devoted exclusively to the subject. The new essay, published in the *American Museum* in July 1788, was, in Rush's opinion, "the boldest attack I have ever made upon a public opinion or a general practice." Angry criticism of the essay caused Rush to add some material and he published the resultant *Considerations on the Injustice and Impolicy of Punishing Murder by*

Death in 1792. Yet another version, "An Enquiry Into the Consistency of the Punishment of Murder by Death, With Reason and Revelation," appeared in a book of essays that Rush published in 1798. All three works are excerpted in this volume.

Although Rush borrowed some of his arguments from Italian jurist Cesare Beccaria's *On Crimes and Punishment,* published in 1764, it is more interesting to note what Rush added. Rush apparently invented his arguments that capital punishment makes convictions harder to obtain, that murderers are usually not hardened criminals likely to murder again, and that the death penalty invites murders by those who want the state to help them commit suicide. More fundamentally, Rush devoted most of his attack to religious arguments, whereas Beccaria ignored God and the Bible completely. In Europe, a reformer could write for the edification of princes and philosophs and restrict himself to utilitarian arguments. In America, however, abolition could come about only with the support of the general reading public, and religious appeals dominated the capital punishment controversy for a century.

Abolish the Absurd and Unchristian Practice (1787, 1792, 1797)

I have said nothing upon the manner of inflicting death as a punishment for crimes, because I consider it as an improper punishment for *any* crime. Even murder itself is propagated by the punishment of death for murder. Of this we have a remarkable proof in Italy. The duke of Tuscany soon after the publication of the marquis of Beccaria's excellent treatise upon this subject, abolished death as a punishment for murder.[1] A gentleman, who resided five years at Pisa, informed me, that only five murders had been perpetrated in his dominions in twenty years. The same gentleman added, that after his residence in Tuscany,

From Benjamin Rush, *An Enquiry into the Effects of Public Punishments Upon Criminals and Upon Society* (Philadelphia: Joseph James, 1787), pp. 15-18.

he spent three months in Rome, where death is still the punishment of murder, and where executions, according to Dr. Moore,[2] are conducted with peculiar circumstances of public parade. During this short period, there were sixty murders committed in the precincts of that city. It is remarkable, the manners, principles, and religion, of the inhabitants of Tuscany and Rome, are exactly the same. The abolition of death alone, as a punishment for murder, produced this difference in the moral character of the two nations.

I suspect the attachment to death, as a punishment for murder, in minds otherwise enlightened, upon the subject of capital punishments, arises from a false interpretation of a passage contained in the old testament, and that is, "he that sheds the blood of man, by man shall his blood be shed."[3] This has been supposed to imply that blood could only be expiated by blood. But I am disposed to believe, with a late commentator[4] upon this text of scripture, that it is rather a *prediction* than a *law*. The language of it is simply, that such will be the depravity and folly of man, that murder, in every age, shall beget murder. Laws, therefore, which inflict death for murder, are, in my opinion, as unchristian as those which justify or tolerate revenge; for the obligations of christianity upon individuals, to promote repentance, to forgive injuries, and to discharge the duties of universal benevolence, are equally binding upon states.

The power over human life, is the sole prerogative of him who gave it. Human laws, therefore, rise in rebellion against this prerogative, when they transfer it to human hands.

If society can be secured from violence, by confining the murderer, so as to prevent a repetition of his crime, the end of extirpation will be answered. In confinement, he may be reformed: and if this should prove impracticable, he may be restrained for a term of years, that will probably, be coeval with his life.

* * *

I shall conclude this enquiry by observing, that the same false religion and philosophy, which once kindled the fire on the alter of persecution, now doom the criminal to public ignominy and death. In proportion as the principles of philosophy and christianity are understood, they will agree in extinguishing the one, and destroying the other. If these principles continue to extend their influence upon government, as they have done for some years past, I cannot help entertaining a hope, that the time is not very distant, when the gallows, the pillory, the stocks, the whipping-post and the wheel-barrow, (the usual engines of public punishments) will be connected with the history of the rack and the stake, as marks of the barbarity of ages and countries, and as melancholy proofs of the feeble operation of reason and religion upon the human mind.

––––––––––––––

I. The Punishment of Murder by Death, is contrary to *reason,* and to the order and happiness of society.

1. It lessens the horror of taking away human life, and thereby tends to multiply murders.

2. It produces murder by its influence upon people who are tired of life, and who, from a supposition that murder is a less crime than suicide, destroy a life (and often that of a near connection) and afterwards deliver themselves up to the laws of their country, that they may escape from their misery by means of a halter.

3. The punishment of murder by death multiplies murders, from the difficulty it creates of convicting persons who are guilty of it. Humanity, revolting at the idea of the severity and certainty of a capital punishment, often steps in, and collects such evidence in favour of a murderer, as screens him from death altogether, or palliates his crime into manslaughter. Even the law itself favours the acquital of a murderer by making the circumstance of premeditation and malice, necessary to render the offence, a capital crime. . . . If the punishment of murder consisted in long confinement, and hard labour, it would be

From Benjamin Rush, "An Enquiry into the Consistency of the Punishment of Murder by Death, with Reason and Revelation," in *Essays, Literary, Moral and Philosophical* (Philadelphia: Bradford, 1798), pp. 164-182.

proportioned to the measure of our feelings of justice, and every member of society would be a watchman, or a magistrate, to apprehend a destroyer of human life, and to bring him to punishment.

4. The punishment of murder by death checks the operations of universal justice, by preventing the punishment of every species of murder.

5. The punishment of murder by death has been proved to be contrary to the order and happiness of society, by the experiments of some of the wisest legislators in Europe. The Empress of Russia, the King of Sweden, and the Duke of Tuscany,[5] have nearly extirpated murder from their dominions, by converting its punishments into the means of benefiting society, and reforming the criminals who perpetrate it.

II. The punishment of murder by death is contrary to *divine revelation*. A religion which commands us to forgive, and even to do good to, our enemies, can never authorise the punishment of murder by death. "Vengence is mine," said the Lord; "I will repay." It is to no purpose to say here, that this vengeance is taken out of the hands of an individual, and directed against the criminal by the hand of government. It is equally an usurpation of the prerogative of heaven, whether it be inflicted by a single person, or by a whole community.

Here I expect to meet with an appeal from the letter and spirit of the gospel, to the law of Moses, which declares, "he that killeth a man shall be put to death."[6] Forgive, indulgent heaven! the ignorance and cruelty of man, which, by the misapplication of this text of scripture, has so long and so often stained the religion of Jesus Christ with folly and revenge.

The following considerations, I hope, will prove that no argument can be deduced from this law, to justify the punishment of murder by death;—on the contrary, that several arguments against it, may be derived from a just and rational explanation of that part of the Levitical institutions.

1. There are many things in scripture above, but nothing contrary to, reason. Now, the punishment of murder by death, is contrary to reason. It cannot, therefore, be agreeable to the will of God.

2. The order and happiness of society cannot fail of being

agreeable to the will of God. But the punishment of murder by death, destroys the order and happiness of society. It must therefore be contrary to the will of God.

3. Many of the laws given by Moses, were accommodated to the ignorance, wickedness, and "hardness of heart," of the Jews. Hence their divine legislator expressly says, "I gave them statutes that were not good, and judgments whereby they should not live." Of this, the law which respects divorces, and the law of retaliation, which required, "an eye for an eye, and a tooth for a tooth," are remarkable instances.

But we are told, that the punishment of murder by death, is founded not only on the law of Moses, but upon a positive precept to Noah and his posterity, that "whoso sheddeth man's blood, by man shall his blood be shed." If the interpretation of this text given in a former essay [7] be not admitted, I shall attempt to explain it by remarking, that soon after the flood, the infancy and weakness of society rendered it impossible to punish murder by confinement. There was therefore no medium between inflicting death upon a murderer, and suffering him to escape with impunity, and thereby to perpetrate more acts of violence against his fellow creatures. It pleased God, in this condition of the world, to permit a less, in order to prevent a greater evil. He therefore commits for a while his exclusive power over human life, to his creatures for the safety and preservation of an infant society, which might otherwise have perished, and with it, the only stock of the human race. The command indirectly implies that the crime of murder was not punished by death in the mature state of society which existed before the flood. Nor is this the only instance upon record in the scriptures in which God has delegated his power over human life to his creatures. Abraham expresses no surprise at the command which God gave him to sacrifice his son. He submits to it as a precept founded in reason and natural justice, for nothing could be more obvious, than that the giver of life had a right to claim it, when and in such manner as he pleased. 'Till men are able to give life, it becomes them to tremble at the thought of taking it away. Will a man rob God? —Yes—he robs him of what is infinitely dear to him—of his darling attribute of mercy, every time he deprives a fellow creature of life.

4. If the Mosaic law, with respect to murder, be obligatory upon Christians, it follows that it is equally obligatory upon them to punish adultery, blasphemy and other capital crimes that are mentioned in the Levitical law, by death. Nor is this all: it justifies the extirpation of the Indians, and the enslaving of the Africans; for the command to the Jews to destroy the Canaanites, and to make slaves of their heathen neighbours, is as positive as the command which declares, "that he that killeth a man, shall surely be put to death."

5. Every part of the Levitical law, is full of types of the Messiah. May not the punishment of death, inflicted by it, be intended to represent the demerit and consequences of sin, as the cities of refuge were the offices of the Messiah? And may not the enlargement of murderers who had fled to those cities of refuge, upon the death of a high priest, represent the eternal abrogation of the law which inflicted death for murder, by the meritorious death of the Saviour of the world?

6. The imperfection and severity of these laws were probably intended farther—to illustrate the perfection and mildness of the gospel dispensation. It is in this manner that God has manifested himself in many of his acts. He created darkness first, to illustrate by comparison the beauty of light, and he permits sin, misery, and death in the moral world, that he may hereafter display more illustriously the blessings of righteousness, happiness, and immortal life. This opinion is favoured by St. Paul, who says, "the law made nothing perfect, and that it was a shadow of good things to come."

How delightful to discover such an exact harmony between the dictates of reason, the order and happiness of society, and the precepts of the gospel! There is a perfect unity in truth. Upon all subjects—in all ages and in all countries—truths of every kind agree with each other. I shall now take notice of some of the common arguments, which are made use of, to defend the punishments of murder by death.

1. It has been said, that the common sense of all nations, and particularly of savages, is in favour of punishing murder by death.

The common sense of all nations is in favour of the commerce and slavery of their fellow creatures. But this does not take away from their immorality. Could it be proved that the Indians punish murder by death, it would not establish the right of man over the life of a fellow creature; for revenge we know in its utmost extent is the universal and darling passion of all savage nations. The practice morever [*sic*], (if it exist) must have originated in *necessity*: for a people who have no settled place of residence, and who are averse from all labour, could restrain murder in no other way. But I am disposed to doubt whether the Indians punish murder by death among their own tribes. In all those cases where a life is taken away by an Indian of a foreign tribe, they always demand the satisfaction of life for life. But this practice is founded on a desire of preserving a balance in their numbers and power; for among nations which consist of only a few warriors, the loss of an individual often destroys this balance, and thereby exposes them to war or extermination. It is for the same purpose of keeping up an equality in numbers and power, that they often adopt captive children into their nations and families. What makes this explanation of the practice of punishing murder by death among the Indians more probable, is, that we find the same bloody and vindictive satisfaction is required of a foreign nation, whether the person lost, be killed by an accident, or premeditated violence. Many facts might be mentioned from travellers to prove that the Indians do not punish murder by death within the jurisdiction of their own tribes. I shall mention only one, which is taken from the Rev. Mr. John Megapolensis's account of the Mohawk Indians, lately published in Mr. Hazard's historical collection of state papers.[8] —"There is no punishment, (says our author) "here for murder, but every one is his own avenger. The friends of the deceased revenge themselves upon the murderer until peace is made with the next a kin. But although they are so cruel, yet there are not half so many murders committed among them as among Christians, notwithstanding their severe laws, and heavy penalties."

2. It has been said, that the horrors of a guilty conscience proclaim the justice and necessity of death, as a punishment for murder. I draw an argument of another nature from this fact. Are the horrors of conscience the punishment that God inflicts

upon murder? Why, then should we shorten or destroy them by death, especially as we are taught to direct the most atrocious murderers to expect pardon in the future world? No, let us not counteract the government of God in the human breast: let the murderer live—but let it be to suffer the reproaches of a guilty conscience; let him live, to make compensation to society for the injury he has done it, by robbing it of a citizen; let him live to maintain the family of the man whom he has murdered; let him live, that the punishment of his crime may become universal? and, lastly, let him live, that murder may be extirpated from the list of human crimes!

Let us examine the conduct of the moral Ruler of the world towards the first murderer.—See Cain, returning from his field, with his hands reeking with the blood of his brother! Do the heavens gather blackness, and does a flash of lightning blast him to the earth? No. Does his father Adam, the natural legislator and judge of the world, inflict upon him the punishment of death? No. The infinitely wise God becomes his judge and executioner. He expels him from the society of which he was a member. He fixes in his conscience a never dying worm. He subjects him to the necessity of labour; and to secure a duration of his punishment, proportioned to his crime, he puts a mark of prohibition upon him, to prevent his being put to death, by weak and angry men; declaring, at the same time, that "whosoever slayeth Cain, vengeance shall be taken on him seven-fold."

But further, if a necessary connection existed between the crime of murder and death in the mind and laws of the Deity, how comes it that Moses and David escaped it? They both imbrued their hands in innocent blood, and yet the horrors of a guilty conscience were their only punishment. The subsequent conduct of those two great and good men, proves that the heart may retain a sound part after committing murder, and that even murderers, after repentance, may be the vehicles of great temporal and spiritual blessings to mankind.

3. The declaration of St. Paul before Festus, respecting the punishment of death, and the speech of the dying thief on the cross, are said to prove the lawfulness of punishing murder by death: but they prove only that the punishment of death was

agreeable to the Roman law. Human life was extremely cheap under the Roman government. Of this we need no further proof than the head of John the Baptist forming a part of a royal entertainment. From the frequency of public executions, among those people, the *sword* was considered as an emblem of public justice. But to suppose, from the appeals which are sometimes made to it as a sign of justice, that capital punishments are approved of in the New Testament, is as absurd as it would be to suppose that horse-racing was a christian exercise, from St. Paul's frequent allusions to the Olympic games.

The declaration of the barbarians upon seeing the snake fasten upon St. Paul's hand, proves nothing but the ignorance of those uncivilized people;—"and when the barbarians saw the venemous beast hang on his hand, they said among themselves, no doubt this man is a murderer, whom, though he hath escaped the sea, yet vengeance suffereth not to live."—Acts xvii. and 4th.

Here it will be proper to distinguish between the sense of justice so universal among all nations, and an approbation of death as a punishment for murder. The former is written by the finger of God upon every human heart, but like his own attribute of justice, it has the happiness of individuals and of society for its objects. It is always misled, when it seeks for satisfaction in punishments that are injurious to society, or that are disproportioned to crimes. The satisfaction of this universal sense of justice by the punishments of imprisonment and labour, would far exceed that which is derived from the punishment of death; for it would be of longer duration, and it would more frequently occur; for, upon a principle formerly mentioned, scarcely any species of murder would escape with impunity.

The conduct and discourses of our Saviour should outweigh every argument that has been or can be offered in favour of capital punishment for any crime. When the woman caught in adultery was brought to him, he evaded inflicting the bloody sentence of the Jewish law upon her. Even the *maiming* of the body appears to be offensive in his sight; for when Peter drew his sword, and smote off the ear of the servant of the high priest, he replaced it by miracle, and at the same time declared,

that "all they who take the sword, shall perish with the sword."
He forgave the crime of murder, on his cross; and after his
resurrection, he commanded his disciples to preach the gospel
of forgiveness, *first* at Jerusalem, where he well knew his murderers still resided. These striking facts are recorded for our
imitation, and seem intended to shew that the Son of God died,
not only to reconcile God to man, but to reconcile men to each
other. There is one passage more, in the history of our Saviour's
life which would of itself overset the justice of the punishment
of death for murder, if every other part of the Bible had been
silent upon the subject. When two of his disciples, actuated by
the spirit of vindictive legislators, requested permission of him
to call down fire from Heaven to consume the inhospitable
Samaritans, he answered them "The Son of Man is not come to
destroy men's *lives* but to save them." I wish these words composed the motto of the arms of every nation upon the face of
the earth. They inculcate every duty that is calculated to preserve, restore, or prolong human life. They militate alike against
war—and capital punishments—the objects of which, are the un-
profitable destruction of the lives of men. How precious does a
human life appear from these words, in the sight of heaven!
Pause, Legislators, when you give your votes for inflicting the
punishment of death for any crime. You frustrate in one instance, the design of the mission of the Son of God into the
world, and thereby either deny his appearance in the flesh, or
reject the truth of his gospel. You, moreover, strengthen by
your conduct the arguments of the Deists against the particular
doctrines of the Christian revelation. You do more, you preserve a bloody fragment of the Jewish institutions.—"The Son
of Man came not to *destroy* men's lives, but to *save* them."
Excellent words! I require no others to satisfy me of the truth
and divine original of the Christian religion; and while I am able
to place a finger, upon this text of scripture, I will not believe
an angel from heaven should he declare that the punishment of
death, for *any* crime, was inculcated, or permitted by the spirit
of the gospel.

The precious nature of human life in the eyes of the Saviour
of mankind, appears further in the comparative value which he

has placed upon it in the following words. "For what is a man profited, if he shall gain the whole world, & lose his life, or what shall a man give in exchange for his *life*." I have rejected the word soul which is used in the common translation of this verse. The original word in the Greek, signifies *life,* and it is thus happily and justly translated in the verse which precedes it.

4. It has been said, that a man who has committed a murder, has discovered a malignity of heart, that renders him ever afterwards unfit to live in human society. This is by no means true in many, and perhaps in most of the cases of murder. It is most frequently the effect of a sudden gust of passion, and has sometimes been the only stain of a well-spent, or inoffensive life. There are many crimes which unfit a man much more for human society, than a single murder; and there have been instances of murderers, who have escaped, or bribed the laws of their country, who have afterwards become peaceable and useful members of society. Let it not be supposed that I wish to palliate, by this remark, the enormity of murder. Far from it. It is only because I view murder with such superlative horror, that I wish to deprive our laws of the power of perpetuating and encouraging it.

It has been said, that the confessions of murderers have, in many instances, sanctioned the justice of their punishment. I do not wish to lessen the influence of such vulgar errors as tend to prevent crimes, but I will venture to declare, that many more murderers escape discovery, than are detected, or punished.— Were I not afraid of trespassing upon the patience of my readers, I might mention a number of facts, in which circumstances of the most trifling nature have become the means of detecting theft and forgery; from which I could draw as strong proofs of the watchfulness of Providence over the property of individuals, and the order of society, as have been drawn from the detection of murder. I might mention instances, likewise, of persons in whom conscience has produced restitution for stolen goods, or confession of the justice of the punishment which was inflicted for theft. Conscience and knowledge always keep pace with each other, both with respect to divine and human laws.

The acquiescence of murderers in the justice of their execution, is the effect of prejudice and education. It cannot flow from a conscience acting in concert with reason or religion—for they both speak a very different language.

The world has certainly undergone a material change for the better within the last two hundred years. This change has been produced chiefly, by the secret and unacknowledged influence of Christianity upon the hearts of men. It is agreeable to trace the effects of the Christian religion in the extirpation of slavery —in the diminution of the number of capital punishments, and in the mitigation of the horrors of war. There was a time when masters possessed a power over the lives of their slaves. But Christianity has deposed this power, and mankind begin to see everywhere that slavery is alike contrary to the interests of society, and the spirit of the gospel. There was a time when torture was part of the punishment of death, and when the number of capital crimes in Great Britain, amounted to one hundred and sixty-one.—Christianity has abolished the former, and reduced the latter to not more than six or seven. It has done more. It has confined, in some instances, capital punishments to the crime of murder—and in some countries it has abolished it altogether. . . .

But I despair of making such an impression upon the present citizens of the united states, as shall abolish the absurd and unchristian practice. From the connexion of this essay with the valuable documents of the late revolution contained in the American Museum,[9] it will probably descend to posterity. To you, therefore, the unborn generations of the next century, I consecrate this humble tribute to justice. . . .

From Benjamin Rush, *Considerations on the Injustice and Impolicy of Punishing Murder by Death* (Philadelphia: Carey, 1792), p. 9.

2 EDWARD LIVINGSTON

Probably no American opponent of capital punishment has been so influential as Edward Livingston (1764-1836). Livingston, a member of one of New York's most prominent families, was building a splendid career in law and politics when a financial scandal forced his flight from the state in 1803. Livingston resettled in the recently acquired territory of Louisiana and within a short time became a prominent lawyer in New Orleans. He returned to politics in 1820 and served as state and national legislator, secretary of state, and minister to France during the remaining sixteen years of his life.

Livingston had a long record of support for criminal law reform when he entered the Louisiana Assembly in 1820. As a result, his colleagues were receptive to his proposal that he undertake a revision of the criminal laws of the state, a task he began in early 1821. A little more than a year later Livingston presented the legislators with his "Report on the Plan of a Penal Code," a portion of which was a long justification for omitting capital punishment from the new laws. The legislature tentatively approved the plan, and Livingston turned to drafting a number of codes, including the "Code of Crimes and Punishments," which he completed in 1825. An "Introductory Report" affixed to this document contained another long defense of the abolition of capital punishment.

Livingston's ideas were too advanced, perhaps, for his fellow Louisianans, for the state never adopted the new criminal code or what the reformer considered the "one most important principle" of the work, abolition of the death penalty. Livingston's writings had an enormous influence outside the state, however, where they were reprinted in a number of editions. European

and American intellectuals praised the boldness of his ideas and
the eloquence of his arguments. More important, reformers in a
number of states mined his writings to strengthen their own
arguments for the limitation or abolition of the death penalty.
In the period 1833-1853, there were hundreds of active anti-
gallows reformers in America. Virtually all used the arguments
—many the exact language—of Edward Livingston.

Livingston's writings on capital punishment showed a debt to
Benjamin Rush, but in their predominately secular approach
were more in the tradition of Beccaria. Most of the arguments,
however, were of Livingston's own devising: the danger of executing the innocent, the inefficacy of capital punishment as a
deterrent, the disruptions which the sanction causes in the administration of justice. That so much of today's debate is discussed in the same terms suggests the importance, the greatness,
of Livingston and his work.

The Crime of Employing the Punishment of Death (1822, 1825)

I . . . [have come] to the conclusion, that the punishment of
death should find no place in the code which you have directed
me to present.

* * *

. . . I proceed therefore to develope the considerations which
carried conviction to my mind, but which being perhaps now
more feebly urged than they were then felt, may fail in producing the same effect upon others. A great part of my task is
rendered unnecessary, by the general acknowledgment, univer-

From Edward Livingston, "Report on the Plan of a Penal Code," in *The Complete
Works of Edward Livingston on Criminal Jurisprudence* (New York: National Prison
Asso., 1873), vol. I, pp. 35-59. Reprinted from Philip English Mackey, ed., "Edward
Livingston on the Punishment of Death," *Tulane Law Review,* 48 (December 1973),
pp. 25-42.

sal, I may say, in the United States, that this punishment ought to be abolished in all cases, excepting those of treason, murder and rape.[1] In some states arson is included; and lately, since so large a portion of our influential citizens have become bankers, brokers, and dealers in exchange, a strong inclination has been discovered to extend it to forgery, and uttering false bills of exchange. As it is acknowledged then to be an inadequate remedy for minor offences, the argument will be restricted to an inquiry, whether there is any probability that it will be more efficient in cases of greater importance. Let us have constantly before us, when we reason on this subject, the great principle, that the end of punishment is the prevention of crime. Death, indeed, operates this end most effectually, as respects the delinquent; but the great object of inflicting it is the force of the example on others. If this spectacle of horror is insufficient to deter men from the commission of slight offences, what good reason can be given to persuade us that it will have this operation where the crime is more atrocious? . . .

It is, on the contrary, a remedy peculiarly inapplicable to those [great] offences. Ambition, which usually inspires the crime of treason, soars above the fear of death; avarice, which whispers the secret murder, creeps below it; and the brutal debasement of the passion that prompts the only other crime, thus punished by our law, is proverbially blind to consequences, and regardless of obstacles that impede its gratification—threats of death will never deter men who are actuated by these passions; many of them affront it in the very commission of the offence, and therefore readily incur the lesser risk of suffering it, in what they think the impossible event of detection. But present other consequences more directly opposed to the enjoyments which were anticipated in the commission of the crime, make those consequences permanent and certain, and then, although milder, they will be less readily risked than the momentary pang attending the loss of life; study the passions which first suggested the offence, and apply your punishment to mortify and counteract them. The ambitious man cannot bear the ordinary restraints of government—subject him to those of a prison; he could not endure the superiority of the most dignified magistrate—force him to submit to the lowest officer of executive justice; he sought, by his crimes, a superiority above all that was most respectable in society—reduce him in his punishment to a level with the most vile and abject of mankind. If avarice suggested the murder—separate the wretch for ever from his hoard; realize the fable of antiquity; sentence him, from his place of penitence and punishment, to see his heirs rioting on his spoils; and the corroding reflection that others are innocently enjoying the fruits of his crime, will be as appropriate a punishment in practical as it was feigned to be in poetical justice. The rapacious spendthrift robs to support his extravagance, and murders to avoid detection; he exposes his life that he may either pass it in idleness, debauchery and sensual enjoyment, or lost it by a momentary pang—disappoint his profligate calculation; force him to live, but to live under those privations which he fears more than death; let him be reduced to the coarse diet, the hard lodging, and the incessant labour of a penitentiary.[2]

Substitute these privations, which all such offenders fear, which they have all risked their lives to avoid; substitute these, to that death which has little terror for men whose passions or depravity have forced them to plunge in guilt, and you establish a fitness in the punishment to the crime; instead of a momentary spectacle, you exhibit a lesson, that is every day renewed; and you make the very passions which caused the offence the engines to punish it, and prevent its repetition.

* * *

In coming to a resolution on this solemn subject, we must not forget another principle we have established, and I think on the soundest reasons, that other things being equal, that punishment should be preferred, which gives us the means of correcting any false judgment, to which passion, indifference, false testimony, or deceiving appearances, may have given rise. Error from these, or other causes, is sometimes inevitable, its operation is instantaneous, and its fatal effects in the punishment of death, follow without delay; but time is required for its correction; we retrace our steps with difficulty; it is mortifying to acknowledge that we have been unjust, and during the time requisite for the discovery of the truth, for its operation on our unwilling minds, for the interposition of that power, which alone can stop the execution of the law, its stroke falls, and the innocent victim dies. What would not then the jurors who convicted; the judges who condemned; the mistaken witness who testified to his guilt; what would not the whole community who saw his dying agonies, who heard, at that solemn moment, his fruitless asseverations of innocence; what would they not all give to have yet within their reach the means of repairing the wrongs they had witnessed or inflicted?

... This consideration alone, then, if there were no others, would be a most powerful argument for the abolition of capital punishments; but there are others no less cogent.

To see a human being in the full enjoyment of all the faculties of his mind, and all the energies of his body; his vital powers attacked by no disease; injured by no accident; the pulse beating high with youth and health; to see him doomed by the cool calculation of his fellow-men to certain destruction, which no courage can repel, no art or persuasion avert; to see a mortal distribute the most awful dispensations of the Deity, usurp his attributes, and fix, by his own decree, an inevitable limit to that existence which Almighty power alone can give, and which its sentence alone should destroy; must give rise to solemn reflections, which the imposing spectacle of a human sacrifice naturally produces, until its frequent recurrence renders the mind insensible to the impression. But in a country where the punishment of death is rarely inflicted, this sensation operates in all its force; the people are always strongly excited by every trial for a capital offence; they neglect their business, and crowd round the court; the accused, the witnesses, the counsel, everything connected with the investigation becomes a matter of interest and curiosity; when the public mind is screwed up to this pitch, it will take a tone from the circumstances of the case, which will rarely be found to accord with the impartiality acquired by justice.

If the accused excite an interest from his youth, his good character, his connections, or even his countenance and appearance, the dreadful consequences of conviction, and that, too, in the case of great crimes as well as minor offences, lead prosecutors to relax their severity, witnesses to appear with reluctance, jurors to acquit against evidence, and the pardoning power improperly to interpose. If the public excitement take another turn, the consequences are worse; indignation against the crime is created into a ferocious thirst of vengeance; and if the real culprit cannot be found, the innocent suffers on the slightest presumption of guilt; when public zeal requires a victim, the innocent lamb is laid on the altar, while the scape-goat is suffered to fly to the mountain. This savage disposition increases with the severity and the frequency of capital inflictions, so that in atrocious as well as in lighter offences, this species of punishment leads sometimes to the escape of the guilty, often to the conviction of the innocent.

Whoever has at all observed the course of criminal proceedings, must have witnessed what I have just endeavoured to describe; undeserved indulgence, unjust severity; opposite effects proceeding from the same cause; the unnecessary harshness of the punishment.

But when no such fatal consequences are to be the result, the course of justice is rarely influenced by passion or prejudice. The evidence is produced without difficulty, and given without reluctance; it has its due effect on the minds of jurors, who are under no terrors of pronouncing an irremediable sentence: and pardons need not be granted, unless innocence is ascertained, or reformation becomes unequivocal.

Another consequence of the infliction of death is, that if frequent it loses its effect; the people become too much familiarized with it to consider it as an example; it is changed into a spectacle, which must frequently be repeated to satisfy the ferocious taste it has formed. . . .

But if this punishment be kept for great occasions, and the people are seldom treated with the gratification of seeing one of their fellow-creatures expire by the sentence of the law; a most singular effect is produced; the sufferer, whatever be his crime, becomes a hero or a saint; he is the object of public attention, curiosity, admiration, and pity. . . .

Thus the end of the law is defeated, the force of example is totally lost, and the place of execution is converted into a scene of triumph for the sufferer, whose crime is wholly forgotten, while his courage, resignation, or piety, mark him as the martyr, not the guilty victim, of the laws.

Where laws are so directly at war with the feelings of the people whom they govern, as this and many other instances prove them to be, these laws can never be wise or operative, and they ought to be abolished.

* * *

I do not urge the doubts which many wise and conscientious persons have entertained of the right of inflicting this punishment, because I am inclined to think that the right can be well established. If this measure be the only one that can prevent the crime, government has a right to adopt it, unless the evil arising from the punishment be greater than that which could be apprehended from the offence. If it were proved, that the fruit in a garden could not be preserved without punishing the boys who stole it with death, the evil to be apprehended from the offence is so much less than that produced by the punishment, that it ought never to be inflicted by the law, much less . . . by the party injured; but on the contrary, it is a less evil to destroy the life of an assassin, than to permit him to take that of a man, whose existence is useful to his country, and necessary to his family. Whenever, therefore, in this latter case, the alternative is proved to be the only one, I do not think that we ought to hesitate from any doubt of the right: but if the necessity of the punishment, as well as the preponderating evil of the crime, cannot be clearly shown, the right cannot exist. The burthen of argument rests here on those who advocate this punishment; they must show that it is the only means of repressing the offence: they must show, that in the cases to which they mean to apply it, the evil of the offence is greater that the punishment. . . .

But . . . we ought to inquire . . . whether the punishment of death is necessary to prevent offences. . . . [S]ome reasons have already been given to show that it is not. Let us examine those which are usually given on the affirmative side of this interesting question.

First. There are those who support it by arguments drawn from religion. The divine spirit infused into the great legislator of the Jews, from whose code these arguments are drawn, was never intended to inspire a system of universal jurisprudence. The theocracy given as a form of government to that extraordinary people, was not suited to any other; as little was the system of their penal laws, given on the mysterious mountain, promulgated from the bosom of a dark cloud, amid thunder and lightning; they were intended to strike terror into the minds of a perverse and obdurate people; and as one means of effecting this, the punishment of death is freely denounced for a long list of crimes; but the same authority establishes the *lex talionis,* and other regulations, which those who quote this authority would surely not wish to adopt. They forget that the same Almighty author of that law, at a later period, inspired one of his prophets with a solemn assurance, that might with propriety be placed over the gates of a penitentiary, and confirmed it with an awful asseveration,—"As I LIVE saith the LORD GOD, I have no pleasure in the DEATH of a sinner, but rather that he should TURN FROM HIS WICKEDNESS AND LIVE." They forget, too, although they are Christians who use this argument, that the divine author of their religion expressly forbids the retaliatory system, on which the punishment of death for murder is founded. . . . Indeed, if I were inclined to support my opinion by arguments drawn from religion, the whole New Testament should be my text, and I could easily deduce from it authority for a system of reform as opposed to one of extermination. But although the legislator would be unworthy of the name, who should prescribe anything contrary to the dictates of religion, and particularly to those of that divine morality on which the Christian system is founded, yet it would not be less dangerous, to make its dogmas the ground-work of his legislation, or to array them in defence of political systems. In a government, where all religions have equal privileges, it would be obviously unjust; it would lessen the reverence for sacred, by mixing them with political institutions, and perverting to temporal uses those precepts which were given as rules for the attainment of eternal happiness.

Secondly. The practice of all nations, from the remotest
antiquity, is urged in favour of this punishment; the fact, with
some exceptions, is undoubtedly true, but is the inference just?
There are general errors, and unfortunately for mankind, but
few general truths, established by practice, in government legislation. Make this the criterion, and despotism is, by many thousand degrees on the scale of antiquity, better than a representative government: the laws of Draco were more ancient than
those of Solon, and consequently better; and the practice of
torture quite as generally diffused as that of which we are now
treating. Idolatry in religion, tyranny in government, capital
punishments, and inhuman tortures in jurisprudence, are coeval
and coextensive. Will the advocates of this punishment admit
the force of their argument in favour of all these abuses? If they
do not, how will they apply it to the one for which they argue?

The long and general usage of any institution gives us the
means of examining its practical advantages or defects: but it
ought to have no authority as a precedent, until it be proved,
that the best laws are the most ancient, and that institutions for
the happiness of the people are the most permanent and most
generally diffused. But this unfortunately cannot be maintained
with truth; the melancholy reverse forces conviction on our
minds. . . .

* * *

The third and last argument I have heard urged, is nearly
allied to the second; it is, the danger to be apprehended from
innovation. I confess, I always listen to this objection with some
degree of suspicion. That men who owe their rank, their privileges, their emoluments, to abuses and impositions, originating
in the darkness of antiquity, and consecrated by time; that such
men should preach the danger of innovations, I can well conceive; the wonder is, that they can find others weak and credu-
lous enough to believe them. But in a country where these
abuses do not exist; in a country whose admirable system of
government is founded wholly on innovation, where there is no
antiquity to create a false veneration for abuses, and no apparent interest to perpetuate them; in such a country, this argu-

ment will have little force against the strong reasons which assail
it. Let those, however, who honestly entertain this doubt, reflect that, most fortunately for themselves and for their posterity, they live in an age of advancement: not an art, not a science,
that has not in our day made rapid progress towards perfection.
The one of which we now speak has received, and is daily
acquiring, improvement; how long is it since torture was abolished? Since judges were made independent? Since personal
liberty was secured, and religious persecution forbidden? All
these were, in their time, innovations as bold at least as the one
now proposed. The true use of this objection, and there I confess it has force, is to prevent any hazardous experiment, or the
introduction of any change that is not strongly recommended
by reason. I desire no other test for the one that is now under
discussion, but I respectfully urge that it would be unwise to
reject it, merely because it is untried, if we are convinced it will
be beneficial. Should our expectations be disappointed, no extensive evil can be done; the remedy is always in our power.
Although an experiment, it is not a hazardous one, and the only
inquiry seems to be, whether the arguments and facts stated in
its favour are sufficiently strong to justify us in making it. Indeed, it appears to me that the reasoning might, with some
propriety, be retorted against those who use it, by saying, "All
punishments are but experiments to discover what will best
prevent crimes; your favourite one of death has been fully tried.
By your own account, all nations, since the first institution of
society, have practised it, but you yourselves must acknowledge, without success. All we ask, then, is that you abandon an
experiment which has for five or six thousand years been pro-
gressing under all the variety of forms which cruel ingenuity
could invent; and which in all ages, under all governments, has
been found wanting. You have been obliged reluctantly to confess that it is inefficient, and to abandon it in minor offences;
what charm has it then which makes you cling to it in those of a
graver cast? You have made your experiment; it was attended in
its operation with an incalculable waste of human life, a deplor-
able degradation of human intellect; it was found often fatal to
the innocent, and it very frequently permitted the guilty to

escape. Nor can you complain of any unseasonable interference with your plan that may account for its failure: during the centuries that your system has been in operation, humanity and justice have never interrupted its course; you went on in the work of destruction, always seeing an increase of crime, and always supposing that increased severity was the only remedy to suppress it: the mere forfeiture of life was too mild; tortures were superadded, which nothing but the intelligence of a fiend could invent, to prolong its duration and increase its torments; yet there was no diminution of crime; and it never occurred to you, that mildness might accomplish that which could not be effected by severity." This great truth revealed itself to philosophers, who imparted it to the people; the strength of popular opinion at length forced it upon kings, and the work of reformation, in spite of the cry against novelty, began. It has been progressive. Why should it stop, when every argument, every fact, promises its complete success? We could not concur in the early stages of this reformation; perhaps the credit may be reserved to us of completing it; and I therefore make no apology to the general assembly for having so long occupied them with this discussion. In imposing so important a change, it was necessary to state the prominent reasons which induced me to think it necessary; many more have weighed upon my mind, and on reviewing these, I feel with humility and regret how feebly they are urged. The nature of the subject alone will, however, create an interest sufficient to promote inquiry, and humanity will suggest arguments which I have not had sagacity to discover or the talent to enforce.

[T]he right to inflict death exists, but . . . it must be in defence, either of individual or social existence; and . . . it is

From Edward Livingston, "Introductory Report to the Code of Crimes and Punishments," in *The Complete Works of Edward Livingston on Criminal Jurisprudence,* vol. I, pp. 194-224. Reprinted from Philip English Mackey, ed., "Edward Livingston on the Punishment of Death."

limited to the case where no other alternative remains to prevent the threatened destruction.

In order to judge whether there is any necessity for calling this abstract right into action, we must recollect the duty imposed upon society of protecting its members, derived, if we have argued correctly, from the social nature of man, independent of any implied contract. While we can imagine society to be in so rude and imperfect a state as to render the performance of this duty impossible without taking the life of the aggressor, we must concede the right. But is there any such state of society? Certainly none in the civilized world, and our laws are made for civilized man. Imprisonment is an obvious and effectual alternative; therefore, in civilized society, in the usual course of events, we can never suppose it necessary, and of course never lawful: and even among the most savage hordes, where the means of detention might be supposed wanting, banishment, for the most part, would take away the necessity of inflicting death. . . .

* * *

. . . Society has the right only to defend that which the individuals who compose it have a right to defend, or to defend itself—that is to say, its own existence, and to destroy any individual, or any other society which shall attempt its destruction. But this, as in the case of individuals, must be only while the attempt is making, and when there is no other means to defeat it. And it is in that sense only that I understand the word so often used, so often abused, so little understood, *necessity*. It exists between nations during war; or a nation and one of its component parts in a rebellion or insurrection; between individuals during the moment of an attempt against life, which cannot otherwise be repelled; but between society and individuals, organized as the former now is, with all the means of repression and self-defense at its command, never. I come, then, to the conclusion, in which I desire most explicitly to be understood that, although the right to punish with death might be abstractedly conceded to exist in certain societies, and under certain circumstances, which might make it necessary; yet, composed as society now is, these circumstances cannot reasonably be even supposed to occur—that therefore no necessity, and, of course, no right to inflict death as a punishment does exist.

There is also great force in the reasonings which have been used to rebut that, which founds the right to take life for crimes on an original contract, made by individuals on the first formation of society. First, that no such contract is proved, or can well be imagined. Secondly, that if it were, it would be limited to the case of defence. The parties to such contract could only give to the society those rights which they individually had; their only right over the life of another is to defend their own; they can give that to society, and they can give no more. In this case also, therefore, the right resolves itself into that of doing what is necessary for preservation. The great inquiry then recurs—is the punishment of death in any civilized society necessary for the preservation either of the lives of its citizens individually or of their social collective rights? If it be not necessary, I hope it has been proved not to be just; and if neither just nor necessary, can it be expedient? To be necessary, it must be shown that the lives of the citizens and the existence of society cannot be preserved without it. But can this be maintained in the face of so many proofs? Egypt, for twenty years, during the reign of Sabaco—Rome, for two hundred and fifty years—Tuscany, for more than twenty-five—Russia, for twenty-one, during the reign of Elizabeth—are so many proofs to the contrary. . . .

Societies have, then, existed without it. In those societies, therefore, it was not necessary. Is there anything in the state of ours that makes it so? It has not, as far as I have observed, been even suggested. But if not absolutely necessary, have its advocates even the poor pretext that it is convenient; that the crimes for which it is reserved diminish under its operation in a greater proportion than those which incur a different punishment? The reverse is the melancholy truth. Murder, and those attempts to murder, which are capitally punished, have increased in some of the United States to a degree that not only creates general alarm, but, by the atrocity with which they are perpetrated, fix a stain on the national character which it will be extremely difficult to efface. I might rely for this fact on the general impression which every member of the body I address must have on the subject; but as the result is capable of being demonstrated by figures, I pray their attention to the tables annexed to this report, in which, although they are far from being as complete as could be wished, they will see an increase of those crimes that demonstrates, if anything can do it, the inefficiency of the means adopted and so strangely persisted in, of repressing them. The small number of executions compared with the well authenticated instances of the crime, shows that the severity of the punishment increases the chance of acquittal; and the idle curiosity which draws so many thousands to witness the exhibition of human suffering at the executions; the levity with which the spectacle is beheld, demonstrates its demoralizing and heart-hardening effects; while the crimes committed at the very moment of the example intended to deter from the commission, shows how entirely inefficient it is. . . .

* * *

. . . The most serious and intense reflection has brought my mind to the conclusion, not only that it fails in any repressive effect, but that it promotes the crime. The cause it is not very easy to discover, and still more difficult to explain; but I argue from effects—and when I see them general in their occurrence after the same event, I must believe that event to be the efficient cause which produces them, although I may not be able to trace exactly their connection. This difficulty is particularly felt in deducing moral effects from physical causes, or arguing from the operation of moral causes on human actions. The reciprocal operations of the mind and body must always be a mystery to us, although we are daily witnesses of their effects. In nothing is this more apparent, or the cause more deeply hidden, than in that propensity which is produced on the mind to imitate that which has been strongly impressed on the senses, and that frequently in cases where the first impression must be that of painful apprehension. It is one of the earliest developments of the understanding in childhood. Aided by other impulses, it conquers the sense of pain and the natural dread of death. . . . The lawgiver, therefore, should mark this, as well as every other propensity of human nature; and beware how he repeats, in his punishments, the very acts he wishes to repress, and makes them examples to follow rather than to avoid.

Another reason, perhaps not sufficiently enlarged upon in the former report, to show that it cannot be efficient, is drawn from the uncertainty of its infliction—an uncertainty which reduces the chance of the risk to less than that which is, in many instances, voluntarily incurred in many pursuits of life. Soldiers march gaily to battle with the certainty that many of them must fall—those who commit a crime punishable with death always proceed with the hope that they will avoid detection. . . . The great error of our laws is, an obstinate refusal to consider an offender against them as moved by the same impulses, guided by the same motives, with the rest of the community; refusing, in short, to consider him as a man. They suppose him a demon or an idiot, and their provisions are, accordingly, for the most part calculated for a being actuated by perversity too incorrigible to be amended, or by folly incapable of pursuing his own happiness when the path is pointed out. If we, on the contrary, were to frame our laws for man as he is, should we consider that the threat of death would be an efficient restraint to him who, before he commits the crime, takes every measure that prudence can dictate to avoid discovery; and who, after that, calculates on the proverbial uncertainty of the law; while many of us are not deterred by a risk which we cannot flatter ourselves to avoid, for a trifling gain or a momentary gratification. Yet it may be said the good citizen incurs the risk of death, but not of death in such a form; he would not, for the gratification or reward you speak of, incur the slightest risk of infamy, although the greatest that can be presented of honourable death does not affright him. This is most true, and this is most conclusive in the argument. It is not death, then, that is feared; it is death with ignominy. But if it be that which makes death dreadful, will it not make life intolerable? If the suffering of shame cannot be endured during the short interval between conviction and execution, how can it be borne spread over a whole life?

* * *

There is no point in the argument on which stronger reasoning and more persuasive authority could be produced than on this, which has more than once been necessarily introduced, for it connects itself with every other. From the operation of the earliest written laws of which history gives us any account, down to the present day, it has been invariably observed by all who would take the trouble to think, that the inexecution of penal laws was in exact proportion to their severity. . . . I make no quotations from modern writers on penal law to this point, for there is not one who has not given his testimony in favour of the position I have taken; and yet, by a most singular incongruity, each of them has a favourite crime to which he thinks it inapplicable.

This is not an essay to prove the inutility, the danger, and, if these are admitted, the *crime* of employing the punishment of death. Such a work would require a methodical arrangement, and a research into the first principles of penal law, which cannot be expected from a mere explanatory report, in which heads of argument are suggested without much order and with little development, leaving to the enlightened minds to which they are addressed the task of pursuing, to all their consequences, the topics which are raised for consideration. With this understanding, I shall add a few more reflections on this subject, so interesting to our best feelings.

All nations, even those the best organized, are subject to political disorders, during which the violent passions that are excited avail themselves of every pretext for their indulgence; and parties, animated with the rage of civil discord, mutually charge each other with the worst intentions and blackest crimes; but even in the hottest warfare of party rage, the destruction of a rival faction or a dangerous leader is seldom attempted but by the imputation of some crime; new laws are not made on such occasions, but the existing laws are perverted and misapplied;

new punishments are not invented, but those already known are rigorously enforced against the innocent.

* * *

. . . In the times I have supposed—and they may afflict our country as they have all others—it is of importance to sanction no penalty that may be used to the destruction of your best citizens; they are the most obnoxious to all parties; not partaking the violence of either, they are suspected by both, and become the first victims; and never has any revolutionary or factious storm desolated any land, without the loss of men lamented even by their mad executioners after the calm of peace had restored them to their senses. Beware, then, how you sharpen the axe, and prepare the other instruments of death, for the hand of party violence. Beware how you so accustom the people to their use, that whenever their judgment may be led astray so as to think the innocent guilty, they may feel no shock in witnessing the last agonies of a man whom they may afterwards deplore as a national loss, and whose death they may feel as a national disgrace. I dwell upon this, because I deeply feel its force.

History presents to us the magic glass on which, by looking at past, we may discern future events. It is folly not to read; it is perversity not to follow its lessons. If the hemlock had not been brewed for felons in Athens, would the fatal cup have been drained by Socrates?

* * *

. . . Sometimes, indeed, we are asked, are you sure that if we give up this punishment, your substitute will prove effectual? If you mean so effectual as to eradicate the crime, I answer, No! But I am as sure as experience and analogy, and reasoning united, can make me, that it will be more effectual. What is it we fear? Why do we hesitate? You know, you cannot deny, that the fear of the gallows does not restrain from murder. We have seen a deliberate murder committed in the very crowd assembled to enjoy the spectacle of a murderer's death; and do we

still talk of its force as an example? In defiance of your menaced punishment, homicide stalks abroad and raises its bloody
hand at noon-day in your crowded streets; and when arrested in
its career, takes shelter under the example of your laws, and is
protected by their very severity, from punishment. Try the efficacy of milder punishments; they have succeeded. Your own
statutes, all those of every state in the union, prove that they
have succeeded, in other offences; try the great experiment on
this also. Be consistent; restore capital punishments in other
crimes, or abolish it in this. . . .

I cannot, I ought not, to dismiss this subject without once
more pressing on the most serious consideration of the legislature an argument which every new view of it convinces me is
important; and, if we listen to the voice of conscience, conclusive: the irremediable nature of this punishment. Until men
acquire new faculties, and are enabled to decide upon innocence
or guilt without the aid of fallible and corruptible human evidence, so long will the risk be incurred of condemning the
innocent. Were the consequence felt as deeply as it ought to be,
would there be an advocate for that punishment, which, applied
in such case, has all the consequences of the most atrocious
murder to the innocent sufferers—worse than the worst murderer! He stabs, or strikes, or poisons, and the victim dies—he dies
unconscious of the blow—without being made a spectacle to
satisfy ferocious curiosity, and without the torture of leaving
his dearest friends doubtful of his innocence, or seeing them
abandon him under the conviction of his guilt; he dies, and his
death is like one of those inevitable chances to which all mortals
are subject; his family are distressed, but not dishonoured; his
death is lamented by his friends, and, if his life deserved it,
honoured by his country. But the death inflicted by the laws,
the murder of the innocent under its holy forms, has no such
mitigating circumstances. Slow in its approach, uncertain in its
stroke, its victim feels not only the sickness of the heart that
arises from the alternation of hope and fear, until his doom is
pronounced, but when that becomes inevitable, alone, the tenant of a dungeon during every moment that the cruel lenity of
the law prolongs his life, he is made to feel all those anticipa-

tions, worse than a thousand deaths. The consciousness of innocence, that which is our support under other miseries, is here
converted into a source of bitter anguish, when it is found to be
no protection from infamy and death; and when the ties which
connected him to his country, his friends, his family, are torn
asunder, no consoling reflection mitigates the misery of that
moment. He leaves unmerited infamy to his children; a name
stamped with dishonour to their surviving parent, and bows
down the grey hairs of his own with sorrow to the grave. As he
walks from his dungeon, he sees the thousands who have come
to gaze on his last agony; he mounts the fatal tree, and a life of
innocence is closed by a death of dishonour. This is no picture
of the imagination. Would to God it were! Would to God that,
if death must be inflicted, some sure means might be discovered
of making it fall upon the guilty. These things have happened.
These legal murders have been committed! and who were the
primary causes of the crime? Who authorized a punishment
which, once inflicted, could never be remitted to the innocent?
Who tied the cord, or let fall the axe upon the guiltless head?
Not the executioner, the vile instrument who is hired to do the
work of death; not the jury who convict, or the judge who
condemns; not the law which sanctions these errors, but the
legislators who made the law; those who, having the power, did
not repeal it. These are the persons responsible to their country,
their consciences, and their God. These horrors not only have
happened, but they must be repeated: the same causes will
produce the same effects. The innocent have suffered the death
of the guilty; the innocent will suffer. We know it. The horrible
truth stares us in the face. We dare not deny, and cannot evade
it. A word, while it saves the innocent, will secure the punishment of the guilty, and shall we hesitate to pronounce it? Shall
we content ourselves with our own imagined exemption from
this fate, and shut our ears to the cries of justice and humanity?. . . I urge this point with more earnestness, because I have
witnessed more than one condemnation under false construc-
tions of law, or perjured, or mistaken testimony; sentences that
would now have been reversed if the unfortunate sufferers were
within the reach of mercy. I have seen, in the gloom and silence

of the dungeon, the deep concentrated expression of indignation which contended with grief; have heard the earnest asseverations of innocence, made in tones which no art could imitate; and listened with awe to the dreadful adjuration, poured forth by one of these victims with an energy and solemnity that seemed superhuman, summoning his false accuser and his mistaken judge to meet him before the throne of God. Such an appeal to the high tribunal which never errs, and before which he who made it was in a few hours to appear, was calculated to create a belief of his innocence; that belief was changed into certainty; the perjury of the witness was discovered, and he fled from the infamy that awaited him; but it was too late for any other effect than to add one more example to the many that preceded it of the danger, and I may add impiety, of using this attribute of the divine power, without the infallibility that can alone properly direct it. And this objection alone, did none of the other cogent reasons against capital punishment exist, this alone would make me hail the decree for its abolition as an event, so honourable to my country and so consoling to humanity, as to be cheaply purchased by the labour of a life.

* * *

Conscious of having been guilty of much repetition, and certain that I have weakened, by my version of them, arguments much better used by others, I am yet fearful of having omitted many things that might have an effect in convincing any one of these to whom this report is addressed. The firm religious belief I have of the truth of the doctrine I advance, contrasted with the sense of my incapacity to enforce it upon others, must have produced obscurity where the interests of humanity require there should be light, and confusion where the performance of my great duty demands order. But the truth will appear in spite of these obstacles. From the midst of the cloud, with which human imperfection has surrounded her, her voice, like that of the Almighty from the mount, will be heard reiterating to nations as well as to individuals, the great command, "THOU SHALT NOT KILL."

3 ROBERT RANTOUL, Jr.

America's most active and renowned opponent of capital punishment in the late 1830s was Robert Rantoul, Jr. (1805-1852), of Massachusetts. Born in Beverly of liberal Unitarian parents, he attended Phillips Academy in Andover and Harvard College before beginning a career as a lawyer in Salem in 1829. Following in the footsteps of his reformer-politician father, Rantoul gained election to the Massachusetts House in 1834 and attached himself to a host of causes. In a few years, he was one of the leaders of the Democratic Party in Massachusetts.

After 1838, Rantoul left the legislature to pursue a successful career in law and to plan business ventures in the Mississippi Valley. His continuing political influence gained him posts as customs collector for the port of Boston and United States district attorney for Massachusetts. In 1851, he was elected to the United States Senate to serve out the unexpired term of Daniel Webster and also secured election to a full term in the House of Representatives, where he planned to join the fight against the expansion of slavery. Rantoul's premature death was mourned by humanitarians and reformers throughout the free states.

Rantoul formed his opinions about the gallows at an early age. Both his parents were profoundly opposed to capital punishment, and Rantoul's father, while serving in the Massachusetts legislature, sought repeatedly to strike it from the laws. But it was probably the young lawyer's involvement in a famous murder trial in 1830 which made him such an active advocate of abolition. Rantoul was convinced that his client, John Francis

Knapp, was innocent of murder and was appalled by Knapp's conviction and execution.

Rantoul proposed measures to abolish or limit capital punishment during each of his four years in the Massachusetts legislature, 1835-1838. In two of those sessions, the House passed bills eliminating some of the state's six capital crimes, but in both cases, the Senate would not concur. The arguments Rantoul put forth in his four committee reports and in debate remained after the reformer left the legislature, however, and in 1839, both houses agreed to end the death penalty for burglary and highway robbery. In the 1840s, Rantoul, although less active, remained committed to the reform, writing letters to newspapers, assisting other reformers, and serving as president of the Massachusetts Society for the Abolition of Capital Punishment.

Of Rantoul's four reports to the legislature, those of 1836 and 1837 were superior in style and argumentation. The report of 1836, excerpted here, was his most complete and most famous. In its unusual length, Rantoul repeated most of the arguments of Livingston and Rush and added new ones of his own. In these excerpts, the religious and utilitarian arguments have been reduced to mere samples in order to feature the more original discussion of the right of society to inflict the death penalty. Here the political philosophy was Jeffersonian, the mood Jacksonian, the result highly effective.

Has Society the Right to Take Away Life? (1836)

Though it may not be necessary for your committee to express an opinion upon the right, if, after admitting the right, it should be found that upon grounds of expediency alone this punishment ought to be entirely dispensed with, yet as the right itself to take away life is now utterly denied by many thousand citizens of this Commonwealth, whose number seems to be ra-

From Luther Hamilton, ed., *Memoirs, Speeches and Writings of Robert Rantoul, Jr.* (Boston: Jewett 1854), pp. 436-492.

pidly increasing, your committee have thought it proper to state, so far as they understand them, the principles upon which this denial rests, leaving it to the wisdom of the legislature to allow those principles due weight in its deliberations.

It is said, then, that society is nothing but a partnership, and further, that it may with propriety be styled a *limited partnership*, created and continued for *specific purposes*,—for purposes which are easily defined. These purposes are all of them benevolent and philanthropic, and it is the continual boast of Americans that we have succeeded in accomplishing them more uniformly and completely, and with less unnecessary suffering or avoidable injustice, than any association of men that has ever preceded us. This proud assumption of superiority rests, we believe, upon a foundation of truth, and is established impregnably in our history. Your committee would be among the last to deny or to doubt it: yet it is impossible that our system should be by any means perfect, since it is the work of finite human faculties, and since that approach towards perfection which is within the compass of human capacity must always be the tardy growth of many ages of gradual, irregular, and often interrupted improvement. The class of reasoners of whom we are speaking, hold the infliction of capital punishment to be one of the most obvious vices in our present mode of administering the common concerns.

We are all of us members, say they, of the great partnership. Each one of us has not only an interest, but an influence, also, in its proceedings. Shall the partnership, under certain circumstances which will probably happen now and then, proceed deliberately, with much ceremony, and in cold blood, to strangle one of the partners? Has society the right to take away life?

The Whole Object of Government Is Negative

It is for the protection of property, life, and liberty. It is not for the destruction of any of them. It is not to prescribe how any one may obtain property, how long one may enjoy life, under what conditions he may remain at liberty. It was precisely to prevent the strong from controlling the weak in all these particulars, that government was instituted. It is to take care that no man shall appropriate the property of another, that no man shall restrain the liberty of another, that no man shall injure the person, or shorten the life of another. Having performed these duties, its office is at an end. . . .

Government Is a Necessary Evil

It is for our ignorance, for our folly, and our wickedness, that we are shackled with its control; and we submit to it only that it may shield us from the heavier curse, the eternal and deadly warfare which men must wage against one another, if left in a state of total anarchy, without the possibility of a common arbiter of differences, or a mutual protector from each other's aggressions. Protection being the only object of society, it follows that we surrender to it, for the purpose of preserving our natural rights as nearly unimpaired as conflicting claims will in the nature of things admit, only so much liberty as it is necessary should be relinquished to that end. To give up more, by the division of a hair, would be to counteract so far the very endeavor we are making when we are forming the social compact to secure the full enjoyment of our natural rights. It needed not, therefore, the authority of Montesquieu, or of Beccaria, to give weight to the maxim, that every punishment which does not arise from absolute necessity; and even every act of authority of one man over another, for which there is not an absolute necessity, is tyrannical. The right to punish crimes is founded upon the necessity of defending the public liberty, and is coextensive only with that necessity.

To suppose that any people has entered into a compact giving unlimited powers for all possible purposes to its government, would be to suppose an obvious absurdity; yet this is what most governments assume as far as they dare, never admitting any limits to their prerogative except those which are forced upon them by resistance, or the immediate apprehension of resistance. To suppose that limited grants of power are to be used for any other than the purposes for which they were made, is almost equally absurd; yet this is the supposition constantly acted on in the practice of almost every government that ever existed.

Whether, in entering into the social compact, we gave up our lives, to be thrown into the common stock and disposed of as society might will, is a question to be decided with reference to these principles, and it may be thought to be quite settled, beyond dispute, by the bare statement of these principles. Philosophers and jurists of the highest reputation have, however, disagreed in the inferences which we should draw from them. Rousseau supposes that in consequence of the social contract between the citizens and society, life becomes "a conditional grant of the State," to be given up whenever the State shall call for it. This theory has the merit of being consistent and intelligible, but it is anti-republican and slavish. . . .

When we surrendered to society the smallest possible portion of our liberty, to enable us the better to retain the aggregate of rights which we did not surrender, did we concede our title to that life with which our Creator has endowed us? Is it to be conceived that we have consented to hold the tenure of our earthly existence at the discretion, or the caprice of a majority, whose erratic legislation no man can calculate beforehand? While our object was to preserve, as little impaired as might be possible, all our rights, which are all of them comprehended in the right to enjoy life, can we have agreed to forfeit that right to live while God shall spare our lives, which is the essential precedent condition of all our other rights? Property may be diminished, and afterwards increased. Liberty may be taken away for a time, and subsequently restored. The wound which is inflicted may be healed, and the wrong we have suffered may be atoned for; but there is no Promethean heat that can rekindle the lamp of life if once extinguished. Can it be, then, that while property, liberty, and personal security are guarded and hedged in on every side, by the strict provisions of our fundamental constitution, that life is unconditionally thrown into the common stock, not to be forfeited in a specific case, agreed upon beforehand at the organization of our society, but in all such cases as the popular voice may single out and make capital by law? Have we entered into any such compact?

The burden of proof is wholly upon those who affirm that we have so agreed. Let it be shown that mankind in general, or the inhabitants of this Commonwealth in particular, have agreed to hold their lives as a conditional grant from the State. Let it be shown that any one individual, understanding the bargain, and being free to dissent from it, ever voluntarily placed himself in such a miserable vassalage. Let there, at least, be shown some reason for supposing that any sane man has of his own accord bartered away his original right in his own existence, that his government may tyrannize more heavily over him and his fellows, when all the purposes of good government may be amply secured at so much cheaper a purchase. In no instance can this preposterous sacrifice be implied. It must be shown by positive proof that it has been made, and until this is undeniably established, the right of life remains among those reserved rights which we have not yielded up to society.

It belongs to those who claim for society the rightful power of life and death over its members, as a consequence of the social compact, to show in that compact the express provisions which convey that power. But it cannot be pretended that there are or ever were such provisions. It is argued, as boldly as strangely, that this right is to be implied from the nature of the compact. It may seem unnecessary to reply to such an assumption; but it has often been advanced, and for that reason deserves our notice. In point of fact, there is no social compact actually entered into by the members of society. It is a convenient fiction,—a mere creature of the imagination,—a form of expression often used to avoid long and difficult explanations of the real nature of the relation between the body politic and its individual members. This relation is not, strictly speaking, that of a compact. It is not by our voluntary consent that we become each one of us parties to it. The mere accident of birth first introduced us, and made us subject to its arrangements, before we were in any sense free agents. After we had grown to the age of freemen, and had a right to a voice in the common concerns, what alternatives had we then left? Simply these: Resistance to the social compact, as it is called, under the prospect of producing ruin, confusion, anarchy, slaughter almost without bounds, and finally ending in a new form of the social compact much more objectionable than that which had been destroyed, if the resistance should prove successful: should it fail of success, incurring the penalty of treason, a cruel death, to such as have not been fortunate enough to fall in the field of battle. Flight from the social compact, that is to say, flight not only from one's home, friends, kindred, language, and country, but from among civilized men, perhaps it may be said from the fellowship of the human race. Or, lastly, submission to the social compact as we find it, taking the chance of our feeble endeavors to amend it, or improve the practice under it. To this result almost every man feels compelled by the circumstances in which he finds himself; circumstances so strong as to force from an inspired apostle the declaration, though he wrote under the tyrant Nero, a monster of depravity, "the powers that be are ordained of God; whosoever therefore resisteth the power, resisteth the ordinance of God; and they that resist shall receive unto themselves damnation."[1] With whatever latitude this is to be understood, and there are cases generally supposed to justify resistance to the utmost extremity, it is certain that submission to the existing constitution of society is, in ordinary cases at least, a duty and a necessity also. How then can that be a compact into which we are forced by the irresistible influence of our circumstance, and how can submission be regarded as a voluntary acquiescence, when there is no door open to avoid submission, except such resistance, or such a flight as has been described? It is a palpable folly to pretend that an actual, voluntary compact exists, and they who derive the right to punish capitally from any supposed social compact, must first suppose an agreement which the facts in the case show was not and never could be freely entered into by the individual members of society; and then from that purely imaginary agreement proceed to draw an implication, also purely imaginary, and which it would be absurd and monstrous to derive from such premises, even if such a general compact as is supposed in arguments like these had been actually formed. To state this theory is sufficiently to refute it, yet it is that which has been most frequently relied on.

But let us carry this examination one step further. Not only has no man actually given up to society the right to put an end to his life, not only is no surrender of this right under a social compact ever to be implied, but no man can, under a social contract, or any other contract, give up this right to society, or to any constituent part of society, for this conclusive reason, that the right is, not his to be conveyed. Has a man a right to commit suicide? Every Christian must answer, no. A man holds his life as a tenant at will,—not indeed of society, who did not and cannot give it, or renew it, and have therefore no right to take it away,—but of that Almighty Being whose gift life is, who sustains and continues it, to whom it belongs, and who alone has the right to reclaim his gift whenever it shall seem good in his sight. A man may not surrender up his life until he is called for. May he then make a contract with his neighbor that, in such or such a case, his neighbor shall kill him? Such a contract, if executed, would involve the one party in the guilt of suicide, and the other in the guilt of murder. If a man may not say to his next neighbor, "when I have burned your house in the night time, or wrested your purse from you on the highway, or broken into your house in the night, with an iron crow, to take a morsel of meat for my starving child, do you seize me, shut me up a few weeks, and then bring me out and strangle me, and in like case, if your turn comes first, I will serve you in the same way," would such an agreement between ten neighbors be any more valid or justifiable? No. Nor if the number were a hundred instead of ten, who should form this infernal compact, nor if there should be six hundred thousand, or seven hundred thousand, or even fourteen millions, who should so agree, would this increase of the number of partners vary one hair's breadth the moral character of the transaction. If the execution of this contract be not still murder on the one side and suicide on the other, what precise number of persons must engage in it, in order that what was criminal before may become innocent, not to say virtuous,—and upon what hitherto unheard of principles of morality is an act of murder in an individual, or a small corporation, converted into an act of justice whenever another subscriber has joined the association for mutual sacrifice? It is a familiar fact in the history of mankind, that great corporations will do, and glory in, what the very individuals composing them

would shrink from or blush at; but how does the division of the
responsibility transform vice into virtue, or diminish the
amount of any given crime? The command, "Thou shalt not
kill," applies to individual men as members of an association,
quite as peremptorily as in their private capacity; and although
men in a numerous company may keep one another in countenance in a gross misdeed, and may so mystify and confuse their
several relations to it, as that each one may sin ignorantly, and
therefore in the sight of the Searcher of Hearts be absolved
from intentional guilt, still that it does not alter the true nature
of the act must be obvious, as also that it is equally our duty to
abstain from a social as from a personal crime, when once its
criminality is clearly understood.

It is not, however, from any social compact, either actual or
implied, comprehending the whole body of the people, that the
practice of putting to death particular members of the community, grew up. It was from a compact of the opposite character,
the league of the oppressors against the oppressed. "If we look
into history, we shall find," says Beccaria, "that laws which are,
or ought to be, conventions between men in a state of freedom,
have been, for the most part, the work of the passions of a
few,—not dictated by a cool examiner of human nature, who
had this only end in view, *the greatest happiness of the greatest
number.*" This principle, adopted by Bentham, and made the
foundation of his theoretical system of government and legislation, his Excellency considers to be practically in operation in
our own institutions. "Our system looks to the people," says
the address, "not merely as a whole, but as a society composed
of individual men, whose happiness is the great design of the
association. It consequently recognizes the greatest good of the
greatest number, as the basis of the social compact." [2]

The leading idea of the American policy is freedom. Other
nations have forms of government intended and suited solely to
secure the interests of the ruling classes. Here, for the first time
in the history of the world, a written Constitution was adopted,
establishing a government for the security of the rights and
liberties of the whole people. This is the first true social compact, if any such compact be in existence, and it should be

construed in the spirit in which it was made. Other Constitutions have been compacts of aristocracies parcelling out among themselves their prerogative to plunder and oppress; compacts to take all that could be wrested from the producer, and to guard against his resistance. Ours is a compact which protects whatever we have, or may acquire, and provides for mutual defence against any invasion of the rights of a citizen. And this is all that it aims to accomplish, all that any government can accomplish for the benefit of the people, and more than any other ever yet did effect, for in aiming at other, and unattainable ends, every government except, let us hope, our own, has failed partially of fulfilling what ought to be its legitimate purpose, and has visited its unhappy subjects with miserable evils, instead of the blessings which it promised.

There is no departure from the proper sphere of government which has been more fruitful in misery than the attempt to sit in judgment on the hearts and consciences of men, and to measure out punishments according to the supposed degrees of moral guilt, instead of punishing merely to protect. . . . Society should at length cease to be vindictive. In fixing the punishment we should weigh, not the ill desert of the criminal, which can in no case be truly and exactly known, and which if known would vary almost infinitely in crimes of the same legal description, but the melancholy necessity of painful precautions against the moral maniac who endangers our safety.

* * *

When the favored few governed for their own exclusive advantage the subject many, whom they held to be created out of a different clay, they naturally made their own opinions, comfort, and interest, the sole standard of right and wrong. Possessing such unbounded power, they would have been virtuous beyond human virtue, if they had not signally abused it. Accordingly we find that they sported in perfect wantonness with both the liberties and lives of the people. No wonder that vulgar life was cheap, when the noble could impose laws upon vassals and villains, when he could be tried only by his peers, and when there was little sympathy between the ruling and the suffering classes. The game laws are only one of the consequences to be expected from such a state of things. There was a time, we are told, when by the law of England the killing of a man was permitted to be expiated by the payment of a fine, while the killing of a wild boar, by one not qualified to hunt, was punishable with death. It happened then, so the anecdote has come down to us, that a man charged with killing a wild boar, and put on trial for his life, plead in his defence that he did it by mistake, for that he really thought the beast was only a man. It was from times when the conquerors, who held in military subjection the people they had overrun, thus sacrificed life to their own pleasures or caprices, that its cheap estimate came down to a later stage of society, when the moneyed aristocracy wasted it as lavishly and unscrupulously for the protection of property from even slight aggressions, as ever the iron-clad barons that preceded them, had for the protection of their privileges. The humanity of our day has made these laws for the most part, in most countries, inoperative, where they have not been repealed; but it is difficult to divest us so far of the impressions they have left behind them, as to see the punishment of death in its true light, a mere remnant of feudal barbarity. We are apt to think, so great is the reform already made in this respect, that we have gone far enough; and our conservatives cling to the surviving instances of this abuse, with as ardent attachment, as the crown lawyers, in more countries than one, did to the practice of torture, when philanthropy and philosophy waged a successful warfare against that characteristic vestige of the wisdom of antiquity. This claim of right, however, to put to death, implies the aristocratic contempt for mere naked humanity, which once was universally prevalent through the law-making classes. When the feeling is entirely extinct, we may hope that the claim itself will be abandoned. It has no place in a social compact founded in principles of equality.

There remains one ground on which this right is sometimes rested,—the right of self-defence. But this cannot give the right to put to death, lest he might possibly repeat the crime, one who has once committed a murder, and in no other case than murder does the argument apply. You cannot defend the victim of the crime, for he is gone already. To put to death the criminal because you have strong reason to suspect he might be guilty of the same offence again under similar circumstances, would be to punish, not a crime, nor even the intention to commit it, but a suspected liability to fall under future temptation, which may or may not assail him, and which he may be effectually precluded from, if society so wills. No man has agreed that for the purpose of self-defence, society may seize him and put him to death, to prevent others from following his example, or to prevent him from repeating it; neither is this ground of self-defence sincerely believed to be sound by the community, or any considerable portion of it, for if it were, we should execute the monomaniac who evinces a disposition to kill, yet the proposition to do so would be rejected with unanimous indignation, even after he had committed more than one murder. But it is more necessary to defend ourselves against such a man, inaccessible to the ordinary motives of hope and fear, the avenues of whose heart are closed against the approaches of repentance, than against any other murderer. Yet we do not hang the maniac. Some other feeling then must actuate us, other than the desire of self-defence, when we consign the murderer to the gallows.

Indeed, how can it be pretended that death is a necessary measure of self-defence, when we have prisons from which escape is barely possible, and when tenfold more of the most dangerous criminals now go wholly unpunished, from the repugnance of witnesses, jurors, judges, executive magistrates, and the public, at capital punishments, than could ever make their way from prisons, such and so guarded, as the practical science of the present day can construct for their safe keeping. However, it might be in a state of imperfect civilization, among us, the right of self-defence furnishes no foundation whatever, much less any solid basis, upon which to establish the right to take away life.

* * *

The fundamental article in the American political creed is, that governments ought to be strictly confined within their proper sphere. The propensity to exercise power, results from the

passions which impel the holder to increase it. Temptation to
abuse it will arise, too strong for human frailty, where it is
suffered to be accumulated beyond the absolute necessity for
intrusting it. There is no power more flattering to ambition,
because there is none of a higher nature, than that of disposing
at will of the lives of our fellow-creatures. Accordingly, no
power has been more frequently or more extensively assumed,
exercised, and abused. When we review the past, history seems
to be written in letters of blood. Until within a very short
period, the trade of government has been butchery in masses,
varied by butchery in detail. The whole record is a catalogue of
crimes, committed for the most part under legal forms, and the
pretence of public good. . . . That such scenes are no longer to
be witnessed must be attributed to changes similar in principle
and tendency to the total abolition of capital punishment. It is
because the powers of governments and of the few have been
greatly abridged and restricted, and particularly the very power
in question. It is because the rights of the many, and of individuals have been better ascertained and secured, and especially the right of life. . . .

Not only are the general nature and purpose of government
such as have been described, but it is argued that they are
expressly recognized in our constitutions, all of which create
governments intended to operate only within limited spheres,
for specified objects, and with specified and rigorously restricted powers. . . . The Constitution of Massachusetts begins
with promulgating in its first sentence the general theory of
government which has been laid down. "The end of the institution, maintenance, and administration of government," says
that celebrated instrument, "is to secure the existence of the
body politic; to protect it, and to furnish the individuals who
compose it, with the power of enjoying, in safety and tranquillity, *their natural rights, and the blessings of life.*" It is no part
of its end, then, to surrender, or to take away any natural right
of an individual, much less the last and dearest, or to debar him
not only from the blessings of existence, but from life itself. . . .
Let it not be said our Constitution does not forbid capital punishment; for neither does it, by that name, forbid slavery, or the

whipping-post, or the pillory, or mutilation, or torture, yet all these are confessedly contrary to the spirit of the Constitution. The grand, the comprehensive principle is there. The sages who proclaimed it, before the world was ripe to realize it in all its bearings, left it, unavoidably left it, to the wisdom and humanity of their posterity to receive its full application in all its important consequences. The sublime truth, that all men are by their birthright free and equal, had been asserted for some years by Massachusetts, before the non-existence of slavery within the Commonwealth was adjudged to follow as a necessary corollary from that dogma. The whipping-post and the pillory survived, for a period, the constitutional prohibition of cruel and unusual punishments. They have disappeared, and the gallows, which is more unusual than either of those barbarities had been, and infinitely more cruel and revolting, must soon follow in their train. After the reformation shall have been accomplished, mankind will look back with astonishment at its tardy progress. They will be unable to comprehend how or why it was delayed so long.

* * *

Beccaria sums up the result of his inquiries upon the subject of crimes and punishments in this theorem: "That a punishment may not be an act of violence against a private member of society, it should be public, immediate, and *necessary; the least possible in the case given;* proportioned to the crime, and determined by the laws." Under such a rule society might keep within the boundary of its undisputed rights, and refrain altogether from inflicting the punishment of death.

These remarks upon the abstract question of right in this case are submitted by your committee as the fairest statement they have been able to draw up of the argument against the right denied. They repeat, that they submit it without any expression of opinion how far the reasoning may be sound or otherwise. They thought it due to the number and excellent character of the citizens who profess these sentiments, to communicate them to the legislature, and through them to the public. If correct, they will have their proper influence; if erroneous, they will have an ordeal to pass through which will expose and refute them. Your committee have gone the more at large into the argument, because they know of no work in common circulation, from which one may collect even a tolerable idea of it, while at the same time, and from very imperfect statements, or rather hints, it is everywhere the topic of eager discussion. Having drawn an outline, without pretending to exhaust the subject, they leave it with the house, and pass to the consideration of the expediency of capital punishments, supposing society to possess the abstract right.

Upon this branch of the inquiry, your committee have no hesitation in expressing the most decided conviction, that whatever may have been the case in a state of imperfect civilization, or whatever may be the duty of another government with regard to certain other crimes not falling within the jurisdiction of this Commonwealth, questions not necessary to be discussed here, it is inexpedient, in this State, at this time, to provide by law for the punishment of death. In their opinion, this punishment is in no case necessary for the preservation of property, or of honor, or of life, or of good government. And if it be not necessary, certain they are, that no member of this house would wish that it should be wantonly or gratuitously inflicted.

There are three crimes against property punishable with death by the laws of this State,—arson, burglary, and highway robbery.[3] The reason for so distinguishing these three crimes is usually alleged to be, that they, in a peculiar manner, endanger life. This is the most preposterous reason that can be given for affixing to them a punishment which renders them much more dangerous to life than they would be under any other modification of the law. It would almost seem as if the law had been first framed in solemn mockery, professing to guard life with jealous tenderness, yet in fact intending not to save life, but to kill. In case there be any witness of either of these crimes, the law prompts the criminal not to stop short at an aggression upon property, but tempts him to go on to the commission of murder; and it tempts him to do this as he values his own life. It says to him in plain and intelligible language, you are now face to face with your mortal enemy. One of you must die. It is for you to choose whether the doom shall fall upon your own head, or upon that of your adversary. Kill him, or he will kill you. If you, already plunged so deep in crime, through the tenderness of conscience, choose to make yourself a martyr by the most cruel and ignominious death, and without the sympathy and admiration of his fellows, which supports the martyr,—if you choose to throw away your own life, for the sake of the life of this man who stands before you, obey the call of duty, and in return, I, the law, will lay my hand upon you, and drag you to a certain execution; but if you prefer security both of your person and character, to the impending destruction and disgrace, go on boldly, imbrue your hand in the blood of your fellow, and you will escape my grasp: your crime will be shrouded in darkness impenetrable to human eyes: this is the voice of the law. . . .

* * *

It has been said, but it is the language of unreflecting levity, that the criminal convicted of a capital offence, under our laws, is generally depraved and worthless, and that, therefore, the sacrifice of a few such lives is of very little consequence to society, and it is not an object fit to engage the attention of the government of a great State, even if these laws might be repealed without injury. It is impossible that any member of this legislature can entertain so inhuman a sentiment. Felons, however fallen, still are men, and have the better title to commiseration the more deeply they are sunk in guilt. . . . Suppose that one only may be caught up from the gulf of vice, misery, and perdition, and restored to repentance, virtue, and usefulness, this would be gain enough to reward all the exertions that may be made to effect the reform, for there is upon earth no gem so precious as the human soul.

* * *

Of the crime against female honor, we shall say but few words. It is now generally unpunished, from the difficulty of obtaining a capital conviction. When we consider the tremendous power which this law would put into the hands of a bad and revengeful woman, if jurors were not unwilling to convict, we cannot wonder at their reluctance. There is generally but one witness, and the acquittal of the accused after her testimony has been heard, where it is clear and conclusive, seems to add a new burden of dishonor to a wrong already too great to be endured; while a conviction and execution only agonizes the injured party with the idea, that through her instrumentality, a wretch has been prematurely launched into eternity, and that the outrage she has suffered, and the evidence she has given, which she would wish to be buried in oblivion, are the subjects of general conversation, perhaps of misconstruction, certainly of levity and ribaldry, among the abandoned and vicious through a wide region. The mere chance of loss of life which a soldier will brave for sixpence a day, and which cannot prevent a crime carried on as deliberately as larceny, and for as small temptation, cannot have much effect in restraining those insensible to higher motives. An execution which took place at Worcester, for this crime, on the 8th of December, 1825, was soon afterwards followed by an attempt, by a brother of the criminal, to commit the same crime for which his relative had just suffered the loss of his life. The experience of England, Ireland, and France, does not show that the fear of death is a preventive of this crime, but does show, that capital punishment for the offence often causes the murder of the victim of the outrage. Several cases of this effect have been known in the United States; and one not long ago excited much attention in a neighboring State. To substitute a punishment which would not lead to murder, and which being more likely to be inflicted, would be more effectual, would be a most salutary reform.[4]

The crime of treason, under monarchical governments, and by the advocates of arbitrary power, has been magnified into guilt of the most malignant dye. But a little reflection upon the nature of the various revolutions recorded in history, will show us that treason and patriotism have often been convertible terms, and that it depends upon the failure or the success of his undertaking whether the adventurer shall be crowned with laurel or branded with infamy, so far as government is the dispenser of good and evil fame. . . . Treason, then, is the crime of being defeated in a struggle with the government, whether wrongfully undertaken, or in a just and holy cause. . . .

* * *

If a law against treason be needed, still there is no need that the punishment should be capital. The class of men who take the lead in such enterprises are not to be deterred by the fear of death; but the prospect of it only makes them more desperate, after they have once embarked. The government cannot go through the judicial forms, and execute the sentence against a traitor, while he continues to be dangerous: after the danger is over, they may, but it would then be a gratuitous cruelty.

* * *

. . . Your committee suggest, respectully, whether it be wise and prudent to place in the hands of government an instrument, which in a period of excitement may be employed to inflict a lasting injury, and which can never, under any circumstances, be necessary or useful. Either the State treason law should be struck from the statutes entirely, or the crime should cease to be capital.[5]

The case of wilful murder remains to be considered. It is not necessary to hang the murderer in order to guard society against him, and to prevent him from repeating the crime. If it were, we should hang the maniac, who is the most dangerous murderer. Society may defend itself by other means than by destroying life. Massachusetts can build prisons strong enough to secure the community forever against convicted felons.

Some will justify capital punishment on the ground that it may prevent the perpetration of the crime by others; a most shocking sort of experimenting upon human nature, to kill one man in order to reform or confirm the virtue of another! This idea seems to involve an absurd, but an awful perversion of all moral reasoning. Of all the means of exerting a good moral influence upon society, that of shedding human blood would seem to be the wildest and the worst that has ever been resorted to by reformers and philanthropists!

But if any thing can be judged by history, observation, and experience, it has long been demonstrated that crimes are not diminished, but, on the contrary, increased by capital punishments. Whenever and wherever punishments have been severe, cruel, and vindictive, then, and there, crime has most abounded. They are mutually cause and effect. If severe punishments do not tend directly to produce the very crimes for which they are inflicted, as in some cases it may be shown statistically that they have done, they indirectly, by ministering to bad passions, and diminishing the natural sensibility of man for the sufferings of his fellow man, induce that hardness of heart which prepares the way for the commission of the most ferocious acts of violence. Under no form of government have severe corporal punishments, frequently and publicly administered, improved the public morals. The spectacle of capital punishments is more barbarizing, and promotive of cruelty and a disregard of life. Whoever sees life taken away by violent means, experiences a diminution of that instinctive horror which for wise purposes we are made to feel at the thought of death. Let the idea of crime, horrible crime, be indissolubly and universally associated with the voluntary and deliberate destruction of life under whatever pretext. Whoever strengthens this association in the public mind, does more to prevent murders than any punishment, with whatever aggravation of torture, can effect through fear. The denomination of Friends have always been educated in this idea, and among them murders are unknown. The strongest safeguard of life, is its sanctity; and this sentiment every execution diminishes.

* * *

That hanging adds no new terrors to that death which all must sooner or later meet, is evident from its having become so common a mode of suicide, for which purpose it was almost unknown among the ancients. Not only the mode is borrowed, but the act itself is often suggested, from public executions. Often, very often has it happened, that an execution has been followed on the next day, or within a few weeks by suicides among those who witnessed the scene. It cannot be expected, therefore, that it should have any peculiar virtue to deter from crime; least of all from that crime for which it steels the breast, and braces up the nerves. . . .

* * *

This punishment is not only unnecessary for protection, which would seem to be its only legitimate object, but so crude and ill considered have been the opinions heretofore entertained upon the subject, that this committee feel compelled to go one step further, and urge, that it is not justifiable for revenge. This may appear to some superfluous, but there is strong ground to believe, that the vindictive feelings are at the bottom of much of the zeal manifested in favor of "cruel and unusual punishments," among those who do not weigh their opinions so carefully as the members of this house. There can be no need to prove, it suffices to suggest, that revenge is an unholy passion, itself the parent of many crimes, often of the crime of murder, and that it cannot be that the law should gratify and foster in the breasts of men the spirit of demons. The law should be wholly passionless, unbiased by resentment or partiality, sitting in calm serenity in the temple of justice, to mete out penalties by the measure of absolute necessity, and staying the hand of the wrong doer: thus, and thus only, should it guard the public good, and protect individual rights. There may have been many cases where government found it expedient to employ revenge, as well as other bad passions, to execute its decrees: such a necessity is to be regretted, and the practice abandoned as soon as the necessity ceases. Encouraging common informers was an expedient of this sort, very common in our own laws, but it has been wisely stricken out in almost every instance from the Revised Statutes. Fixing a price upon the head of a refugee was once thought just and useful, but is now condemned. Promising pardon to an accomplice, to induce him to testify against his fellow criminal, is a use now made of the treachery which is despised while it is used.

In a state of nature, every man revenges to the utmost of his power the injury that he has received: retaliation is the only rule of punishment. In a rude state of society these practices are suffered to continue, because they cannot be prevented. The law only undertakes to restrict them within certain limits, and to forbid their most cruel excesses. The legislator who should enact laws which presuppose a more elevated standard of morality, would find that public opinion did not sustain him, and that his statutes would remain inoperative and useless. It has been observed, that among a people hardly yet emerged from barbarity, punishments should be most severe, as strong impressions are required; but in proportion as the minds of men become softened by their intercourse in society, the severity should be diminished, if it be intended that the necessary relation between the infliction and its object should be maintained. For this reason, the indulgence of individual revenge is much less an evil while society is obliged to tolerate it, than it would be in a later stage, when it might be, and ought to be suppressed. We must carry these ideas with us, while we inquire whether regulations promulgated in the infancy of our race, or adapted afterwards to a peculiarly stiff-necked and obdurate people, are obligatory upon mankind in their present refinement and civilization.

Sundry passages in the Jewish Scriptures have been adduced, as authorizing and enjoining capital punishments. These injunctions were addressed to people but a few removes from the condition of savages, and almost universally addicted to the most heinous acts of wickedness. For the hardness of their hearts, their great lawgiver wrote them the sanguinary precepts, which a blind attachment to antiquity still invokes, in part, though all of them unsuited to our circumstances, and most of them universally confessed to be so. . . . There was then no fit substitute for capital punishments, and they were resorted to almost of necessity. But, because a peculiar people, under the most peculiar circumstances, by as express an interposition of heaven, as that which directed Abraham to offer up Isaac, were commanded to punish certain crimes with death, shall we, a polished and humane people, whose moral sensibility is deeply wounded by the spectacle, under circumstances essentially opposite to theirs, without warrant, violate the great command, which says to the legislator as well as to the subject, thou shall

not kill? This is the command both of nature and of revelation;
it grows out of no local or temporary occasion, but is eternal
and universal in the obligation it imposes. How, then, dare any
man disobey it; and how is it an excuse for our disobedience,
that the man we kill has broken this law before we break it, and
that we have taken into our own hands to exercise upon him
that vengeance which the Almighty has declared belongs to himself, because he, in his inscrutable purposes, some thousands of
years ago, specially authorized a particular people, in specified
cases, to be the executors of his vengeance? . . .

* * *

Your committee have confined themselves to the discussion
of three questions: 1. Has society a right, from the social compact, to take away life? 2. Is there any thing peculiar to either
of our six capital crimes which requires the punishment of
death? 3. Is there any command in Scripture which enjoins on
us to inflict that punishment in any case? They have preferred
to give somewhat thorough and extended answers to each of
these questions, rather than to go over the whole ground which
they might have occupied. To enter upon important considerations which remain untouched, would enlarge the limits of this
report beyond what customary usage would justify. They therefore conclude with the words of his Excellency, "the people of
America should be the last blindly to adhere to what is established merely as such; and it may sometimes be our duty to
imitate our forefathers in the great trait of their characters,—the
courage of reform,—rather than to bow implicitly to their authority in matters in which the human mind has made progress
since their day." [6]

4 JOHN L. O'SULLIVAN

When Robert Rantoul slackened his anti-gallows activity in the 1840s, a young New York editor rapidly rose to leadership of the reform. John L. O'Sullivan (1813-1895) was educated in Britain and France and at Columbia College. He practiced law in New York City from 1834 to 1837 before founding the *United States Magazine and Democratic Review,* one of the leading periodicals of the antebellum period. The magazine brought O'Sullivan into contact with the great literary and political figures of the day and he became influential in New York and national Democratic politics.

O'Sullivan was a champion of nationalism and expansion (indeed, he coined the term "manifest destiny"), but his unbounded devotion to that cause eventually got him into serious trouble. His illegal actions in support of Narciso Lopez' filibustering invasions of Cuba in 1849 and 1850 led to federal prosecution, and he escaped conviction only after great expense of time and money. O'Sullivan spent most of the next twenty-five years in Europe, first as Franklin Pierce's minister to Portugal, then as a pro-Southern spectator of the Civil War. He returned to the United States only in the 1870s and lived out the remainder of his life in obscurity in New York City.

By the late 1830s, O'Sullivan had become convinced that the "democratic genius" of the United States demanded the complete abolition of capital punishment. He sought and won election to the New York Assembly in 1840 with the primary motive of effecting this reform; during the two years he spent in the legislature, he devoted the major part of his efforts to that goal. In the 1841 session, O'Sullivan secured chairmanship of a special committee to consider capital punishment and after three months of feverish work presented a book-length report and an abolition bill to his colleagues. After much delay, the Assembly defeated the bill by a narrow margin. O'Sullivan expected more success in the 1842 session, but the Assembly rejected his new bill by almost the same margin.

O'Sullivan left the legislature when his term expired, but continued to fight for abolition as a private citizen. Active in anti-gallows societies, supportive in his opinion-shaping magazine, tireless in his efforts to rally other reformers, O'Sullivan for four years did more than any other American to discredit capital punishment. After the Mexican War began, he became too involved in foreign affairs to devote much time to the reform.

O'Sullivan's report of 1841, though one of the most eloquent and influential of all American appeals against the death penalty, was far from an original document. In writing the report, the reformer borrowed extensively from Livingston and Rantoul and quoted scores of other writers—penologists, theologians, jurists, and doctors. The following excerpts present three of the strongest and most original topics: the problem of juror reluctance, the history of abolition experiments, and the vexing problem of insanity and criminal responsibility.

The Hideous Stain of Blood (1841)

The *uncertainty of conviction*, by juries, for capital offences, has grown almost into a proverb. There can be no criminal lawyer in this State, of any extended practice or observation, by whom this remark will not be received as a truism. Even after the rejection from the panel, by challenge, of all who have formed a decided principle of action or opinion on this subject, juries are always, and will always be, powerfully swayed in their judgment, as well as in their feelings, by that horror of shedding

From John L. O'Sullivan, *Report in Favor of the Abolition of the Punishment of Death by Law*, 2d ed. (New York: n.p., 1841), pp. 72-77, 98-116, 138-139.

the blood of their fellow-man, which the laws of God have planted too deeply in the hearts of all to be eradicated, however it may be weakened, by the influence of any laws of man. In the clearest cases, it is constantly seen they *will not* convict; and the criminal, whatever both the heinousness and the certainty of his guilt, must be singularly unfortunate indeed, if the ingenuity and eloquence of an able advocate cannot find, in the circumstances of the case, some point or other, great or small, on which he can urge to the hearts or the imagination of the jury such appeals, as cannot be counteracted without extreme difficulty by the sober voice of truth and justice. It is vain to talk of the juror's oath. They *will* violate them, by what their consciences regard as only pious perjuries, under a thousand pleas of technical deficiencies or imperfections of evidence, however immaterial in their nature. In strong cases they will do it openly, and without even a shadow of other reason or justification, than simply this invincible repugnance which holds back their hands from the deed of blood.

* * *

None that have ever attended our criminal courts, in capital cases, can have failed to notice the operation of the principle here referred to, in a manner the most subversive of the ends of justice, and the most dangerous to the security of the community. In nine cases in ten, the prisoner is converted into an object of all but universal sympathy and interest. The heinousness of his crime is half forgotten; the dread and unnatural awfulness of the doom depending on the issue of his case is alone remembered,—especially if he has youth or any other circumstance in his favor calculated in the least degree to touch the heart of man or woman; and every effort is exhausted to save him, by court, jury, witness, and public, who all become enlisted in one common though tacit conspiracy against the cause of the public justice and the public security; the prosecuting attorney usually standing alone—alone with the law—to resist the one, and protect the other. More or less of the jury, too, often find their minds so disturbed by the reflections on the subject of the lawfulness of capital punishment, which have been stimulated by counsel, but which had never before assumed any such distinct and definite form as to prevent them from taking their seats as jurors, that they will not, under any circumstances, convict; and in the choice between the two, regard the perjury, on such an occasion, as the less offence in the eye of the God in whose name they took the oath they thus directly violate. On this point it is unnecessary to dwell. None will question the truth here presented. And none can either compute the number of criminals who have thus been let loose on society, scot free of all penalty, and emboldened and hardened by a first impunity; nor form any conception of the amount of evil which has had its origin in this cause, in casting upon the administration of the law an uncertainty in the last degree prejudicial to all the policy of penal justice. That this important chance of escape enters largely into the calculations of those who may meditate the commission of crimes bringing them within its application, who can doubt? And he must be very slenderly endowed with inventive powers who could not, in his preparations for a murder, so combine his circumstances—by a feigned insanity or eccentricity of conduct, in advance, for instance, or by leaving open some avenue for the possibility of a doubt of his identity or guilt,—as to secure to himself before a jury, in the event of a detection, a chance of an acquittal which it would require no great degree of daring to risk.

* * *

Nor have we to regard this evil merely in the degree in which we are at present, and have long been, compelled to recognise its existence. It is one which is daily increasing, as the sentiment which is its source is daily extending and deepening its hold upon the minds and hearts of the community. And, independently of its notorious and powerful influence on juries, who can say how large the number is already, whom no considerations of either private resentment or public duty could tempt to become accessories to one of these "judicial murders" of a fellow-man, guilty and blood-stained though he may be, in the capacities of informers or prosecuting witnesses?

Were the punishment imprisonment for life, a very different

spirit would pervade judge, jury, witness, prosecutor—in a word, the whole community. While we can never have any reason to apprehend any undue extreme of severity against a prisoner, the minds of all would be earnestly bent on establishing the truth and validity of his guilt or innocence, with a determination—prompted by the principle of self-defence, and unaffected by any counteracting influence—in case of his guilt, to place him by the verdict and judgment beyond the possibility of doing farther evil to the society he has already once outraged; and the plea of insanity would rather tend to serve as an additional motive, than as a check to the stern and unrelenting enforcement of the law. The effect that would be thus produced on the minds of those whom it is desired to influence by the salutary fear of that law, may well be left to the reflections of every reader. The maxim of all penal jurisprudence, that it is far more the *certainty* than any *severity* of punishment that deters from crime, is too familiar to all to claim more than this allusion; while the following testimony from Mr. Lownes' work on the Prison (p. 93)[1] will not be deemed irrelevant to the point: "Some old offenders have chosen to run the *risk* of being hanged in other States, rather than encounter the certainty of being confined in the penitentiary cells of this."—(Pennsylvania.)

What more, then, remains to be done, after having thus shown, not only the superior terrors of the proposed perpetual solitary imprisonment at labor over that of capital punishment, on the basis of an equal probability of their being incurred—but also the immense advantage that would be gained to the public in preventing the acquittals now prompted by an unwise weakness of mercy, and in the moral influence of the greatly increased certainty of conviction in the one case over the other?

Then, too, would cease the state of things now existing, in which a higher duty to their consciences, than that which they all owe to their country, excludes from the jury-box, in all cases of capital indictment, a large portion of those members of the community the best qualified by education, character, and habits of reflection, to perform its important office the most wisely and well. In one of the cases which have been brought particularly under the committee's notice, as occurring within the past two years, in which the judge's return to the Governor exhibits the process of the impannelling of the jury, before the requisite twelve could be found to fill it, ten had been excused on the ground of opposition to capital punishment for any cause whatever.

* * *

Nor is it an untried experiment on which it is here proposed to enter. Other communities, when in a stage of civilization, and of general moral culture, far inferior to that which invites us now no longer to delay in following their example, have abolished the punishment of death—and with such a success as amply to justify us in the great reform proposed by the committee. If it can be shown that a single community has ever existed, which has been able to sustain itself against the dangers apprehended by the opponents of this reform—whose statute-books have been kept pure from the hideous stain of blood which it is our object now to erase from ours, and where the life of the citizen and the general order and security of the society have yet been not less safe than they are ever made by the presumed protection of the penalty of death—the sole ground will be swept away on which the great public crime of its continuance can be even attempted to be palliated this ground of a supposed "social necessity."

Now we know that throughout all the better age of the Roman republic, for a period of about two centuries and a half, the infliction of the punishment of death upon a Roman citizen for any cause whatever, was expressly forbidden by the famous Porcian Law—a *democratic* law, passed in 454th year of Rome, by the tribune Porcius Lecca.... The exile of Cicero turned upon his violation of this law, as regarded his arbitrary and strong-handed, however patriotic, infliction of the punishment of death upon the Catilinarian conspirators. The practicability of maintaining order and good government in a community without the punishment of death, is sufficiently proved by this example alone—the force of which argument is not affected by its exclusion of slaves and foreigners; nor by the fact of its

occasional violation in cases of high political excitement and
moments of public danger. . . . And if the simple respect for the
native majesty of the free citizen of a free republic, could teach
this sacred principle and wise practice to stern and cruel Rome
—if her Cicero could exclaim, "Away with the executioner and
the execution, and the very name of its engine! not merely from
the limbs, but from the very thoughts, the eyes, the ears, of
Roman citizens!—for not alone the occurrence and the endur-
ance of all these things, but also the liability, the apprehension,
even the mere mention of them, are unworthy of a Roman
citizen and a free man!"—what, then, should be the principle,
what the practice, of our far truer and higher democracy, elevated and purified as it has been by that Christianity which had
then not yet dawned upon the world for Jew or Gentile? [2]

In ancient Egypt under Sabaco, for a period of fifty years, as
we are informed by both Herodotus and Diodorus Siculus, no
capital punishments were inflicted, those penalties being
changed, with much success, into stated kinds of labor. . . . [3]

The Empress Elizabeth of Russia, on ascending the throne,
pledged herself never to inflict the punishment of death; and
throughout her reign, twenty years, she kept the noble pledge.
And so satisfactory was found its operation, that her successor,
the great Catherine, adopted it into her celebrated Code of
Laws, with the exception of very rare cases of offences against
the state. "Experience demonstrates," is the language of her
"Grand Instructions for framing a new code of laws for the
Russian Empire," Article 210, "that the frequent repetition of
capital punishments has never yet made men better. If, therefore, I can show that in the ordinary state of society the death
of a citizen is neither useful nor necessary, I shall have pleaded
the cause of humanity with success. . . ."

. . . The Count de Ségur, on his return from his embassy at
St. Petersburgh, in a letter published in the *Moniteur,* in June,
1791, declared that Russia, under the operation of this law, was
one of the countries in which the least number of murders was
committed,—adding that Catherine herself had several times said
to him: *We must punish crime without imitating it; the punishment of death is rarely anything but a useless barbarity.*" [4]

* * *

From Howard's well known work on Prisons,[5] the following facts are derived: In Leeuwarden, at the date of his visit, in 1783, there had been no execution for fourteen years, and there were in the prison only a few persons confined for petty offences. At Utrecht there had not been an execution in the city or province for twenty years; and in 1776, there were no prisoners,—in 1778, no debtors, and only one criminal, and his offence not capital,—in 1781, no debtors, and but five offenders, —and in 1783, only three prisoners. In Brunswick there had not been an execution for fourteen years; and in the *tower,* or prison for capital offences, which was over one of the gates, and consisted of three rooms, none of them had been occupied for a considerable time. In Denmark, where executions were rare, a great number for child-murder were condemned to work in spin-houses for life, and to be whipped annually on the day when, and the spot where, the crime was committed; that this mode of punishment *was dreaded more than death,* and since it was adopted *had greatly diminished the frequency of the crime.*

* * *

During the seven years (1804-1811) of the recordership of the celebrated Sir James Mackintosh, at Bombay, in India, the punishment of death was never once inflicted in the court over which he presided. The following [conclusion is] from his parting charge to the grand jury, (July 20th, 1811,) in reviewing the administration of the law during his presidency of the court:

"Since my arrival here in May, 1804, the punishment of death has not been inflicted by this court. . . .

* * *

"This small experiment has . . . been made without any diminution of the security of the lives and property of men. Two hundred thousand men have been governed for seven years without a capital punishment, and without any increase of crimes.—If any experience has been acquired, it has been safely and innocently gained."

In Tuscany the abolition of capital punishment has received perhaps the fairest and most satisfactory experiment known to the committee to have anywhere been made. The Grand Duke Leopold ascended the throne in 1765, and immediately, under the influence of the enlightened counsels of Beccaria, instituted a general reform of the penal code of the country, abolishing the torture and the punishment of death—the latter provisionally and experimentally. An idea of the success which attended the wise humanity of this experiment may be best had from the solemn edict issued by him twenty-one years after, in 1786. After referrring to his former provisional acts, and expressing his satisfaction at the happy results which had attended the experiment which they made,—as having, "instead of increasing the number of crimes, considerably diminished that of the smaller ones, and rendered those of an atrocious nature very rare,"—he proceeds:

"In consideration (Article 51) of the proper objects of punishment, the redress of the injury sustained by the public or the individual; the correction of the delinquent, who is still, notwithstanding, to be regarded as a child of the state, whose amendment ought never to be abandoned in despair; the certainty that he shall never again have the power of repeating his atrocities; and lastly, the public example; and that the government, in the punishment of crimes, and in adapting such punishment to the object toward which alone it should be directed, ought always to employ those means which, while the most efficacious, are the least hurtful to the offender; that this combined efficacy and moderation are found to consist, more in condemning him to hard labor than in putting him to death; since the former serves as a lasting example, and the latter only as a momentary object of terror, which often merges into compassion; and since, while the former takes from him the possibility of repeating his crime, it does not destroy the hope of his reformation, and of his becoming once more a useful and chastened subject; in consideration, likewise, that a very different legislation from that formerly prevailing will better agree with the gentle manners of the present age, and especially of the people of Tuscany, *we have resolved to abolish, and by the present law do abolish, forever, the punishment of death, . . ."*

* * *

"It is difficult for me," says the Marquis de Pastoret, Vice-President of the French Chamber of Peers, in a letter to the Count de Sellon, of Geneva, in about 1828, in reply to a request for some *official documents* respecting this experiment in Tuscany, "to give you *official documents*, as you call them, of the happy effects produced in Tuscany by the abolition of the punishment of death. It was a fact *so fully recognised,* when I wrote, when Leopold was still on the throne, that I could not think of seeking the means of proving what no one thought of disputing. Twice proscribed, and having first sought refuge in Switzerland, and afterward in Italy, I spent in those unhappy days a period of considerable length at Florence, and I often there have heard the praises by its inhabitants of the mildness of their laws, and the efficacious influence it had *in diminishing the number of crimes.".* . .

In Belgium capital punishment has been almost, if not entirely, disused since 1829. . . . The following tabular statement will explain itself to every eye at a glance:

Abstract of Returns printed for the Chamber of Deputies.

PERIODS.	CAPITAL CONVICTIONS.			EXECUTIONS.
Five years ending.	Murder.	Other crimes.	Total.	
With 1804	150	203	353	235
" 1809	82	70	152	88
" 1814	64	49	113	71
" 1819	42	29	71	26
" 1824	38	23	61	23
" 1829	34	40	74	22
" 1834	20	23	43	None.

From these returns it appears (to go no farther back in the comparison than the last two periods) that, while the number of executions was, in the period ending in 1829, *twenty-two,* the number of murders committed was *thirty-four,* and of other capital crimes *forty;* in the period ending in 1834, when *no executions took place,* capital punishment being practically abolished, and imprisonment for life at hard labor substituted, instead of an increase of violence and license as its consequence, the number of murders was reduced to *twenty,* and of other capital crimes to *twenty-three.* What more can be required to satisfy the most obstinate perversion of prejudice against the proposed measure?

It is frequently stated that, since the year here referred to, (1829,) capital punishment has been *abolished* in Belgium. This is believed to be a mistake, so far as regards any formal legal abolition, though in practice such may indeed be said to be the case. Nor, although other countries may have thus afforded us all the benefit of the experiments, more or less complete, which they have made, are the committee aware of any which, by an anticipation of the action proposed by them to the present Legislature, can bear off from the State of New York the honor, which will shine throughout all future time as the brightest jewel on her brow, of being the first to lead the way to the nations in the movement of this noble reform—a movement which, it is confidently believed, the rest will not thereafter be slow, joyfully and gratefully, to follow.

* * *

There is one topic connected with this general subject, not yet adverted to, which the committee regret to feel compelled, by the length into which they have been already led on other branches of their inquiry, to pass over with only a notice very unequal to its importance or its interest—they refer to that *insanity* which is so often the unsuspected origin of crime. What insanity is—where the dividing line at which reason ceases and it begins—how its subtle presence is to be always detected—when the influence of the physical causes to which its origin is almost always to be ascribed, commences to disturb the clearness of the operation of our mental processes and moral sentiments, with a sufficient degree of derangement to affect our just responsibility for the actions to which it impells or incites us— who can undertake to say? . . .

"Whatever may have been the decisions of courts of judica-

ture," says Dr. Prichard, in his valuable treatise on insanity,[6] "or
the opinions of lawyers on the subject, certain it is, as a matter
of fact, *idiotism,* or mental incapacity depending on congenital
formation, is not a thing to be pronounced absolute and complete within a definite degree. It exists in various shades and
modifications, from the last stage of fatuity which places human beings far below the brute in regard to manifestations of
mind, up to an almost imperceptible inferiority in comparison
with the ordinary power of understanding. There are some idi-
ots whose degradation is of so decided a character, and whose
defect is so strikingly displayed by the expression of countenance and manner, that no person could hesitate a moment to
pronounce upon their state; but the number is much greater of
those whose affection is of such a kind as to leave room for
doubt, and to require attentive examination. Yet it is no less
truly the fact that these individuals are by nature incompetent
to govern their conduct, or if left to themselves amid the colli-
sions and accidents of life to prevent the ruin of their families
or relations. Whatever the law of precept or custom may be,
with respect to those unfortunate persons, common sense and
humanity indicate most plainly, that they ought to be protected.". . .

It is recognised by all the writers on this subject, that there is
no branch of human science over which rests a greater degree of
mystery and uncertainty. One point, at least, may be regarded
as established, that, in the vast majority of cases, insanity is
directly ascribable to internal physical derangement, organic or
functional, and that it is generally, in its early stages, as open to
cure by medical treatment as almost any other disease. It is
ususally, at these periods, extremely irregular and intermitting
in its action—its illusions generally partial—and its presence very
often entirely unsuspected till it breaks out for the first time
into violent open manifestation. It may often exhaust itself for
the time in the very act, and a state of perfect mental composure may follow, as it may seem to have preceded, the crime
to which it may have impelled the half unconscious and unre-
sisting hand. It may have been insanity itself which stimulated
the morbid action of the very passions by which the act was

prompted; while the judicial investigation which confines itself
to the question of its malice prepense, has no means of going
farther,—no means of ascending from the apparent moral causes
of the act, to the hidden physical causes of those causes themselves. The existence of native propensies, to particular direc-
tions of good and evil, based upon organization, for which a
long line of dead ancestry is more responsible than the individual who is their unfortunate victim, is generally recognised
alike by the science and the common practical sense of the
present day. And although we do not admit in this fact any
relaxation of our moral responsibility, so long as a perfect state
of health gives full vigor and freedom of scope to that counteracting moral energy resident in our own controlling will; yet it
is undeniable, that we are constantly subject to the influence of
a thousand unseen internal causes over which we can have no
control, deranging, impairing, and often destroying—in greater
or less degree—the healthy action of that self-regulating moral
power to which alone such responsibility can attach.

* * *

"There is so much evil," says Mr. Simpson, in his excellent
work on the Necessity of Popular Education,[7] "in the very risk
that man's vengeance should follow God's visitation, that all
cases of crimes of violence, I repeat, in which mental disease is
unequivocally proved, should have the whole benefit of the
presumption that such disease may at any moment run into
irresponsible mania, and the unhappy patient be judged fit for
confinement and not for punishment." And none will deny that
a very strong argument is involved in the consideration here
presented, against the infliction of the irreparable punishment
of *death* for offences of this nature, of which in so many cases
the true origin must be buried in a depth of uncertainty far
beyond the ken of judge or jury, and open to the eye of that
intelligence alone which created man, alike in his moral and
physical constitution, the infinite and awful mystery that he is.
"The difficulties with which administrators of public justice
have to contend," says Dr. Prichard, "in distinguishing crimes
from the result of insane impulse, will never be entirely re-

moved, but they will be rendered much less important when the good sense of the community shall have produced the effect of abolishing all capital punishments. That this will sooner or later happen, I entertain no doubt."

The imagination is appalled at the thought of the untold numbers of our fellow-men who have been made, by the ignorant cruelty of a society yet clinging, in the maturity of its civilization, to the foolish and wicked practices of its barbarian childhood, to expiate on the scaffold crimes which have had their true origin in little else than an unconjectured internal derangement of the stomach or the brain. . . . .

* * *

[The committee believes] that a very large majority of the people of this State are at heart decidedly opposed to capital punishment,—that the number would be exceedingly small who would not hail with high gratification at least the trial of the proposed reform as an experiment, an experiment that may be with perfect ease abandoned by the next or any succeeding Legislature,—and that after the attention which has been drawn to the subject at the present session, a very profound dissatisfaction and disappointment would pervade the public mind, if any causes were allowed by this body to frustrate or delay a definite action upon it. It behoves, and will well become, the State of New York to take the initiative in this wise and sacred philanthropy,—the State from whose example and lead have already proceeded two of the most important popular and legal reforms that have made, and are rapidly making, their way, far and wide, throughout both her sister States in this great republican Union, and even the nations separated from us by three thousand miles of ocean, namely, the great Temperance Reform and the Abolition of Imprisonment for Debt,—the State, too, that has given birth to many a noble son who have advocated this reform, of whom two alone need here be referred to, a Tompkins and a Livingston,[8] and to whose memories no worthier monument, than the proposed law, could be erected by a proud and grateful country.

5 JOHN GREENLEAF WHITTIER

Quaker poet John Greenleaf Whittier (1807-1892) was an active reformer for much of his life, often infusing his poems with his social and political beliefs. Born in Haverhill, Massachusetts, Whittier began to write poetry at age fourteen and succeeded four years later in getting his early work published. William Lloyd Garrison, who admired the young man's writing, helped Whittier in 1829 secure the first of his many editorial positions. During the next several decades Whittier earned a living by working for reform newspapers and journals in Massachusetts, Connecticut, New York, and Pennsylvania. He continued writing poems and articles, many of them supporting the abolition of slavery, a cause to which he was passionately devoted. Whittier's abhorrence of slavery also drove him to the lecture circuit and to dabble in politics. The early 1840s saw Whittier win national acclaim as a poet, and his reputation continued to grow over the next thirty years. After the Civil War, Whittier curtailed his reform activity and, secure in his reputation as one of America's greatest poets, continued to write until his death.

Whittier's dislike of capital punishment was probably nurtured in childhood by his Quaker parents. He must have been influenced, too, by the man with whom he shared a room while both served in the Massachusetts legislature in 1835—Robert Rantoul, Jr. (see selection 3). Thus, when opponents of capital punishment began to campaign in the early 1840s, Whittier paused in his anti-slavery efforts to write several poems on the subject and enrolled himself as a charter member and officer of the Massachusetts Society for the Abolition of Capital Punishment.

The poem of 1843, reprinted here, was occasioned by the appearance in several religious newspapers of a pro-gallows letter by a clergyman. The minister described an execution he had recently attended and eulogized hanging and its beneficent effects. Deeply disturbed by the juxtaposition of gallows and gospel, Whittier responded with sometimes acid verse.

The Human Sacrifice (1843)

I

Far from his close and noisome cell,
   By grassy lane and sunny stream,
Blown clover field and strawberry dell,
And green and meadow freshness, fell
   The footsteps of his dream.
Again from careless feet the dew
   Of summer's misty morn he shook;
Again with merry heart he threw
   His light line in the rippling brook.
Back crowded all his school-day joys;
   He urged the ball and quoit again,
And heard the shout of laughing boys
   Come ringing down the walnut glen.
Again he felt the western breeze,
   With scent of flowers and crisping hay;
And down again through wind-stirred trees
   He saw the quivering sunlight play.
An angel in home's vine-hung door,
He saw his sister smile once more;
Once more the truant's brown-locked head
Upon his mother's knees was laid,
And sweetly lulled to slumber there,
With evening's holy hymn and prayer!

From John Greenleaf Whittier, "The Human Sacrifice," in *Anti-Slavery Poems: Songs of Labor and Reform* (Cambridge, Mass.: Riverside, 1888), pp. 282-289.

II

He woke. At once on heart and brain
The present Terror rushed again;
Clanked on his limbs the felon's chain!
He woke, to hear the church-tower tell
Time's footfall on the conscious bell,
And, shuddering, feel that clanging din
His life's last hour had ushered in;
To see within his prison-yard,
Through the small window, iron barred,
The gallows shadow rising dim
Between the sunrise heaven and him;
A horror in God's blessed air;
    A blackness in his morning light;
Like some foul devil-altar there
    Built up by demon hands at night.
    And, maddened by that evil sight,
Dark, horrible, confused, and strange,
A chaos of wild, weltering change,
All power of check and guidance gone,
Dizzy and blind, his mind swept on.
In vain he strove to breathe a prayer,
    In vain he turned the Holy Book,
He only heard the gallows-stair
    Creak as the wind its timbers shook.
No dream for him of sin forgiven,
    While still that baleful spectre stood,
    With its hoarse murmur, *"Blood for Blood!"*
Between him and the pitying Heaven!

III

Low on his dungeon floor he knelt,
    And smote his breast, and on his chain,
Whose iron clasp he always felt,
    His hot tears fell like rain;
And near him, with the cold, calm look
    And tone of one whose formal part,

Unwarmed, unsoftened of the heart,
Is measured out by rule and book,
With placid lip and tranquil blood,
The hangman's ghostly ally stood,
Blessing with solemn text and word
The gallows-drop and strangling cord;
Lending the sacred Gospel's awe
And sanction to the crime of Law.

IV

He saw the victim's tortured brow,
    The sweat of anguish starting there,
The record of a nameless woe
    In the dim eye's imploring stare,
        Seen hideous through the long, damp hair,—
Fingers of ghastly skin and bone
Working and writhing on the stone!
And heard, by mortal terror wrung
From heaving breast and stiffened tongue,
    The choking sob and low hoarse prayer;
As o'er his half-crazed fancy came
A vision of the eternal flame,
Its smoking cloud of agonies,
Its demon-worm that never dies,
The everlasting rise and fall
Of fire-waves round the infernal wall;
While high above that dark red flood,
Black, giant-like, the gallows stood;
Two busy fiends attending there:
One with cold mocking rite and prayer,
The other with impatient grasp,
Tightening the death-rope's strangling clasp.

V

The unfelt rite at length was done,
    The prayer unheard at length was said,
An hour had passed: the noonday sun

Smote on the features of the dead!
And he who stood the doomed beside,
Calm gauger of the swelling tide
Of mortal agony and fear,
Heeding with curious eye and ear
Whate'er revealed the keen excess
Of man's extremest wretchedness:
And who in that dark anguish saw
    An earnest of the victim's fate,
The vengeful terrors of God's law,
    The kindlings of Eternal hate,
The first drops of that fiery rain
Which beats the dark red realm of pain,
Did he uplift his earnest cries
    Against the crime of Law, which gave
    His brother to that fearful grave,
Whereon Hope's moonlight never lies,
    And Faith's white blossoms never wave
To the soft breath of Memory's sighs;
Which sent a spirit marred and stained,
By fiends of sin possessed, profaned,
In madness and in blindness stark,
Into the silent, unknown dark?
No, from the wild and shrinking dread,
With which he saw the victim led
    Beneath the dark veil which divides
Ever the living from the dead,
    And Nature's solemn secret hides,
The man of prayer can only draw
New reasons for his bloody law;
New faith in staying Murder's hand
By murder at that Law's command;
New reverence for the gallows-rope,
As human nature's latest hope;
Last relic of the good old time,
When Power found license for its crime,
And held a writhing world in check
By that fell cord about its neck;

Stifled Sedition's rising shout,
Choked the young breath of Freedom out,
And timely checked the words which sprung
From Heresy's forbidden tongue;
While in its noose of terror bound,
The Church its cherished union found,
Conforming, on the Moslem plan,
The motley-colored mind of man,
Not by the Koran and the Sword,
But by the Bible and the Cord!

VI

O Thou! at whose rebuke the grave
Back to warm life its sleeper gave,
Beneath whose sad and tearful glance
The cold and changëd countenance
Broke the still horror of its trance,
And, waking, saw with joy above,
A brother's face of tenderest love;
Thou, unto whom the blind and lame,
The sorrowing and the sin-sick came,
And from Thy very garment's hem
Drew life and healing unto them,
The burden of Thy holy faith
Was love and life, not hate and death;
Man's demon ministers of pain,
    The fiends of his revenge, were sent
    From thy pure Gospel's element
To their dark home again.
Thy name is Love! What, then, is he,
    Who in that name the gallows rears,
An awful altar built to Thee,
    With sacrifice of blood and tears?
Oh, once again Thy healing lay
    On the blind eyes which knew Thee not,
And let the light of Thy pure day
    Melt in upon his darkened thought.

Soften his hard, cold heart, and show
   The power which in forbearance lies,
And let him feel that mercy now
   Is better than old sacrifice!

VII

As on the White Sea's charmëd shore,
   The Parsee sees his holy hill
With dunnest smoke-clouds curtained o'er,
Yet knows beneath them, evermore,
   The low, pale fire is quivering still;
So, underneath its clouds of sin,
   The heart of man retaineth yet
Gleams of its holy origin;
   And half-quenched stars that never set,
Dim colors of its faded bow,
   And early beauty, linger there,
And o'er its wasted desert blow
   Faint breathings of its morning air.
Oh, never yet upon the scroll
Of the sin-stained, but priceless soul,
   Hath Heaven inscribed "Despair!"
Cast not the clouded gem away,
Quench not the dim but living ray,—
   My brother man, Beware!
With that deep voice which from the skies
Forbade the Patriarch's sacrifice,
   God's angel cries, Forbear!

6 CHARLES SPEAR

Among the many humanitarian reformers of the antebellum period, few were more dedicated to their causes than Universalist minister Charles Spear (1801-1863). Spear was born and lived much of his life in Boston, though his early ministerial duties carried him to temporary residence in Brewster and Rockport, Massachusetts. His profound sympathy for the poor and especially the imprisoned led him to undertake an unusual ministry. He had no church after 1839, but chose as his congregation the inmates of nearby jails. Throughout the 1840s and 1850s, Spear visited prisons, literally begged funds to assist discharged convicts (many of whom found temporary quarters in his humble house), harangued politicians and clerics in behalf of penal reform, and edited a struggling periodical devoted to his cause. Upon the outbreak of the Civil War, Spear became a hospital chaplain in Washington, where within a short time he contracted a disease and died.

Though Spear first spoke out against the death penalty in a sermon of 1830, his great work for the reform took place during the early 1840s. In 1844, he published *Essays on the Punishment of Death,* a popular book, and began to plan a reform newspaper. This work, at first called *The Hangman,* later, *The Prisoner's Friend,* appeared for the first time in January 1845 and struggled financially for twelve years. The anti-gallows crusade of the 1840s would not have been so active nor so widespread without Spear's weekly, later monthly, exhortations and news of the reform's successes and failures.

Essays on the Punishment of Death was a success although it was of indifferent literary quality. Spear devoted considerable space to the conventional secular arguments against the punishment, yet the greatest attraction of the book was its devout, if naive, religious appeals. The portions reproduced here are a fair sample of the reform response to the ubiquitous biblical defenses of the gallows in the antebellum period.

Thou Shalt Not Kill (1844)

Having presented various facts and arguments from history and observation, we now approach the sacred volume; that volume which must decide all moral questions, and by which every system of Moral Philosophy is to be tried. Let us go then to its sacred pages, solemnly and reverently asking for light from Him who is the source of all moral and spiritual light. . . .

* * *

Let us then turn back the page of history, and look into the first family that inhabited our fair world. . . .

. . . 'And Cain talked with Abel his brother, and it came to pass, when they were in the field, that Cain rose up against Abel his brother and slew him.'. . .

* * *

There was no trial . . . ; there were no witnesses, no judge with his ermine robe, no gathering of spectators, no prison, no fetters forged for the culprit. No. The Great Lawgiver himself presided, and pronounced the sentence. And what a lesson of calmness! What mingling of mercy and justice! And what a beautiful example for legislation in all ages!

We have seen the *deed;* we have learned the *motive,* and now the *sentence!* 'And now art thou cursed from the earth, which hath opened her mouth to receive thy brother's blood from thy hand. When thou tillest the ground, it shall not henceforth yield

From Charles Spear, *Essays on the Punishment of Death* (Boston: Spear, 1844), pp. 125-191.

unto thee her strength. A fugitive and a vagabond shalt thou be in the earth.'. . .

* * *

Amidst all the guilt and sufferings of the murderer, still both life and liberty were held sacred. 'And the Lord said unto him, Therefore, whosoever slayeth him, vengeance shall be taken on him seven-fold. And the Lord set a mark upon Cain, lest any finding him should kill him.' How remarkable! The first law on record against murder, is to preserve the life of the murderer himself! If the gallows is so sanctifying, why was it not reared at that early period in the history of man? . . .

* * *

[The covenant with Noah is] a portion of Scripture on which the advocates for the punishment of death place great confidence. The Rev. Mr. Cheever [1] calls it 'the citadel of the argument, commanding and sweeping the whole subject.'

'The hand,' he continues, 'that drew the rainbow over the sky, in sign "that storms prepare to part," wrote this statute in lines no more to be effaced till the destruction of all things, than the colors of the rainbow can be blotted from the sky, while lasts the constitution of this physical universe. And, as in every conflict of the elements that might fill men's souls with terror of another deluge, this bow of mercy, this vision of delight, should span the clouds with the glittering arch, so, in every storm of human passion, that rises to the violence of death, this statute, as a bow of promise, is God's assurance to the world, against the anarchy of murder. There probably never was an instance of murder in the Christian world, in which men did not think of it; nor ever an instance in the heathen world, in which the voice of conscience did not echo its assurance. As it stands in the Scriptures, it is one of the planets in the firmament of revealed truth; to strike it out from its place, and from its authority for the guidance of human legislation, would be like striking the constellation of the Pleiades, or the bright North Star, from heaven. . . . Its light, like that of the planets, has travelled unaltered and unabated across the storms and changes

of thousands of years; and still it shines, and still will it shine to
the end of the world; for as sure as we are that a God of mercy
gave this comprehensive element of law to Noah, so sure we are
that he will never suffer it to be blotted from human statute
books by the presumptuous tampering of a single generation.'

Such is the boasting, extravagant manner in which this reverend divine speaks of the covenant of Noah. He even goes farther, and endeavors to show that it is inhuman to strike out the
penalty of death. This is only a reiteration of the same argument that has always been employed by the advocates of sanguinary laws. . . .

Let us take a general view of the use made of this covenant.
We find that many writers confound it with the Mosaic code,
which was not given till nearly a thousand years after. Strictly
speaking, the passage on which we are now commenting was not
a code. It was a law or prophecy connected with regulations of
another kind. The advocates for the Punishment of Death often
use it both as a command and prophecy. But the most singular
reason for this covenant is that given by the Rev. Mr. Cheever,
in the introduction of his reply to O'Sullivan.[2] 'I have argued
that in consequence of the divine lenity in the case of Cain, the
crime of murder had become frightfully common, the earth
being filled with violence. The assurance that his own life would
not be taken, with which Lamech, whether a murderer or a
homicide, comforted himself and his wives by the example of
Cain's preservation, shows how men reasoned from that lenity;
and that the consequence of it would be a great cheapness in
the estimate of human life, a great freedom in the indulgence of
violent passion, unrestrained by consequences, and a perfect
carelessness and recklessness in bloodshed.' Indeed, then, the
Deity must have been a poor legislator! What a mistake! How
short-sighted! Not to see that, even in a period scarcely covering
the life of a patriarch, in passing sentence upon Cain, the result
would be 'a great cheapness in the estimate of human life,' 'a
perfect carelessness and recklessness in blood-shed!' And pray
what certainty have we, on this ground, that, in future legislation, God may not make a similar mistake! And how are we to
know but he has been mistaken in every age, and that even in

sending Christianity from heaven, He may fail in making it effectual in the redemption of man! But we cannot pursue this author in such a strain of remark. The idea that God was thus trying, as it were, the experiment of dispensing with Capital Punishment, for the experimental instruction of the human race itself, certainly seems puerile and absurd in the extreme.

Let us look at the circumstances connected with this passage. Its history is solemn and unspeakably important. 'The earth was filled with violence.' 'All in whose nostrils was the breath of life, of all that was in the dry land died.' . . 'Noah only remained alive, and they that were with him in the ark.' . . .

At last, 'the windows of heaven were stopped,' and the ark rested upon the mountains of Ararat. . . .

Now, as the last wave of the deluge swept over the earth, and man was again to re-people its surface, God establishes his covenant with his chosen servant. 'And the fear of you, and the dread of you, shall be upon every beast of the earth, and upon every fowl of the air, upon all that moveth upon the earth, and upon all the fishes of the sea; into your hand are they delivered. Every moving thing that liveth shall be meat for you; even as the green herb have I given you all things. But flesh with the life thereof, which is the blood thereof, shall ye not eat. And surely your blood of your lives will I require: at the hand of every beast will I require it, and at the hand of man; at the hand of every man's brother will I require the life of man. Whoso sheddeth man's blood, by man shall his blood be shed; for in the image of God made he man.'³ Then was established the token of the covenant, 'the bow in the cloud.' . . . Such is the history of the covenant with Noah. Let us proceed to discover its true meaning. And if we can but show, by fair interpretation, that it does not sanction the law of the Punishment of Death, then its advocates must remain content; for here, Mr. Cheever says, is the citadel of the argument; 'all else is a mere *guerilla* warfare, if you cannot carry this entrenchment.' To give our remarks order and precision, we will present them under two different views. . . .

I. The true rendering. Some commentators have given a different view from our common English translation. . . .

Mr. Rantoul,[4] to whom we are greatly indebted for many valuable facts, says, 'that the Hebrew participle translated "whoso sheddeth," answers to our English word "shedding," and might, with quite as much or more propriety, be rendered "whatsoever sheddeth;" and the grammatical construction will be consulted by substituting "its" for "his." The clause will then read, "whatsoever sheddeth man's blood, by man shall its blood be shed." ' He then shows that this rendering makes it consistent with the context, which was to show the sanctity of human life. 'The fear and dread of man shall be upon every beast. The beasts may be eaten for food, but not with the sacred principle of life, the blood; for life is sacred, and if your blood of your lives shall in any case be shed, I will require a strict account of it, whether it be shed by beast or man. I will myself call to a strict account the *man* who shall shed the blood of his brother, but if a *beast* has shed man's blood, by man let that beast be slain, because that beast has profanely marred the image of God in the human frame.' Mr. O'Sullivan says the literal rendering is, 'Shedding blood of man in man his (or its) blood will be shed.' He then endeavors to show the difficulties attending the common translation. He, however, does not rest his argument upon the mere rendering of the passage. 'That of the Septuagint would alone suffice, as it is not to be supposed that the seventy-two learned Jews of Alexandria, two hundred and eighty-seven years before Christ, would have misunderstood the Hebrew expression; . . . "Whoso sheddeth a man's blood, *for* his blood (i.e. the blood of the slain) will have his own shed." So also the Samaritan version, . . . "*for* the man his blood will be shed." While the Latin Vulgate renders it simply: . . . "Whoso sheddeth human blood, his blood will be shed,"—omitting our "by man" altogether.' Calvin says, 'to render it "by man," is a "forced" construction.' And he interprets it rather in a denunciatory than in a mere legislative sense.[5] Le Clerc,[6] who is certainly high authority, in a note on the word, says, 'that while some translate it "*per* hominem," i.e. *through* or *by* man, and that the preposition *beth* is constantly to be found in the sense of *per,* yet, "in accordance with the most frequent usage of the Hebrew language, it would have been said BJAD ADAM, *by the hand of man.* Yet it is always read BAADAM, or *in man,* or *among men.*" "As *in man* (continues Le Clerc) would scarcely make any sense, we are led to adopt the other signification, *among men*; whence arises a plain proposition, which is the same as that of the words immediately preceding, but more clearly expressed. God has said that *he will require* the life of the man slain from the slayer, among men or among beasts; he here more fully sets forth the same truth when he says that the blood of the slayer will be shed. . . . Homicides generally suffer a retributive punishment for their crime, whether they fall into the hands of the law, or, by the just providence of God, perish by some violent death." ' Such authority ought to settle forever the true rendering. Professor Upham,[7] one of the first Hebrew scholars in this country, says, 'that the passage may read, "whoso sheddeth man's blood, by man WILL his blood be shed." ' He adds that the expressions 'are obviously not to be understood as a command, authorizing and requiring every one, by his own act, and in his own person, to put to death any and every other individual who has been guilty of murder. Such an interpretation would fill the world with violence and confusion.'

II. The passage may be considered as a denunciation or prediction. We know that the advocates of the law of death will look on such a view with suspicion, or as an evasion of its true meaning. But we leave them in the hands of commentators of their own school. When men like Le Clerc, Michaelis,[8] Calvin, and Upham favor such a rendering, it is certainly entitled to respect. . . . We sincerely believe that our views are confirmed by history, both sacred and profane. The passage expresses a great retributive fact revealed in the moral world, and in the Word of God. He who wickedly takes human life will meet with severe punishment, and come to a miserable end. It may be understood in the same general sense as that in the fifty-fifth Psalm: 'Bloody and deceitful men shall not live out half their days.' It is so arranged in the constitution of things, and in the providence of God, that bloody and deceitful men do not prosper, but always meet with disappointment and suffering. . . .

* * *

There is one consideration which ought to have great weight
with those who advocate the penalty of death from the covenant of Noah. It seems, however, to have been entirely overlooked by them. We refer to the fact, that even in the patri-
archal age, it was not understood as a command to take life. We
have an account 'of the murder of Shechem and the people of
his city, by Simeon and Levi, the sons of Jacob, under circumstances of a most treacherous ferocity. Had the covenant with
Noah been understood in that day as requiring the retribution
of blood for blood, it is not to be supposed that the patriarch
Jacob—combining the character of ruler with that of parent—
would have left unexecuted the mandate so directly and imperatively given by the recent voice of God himself. His grief and
anger for their crime are shown in Gen. xxxiv. 30. He nowhere
intimates any feeling of remorse for the neglect of what would
otherwise have been a high and solemn duty incumbent on him
as a patriarch. While in his denunciation, on his death-bed, of
the future retribution yet to overtake the seed of the guilty
brothers, (Gen. xlix. 6, 7,) he makes no allusion to any such
penalty, upon them or theirs, as that which must have been
regarded as inevitable, had *he* understood the passage in question according to the modern interpretation of the advocates of
Capital Punishment.' We forget that Moses himself was a murderer, even while this covenant was the only law.

* * *

The advocates of Capital Punishment have invariably appealed to the code of Moses. It has been to them a 'city of
refuge.' It is worthy of remark that the opposers of every moral
improvement have gone at once to the types and shadows of the
old dispensation. The advocates for Slavery, the supporters of
War, and the opposers of Temperance, have all sought rest amid
its shadows and darkness; and whoever has even suggested that
its essential features have passed away, has been deemed an
innovator or a skeptic. . . .

* * *

We will present the code itself, or rather its various capital offences. It is remarkable that no writer with whom we have met has performed this labor. We feel that it will do more to settle the question of its adoption by any civilized community than all other considerations:

Number of Capital Offences in the Mosaic Code.

Touching the Mount,	Exod. xix. 12.
Murder,	" xxi. 12.
Kidnapping,	" 16.
Eating leavened bread during the Passover,	" xii. 15.
Suffering an unruly ox to be at liberty, if he kill; the ox also to be stoned,	" xxi. 29.
Witchcraft,	" xxii. 18.
Beastiality, the beast put to death,	" xxii. 19.
Idolatry,	" xxii. 20.
Oppression of Widow and Fatherless,	" xxii. 22.
Compounding holy ointment, or putting it on any stranger,	" xxx. 33.
Violation of the Sabbath,	" xxxi. 14.
Smiting of father or mother,	" xxi. 15.
Sodomy,	Lev. xx. 13.
Eating the flesh of the sacrifice of peace offerings with uncleanness,	" vii. 20.
Eating the fat of offered beasts,	" vii. 25.
Eating any manner of blood,	" vii. 27.
Offering children to Moloch,	" xx. 2.
Eating a sacrifice of peace-offering,	" xix. 8.
Screening the idolater,	" xx. 4.
Going after familiar spirits and wizards,	" xx. 6.
Adultery, [both parties, if female married, and not a bond-maid,]	" xx. 10.
Incest, [three kinds,]	" xx. 11.
Cursing of parents,	" xx. 9.
Unchastity in a priest's daughter,	" xxi. 9.
Blasphemy,	" xxiv. 16.
Stranger coming nigh the tabernacle,	Numb. i. 51.
Coming nigh the priest's office,	" iii. 10.
Usurping the sacerdotal functions,	" iv. 20.
Forbearing to keep passover, if not journeying,	" ix. 13.
Presumption, or despising the word of the Lord,	" xv. 30.
Uncleanness, or defiling the sanctuary of the Lord,	" xix. 13.

False pretension to the character of a divine
messenger, ...Deut. xiii. 5.
Opposition to the decree of the highest judicial
authority, ... " xvii. 12.
Unchastity before marriage, when charged by a
husband, ... " xxii. 13.

Modes of Punishment for Capital Offences.

Sword, ...Exod. xxii. 24.
Stoning, ... Lev. xx. 2.

Posthumous Insults.

Burning of the body, ...Lev. xx. 14; Josh. vii. 15.
Hanging of the body, ...Deut. xxi. 22.
Heaping of stones over the body or place of burial, Josh. vii. 25

Modes Introduced from Other Nations.

Decapitation, ...2 Sam. iv. 7.
Sawing asunder, ... Heb. xi. 37.
Strangulation.
Crucifixion.

What a dark catalogue! How minute in its delineation of offences! Every avenue of passion seems to have been guarded by a severe penalty. We ask its advocates if they are willing to take it entire for a guide to morals? Or will they contend that a part only is binding at the present day? If so, what part? Shall 'he that smiteth father or mother be put to death?' Shall this penalty be inflicted on 'the man that gathers sticks upon the Sabbath day?' Shall it be inflicted on him who 'stealeth a man and selleth him?' Or on him 'who afflicts any widow or father-less child?' Alas! if we were tried by this standard, imperfect as it was, we should find we were weighed in the balance and found wanting!

* * *

Whatever is immutably right, in that ancient dispensation, will stand forever; not because we find it there, but because truth, like its great Author, is imperishable. Whatever was based upon the peculiar situation of Israel, has passed away. Its rites and ceremonies are lost in the more perfect system of Christianity.... He who received the law upon the Mount bid the people look to a higher and more perfect dispensation. 'The Lord thy God will raise up unto thee a Prophet from the midst of thee, of thy brethren like unto me; unto him shall ye hearken.' When that Prophet came, he abolished the penal and ceremonial part of the old dispensation, and summed up the whole decalogue in two simple precepts: 'Thou shalt love the Lord thy God with all thy heart, and with all thy soul, and with all thy mind.... Thou shalt love thy neighbor as thyself.' Having thus condensed or simplified the moral part of the ancient code, he declared, 'On these two commandments hand all the law and the prophets.'

Let it be remembered, however, that there was in that code a great command, 'Thou shalt not kill.' This is the sixth commandment. It is addressed to all men; to sovereigns as well as subjects. Thou shalt not commit homicide. Such is the strict translation: the Hebrew verb signifying strictly to commit homicide; not always homicide with malice, which is the mere interpretation of our English word *murder,* nor the mere act of killing, which may be applied to the destruction of animals as well as man. Homicide, then, is forbidden without any qualification. We might as well talk of qualifying or repealing the first or second, third, fourth or fifth, in short, the whole decalogue, as this commandment. He who breaks this law will be held accountable. Life is sacred, inviolable. It is not to be taken even by the individual himself, nor by any earthly power....

* * *

After wandering among the types and shadows of the Mosaic dispensation, it is refreshing to come to that more excellent ministry; to him who is the Mediator of a better covenant. We feel as though we had crossed the desert, and were about entering Canaan. As we approach, we hear the song, not of Moses and his host, but of angels uttering, in strains unheard before, PEACE ON EARTH, GOOD WILL TO MEN. We place our feet on the plain of Bethlehem, beside the cradle of the great

Christian Legislator, with an illuminated sky above us. Here are no gibbets, no ruthless desolations, but all is lovely and refreshing. . . .

*   *   *

Had Jesus been governed by human wisdom, he would have pronounced blessings upon the proud, the rich and the popular. His first labor was to abrogate forever the law of retaliation. 'It hath been said, thou shalt love thy neighbor and hate thine enemy, but I say unto you, love your enemies, bless them that curse you, do good to them that hate you.' But can we love another, and put him to death? How much love does the government feel when the unhappy culprit is forced from his cell to the place of execution? . . .

A solitary case occurs in the eventful life of the Son of God, in which a capital offender was brought before him. 'And the Scribes and Pharisees brought unto him a woman taken in adultery.' The object was rather to ensnare him than to obtain a just decision. 'This they said tempting him, that they might have to accuse him.' 'He knew what was in man.' He penetrated into the very depths of the heart. In this instance, what a sublimity of action! What brevity in his language! What inexpressible tenderness! What a benignity of spirit! While he rebukes the severity of the law on the one hand, he puts her accusers to flight on the other. What a rebuke to self-righteousness! 'He that is without sin among you, let him first cast a stone at her.' Then leaving the rebuke to find its way to their hearts, he stooped down and wrote on the ground. 'And they which heard it, being convicted by their own conscience, went out one by one, beginning at the eldest, even unto the last: and Jesus was left alone, and the woman standing in the midst. When Jesus had lifted up himself, and saw none but the woman, he said unto her, Woman, where are those thine accusers? hath no man condemned thee? She said, No man, Lord. And Jesus said unto her, Neither do I condemn thee: go, and sin no more.' How admirably did Jesus turn the thoughts of these accusers inward! Would it not be well, when we look upon the miserable culprit, to turn our thoughts in upon our own hearts? A certain divine used to exclaim, when he saw a criminal carried to execution, 'There goes my wicked self.' And when the advocates for blood come forward in their zeal, would it not be well to pause and remember the words of Jesus? 'He that is without sin among you, let him cast the first stone.' Let those who cry for blood, erect the gibbet and place the halter! How many would then be executed?

* * *

It is said that the Christian precepts were designed for individuals, not nations. This has always been urged against every attempt to make an application of Christianity to the life and conduct. The popular distinction between political and moral right, or between political expediency and Christian duty, is dangerous in the extreme. On this principle, political bargains are often made, and as often broken. By what authority do we limit the precepts of Christ? 'No prophecy of the scripture is of private interpretation.' If individuals are bound to act up to Christian rules, societies are subject to the same. If not, how many individuals must associate before the precepts of Jesus cease to be binding? Were Robinson Crusoe and his man Friday a nation? If not, when would they have begun to be a nation, provided successive ships had been cast away on his island, and successive savages enslaved? How populous must the island become before their members would sanction sin? . . .

Jesus, it is said, did not condemn the law against which we have been laboring. . . . Hear, then, his commands: 'Ye have heard that it hath been said, An eye for an eye, and a tooth for a tooth. But I say unto you, That ye resist not evil: but whosoever shall smite thee on thy right cheek, turn to him the other also. And if any man will sue thee at the law, and take away thy coat, let him have thy cloak also.' These prohibit, decisively and positively, all acts of retaliation and violence. If carried out, not a single execution would ever again disgrace humanity. Such declarations, it is said, are not to be understood literally. Indeed! Is Christ divided? Did he not, when smitten on the one cheek, turn the other? Did he not even die on Calvary for his enemies? . . .

* * *

... Go, ye advocates for blood! go, stand at the foot of that cross! Go, imbibe its spirit of forgiveness and forbearance! Go, while the blood flows fresh from the wounded Saviour! Go! and then take your fellow-man, one for whom Christ died; one, weak, helpless, tempted, frail, like yourself; one made in the image of God; go, and erect your scaffold; and, amid his shrieks and groans, innocent though he may be, hurl him into the presence of his God!

7 CHARLES C. BURLEIGH

Charles C. Burleigh (1810-1878), trained as a lawyer, spu: his profession to become one of the leading anti-slavery a tors in America. Beginning in 1833, Burleigh edited a serie anti-slavery newspapers and journals, at first in his native (necticut, later in Boston and Philadelphia. A friend and all William Lloyd Garrison and Samuel J. May, he earned a rep tion as a fine writer and an unsurpassed orator.

The abolition of capital punishment was one of Burle peripheral reform interests, but he devoted a consider amount of time to it in the mid-1840s. In 1845, he publi: *Thoughts on the Death Penalty*, which attacked the gall essentially by attacking the writings of its chief defer George B. Cheever. In the following year, he devoted six e ings to heated debate with Philadelphia's Frederick Plum: another clerical champion of hanging.

Most of Burleigh's *Thoughts* merely summarized the ι tarian arguments of O'Sullivan and Spear. More interesting Burleigh's attack on a new argument which Cheever and ot had devised only a few years before. Capital punishm Cheever had claimed in his *Punishment By Death* of 1842, inherently just, apart from all claims of expediency. Man': stract sense of justice demanded that murder be punished ' nothing short of the death of the criminal. Burleigh was on the first reform writers to grapple with this slippery m physical position and he did so with great success.

Where is the Boasted Justice (1845)

"UTILITY NOT THE GROUND OF PUNISHMENT"

But death to the murderer is demanded on other grounds than those of expediency. "Punishment," says Cheever, "is sometimes called for, apart from the question whether it be useful or not." And again; "there is such a thing as retributive justice, apart from the purpose of security against crime, or the necessity of the guardianship of society and the universe." "The culprit," says Theodore Frelinghuysen,[1] "is doomed to suffer, because *he deserves to suffer.*" Hence it is argued, that as the murderer deserves to die, it is the right and duty of the State to kill him.

DESERT OF DEATH NO PROOF OF RIGHT TO KILL

Now without calling in question the premises of this argument, I dissent from its conclusion. Whether the murderer is worthy of death or not, we need not determine; for granting that he is, it by no means follows that we are bound, or have a right, to give him his desert. Not even the warmest friend of the gallows will maintain that human tribunals ought *always* to award, to every offender, all the suffering he deserves; or that mercy should never be shown, however safe, or even generally beneficial, it might be in any particular case. Nor will it be denied that cases may and do occur, in which mercy is both safe and conducive to the common good. But if this is admitted, then the criminal's desert of death is, in no case, of itself enough to justify the State's infliction of it. Not only must his desert be proved, but also that the infliction will do more good than harm; since the latter is not implied in the former, and both are needed, to authorize the death-doom.

And what are we, that we should demand the stern award of

From Charles C. Burleigh, *Thoughts on the Death Penalty* (Philadelphia: Merrihew and Thompson, 1845), pp. 107-119.

strictest justice against our offending brother? Who of us would stand forth to execute it, if the warrant ran, as once of old, "let him who is without sin" strike the first blow? Shall they who own themselves transgressors daily of that perfect law which justly claims their full obedience, and who rely on sovereign grace alone for all they hope here or hereafter, refuse the lenity they crave, and, like the forgiven debtor of ten thousand talents, drag to inexorable judgment the poor fellow servant who owes a hundred pence. . . .

. . . To doom our brother to "the most terrible of all penalties" in human power, while we put up that beautiful petition which Jesus taught us—"forgive, *as we forgive*,"—what is it but to turn the prayer for pardon into a dreadful imprecation, calling down God's heaviest judgments on our own heads? For if our way of forgiving is to punish as severely as we can, and we ask God to forgive *as* we do, do we not ask him to punish with the utmost severity in his Almighty power? How the use of this petition can be reconciled with the infliction of suffering, merely because it is deserved, and "apart from the question" of its utility either to the sufferer or the community, is a problem which I am glad it is not my task to solve. However just such retribution, for retribution's sake, may be esteemed, I cannot but think that the disciple of Jesus, filled with the spirit of his master, would choose to leave it in the hands of Him "to whom vengeance [i.e., retribution] belongeth;" who claims it as His own prerogative.

But if these considerations are urged in vain; if it is still insisted that mercy must not be suffered to "rejoice against judgment," but justice, severe and unrelenting, must have its course; then it behooves us at least to be sure that what we propose to do *is* just;—just not merely *towards others*, but also *in us*. For the practical question before us is not, what is just for the criminal to suffer?—but what is just for society to inflict? Now I maintain that justice, as well as mercy, forbids our indicting any punishment for the sake of mere retribution, "apart from the question" of its usefulness. We have no right to make men suffer solely "because they deserve to suffer." If we had, it would be right for us to punish all transgressions of the Divine law, natural or revealed, those which are not, no less than those which are, direct invasions of the rights of man. Not only crime, but every form of sin, would be within the proper scope of human penalties;—a doctrine which, carried to its legitimate conclusions, would turn our law-courts into courts of conscience, literally, "with a vengeance;" make morals and religion, in their minutest details, the subject of penal legislation, and enact into statutes the teachings of physiology touching diet, exercise and habits of life; menace impiety with dungeon and halter; set censors over table, toilet, field and workshop, to watch against intemperance in food and drink, extravagance or conformity to hurtful fashions in dress, indolence or wanton over-exertion in labor; and in a word enforce sinless perfection with the terror of the magistrate's sword. Rather more work than our republican rulers would care to assume, in these days when the favourite democratic motto is, "that government is best which governs least." And seriously, can that be a true doctrine, of which the consequences are so absurd?

Again. However worthy of retributive punishment the criminal may be, all doubtless will admit that his partners in the crime cannot claim the right to award it to him. A child may "deserve to suffer" for lying or stealing; but should his father, who had taught him theft and falsehood, and tempted him to their commission, "doom him to suffer," and that too, not for the child's good, or his own, or any other's, but purely for the sake of "retribution," who would not cry out upon the act as cruelly unjust? Yet how much does the relative position of society and the criminals it punishes differ from this? What has it done for them, and for the degraded class whence generally they come? Has it surrounded their childhood with healthy moral influences, or done aught to prevent them from drawing their first breath in a tainted moral atmosphere, and being moulded to vicious tastes and habits while yet too young to choose any circumstance of their condition? When choice seemed in their power, but the "second nature" already wrought into them, inclined their choice to evil, has it then been diligent to repair the wrong of its former neglect? When they had wandered far in the way of vice, wherein their feet had first been set, has it sought them out, and, with kind words and deeds of love and wholesome counsel and instruction, laboured to lead them to the better path? Has it been careful so to dispense its wealth that none should be shut out, by abject poverty, from the means of moral culture; or tempted to crime by pinching want and sore distress? Have its laws, and usages, and institutions all been fitted to inspire a deep abhorrence of bloodshed and violence, and to cherish a gentle and loving spirit, and so to make men heartily averse to evil-doing? Far otherwise.

SOCIETY TRAINS MEN TO CRIME

Instead of doing what it should for the prevention of crime by improving the character and condition of those most likely to commit it, and thus hindering the growth of criminal disposi-tions and removing the temptations to their indulgence, it is too often working out the very opposite results. By its too unequal distribution of the good things of life, some, deprived at once of bodily comforts and necessaries, and the means of improvement for mind and heart, are made reckless and desperate by igno-rance and suffering; while in others are nourished all the vices bred of luxury and over-abundance. Its gross neglect, too, of the ignorant and wretched, for whose wants of body and soul it has made no adequate provision, aggravates the evils of this inequality.

Nor is its mere neglect the worst. It has open schools of vice, potent agencies of demoralization. For its state-licensed grog-shops, its theatres, puffed by the popular press and patronized by the "genteel" and "respectable," as well as the vile, its gam-bling houses frequented and countenanced by those who never-theless wear its civic and social honors and stand high in public esteem; for all these—not to name other fountains of corrup-tion—and for their influence in training men for crime, society [is] as truly answerable as individual offenders. By its artificial distinctions, also, which rate birth, and possessions, and out-ward appearance, above moral worth, and prefer eminence in comparatively useless and even positively hurtful employments,

to skill and industry beneficially directed; glorifying the spirit
of slaughter embodied in military heroes, and holding the peaceful virtues and honest toil of artisans and tillers of the earth as
ignoble; it perverts the sense of right, lessens the natural horror
at the thought of shedding human blood, and by insensible
degrees prepares the mind to yield, when unpropitious circumstances or evil passions beset it with temptations. Moreover, as
has heretofore been shown, the penal code itself, while it retains
the stain of blood, teaches a doctrine and sets an example which
help to form men for the commission of murder. And the treatment meted out to less offenders, but too often tends to deepen
their depravity and fit them for yet darker deeds. After suffering some ignominious penalty, perhaps imprisonment among
older, and hardier, and more expert transgressors, of whom they
learn new arts of wickedness; they are sent forth friendless and
destitute, with a stain on their characters which makes it difficult to obtain honest means of support, a consciousness of disgrace which robs them of self-respect, and a sense of discourage-
ment which prevents almost the effort thenceforward to do
better; shunned by the virtuous for fear of contamination, and
left if not driven to the companionship of vice and crime, so
that reformation is hardly to be looked for, however sincerely it
may be desired. A change for the better is indeed beginning to
appear, and convicts have a brighter prospect than in former
times of winning back their way to virtue, usefulness and peace;
but still society is very far from having done its duty toward
them, either before or after their first false step. Such being the
case, ought it not first to make amends for its own faults,
whether of doing or not doing, before it claims a right to punish
for the sake of *retribution* those very crimes which it fosters, at
least, if not creates?

 DANGER OF IRRETRIEVABLE ERRORS

Yet again. Whatever are its rights toward the criminal, has it
any right to endanger the lives of the innocent? Can it justly
seek retribution at the risk of inflicting a great and *irreparable*

wrong? Human tribunals are always liable to err, and error in a case like this admits of no remedy. Other penalties leave a chance for the discovery of mistakes before it is too late to repair, in part, if not wholly, the injustice they may have done; but, to the victim of an unjust death-sentence, no shadow of requital can be made. The memory of the wrong remains to torment its authors with vain regrets, and perhaps to unnerve the arm of justice with the dread of like mistakes in future, so that transgressors will grow bold with the hopes of impunity; but regret and remorse can never "sooth the dull, cold ear of death," or breathe new life into the senseless clay. How many have died for crimes which they never committed, none can tell; but the many *known* instances give reason to suspect that many more have occurred which never came to light. One discovered error makes us justly apprehensive of others undiscovered.

* * *

CONFESSION NOT ALWAYS TO BE TRUSTED

... Even confession is no certain proof of guilt, for crimes have been confessed which had not been committed. Most readers are familiar with the case of Bourne, in Vermont, who confessed a murder of which he had been convicted on circumstantial evidence, and would have been hung, had not his supposed victim returned alive and well, just in time to save him.[2] How many too have confessed the impossible crime of witchcraft, and died sacrifices to a now exploded superstition! But illustrations need not be farther multiplied, of what no candid reasoner will deny,—the ever imminent danger of inflicting, by the doom of death, an immeasurable and utterly remediless wrong. As Dymond well says, "a jury or court of justice never *know* that a prisoner is guilty."[3] Their condemnation is therefore in some sort a shot at random, or at best, with a doubtful aim. Now, however just it may be that a murderer should die, it surely is not just to fire at a venture into the crowd where he is, in order to kill him. La Fayette spoke the language no less of justice than of humanity, when he said, "Till the infallibility of human judgments shall have been proved to me, I shall demand the abolition of the penalty of death."[4]

CHEEVER'S REPLY

If any thing could add strength to this argument from the danger of fatal and irreparable mistakes, Cheever's reply would do it. He says the penalty has saved a hundred innocent persons from murder, where it has cut off ten by mistake. But I have shown that, instead of saving from murder, it causes more murders than it punishes, and is therefore to be charged with the death both of its own innocent victims, and of those who by reason of its influence, fall a prey to the murderer. He says there is the same danger of mistake in all punishments. True, but in all others it can be remedied, in part at least, if not wholly. His argument is good to prove that necessity alone can justify any punishment, and that such only should be chosen as allow mistakes to be corrected, fully if possible, but if not, then partially at all events. It weighs against the gallows, therefore, and not for it. He says that, "in almost every instance" of fatal error, "except where no murder had been committed, the real culprit had taken the life of the accused by perjury;" that is, "had used an institution of justice, instead of the assassin's knife, to perpetrate another" murder. A very good reason for abolishing, but a marvellously poor one for retaining "an institution of justice" (*in*justice, rather,) which can be so easily, and has been so often, turned into "an assassin's knife." And in those cases "in which no murder had been committed," is the loss of an innocent man's life, through the erroneous belief that there had been murder, so trivial an affair as to be worthy of only a mere parenthetical notice? Shall we still uphold a penal system, which sacrifices the innocent on suspicion of crime when none has been committed, and gives the perpetrator of one murder a weapon to commit another with? But, says Cheever, "If you abolish the penalty of death to avoid these murders in the second instance you increase the number of murders in the first instance." This is answered by the proof already given, that abolishing the death penalty *diminishes,* instead of increasing, murders.

DIFFICULTY OF ESTIMATING GUILT

Another thought is perhaps worth suggesting in this connection. Even if the deed were traced with absolute certainty to the doer, the amount of his guilt is known only to the Searcher of hearts; and only he who knows that, can measure out the just degree of punishment. What has been his previous training, what circumstances beyond his control have modified his character, what temptations have beset and what provocations have maddened him; in a word, what influences without himself have combined to shape his course, can be but imperfectly known, if at all, by any human tribunal. Yet all this must be perfectly known before his just desert can be awarded him. Are they the proper dispensers of retributive justice, who do not and cannot, in a single case, know what *is* a just retribution; and who in many cases fail of even approaching to such knowledge?

AND OF MEASURING PUNISHMENT

Again. A right measure of punishment is as hard to attain as a right estimate of guilt. The same infliction will be far severer to some than to others; hence, even if the criminal's exact desert were ascertained, it could not be known whether he was adequately punished, unless it were first known how much a given infliction would make him suffer. But the code of blood forbids the graduation of punishment to the varying grades of guilt. It has the same penalty, for the same outward crime, however unlike the circumstances of its commission, or the character of its authors, or their susceptibility of pain from that particular infliction. For the least guilty, its doom is death; for the most guilty, only death. Yet some, in their brutal stupidity, like Shakespeare's Barnardine, "apprehend death no more dreadfully but as a drunken dream; careless, reckless and fearless of what's past, present or to come;"[5] while others die a thousand deaths in fearing one, feeling keen agony in every moment's anticipation of their fate. To some, death comes a welcome deliverer from a life of complicated misery; others it tears from family and friends, from many comforts, from bright hopes which made life sweet and sunny, and the prospect of the cold, dark grave very terrible. One dies impenitent in a horror of despair, felt as the foretaste of endless woe; another, whose crime was perhaps more aggravated, and involved deeper guilt, goes away rejoicing in the hope of a blessed immortality, which makes death no punishment to him, but rather a speedier dismissal from a world of sin and sorrow to eternal bliss. As the most hardened and depraved, in general, dread death the least, it punishes the least guilty the most severely. Where then is the boasted justice of a penalty which, always so unequal in its bearing, and so incapable of adjustment to different degrees of guilt, must often produce suffering in inverse proportion to desert? . . .

INJUSTICE TO THE MANY

But I have yet another objection to that penalty, on the ground of justice; or rather have to apply more distinctly to this point, an objection already stated under another head. Be the criminal's desert what it may, and be the right of society toward him what it may, it has no right to impair the general security of life, or lower the tone of public morals. The state, the criminal, and the innocent accused of crime, are not the only parties to whom justice has regard. The great body of unoffending citizens have their rights also; rights which are invaded by whatever puts in needless peril their lives, their property, their peace of mind, or their purity of morals. But it has been shown that the penalty of death has this effect; that it is fearfully demoralizing, that it weakens the strongest barrier against crime, especially crimes of blood, increases the chances of impunity, and in various ways tends to the multiplication of murders, as well as of less enormous offences. It is, therefore, gross injustice to the mass of the people, whatever it may be to the immediate sufferer. The incendiary may deserve, if you will, to have his house burnt down but if it stands where the flames will endanger other houses, is it *just* to *their* inmates to set it on fire? So neither is it just to the unoffending many, to punish the offending few in such a way as will lessen the general safety.

* * *

We have now seen that to the question with which we started—ought human hands to punish crime with death?—both expediency and justice answer with an emphatic NO: The one condemning such a punishment as opposed in tendency to every object of penal law of which it can take cognisance; the other pronouncing its infliction, by erring man, a usurpation of the prerogative of the Infallible, and an invasion of the rights of the many, in a vain attempt to deal out retribution for the crimes of the few.

8 WALT WHITMAN

Walt Whitman (1819-1892), newspaper editor and poet, was born in Huntington, Long Island, and spent most of his early life in Brooklyn and New York City. At age thirteen, Whitman began his long association with journalism, which was to provide his livelihood for the next thirty years. By 1846, he was editor of the *Brooklyn Eagle,* where his editorials rallied reformers to a wide variety of causes. Too great enthusiasm for the free-soil movement, in fact, cost him his editorship two years later. Other newspaper jobs followed, however, including editorship of the *Brooklyn Times* from 1857 to 1859, before Whitman abandoned journalism and reform to follow his poetic muse.

Of the many reforms Whitman espoused in his newspaper years, none stirred him more than the campaign to abolish capital punishment. He contributed numerous articles on the subject to newspapers and magazines and, in 1846, was a founding member of the Brooklyn Association for the Abolition of the Death Penalty. Probably his most influential anti-gallows article was written for the November 1845 issue of the *United States Magazine and Democratic Review.* This famous journal, edited by Whitman's political ally and fellow reformer John L. O'Sullivan, won the Brooklyn editor a prestigious national audience for his views on the punishment of crime.

Whitman's arguments added little to those of Livingston and Rantoul, but his manner of presenting them was original and effective. His concluding remarks reveal, perhaps even better than Whittier's poem (see selection 5), the bitterness reformers felt toward the pro-gallows clergy.

A Dialogue (1845)

What would be thought of a man who, having an ill humor in his blood, should strive to cure himself by only cutting off the festers, the outward signs of it, as they appeared upon the surface? Put criminals for festers and society for the diseased man, and you may get the spirit of that part of our laws which expects to abolish wrong-doing by sheer terror—by cutting off the wicked, and taking no heed of the causes of wickedness. I have lived long enough to know that national folly never deserves contempt; else should I laugh to scorn such an instance of exquisite nonsense!

Our statutes are supposed to speak the settled will and voice of the community. We may imagine, then, a conversation of the following sort to take place—the imposing majesty of the people speaking on the one side, a pallid, shivering convict on the other.

"I have done wrong," says the convict; "in an evil hour a kind of frenzy came over me, and I struck my neighbor a heavy blow, which killed him. Dreading punishment, and the disgrace of my family, I strove to conceal the deed, but it was discovered."

"Then," says society, "you must be killed in return."

"But," rejoins the criminal, "I feel that I am not fit to die. I have not enjoyed life—I have not been happy or good. It is so horrid to look back upon one's evil deeds only. Is there no plan by which I can benefit my fellow-creatures, even at the risk of my own life?"

"None," answers society; "you must be strangled—choked to death. If your passions are so ungovernable that people are in danger from them, we shall hang you."

"Why that?" asks the criminal, his wits sharpened perhaps by his situation. "Can you not put me in some strong prison, where no one will be harmed by me? And if the expense is anything against this, let me work there, and support myself."

From Walt Whitman, "A Dialogue," *United States Magazine and Democratic Review,* 17 (November 1845), pp. 360-364.

"No," responds society, "we shall strangle you; your crime deserves it."

"Have you, then, committed no crimes?" asks the murderer.

"None which the law can touch," answers society. "True, one of us had a mother, a weak-souled creature, that pined away month after month, and at last died, because her dear son was intemperate, and treated her ill. Another, who is the owner of many houses, thrust a sick family into the street because they did not pay their rent, whereof came the deaths of two little children. And another—that particularly well-dressed man —effected the ruin of a young girl, a silly thing who afterward became demented, and drowned herself in the river. One has gained much wealth by cheating his neighbors—but cheating so as not to come within the clutches of any statute. And hundreds are now from day to day practising deliberately the most unmanly and wicked meannesses. We are all frail!"

"And *these* are they who so sternly clamor for my blood!" exclaims the convict in amazement. "Why is it that I alone am to be condemned?"

"That they are bad," rejoins society, "is no defence for you."

"That the multitude have so many faults—that none are perfect," says the criminal, "might at least make them more lenient to me. If my physical temperament subjects me to great passions, which lead me into crime, when wronged too—as I was when I struck that fatal blow—is there not charity enough among you to sympathise with me—to let me not be hung, but safely separated from all that I might harm?"

"There is some reason in what you say," answers society; "but the clergy, who hate the wicked, say that God's own voice has spoken against you. We might, perhaps, be willing to let you off with imprisonment; but Heaven imperatively forbids it, and demands your blood. Besides, that you were wronged, gave you no right to revenge yourself by taking life."

"Do you mean me to understand, then," asks the convict, "that Heaven is more blood-thirsty than you? And if wrong gives no right to revenge, why am I arraigned thus?"

"The case is different," rejoins society. "We are a community—you are but a single individual. You should forgive your enemies."

"And are you not ashamed," asks the culprit, "to forget that as a community which you expect me to remember as a man? While the town clock goes wrong, shall each little private watch be abused for failing to keep the true time? What are communities but congregated individuals? And if you, in the potential force of your high position, deliberately set examples of retribution, how dare you look to me for self-denial, forgiveness, and the meekest and most difficult virtues?"

"I cannot answer such questions," responds society; "but if you propose no punishment for the bad, what safety is there for our citizens' rights and peace, which would then be in continual jeopardy?"

"You cannot," says the other, "call a perpetual jail no punishment. It is a terrible one. And as to your safety, it will be outraged less by mild and benevolent criminal laws than by sanguinary and revengeful ones. They govern the insane better with gentleness than severity. Are not men possessing reason more easily acted on through moral force than men without?"

"But, I repeat it, crimes will then multiply," says society (not having much else to say); "the punishment must be severe, to avoid that. Release the bad from the fear of hanging, and they will murder every day. We must preserve that penalty to prevent this taking of life."

"I was never ignorant of the penalty," answers the criminal; "and yet I murdered, for my blood was up. Of all the homicides committed, not one in a hundred is done by persons unaware of the law. So that you see the terror of death does not deter. The hardened and worst criminals, too, frequently have no such terror, while the more repentant and humanised suffer in it the most vivid agony. At least you could try the experiment of no hanging."

"It might cost too much. Murder would increase," reiterates society.

"Formerly," replies the criminal, "many crimes were punished by death that now are not; and yet those crimes have not increased. Not long since the whipping-post and branding-iron stood by the bar of courts of justice, and were often used, too. Yet their abolition has not multiplied the evils for which they were meted out. This, and much more, fully proves that it is by no means the dread of terrible punishment which prevents crime. And now allow me to ask you a few questions. Why are most modern executions private, so called, instead of public?"

"Because," answers society, "the influence of the spectacle is degrading and anti-humanising. As far as it goes, it begets a morbid and unhealthy feeling in the masses."

"Suppose all the convicts," goes on the prisoner, "adjudged to die in one of your largest States, were kept together for two whole years, and then in the most public part of the land were hung up in a row—say twenty of them together—how would this do?"

"God forbid," answers society, with a start. "The public mind would revolt at so bloody and monstrous a deed. It could not be allowed!"

"Is it anything less horrible," resumes the questioner, "in the deaths being singly and at intervals?"

"I cannot say it is," answers society.

"Allow me to suppose a little more," continues the criminal, "that all the convicts to be hung in the whole republic for two years—say two hundred, and that is a small estimate—were strangled at the same time, in full sight of every man, woman and child—all the remaining population. And suppose this were done periodically every two years. What say you to that?"

"The very thought sickens me," answers society, "and the effect would be more terrible and blighting upon the national morals and the health of the popular heart, than it is any way possible to describe. No unnatural rites of the most barbarous and brutal nations of antiquity ever equalled this; and our name would always deserve to be written literally in characters of blood. The feeling of the sacredness of life would be utterly destroyed among us. Every fine and Christian faculty of our souls would be rooted away. In a few years, this hellish oblation becoming common, the idea of violent death would be the theme of laughter and ribald jesting. In all the conduct and opinions of men, in their every-day business, and in their private meditations, so terrible an institution would some way, in some method of its influence, be seen operating. What! two hundred miserable wretches at once! The tottering old, and the youth not yet arrived at manhood; women, too, and perhaps girls who are hardly more than children! The spot where such a deed should be periodically consummated would surely be cursed forever by God and all goodness. Some awful and poisonous desert it ought to be; though, however awful, it could but faintly image the desert such horrors must make on the heart of man, and the poison it would diffuse on his better nature."

"And if all this appalling influence," says the murderer, "were really operating over you—not concentrated, but cut up in fractions and frittered here and there—just as strong in its general effect, but not brought to a point, as in the case I have imagined—what would you then say?"

"Nay," replies society, with feverish haste, "but the executions are now required to be private."

"Many are not," rejoins the other; "and as to those that are nominally so, where everybody reads newspapers, and every newspaper seeks for graphic accounts of these executions, such things can never be private. What a small proportion of your citizens are eye-witnesses of things done in Congress; yet they are surely not private, for not a word officially spoken in the Halls of the Capitol, but is through the press made as public as if every American's ear were within hearing distance of the speaker's mouth. The whole spectacle of these two hundred executions is more faithfully seen, and much more deliberately dwelt upon, through the printed narratives, than if people beheld it with their bodily eyes, and then no more. Print preserves it. It passes from hand to hand, and even boys and girls are imbued with its spirit and horrid essence. Your legislators have forbidden public executions; they must go farther. They must forbid the relation of them by tongue, letter, or picture; for your physical sight is not the only avenue through which the subtle virus will reach you. Nor is the effect lessened because it is more covert and more widely diffused. Rather, indeed, the reverse. As things are, the masses take it for granted that the system and its results are right. As I have supposed them to be, though the nature would remain the same, the difference of the form would present the monstrous evil in a vivid and utterly new light before men's eyes."

"To all this," says society, "I answer—" *what*? What shall it be, thou particular reader, whose eyes now dwell on my fanciful dialogue? Give it for thyself—and if it be indeed an *answer*, thou hast a logic of most surpassing art.

O, how specious is the shield thrown over wicked actions, by invoking the Great Shape of Society in their defence! How that which is barbarous, false, or selfish for an individual becomes singularly proper when sanctioned by the legislature, or a supposed national policy! How deeds wicked in a man are thus applauded in a number of men!

What makes a murder the awful crime all ages have considered it? The friend and foe of hanging will unite in the reply— Because it destroys that cunning principle of vitality which no human agency can replace—invades the prerogative of God, for God's is the only power that can give life—and offers a horrid copy for the rest of mankind. Lo! thou lover of strangling! with what a keen razor's sharpness does every word of this reply cut asunder the threads of that argument which defends thy cause! The very facts which render murder a frightful crime, render hanging a frightful punishment. To carry out the spirit of such a system, when a man maims another, the law should maim him in return. In the unsettled districts of our western states, it is said that in brutal fights the eyes of the defeated are sometimes torn bleeding from their sockets. The rule which justifies the taking of life, demands gouging out of eyes as a legal penalty too.

I have one point else to touch upon, and then no more. There has, about this point, on the part of those who favor hanging, been such a bold, impudent effrontery—such a cool sneering defiance of all those greater lights which make the glory of this age over the shame of the dark ages—a prostitution so foul of names and influences so awfully sacred—that I tremble this moment with passion, while I treat upon it. I speak of founding the whole breadth and strength of the hanging system, as many do, on the Holy Scriptures. The matter is too extensive to be argued fully, in the skirts of an essay; and I have therefore but one suggestion to offer upon it, though words and ideas rush and swell upon my utterance. When I read in the records of the past how Calvin burned Servetus at Geneva, and found his defence in the Bible—when I peruse the reign of the English Henry 8th, that great champion of Protestantism, who, after the Reformation, tortured people to death, for refusing to acknowledge his spiritual supremacy, and pointed to the Scriptures as his authority—when, through the short reign of Edward 6th, another Protestant sovereign, and of the Bloody Mary, a Catholic one, I find the most barbarous cruelties and martyrdoms inflicted in the name of God and his Sacred Word—I shudder and grow sick with pity. Still I remember the gloomy ignorance of the law of love that prevailed then, and the greater palliations for bigotry and religious folly. I bethink me how good it is that the spirit of such horrors, the blasphemy which prostitutes God's law to be their excuse, and the darkness of superstition which applauded them, have all passed away. But in these days of greater clearness, when clergymen call for sanguinary punishments in the name of the Gospel—when, chased from point to point of human policy, they throw themselves on the supposed necessity of hanging in order to gratify and satisfy Heaven—when, instead of Christian mildness and love, they demand that our laws shall be pervaded by vindictiveness and violence—when the sacrifice of human life is inculcated as in many cases acceptable to Him who they say has even revoked his consent to brute sacrifices—my soul is filled with amazement, indignation and horror, utterly uncontrollable. When I go by a church, I cannot help thinking whether its walls do not sometimes echo, "Strangle and kill in the name of God!" The grasp of a minister's hand, produces a kind of choking sensation; and by some optical fascination, the pulpit is often intercepted from my view by a ghastly gallows frame. "O, Liberty!" said Madame Roland, "what crimes have been committed in thy name!" "O, Bible!" say I, "what follies and monstrous barbarities are defended in *thy* name!"

9 HORACE GREELEY

Few Americans of the mid-nineteenth century were better placed to help a reform movement than Horace Greeley, indefatigable lecturer, editor of the country's most influential newspaper, and, in a sense, moral educator of the nation. Greeley (1812-1872) was born on a New Hampshire farm, the child of poor parents. When he arrived in New York City in 1831, he brought with him little formal education, but he had some newspaper experience and managed to gain employment with several renowned editors. Through his own weekly, *The New Yorker,* which he founded in 1834, Greeley established some important contacts and, by 1840, he was a man to reckon with in both journalism and Whig politics. In 1841, Greeley launched the *New York Tribune* which, in a few years, gained the reputation of the finest paper in the city. By the 1850s, its many editions and the United States mails gave it a national influence superior to any other newspaper's in the country.

An avid and seemingly universal reformer, Greeley devoted much of his life to a host of causes, among them temperance, Fourierism, penal reform, women's rights, and, above all, antislavery. An ardent Whig and Republican, he campaigned for his party at every election, but suffered repeated setbacks as a candidate. Greeley sought office in five elections during the 1860s, though he was unsuccessful each time partly because of his erratic or unpopular views about Lincoln, the Civil War, and Reconstruction. His political quest and his life ended tragically in 1872, when he was badly beaten as the Liberal Republican-Democratic candidate for the presidency—he died insane less than a month later.

Greeley showed some interest in capital punishment in the late 1830s, but did not become a strong advocate of abolition until after the appearance of O'Sullivan's report of 1841. In the following decade, he supported the reform in countless articles and lectures and was generous with his time, his presses, and his money. In 1844, he and O'Sullivan helped found the New York State Society for the Abolition of Capital Punishment. None of the illustrious and influential members of that society worked any harder than Greeley to achieve its goal. Greeley's other humanitarian interests sometimes diverted his attention from the movement to abolish the death penalty, especially after 1850, but he remained dedicated to the reform throughout his life.

Tens of thousands of rural Americans first heard of the evils of capital punishment while attending Horace Greeley's lyceum lectures. The following selection incorporated the contents of these speeches but was "recast" by its author for inclusion among some essays published in 1850. Its most notable features are Greeley's use of the frontier experience to make his case and the prevailing secular, utilitarian tone of the arguments.

Death by Human Law (1850)

Death is the universal doom. The time, the mode of individual decease are to human vision inscrutable; the event is inevitable. We do not know whether it is better for us to die early or later—by sudden violence or slow decay. Many who die at twenty are doubtless more fortunate in life and death than others who lived to eighty. Many who perished by flood or fire, by famine or frost, by rack or poison, by ax or halter, are more to be envied than the mass of those who lounged through a long life of pomp and ease, and breathed their last on beds of down amid the tears of idolizing thousands. Who can say that a man

From Horace Greeley, *Hints Toward Reforms,* 2d ed. (New York: Fowler and Wells, 1853), pp. 301-310; first published in 1850.

should be pitied or congratulated that he is doomed to die
to-morrow?

Society must live though individuals should die. All specula-
tion on the *right* of the community to take human life is preposterous. Self-preservation is the primal law; and if the death
of any individual is necessary to the safety of the commonwealth, he must die. I doubt whether there is one theoretical
denier of the right of society to take life who—if he saw a man
forcing his way into the window of his family's sleeping apart-
ment, and knew that the ruffian would, in order to rob secure-
ly, murder the mother and babes there lying in unconscious
slumber—would hesitate to catch up a rifle and shoot the burglar dead on the spot. This would imply no malice toward the
victim of his own evil designs—no desire to harm him—no wrath,
even—but a simple choice that of two evils the greater should be
averted by interposing the lesser.

Thus we hear that in the California of 1849 men were frequently hung by a summary process for simple theft—I do not
say wantonly, nor cruelly. There were no courts, no sheriffs, no
prosecutors, grand juries, police, nor prisons. The legal forms of
indictment, arraignment, trial, sentence, and punishment, were
clearly unattainable. Yet theft must somehow be repressed,
though at the cost of guilty or even innocent lives. To allow it
impunity and triumph would be to arrest the arm of Labor,
palsy Production, Transportation, Commerce, and doom the entire community to ruin and starvation. Yes, though it were
certain that a dozen innocent men would be put to death under
the Lynch-law which precedes and partially subserves the end of
the regular Administration of Justice, we must still say, Welcome this dire alternative—welcome anything rather than Anarchy, chaos, and the unchecked domination of devils!

In such a state of things, it is idle to talk of the duty of
Society toward its erring, sinful members—for Society's first
duty is to exist. That it can not do if the lazy villain may break
at pleasure into the frail shanty of the delving miner and carry
off the fruits of his patient, exhausting toil. The moment it is
established that this is a safe operation, the vicious and unprin-
cipled will hasten to ravage and rob, while the honest and indus-

trious must inevitably cease to dig. They will hasten to collect their valuables in some strong position, to strengthen it with fortifications and defend it by arms. They can do nothing as yet with the rascal but to make him keep his distance, or, if he *will* persist in robbing, to deprive him of the ability in the only way yet practicable, by depriving him of life.

The condition of the Children of Israel at the time the Law was given through Moses was not unlike that of California in 1849. Fugitives and wanderers in a rugged wilderness, surrounded by hostile tribes, and soon to engage in a protracted, exterminating warfare for the land destined to be their home for many centuries—a land certain to be frequently overrun by invading hosts and to be harassed by robber hordes from the adjacent desert—it would have been idle for a people so situated to talk of perpetual imprisonment or anything of the kind. They could treat offenders no otherwise than with severity. Punishment must be prompt or it could not be inflicted, for no prisons existed, nor could any be constructed which could be reasonably expected to hold prisoners through a lifetime. A wise Lawgiver could not overlook these facts. He could give no other laws than such as his people's condition and circumstances required, leaving to later times and a Diviner guide the announcement of the Law of the Universe—of Eternity.

—The infliction of Death on flagrant offenders is not, under such circumstances, necessarily nor naturally an act of vengeance any more than the farmer's destruction of the weeds, briars, and thistles which infest his fields and meadows is. Man must live—Society must exist—the Right must maintain its ascendency—Cultivation and Food-producing must have scope, though robbers should die, the wrong should suffer, and weeds be exterminated in consequence. Whatever degree of severity and amount of destruction may at any time be necessary to maintain this rightful supremacy of good over evil stands justified by the constitution of the universe. It is not cruel but merciful; not wrathful and vindictive but benignant and humane. —

The moral guilt or innocence of the causer of evil is not material to the issue. Suppose an insane man were now wandering and skulking among the mountains and ravines of interior California, so possessed by the spirit of destruction, of slaughter, that he missed no opportunity to kill a human being whom he could surprise when defenseless and alone. He could not be taken, and, if taken, could not be kept secure. He has killed several already, and every week adds to the number of his victims. Now the miners would say, 'True, we know this man is insane and morally irresponsible—that there is no essential guilt in his homicidal frenzy; but we know also that many of us must die by his hands if he does not by ours. We know that life is unsafe and rendered hideous by terror, so long as we remain exposed to his destroying fury. Therefore, the first man among us who gets within rifle-range of him will shoot him down as if he were a wolf'—which he would do, and be perfectly justified in doing—not in revenge for past but in deprecation of future killing.

So with regard to War. If a farmer were to shoot a boy whom he caught robbing his orchard or fleeing from such robbery, the whole country would cry Shame, and the law would not hold the slayer guiltless. But if that youth were an avowed burglar, robbing the farmer's dwelling at midnight and threatening death to all who resisted, shooting him would be deemed justified, not by the robber's guilt but the farmer's peril. The principle is the same with regard to nations as individuals. A nation which should declare war and proceed to invade another's territory, burn its towns and slaughter its resisting people, because of past depredations on the property or outrages on the persons of some of the citizens of the former within the territory of the latter, would surely be guilty of a wanton and inexcusable resort to bloodshed. True, if these depredations and outrages were defiantly proclaimed and gloried in by the offending nation, they might afford some pretext for hostilities—or rather, the *spirit* evinced in their perpetration might be esteemed dangerous to the National and individual security, and so demanding resistance with a view to repression. To embark in wholesale slaughter simply because those outrages had been committed would be wanton and inexcusable crime.

But a nation is invaded and its very existence threatened by some powerful neighbor—as that of Greece was by Xerxes, that of France by the Saracens, that of Russia by Napoleon. It is the plain duty of its people to resist with all their might, and roll back the tide of invasion across their frontiers. It is better for Humanity that thousands should die than that millions should be made slaves, and their children after them. But there is necessarily and properly no vengeful feeling on their part—no wish to harm an individual of the invading host—nothing but submission to the stern, sad necessity of sacrificing the invaders or themselves to the preservation of the most sacred Rights of Man. Since the path to security and perpetuated Freedom lies through the center of that invading, advancing host, the patriot pursues and clears that path, though in so doing he should cleave an invader's heart on the point of his bayonet. Yet he may very probably regard the individuals composing the invading army with pity rather than wrath—may consider that they are, nevertheless, men and brethren, whom deceit and constraint and a perverted love of country have thus armed and impelled on their errand of devastation and enslavement. He must resist and even slay them so long as no other way lies open to him of defeating the baleful purpose whereof they are instruments; but, the moment that peril is averted, by their capture or discomfiture, that moment his acquiescence in this sad necessity of doing them physical harm is at end. To kill one of them now would be a crime—a wanton and guilty effusion of human blood. He is henceforth their friend, their host, their good Samaritan, and in due time dismisses them on their homeward road, heartily wishing them a pleasant journey thither and a long and happy sojourn in the land of their fathers.

—And now to killing malefactors by sentence of law. Is it ever justifiable? I answer Yes, *provided* Society can in no other way be secured against a repetition of the culprit's offence. In committing a murder, for instance, he has proved himself capable of committing more murders—perhaps many. The possibility of a thousand murders is developed in his one act of felonious homicide. Call his moral state depravity, insanity, or whatever you please, he is manifestly a ferocious, dangerous animal, who can not safely be permitted to go at large. Society must be secured against the reasonable probability of his killing others, and, where that can only be effected by taking his life, his life must be taken.

—But suppose him to be in New-England, New-York or Pennsylvania—arrested, secured and convicted—Society's rebel, outcast and prisoner of war—taken with arms in his hands. Here are prison-cells wherefrom escape is impossible; and if there be any fear of his assaulting his keeper or others, that may be most effectively prevented. Is it expedient or salutary to crush the life out of this helpless, abject, pitiable wretch?

I for one think it decidedly *is not*—that it is a sorrowful mistake and barbarity to do any such thing. In saying this, I do not assume to decide whether Hanging or Imprisonment for Life is the severer penalty. I should wish to understand clearly the moral state of the prisoner before I attempted to guess; and, even then, I know too little of the scenes of untried being which lie next beyond the confines of this mortal existence to say whether it were better for any penitent or hardened culprit to be hung next month or left in prison to die a natural death. What is best for that culprit I leave to God, who knows when is the fit time for him to die. My concern is with Society—the moral it teaches, the conduct it tacitly enjoins. And I feel that the choking to death of this culprit works harm, in these respects, namely:

1. *It teaches and sanctions Revenge.* There is a natural inclination in man to return injury for injury, evil for evil. It is the exciting cause of many murders as well as less flagrant crimes. It stands in no need of stimulation—its prompt repression at all times is one of the chief trials even of good men. But A.B. has committed a murder, is convicted of and finally hung for it. Bill, Dick and Jim, three apprentices of ordinary understanding and attainments, beg away or run away to witness the hanging. Ask either of them, 'What is this man hung for?' and the prompt, correct answer will be, 'Because he killed C.D.'—not 'To prevent his killing others,' nor yet 'To prevent others from killing.' Well: the three enjoy the spectacle and turn away satisfied. On their way home, a scuffle is commenced in fun, but gradually changes to a fight, wherein one finds himself down with two holding

and beating him. Though sorely exasperated and severly suffering, he can not throw them off, but he can reach with one hand
the knife in his vest pocket. Do you fancy he will be more or
less likely to use it because of that moral spectacle which Society has just proffered for his delectation and improvement?
You may say Less, if you can, but I say More! many times
more! You may preach to him that Revenge is right for Society
but wrong for him till your head is gray, and he perhaps may
listen to you—but not till after he has opened his knife and
made a lunge with it.

2. *It tends to weaken and destroy the natural horror of
bloodshed.* Man has a natural horror of taking the life of his
fellow man. His instincts revolt at it—his conscience condemns
it—his frame shudders at the thought of it. But let him see first
one and then another strung up between heaven and earth and
choked to death, with due formalities of Law and solemnities of
Religion—the slayer not accounted an evil-doer but an executor
of the State's just decree, a pillar of the Social edifice—and his
horror of bloodshed *per se* sensibly and rapidly oozes away, and
he comes to look at killing men as quite the thing provided
there be adequate reason for it. But what reason? and whose?
The law slays the slayer; but in his sight the corrupter or calum-
niator of his wife or sister, the traducer of his character, the
fraudulent bankrupt who has involved and ruined his friend, is
every whit as great a villain as the man-slayer, and deserving of
as severe a punishment. Yet the Law makes no provision for
such punishment—hardly for any punishment at all—and what
shall he do? He can not consent that the guilty go 'unwhipt of
justice,' so he takes his rifle and deals out full measure of it. He
is but doing as Society has taught him by example. War, duel-
ing, bloody affrays, &c., find their nourishment and support in
the Gallows.

3. *It facilitates and often insures the escape of the guilty
from any punishment by human law.*—Jurors (whether for or
against Capital Punishment) dread to convict where the crime is
Death. Human judgment is fallible; human testimony may mis-
lead. Witnesses often lie—sometimes conspire to lie plausibly
and effectively. Circumstances often strongly point to a conclu-

sion which is after all a false one. The real murderers sometimes conspire to fasten suspicion on some innocent person, and so arrange the circumstances that he can hardly escape their toils. Sometimes they appear in court as witnesses against him, and swear the crime directly upon him. . . . And for every such case there have doubtless been many wherein juries, unwilling to take life where there was a *possibility* of innocence, have given the prisoner the benefit of a very faint doubt and acquitted him. Had the penalty been Imprisonment, they would have convicted, notwithstanding the bare possibility of his innocence, since any future developments in his favor, through the retraction of witnesses, the clearing up of circumstances, or the confession of the actual culprit, would at once lead to his liberation and to an earnest effort by the community to repay him for his unmerited ignominy and suffering. But choke the prisoner to death, and any development in his favor is thenceforth too late. Next year may prove him innocent beyond cavil or doubt; but of what avail is that to the victim over whose grave the young grass is growing? And thus, through the inexorable character of the Death-Penalty, hundreds of the innocent suffer an undeserved and ignominious death, while tens of thousands of the guilty escape any punishment by human law.

4. *It excites a pernicious sympathy for the convict.*—We ought ever to be merciful toward the sinful and guilty, remembering our own misdeeds and imperfections. We ought to regard with a benignant compassion those whom Crime has doomed to suffer. But the criminal is not a hero, nor a martyr, and should not be made to resemble one. A crowd of ten to fifty thousand persons, witnessing the infliction of the law's just penalty on an offender, and half of them sobbing and crying from sympathy for his fate, is not a wholesome spectacle—far otherwise. The impression it makes is not that of the majesty and Divine benignity of Law—the sovereignty and beneficence of Justice. Thousands are hoping, praying, entreating that a pardon may yet come—some will accuse the Executive of cruelty and hardness of heart in withholding it. While this furnace of sighs is at red heat, this tempest of sobs in full career, the culprit is swung off—a few faint; many shudder; more feel an acute shock of

pain; while the great mass adjourn to take a general drink, some of them swearing that *this* hanging was a great shame—that the man did not really deserve it. Do you fancy the greater number have imbibed and will profit by the intended lesson?

—But I do not care to pile argument on argument, consideration on consideration, in opposition to the expediency, in this day and section, of putting men to death in cold blood by human law. It seems to me a most pernicious and brutalizing practice. Indeed, the recent enactments of our own, with most if not all of the Free States, whereby Executions are henceforth to take place in private, or in the presence of a few select witnesses only, seem clearly to admit the fact. They certainly imply that Executions are of no use as examples—that they rather tend to make criminals than to reform those already depraved. When I see any business or vocation sneaking and skulking in dark lanes and little by-streets which elude observation, I conclude that those who follow such business feel at least doubtful of its utility and beneficence. They may *argue* that it is 'a necessary evil,' but they can hardly put faith in their own logic. When I see the bright array of many-colored liquor-bottles, which formerly filled flauntingly the post of honor in every tip-top hotel, now hustled away into some side-room, and finally down into a dark basement, out of the sight and knowledge of all but those who especially seek them, I say exultingly, 'Good for so much! one more hoist, and they will be—where they should be—out of sight and reach altogether:'—so, when I see the Gallows, once the denizen of some swelling eminence, the cynosure of ten thousand eyes, 'the observed of all observers,' skulking and hiding itself from public view in jail-yards, shutting itself up in prisons, I say, 'You have taken the right road! Go ahead! One more drive, and your detested, rickety frame is out of the sight of civilized man for ever!'

10 ELIZABETH CADY STANTON

Women's rights advocates have sometimes expressed the belief that capital punishment, like war, is a man's institution, wholly antithetical to woman's temperament. One proponent of this view was Elizabeth Cady Stanton (1815-1902), one of the most prominent leaders of the women's movement in nineteenth-century America. Stanton was born in Johnstown, New York, where she lived until her departure, at age fifteen, for Emma Willard's Troy Female Seminary.

Though Stanton was interested in reform in young adulthood, she did not begin to work actively in any movements until after her marriage in 1840. Then she began to devote time, first to temperance and the abolition of slavery, later to women's rights, often in conjunction with Lucretia Mott and Susan B. Anthony. Stanton's greatest activity came during her tenure as president of the National Woman Suffrage Association, 1869 to 1890. She was an effective and popular speaker and reached millions of Americans with her lyceum lectures and articles.

The letter reprinted in this volume contains what seems to be Stanton's only recorded remarks on capital punishment, although, as the letter itself makes clear, she bitterly opposed the institution from childhood. The letter was addressed to reformer Marvin H. Bovee, who had asked a number of famous Americans to record their opposition to the death penalty. Although it was hardly an "argument" against capital punishment, it provided a moving account of how the institution affected a sensitive young woman in antebellum America.

There Will Be No Gallows When
Mothers Make the Laws (1868)

New York, August 1st, 1868

Marvin H. Bovee—Dear Sir:—You ask me if I believe in capital punishment. Indeed I do not. When men are dangerous to the public, they should be imprisoned; that done, the remaining consideration is the highest good of the prisoner. Crime is a disease; hence our prisons should be moral seminaries, where all that is true and noble in man should be nurtured into life. Our jails, our prisons, our whole idea of punishment is wrong, and will be until the mother soul is represented in our criminal legislation. It makes me shudder to think of the cruelties that are inflicted on criminals in the name of justice, and of the awful waste of life and force—of the crushing out of hundreds and thousands of noble men and promising boys in these abominable bastiles of the nineteenth century.

As to the gallows, it is the torture of my life. Every sentence and every execution I hear of, is a break in the current of my life and thought for days. I make my son the victim. I am with him in the solitude of that last awful night, broken only by the sound of the hammer and the coarse jeers of men, in preparation for the dismal pageant of the coming day. I see the cold sweat of death upon his brow, and weigh the mountain of sorrow that rests upon his soul, with its sad memories of the past and the fearful forbodings of the world to come. I imagine the mortal agony, the death-struggle, and I know ten thousand mothers all over the land weep, and pray, and groan with me over every soul thus lost. Woman knows the cost of life better than man does. There will be no gallows, no dungeons, no needless cruelty in solitude, when mothers make the laws. God bless you in your noble work.

I have felt so much on this subject that I have often said to my husband, if there is such a thing as the transmigration of

From Marvin Bovee, *Christ and the Gallows* (New York: Masonic Publishing Co., 1869), pp. 173-175.

souls, mine has been in some tortured prisoner, for, ever since I began to think, I have felt the most intense sympathy for the inmates of our jails and prisons. When I was a little girl, twelve years old, there was a public hanging in the town where I lived.¦ From the day the man was placed in our county jail he occupied all my thoughts. I went to see him every day, taking him flowers and fruit, cakes and candy; and knowing the jailor's wife she would often let me in the cell to talk and read to him. He was as gentle and tractable as a child; and, as the awful day approached, I felt that I could not let him die; and as every body outside called him a horrible wretch, I saw that he could only be saved by some special interposition, and, fearing he was too wicked for Heaven to make any, I decided to do it myself. I watched the building of the gallows on a distant hill, and decided at the last to cut the rope, so that when he fell it would break. So on the morning of the day I hastened early to the spot. There was no rope there, and nothing that I could do. Oh! how I wept, and prayed, and wondered what I could do on that cold December morning. At length I heard the distant music,¦ saw the military surround the gallows, saw the poor man ascend it, heard the prayer, saw the death-struggle, and in anguish hurried home, and there I lay for many weeks in a terrible fever; and every execution I now read of in our public journals, brings back that terrible memory.

Whenever you visit our legislature, having in view the modification of our penal code, I will gladly do all in my power to help you banish that relic of barbarism from our land.

Sincerely yours,
Elizabeth Cady Stanton

11 MARVIN H. BOVEE

Marvin H. Bovee (1827-1888), reformer and legislator, was born in New York State, but moved with his family to Eagle, Wisconsin, in 1843. Eager to follow in the footsteps of his father, a former Democratic congressman, Bovee sought and won a seat in the state Senate in 1852. There he championed education reform and amelioration of criminal penalties. He introduced and fought for the bill which, with the concurrence of the House, abolished capital punishment in Wisconsin in 1853.

Encouraged by this success, Bovee dedicated himself to ending the death penalty throughout the country, and he devoted much of his next thirty years to that goal. Bovee had not picked an auspicious time in which to carry out such a plan, however. The anti-gallows movement, at its peak in the 1840s, had faded as the country became increasingly caught up in questions about slavery. In the mid-1850s, Bovee found neither the interest nor the organizations which might have greeted his efforts ten years earlier. During and after the Civil War, the atmosphere was still worse. Thus, Bovee's achievements, after the Wisconsin triumph, were limited to laws restricting, rather than abolishing, capital punishment in the states he canvassed.

Bovee's only book on the subject, *Christ and the Gallows,* was a diverse and sometimes haphazard collection of arguments from other reformers and letters from friends of the cause. Bovee's own thoughts and his writing ability were most evident, perhaps, in his plea to Illinois Governor Richard Oglesby for clemency on behalf of two condemned murderers. It was a well-planned, even shrewd petition, especially in its use of arguments relating to the Civil War, which had just ended.

Bovee's appeal met with temporary success. In the absence of Governor Oglesby, the state's lieutenant governor granted the two felons a month's reprieve. However, the governor, upon his return to the state, took no further action, and the two men were hanged July 20, 1866.

Not Punishments but Cruelties (1869)

To His Excellency, Governor Richard J. Oglesby,
Executive Chamber, Springfield, Ill.

Dear Sir:—Through the public journals of the metropolitan city of your State, I learn that, at a recent term of the Sangamon County Circuit Court, Judge Rice presiding, one Barney Vanansdell' and one James Lemon were duly convicted for the crime of murder, one John Saunders being the unfortunate victim of the fatal attack, which occurred on the 7th day of March, 1865, in the said county of Sangamon.

I have no official information of the judicial proceedings of this trial, nor is it important to the object I have in view in addressing you, only so far as it is ever desirable to state facts in a published communication. If, then, the public journals have correctly reported the proceeding of the trial referred to, we are given to understand that the *men* who have been sentenced to die on the gibbet on the 22nd of the present month, are quite young, neither having attained the age of *twenty* years.

I have never, on any occasion, nor under any circumstances, appended my name to a petition asking the Executive of any State to pardon, or commute the sentence, of any individual convicted for crime. I have assumed this attitude, not, I trust, from any lack of benevolence in my composition, but simply from the stern conviction that, in order to effectually secure the

From Marvin Bovee, *Christ and the Gallows* (New York: Masonic Publishing Co., 1869), pp. 271-279.

speedy amelioration of our penal code, odious laws, equally with good ones, should be rigidly enforced. The thorough enforcement of all laws is the best test of their efficacy and virtue, and when severe and cruel laws are thus enforced, they speedily become so abhorrent to the public mind, that other statutes, more benign in their operation, are thereupon substituted. An unjust law, if not enforced, in consequence of a laxity of purpose on the part of its administrators, induced, perhaps, by a dislike of its provisions, is often retained for many years, whereas its thorough enforcement would become so repugnant to the public sense, that its repeal would be thereby insured. In this aspect of the case, and believing that by submitting to temporary evils that final and lasting good may come, I have hitherto declined making efforts in special instances for either pardons or commutation of sentence, believing that every extension of mercy, in either capital or other crimes, only retards progress in the cause of penal reform by the retention of cruel laws which, if uniformly and rigidly enforced, would be more speedily abolished from the very repugnance which their execution incites.

It is, my dear sir, the youthfulness of these condemned criminals that has arrested my attention, and so far enlisted my sympathies as to lead me thus publicly to address you, trusting that, in the clear light of Executive duty, you may be enabled to commute the sentences of these young men from death on the gibbet to imprisonment for life. Were there no other motives to prompt my action than simply asking, in behalf of these young men, a continuation of that lease of life which God has given them, and to which they are entitled by virtue of their creation, I should have remained silent; but there are higher and more sacred considerations involved in this question. You, sir, have the honor of filling the Executive chair of a great and prosperous State—a commonwealth of nearly if not quite two millions of people, a very large proportion of whom are highly intelligent, moral, and upright. This large class of your citizens can not be unmindful of the fact that capital punishment has not accomplished the object for which it was primarily instituted—that in endeavoring to preserve human life, it has only engendered and begot the very crimes it has sought to prevent;

that instead of becoming the represser of crime, it has become the great progenitor of evil.

The unconditional abrogation of the death penalty has taken place in several of the States of this Union, and with the most gratifying and happy results. Indeed, so highly satisfactory has the experiment proven to the people residing therein, that there is scarcely a possibility that capital punishment will ever again be revived where the modified law has been so thoroughly tested. Michigan abolished the death penalty in 1846, and for *twenty* years has successfully demonstrated that the lives and property of her citizens are just as secure *without* as *with* the gibbet. Rhode Island abolished the death penalty in 1852, and for *fourteen* years has been ridden of the law of demoralization and death, and has never shown any evidence of retrogression from the position she so nobly assumed. Wisconsin abolished the death penalty in 1853, and for *thirteen* years has discarded the idea that life can be rendered safe only through the *judicial* murder of the criminal. In all of the States named, repeated and persistent efforts have been made to revive the law of "blood for blood," but each and every effort has been attended with signal and complete failure. Frequent reports from the State Prison Commissioners and Inspectors of the several States referred to, which are in my possession, bear concurrent testimony to the beneficial workings of the law which punishes the crime of murder by imprisonment rather than death; and I would here say that the State of Illinois, with but about twice the population of Wisconsin, has a far *greater number* of murders committed within her borders, *according to her population,* than the State of Wisconsin referred to. This statement is made, not with a view to disparage or underrate the virtue or morality of our sister State, in whose prosperity and advancement I feel a just pride, but simply to illustrate the important fact, that cruel and barbarous punishments, when inflicted by a State, are not the best modes of encouraging or perpetuating virtue among the people. If the taking of life by individual man be called a *crime,* how can a *similar* act by process of law be termed a virtue? If a State can punish crime in no other way than by imitating the crime committed, then, indeed, its penal code has no other foundation except in vengeful retaliation.

It is said that the punishment of crime is *three*fold in its nature, contemplating in its application *three* specific objects, first of which is the *reformation* of the criminal; secondly, the *protection* of society; and thirdly, the *restraint* imposed upon the criminally inclined. If these be the objects of punishment, then, indeed, has the death penalty fallen far short of accomplishing either one of the objects named; for capital punishment *destroys* without *reforming* the criminal, while all history proves that in securing protection to society, or in deterring the commission of crime, its failure has been most marked and conspicuous. Accomplishing but little good and vast injury, it is, indeed, strange that so abhorrent a punishment should still be retained upon the statute books of many States professing high Christian civilization. My theory of punishment would be summed up in these few words: *Penalties that do not contemplate the reformation of the criminal are not punishments, but cruelties.*

It is but a few years since public executions were authorized by the laws of Illinois. These exhibitions of *legal* murder, once witnessed by thousands, are now somewhat exclusive and private in their nature. But few are now admitted to witness the ingenious process by which a human soul is launched from time into eternity. Why the abolishment of these public spectacles? The answer is plain: the State of Illinois lost confidence in the moral efficacy of public executions, and by its abolition *tacitly* admitted its failure to minister to the moral welfare of her people. And yet, sir, if the death penalty, as some allege, possess a restraining influence upon the vicious, why not erect the gibbet in your public marts, and beside your churches, that the rising generation may profit by the moral lessons which the friends of the gallows claim that it inculcates? But, sir, we are all too well aware of the debasing influence and demoralizing effects of public executions, and what is true of these public exhibitions is also true of private executions, only in a lesser degree.

If the penalty of death shall be inflicted upon Vanansdell and Lemon, what will have been gained for morality or justice? The execution of these young men simply destroys their *visibility* to the *physical eye,* but it harms not the spirit which controls and makes use of those physical organizations; neither does their execution blot out their crime, nor the remembrance of it; nor does it restore the unfortunate John Saunders to life, family, or friends. Does, then, the execution of these young men accomplish nothing? On the contrary, a vast deal. Accomplishes *much* evil, but *no* good. The gallows is the brutal assailant of public virtue and private feeling. It disturbs the moral element of society, by its assault upon the feelings of the virtuous, the sympathetic, the noble, and good, while it whets the appetite and arouses the bloody instincts of the groveling and the debased. The gallows essays to perpetuate virtue, and strikes it down in the self same instant. It mocks at Christianity, by destroying the physical organization of the criminal, while urging its *religious agents* to labor for the salvation of the immortal spirit which it has just *forced* from its *earthly tenement.* Hideous spectre of the past! Born in barbarity, cradled in hate, and nursed with blood, it has grown a giant fiend, whose power, once great, now nearly gone, is soon to be dispelled by the light of a higher and more ennobling civilization.

There is one point, my dear sir, to which I would call your especial attention. We have but recently passed through a war of most gigantic magnitude. It has been prosecuted with all the power and vigor which our vast resources of men and money could bring to its support. The loss of life has been fearful to contemplate, while the expenditure of money and waste of property are almost without a parallel. The compensation for these evils rests solely in the triumphant success of that cause for which the God of battles was invoked. War is ever accompanied by innumerable evils. However glorious and patriotic the cause for which war may be prosecuted, the demoralizing effect upon the public mind is ever apparent. Ours has been no exception. Since the breaking out of hostilities, the general respect for human life has been very much lessened, while the debasing effect upon the minds of very many who were immediately engaged, is noticeable by all. The killing of thousands is not well calculated to inspire feelings of reverence for human life, but, on the contrary, often stimulates the worst passions of man.

I know not, nor is it important to know, whether Vanansdell or Lemon, or both, took part in the strife of battle for the maintenance of the Union. Whether they did or did not, it is nevertheless certain that they have been cognizant of the general affairs of our government for the past four years. They may, notwithstanding, be very ignorant young men, and not sufficiently skilled in that branch of governmental science by which an individual is enabled to draw that *very nice distinction* between the *laudable virtue of killing* by national authority, and the *reprehensible criminality of killing* upon individual responsibility. This distinction is accurately made by men of legal acumen, who are well versed in the abstruse science of political ethics, and is generally made clear to those statesmen and diplomatists who are connected with the Government. Vanansdell and Lemon may not have made the distinction. The enormity of their crime may not have been so fully apparent to them before as after the commission of the act, and it is to be hoped that they now see and feel the wrong they have done, not only to community, but to themselves, and that in the prolongation of their existence, which boon to bestow, rests in the hands of your Excellency, they may become wiser and better men.

I have not lost sight of the important fact that your Excellency represents the executive, and not the law-making branch of your State Government; and that while the law of Illinois imposes the penalty of death for the crime of murder, and courts have no alternative but to pronounce sentence when conviction has taken place, I am also conscious that the organic law of your State, the Constitution of Illinois, places within your official keeping, the high and sacred prerogative of life and death in certain cases; and that the proper exercise of the function of mercy is as clearly and indisputably your right, as it is the right and duty of juries to convict, and of courts to sentence. It only remains for you to determine whether the ends of justice will be best subserved by granting a commutation of sentence in the cases of Vanansdell and Lemon. Death is the common lot of all. If you see fit to modify the sentence of the court, no injurious consequences can possibly ensue. You have the power to rob the gallows of its victims, but the grave will eventually claim its own. It is the great leveler of human distinctions and earthly greatness. The kingly robe and beggar's rags find one common level. The pomp and splendor of earth must all pass away, but *good deeds* will live in the *eternal world.*

It is said, "in the beginning God created the heavens and the earth;" and when the Omnipotent hand had prepared the earth for the habitation of the human family, he said, "let us make man;" whereupon Justice, with stern and relentless visage, said, "make him not, O God, for he will disobey thy commandments, and violate thy holy laws; make him not, O God!" But Mercy, with countenance benign, beaming with the radiance of purity and love, in tones of supplication, plead for his creation. "Make him, God, for though he violate thy commands, and transgress thy holy laws, I will be with him in his days of trial and will plead for his forgiveness; I will be with him in his darkest hour and greatest need. Create him, O God!" And God listened to the voice of Mercy, and created man, not only a just, but a merciful being.

If, in the careful consideration of the claims of Barney Vanansdell and James Lemon to a continuation of that life which was given them by their Creator, you shall become satisfied that nothing will be lost to justice, while much may be given to mercy, by a commutation of the sentence of the court in which they were found guilty, rest assured that your official action will be approved by the great majority of the people of your State, and will be especially commended by the virtuous and good.

I am, dear sir, very respectfully,
Your obedient servant,
MARVIN H. BOVEE.

EAGLE, Wis., *June* 14, 1866.

12 EDMUND CLARENCE STEDMAN

Edmund Clarence Stedman (1833-1908), poet, critic, and editor, was born and raised in Connecticut. Stedman bought and edited several small newspapers in that state before selling them and moving to New York City in 1855. There his topical poems began to win him a modest reputation and some influential friends. He solved the problem of financial security in 1864 by opening a brokerage office which provided him an income sufficient to maintain his family. A businessman by day and a poet and critic by night, Stedman enjoyed great popularity in literary circles of New York for the rest of his life.

Stedman was not much interested in reform and does not appear to have written any anti-gallows articles apart from the one reprinted here. He obviously had been studying the subject in the 1860s, however, and may have been stirred to attack capital punishment by his horror at the string of bungled executions he catalogued in this article.

This sometimes grisly article is a fine example of an argument against capital punishment which was in vogue from the middle of the nineteenth to the middle of the twentieth century. By attacking the technology of executions, sometimes a single disgraceful performance, reformers pushed some states toward abolition. More often, of course, they merely prodded searches for supposedly more humane means of executing criminals.

The Gallows in America (1869)

We are close upon the abolition of Capital Punishment throughout the Northern States. Few are now so tenacious as to esteem it a good thing in itself. Most believe that it will some time cease,—though whether by such social changes that violent crimes will not be committed, or by the discovery of wiser modes of punishment, they are variously minded. Is it not at present a necessary evil? I confess to little patience with this phrase. Evils may be unavoidable, but that they should be deliberately assumed as necessities is a melancholy fatalism. When nations or individuals are assailed, counter-violence is forced upon them; but 'tis needless to measure crime for crime that future ills may be prevented. The time for the cessation of War has not yet come, though philosophers see it approaching, both in the unbearable increase of modern armaments, and in the resort to conventions for the settlement of national disputes. But there is no surer way to prevent nations from engaging in War than further to civilize and refine the organization of Peace; to unfamiliarize people with the idea of shedding blood; to impress them with the sacredness of Human Life. Surely governments have reached that plane of experience which should find them other remedies for the disease of crime,—light or severe to suit the gravity of the case,—than that sharp medicine which Raleigh said would cure the worst disorder.[1]

* * *

It is not difficult to forecast the judgment of the future upon this question. We read of the New England Tragedies, and thank Heaven we are beyond all that![2] Our eyes have at last been opened to the curse and crime of Slavery, and by a terrible effort its presence has been swept away. Long before another century shall have rolled its round, a wiser generation will regard our criminal executions as the darkest remnant, save one, of mediaeval barbarism suffered at this date to linger.

From Edmund Clarence Stedman, "The Gallows in America," *Putnam's Magazine,* 13 (February 1869), pp. 225-235.

The grim old fable of the ship-wrecked sailor who, on falling in with a gallows, thanked God he was in a Christian country, ought of itself to have shamed all Christendom into the extirpation of such accursed trees. The difficulty is that society is partly based upon an organization of errors, which, as it grows in perception, it tries to palliate with surface-reform. I need not go over the application of this method to the Death-Penalty, nor again detail the hundred offences for which the latter was inflicted under the Draconian Code of our great-grandfathers; nor exhibit the progress made from the wheel and stake of the sixteenth century to the more merciful gallows and guillotine of our own. For Capital Punishment still rests upon the old idea of terrifying men from the commission of crime. The Marquis of Beccaria[3] knew better than that, five generations ago. If you wish to terrify offenders, make death as merciless as you can: seek out torture-causing rather than torture-saving inventions. But in every period, the more barbarous the punishments the more violent the crimes. Jurists agree that the object of punishment is, solely, the prevention of offences. The fallacy of cruel punishment has insensibly discovered itself to the minds of people, until our measure of each nation's civilization is almost correlative with its reformatory treatment of its convicts. It only remains to get fairly out of mind the idea of frightening men from crime. . . .

Our foremost plea is the baneful and demoralizing effect upon society of the means resorted to for its protection. We would put an end to Capital Punishment, for the sake of the law-abiding classes; just as the abolition of Slavery was wisely urged *for the benefit of the white man.* Death may be a murderer's desert, but for the sake of the community let us reconsider this usage of inflicting it. Whether "the worst use you can put a man to" is, or is not, "to hang him," the worst use to which Society can put itself is the office of the executioner.[4]

* * *

To be very practical, let us here pause from discussing the wisdom of the Death-Penalty, and look at our cruel and abominable method of inflicting it. They, who still cling to the tradi-

tional right of man-killing, will scarcely be enthusiastic over the
barbarous process which we have imported from our English
fatherland, along with the prize-ring and dog-pit. Oh, the gallows! the gallows! What has made the simple upright, and cross-
beam with its dangling noose, more dreadful than the elaborate
guillotine,—the scaffold with block and axe,—than even the fa-
gots and the stake? Dread symbol of death in its foulest, most
uncomely and pestilential form! But this ancient gallows,
—descended from the gibbet black against the moor, where the
raven made riot, and whence the wind bore noisome stenches to
meadows far away—or, still more anciently, from the trees dangling with corpses around the walls of Plessis-les-Tours,[5] and the
English oaks that bore horrible fruit at the will of every petty
baron—this vile, detested gallows still keeps its numerous and
appointed places among us! Its roots have been firmly planted
in our soil, but one by one they surely will be torn away.

Morally considered, death by the gallows may not always
seem the worst of penalties. To die a dog's death is not to be a
dog. Great and good men have been hanged, and it was said of
one, that he "made the gallows glorious, like the Cross."[6] And
professional persons of that class for whom salt-water has no
terrors—and at whose presence Gonzalo in "The Tempest" was
fain to rejoice,—expect in due course the distinction which has
elevated so many Sheppards and Turpins of their ancestral calling.[7]

But death by the gallows is in many, if not most, instances, as
slow and cruel a torment as that by fire or the wheel. This is a
feature of our own mode of execution which people do not
sufficiently realize, while expending their sympathies upon the
subjects of tyranny or justice in by-gone times. . . . We recognize the fact that bodily pain is one of the greatest human evils,
in our paeans over the discovery of anaesthetics; yet we content
ourselves, in the fastidious cities, with hiding the gallows out of
sight, though we must and do know that it is, week after week,
rehearsing its ancient cruelties behind the screen.

The writer's own sensibilities were so affected by this material view of the Death-Penalty, as first to lead him to the questions, Do we realize *how* inhuman this is? Is there an adequate
necessity for it? By the same process I would like to reach the

judgment of the reader, bringing him, through his pity and refinement, to consider whether we must continue a system
against which every natural instinct makes revolt.

During the recent war, newspaper accounts of executions
were mostly confined to brief announcements of official facts.
Previous to 1860, however, no more grave and painful matters
demanded the reporter's attention. And since 1866 we are again
supplied with old full-length descriptions of hangings,—written
in what may be termed an artistic and euphuistic style, but
trust-worthy in the main,—so that an investigator has pretty
correct details within easy reach. The loathly record is set continually before us, sought for with an appetite by the ground-
lings, and avoided with disgust or read with shrinking curiosity
by the more refined. The latter are mainly responsible for the
law, and I should like to place certain details of its operation
plainly before their faces.

* * *

We should fall into shockingly staple phrases, were we to
dwell upon the preliminary horrors of an execution. These all
have to do with the moral torture of the occasion, and the same
is more or less inseparable from the infliction of Capital Punishment in any form. As attendant upon hanging, however, it is in
its extreme degree. But our present concern is with the dreadful, the inconceivable *physical* agonies of men who are hanged
by the neck till they are dead, and the Lord has mercy upon
their souls.

The *theory* of hanging is, that the neck of the culprit should
be broken; and it is stated by competent surgical authority that,
if this be done successfully, the second cervical vertebra is dislocated, its odontoid process rupturing the transverse ligament
of the atlas (the first bone of the neck which sustains the globe
of the head), and compressing the spinal cord against the poster-
ior arch of the vetebra. The cord is here just expanding into the
medulla oblongata, wherein is situated the ganglion that pre-
sides over respiration. Its compression stops respiration at once
by stopping all desire for it; and death in such case would be
immediate and probably painless.

But in hanging, *as practised,* the second vertebra often is only partially dislocated, or not affected at all, and death takes place either from slow and painful suffocation,—the victim getting just air enough through the half-closed wind-pipe to prolong his struggles,—or from apoplexy following the sudden cerebral congestion which is caused both by the suffocation and by the pressure of the rope upon the great veins of the neck.

I do not hesitate to assert, from the facts in my possession, that in at least *sixty per cent.* of reported cases, in spite of every precaution, the neck has not been broken. The sufferers have slowly and in torment choked to death, frequently with such hard breathing, groans, and contortions, as to drive the witnesses from the dreadful scene. I will only quote from reports of one or two representative cases, but will name a few others, of which the details are too harrowing for republication here.

James Stephens, convicted, on circumstantial evidence, of wife-poisoning (and still believed by his spiritual advisers to have been innocent), was hanged in New York, Feb. 3, 1860. Most careful preparations were made by the sheriff, but the hangman blundered, and Stephens was subjected to great suffering. For many minutes his hard breathing was frightful to listen to. On the 12th of January, 1866, Marschall and Frecke were hanged at Pittsburgh, Pa. Frecke's neck was not broken, and he "died horribly of strangulation. His struggles were terrible and long-continued."

One week afterwards, Mrs. Martha Grinder, the confessed poisoness, was executed upon the same gallows for the murder of her last victim,—Mrs. Caruthers. She also suffered terrible and prolonged agonies. An unusual incident of the death-scene is reported by several witnesses: "The rope slipped her cap partially from her face, and, while hanging at the halter's end, *by a mighty effort she put up one of her hands sufficiently to draw it down again over her distorted features,* thus," says the inductive reporter, "in death asserting the native modesty of woman. She struggled fearfully, *and twelve minutes elapsed before her death.*"

The question whether sensation, reflection, and mental horror accompany the physical contortions of those perishing by strangulation, is fairly settled by such a fact as this, and by the conduct of many who have committed suicide. Examples are common of unfortunates who have fastened a noose around the neck and kicked away the support beneath their feet, but who, finding the tortures of strangulation greater than they had conceived, have repented, and made desperate efforts to regain their footing.

Alexander B. Wiley, hanged at Wilkes-barre, Pa., March 21st, 1867; Hiram Coon, hanged on the following day, at Troy, N.Y.; Jeremiah O. Brown, hanged at "The Tombs," Aug. 9th, 1867; and Sylvester Quiller, hanged at Elizabeth, N.J., on the ensuing 14th of November;—all died in great and prolonged agony of strangulation. The reports of the last case are especially poignant. Yet the State of New Jersey, so loyal in maintenance of good old customs, has achieved reputation for the consistency with which her murderers are brought to execution. One would suppose that within her borders, at least, the hangman had mastered his art.

During the year 1868, a kind of professional demoralization has affected the Jack Ketches of this country and England.[8] Whether surfeited with success, or disgusted with their calling, 'tis evident they no longer practise hanging with that enthusiasm and devotion to details required by the connoisseurs of this humanizing art. We, "the latest seed of Time," take little vantage over ruder generations in the adjustment of the noose, the scientific involution of the knot, the adequate balance of the fatal weights. The record of the past year, in fact, is not creditable to the talent of our own and neighboring States. Even in Newgate, that venerable Academy, the hand of the master seems to have lost its cunning: the great Calcraft is blundering like any callow neophyte of our backwoods school.[9]

Thomas Walsh, a boy of 19, hanged at Newark, N.J., January 2d, 1868; Rufus Ludwig, hanged at Salisbury, N.C., on the 26th of June; John Kennedy, hanged at Canton, N.Y., on the 20th of August; and Harrison Young, hanged at Warwick C.H., Va., on the 25th of August;—were all slowly tortured to death. There is no other name for it. The accounts are full and trust-worthy. Ludwig's execution was one of those old-fashioned outdoor festivals which brought together a larger crowd than ever attended a barbacue or circus in that region. He made a desperate and dramatic fight for his life, at the last moment. In Young's case the rope broke, and some time elapsed before he was strung up again and more efficiently.

* * *

On the 25th of September, 1868, Silas James and Charles T. James were executed at Worcester, Mass., for the barbarous murder of Joseph G. Clark. Silas died with little suffering, but of the agonies of Charles, the younger and least guilty of the two, an eye-witness declared:

> "Even while suspended from the terrible scaffolding, he clung to life with the utmost tenacity. He struggled, drew up his legs a dozen times or more, and his whole body shook violently, *while every now and then his groans and occasional long-drawn breaths broke the sad and painful stillness.* The scene was one which could hardly be tolerated, except on recalling the fearful crime of which the men were guilty."

They attended to such matters roughly, but more thoroughly, upon our frontier, so long as Lynch was jury, judge, and hangman.[10] Now that he has been supplanted by the commissioned officers of civilization, and his triple function subdivided, the result is not so gratifying from a scientific point of view. Rufus B. Anderson was executed in Austin, Nevada, on the 30th of last October, for the murder of one Slocum. The newspapers grimly entitle this affair "Another Civilizing Gallows Scene," and from their reports we learn that the rope broke twice, and in spite of the instinctive attempt of the crowd to rescue the wretched victim, they were forced back by the guard, and Anderson was suspended a third time, and thoroughly hanged.

But enough, and more than enough! Let us drop the catalogue of horrors. A strange impression is made upon the searcher among these noisome records when he sees that murder is hydra-headed; that in almost every newspaper which describes an execution, the telegraphic columns report two or three fresh and atrocious homicides.

It may be said that these horrors, of which the reader can hardly endure the recital, are partly obviated by the adoption of the guillotine or garotte. The polite Latin races, certainly, are more advanced than we, who set our teeth together, and resist taste and sensitiveness in the exercise of inherited customs. While there are agonies of a different kind attendant upon these other modes of execution, which render them unnatural to endure or witness, they nevertheless show one form of progress in European civilization. Doubtless, with new scientific knowledge, a painless mode of killing may be discovered,—as by an electric shock, or by the use of some deadly anaesthetic. But the limitation and abolition of the Death-Penalty grow so rapidly that there is small likelihood of its modification by new forms.

* * *

It is not surprising that those under death-sentence should be opposed to Capital Punishment; but . . . let me print a few sentiments from the lips of culprits who, within a moment of death, seemed as much impressed with the irrationality of their taking-off, as with the inconvenience to which themselves were subjected. G.W. Winnemore, hanged at Philadelphia, Aug. 29th, 1867, said: "I hope this will be the last case of this kind; the last time that a man will be hung in this way on such a scaffold!" John W. Hughes, a man of considerable education, was hanged at Cleveland, O., Feb. 10th, 1866, for the murder of Tamzen Parsons, whom he had bigamously married. He made a remarkable speech upon the scaffold, from which the following passage is taken:

"If the people of Bedford had taken my life at the time I committed the awful deed, I would have said, 'that is Nature's law, and came from the heart;' but now, after six months of preparation and deliberation on the matter by those in official position, I say—they murder, they murder! Gentlemen, what is the advantage to society to take my life or any other man's, in comparison to employing him for the rest of his days in some useful employment? If John W. Hughes has any ability for any thing, then keep him in confinement and employ him in useful labor and make a good man of him, and turn him out reformed, and give him an opportunity to atone for all the evil he may have done society. Did I remember this penalty in that wild fit of drunkenness? No, I don't remember the murder to this time."

Mrs. Bilansky, executed at St. Paul, Minn., Mar. 23d, 1860, for poisoning her husband, protested her innocence, and said: "I die prepared to meet my God!" Then, with a woman's spirit and aptness for the *argumentum ad hominum*, she turned to the sheriff, and said: "Dr. Miller! how can you stain your hands by putting that rope around my neck?" Now I call that a pertinent question, though it came from an impeachable source. It is just the question which thoughtful and advanced minds, in this year of grace, are putting to every one officially concerned in the taking of human life, from the hangman up to the Honorable House. "What kind of a fellow are you, Master Ketch, who, for a matter of ten or twenty dollars, hide like a rat in your hole, and cut the last thread which holds Death back from a pinioned fellow-being?" Yes, now, how can you too, Mr. Sheriff, stain your reluctant hands? How can you, Mr. Governor, sign the warrant under which the Sheriff makes bold to slay his prisoner? How can you, Your Honor, pronounce the dreadful sentence? And how, I say, can you, Representatives of humanity, in Legislature assembled, permit the code of blood longer to stand written upon the statute-books of your Commonwealth? For, after all, it is with yourselves, collectively and individually, that the ultimate responsibility rests.

13 NEWTON M. CURTIS

Newton M. Curtis (1835-1910), soldier and politician was born and raised in upstate New York, where he studied law and managed the family farm until the outbreak of the Civil War. Curtis joined the army immediately after the fall of Fort Sumter and served with such distinction that he won a Congressional Medal of Honor and rose to the rank of brigadier-general before his thirtieth birthday. He commanded troops in southwestern Virginia during the first year of Reconstruction, then returned to civilian life and a number of minor government posts in New York. In 1884, Curtis won election as a Republican to the New York Assembly and from 1890 to 1897, served in the United States House of Representatives. In both bodies he led factions agitating for better treatment for prisoners and the mentally ill.

While he was serving in the state legislature, Curtis sponsored several bills for abolition of the death penalty, and in 1890, won a remarkable seventy-five to twenty-nine vote in the Assembly for abolition. The state Senate, however, refused to pass a similar measure. In Washington, Curtis found a fertile field for reform; in 1892, there were over sixty offenses for which federal civil or military courts could command capital punishment. Although Congress would not give serious consideration to his abolition bills, it did enact Curtis' proposal of 1897, which greatly reduced the number of federal capital crimes.

Curtis was faced with an intricate problem in preparing a major speech on abolition for presentation to the House of Representatives. To succeed, it would have to appeal to as diverse a group as was ever asked to consider the reform—wealthy urban conservatives, profoundly religious southern farmers, machine politicians, and midwestern agrarian radicals. The speech, delivered on June 9, 1892, was a sober compilation of arguments, religious and secular, exemplifying the state of the debate at the end of the century. These excerpts sample all of Curtis' arguments except his history of successful experiments with abolition, omitted because of its close similarity to O'Sullivan's remarks on the subject.

Let Us Enact Just Laws (1892)

THE DEATH PENALTY UNDESIRABLE, AND NOT SUSTAINED BY DIVINE AUTHORITY

Mr. Speaker, the principle I wish to have introduced into the Federal Statutes by House bill 7197, the total abolition of the punishment of death, is something more than a mere question of ethics, as stated by my friend from Texas [Mr. CULBERSON]. It is a practical question and is entitled to be considered on its merits. If the introduction of this principle will tend to promote good order in society, improve the administration of justice, and lessen crime we should give it our assent. We should hesitate if it tends to demoralize society, to lessen restraints upon the vicious, weaken administration, or relinquishes any great or actual deterrent from crime. It has its ethical side, but I will not in this discussion use the arguments of the moralists who oppose capital punishment on the ground that it is unauthorized, unjust, and unchristian.

The individual has the natural right to protect himself from assault and death, and all codes protect him in the proper exercise of the right of self-defense. So has the state the right to employ its forces in protecting the individual from violence, and society from the acts of the unbridled and vicious. The individual, at the moment of attack, may employ all means at hand

From Newton M. Curtis, *To Define the Crime of Murder* (Washington, D.C.: G. P. O., 1892), pp. 9-32.

to save his life until rescued; and the state, in defense of the individual, its peace and tranquillity, can go as far in maintaining its authority as civilized nations, in the exercise of just and equal laws, have ever gone. While an individual may use every means for his protection when menaced and in imminent peril, he can not, under the fiction of self-defense, carry it to the destruction of his assailant when the assailant is disarmed and in keeping of the police. Nor can a state find judicious warrant for going beyond the disarming and confining of a disorderly person. A single step beyond the line of safety is one step in the direction of that condition of society where brute force, not reason, rules.

In advocating this principle we are early warned not to legislate against the laws of God and the criminal codes of civilized states, perfected by the wisdom of ages. We are treated to an enumeration of penalties prescribed in codes established in the infancy of the human race as worthy of perpetual observance by enlightened nations, and commanded to hold as binding upon us and all future generations of men, the laws enacted for a rude and barbarous people. This warning would be sufficient to deter if justified by truth. So respectable are the chief advocates of the theory that the instructions given to Noah, or at least such as it suits their convenience to observe, are binding on mankind, and that no state can be well governed unless her laws are enacted in conformity with those instructions, that I prefer to oppose their opinions by the views of men whose learning will command respectful consideration wherever their names are spoken.

Many learned men have disputed the correctness of the translation of the sixth verse of the ninth chapter of Genesis as it appears in the St. James version. Calmet, Osterwald, Wycliffe, and Scio have each rejected the words "by man" in the sixth verse.[1] These words do not appear in the Septuagint. They do not appear in the Vulgate, which is considered by many to be the best translation. It is important to know that this difference of opinion exists among learned men respecting the meaning of the verse, which has been quoted as divine authority for the taking of human life for the shedding of man's blood.

* * *

They who defend this law and regard it of perpetual obligation, they who love to linger in the humid atmosphere of Mount
Ararat, and fondly cling with blind devotion to the ceremonies
instituted for sojourners in the wilderness, slowly emerging
from centuries of slavery, must certainly have refused to trace
with the Magi the course of that star which illumined the world,
have avoided the manger, the carpenter's shop, the fisherman's
cottage; have stuffed their ears with cobwebs of brutal prejudice, that the lessons taught by the Sermon on the Mount might
not enter their hearts; have veiled their eyes with vengeance,
that they might not see how He, in the extreme agony of His
suffering for man, forgave His persecutors, again declared the
law of reform, and took to His home the repentant thief. They
may search in vain through the chronicles of the theocracy for
the record of a single execution for murder under His administration of nearly thirty centuries. It is recorded that Levi,
Absalom, and David, and other men of renown offended against
this law, yet they died "in battle or in bed."

That this punishment has come down to us from the earliest
period of time, that it has been sanctioned by the criminal
codes of all races and nations of men, is no just reason for its
continuance in the polity of a free and enlightened state. If age
and universality are sound arguments to be offered for the continuance of this ancient principle, so they are equally sound and
conclusive against every effort for progress, against every discovery in science, the perfection of the arts, the use of inventions,
and the employment of the fruits of genius. Age and universality have ever been the ready arguments of those who have stood
in the way of progress. Every invention, every discovery has
been compelled to fight its way to recognition against ancient
theories, through convictions maintained and protected by punishments, proscriptions, and abuse.

* * *

INEFFICIENCY OF THE DEATH PENALTY

No one will maintain that our criminal laws are enacted on
the principle of giving the greatest protection to the well-

disposed from the acts of the unbridled and vicious. The orderly are not secured that safety and protection to life and property which wise laws should afford. The vicious are held to no certain account for their most atrocious acts. Our laws are not enforced because the sentiments of our people rise in rebellion against the infliction of irredeemable penalties. Let the criminal laws be revised so that certainty of punishment will take the place of severe penalties, now seldom awarded and next to impossible to have inflicted, first, because of the reluctance of juries to convict, and, second, by the exercise of executive clemency—granted not on account of the innocence of the prisoner, but because a concentration of social and political influence is found to be a stronger power to override and strike down the hand of justice than the simple plea of innocence.

We are daily informed by the public journals that the most atrocious offenses are committed with impunity, and that homicidal crimes have increased out of all proportion to the population. While the population of the United States within the last decade has increased about 20 per cent, the number of homicidal crimes had increased more that 400 per cent. During these years the nation has been singularly free from great calamities, war, pestilence, and famine, conditions that disrupt society and paralyze administration. Yet, in a period of unparalleled financial prosperity, homicidal crimes have increased from 1 in 35,000 in 1882 to 1 in 10,000 in 1891, as shown by statistics collected by the Chicago Tribune, which are approximately correct and entitled to the fullest credit. They are accepted as the most complete to be obtained in this country. . . . These statistics show not only a rapid increase in homicidal crimes, but the more rapid decline in awarding and inflicting the prescribed punishments therefor.

* * *

In 1882, 8 per cent of those who committed homicidal crimes suffered the extreme penalty of the law. In 1891 only 2 per cent suffered that penalty.[2]

* * *

'If capital punishment did in fact deter from crime, it might be continued as a measure of expediency; but when it affords no protection to society, and all its tendencies are to debase and demoralize, what reason have we for continuing it in our criminal statutes? I do not claim, nor do the advocates of capital punishment claim, that penalties are in themselves sufficient to prevent crime, or that any punishment, however severe or certain in its infliction, will altogether banish crime. We all believe, I doubt not, that prompt trial and the certain infliction of specific penalties will do all that laws can accomplish for the suppression of crime. The character of a nation's laws reflect the moral and social condition of its people. Nor have the people of any nation risen higher than the spirit of the laws by which they have been long governed. Laws should be a crystallization of the best sentiment of the people, and calculated to lead the nation to a higher plane of administration.

Such systems have promoted civilization, and it is the only sure method by which to secure progress in the future. Prescribe mild penalties and provide for their certain enforcement, which can never be done unless the laws command the respect and approval of the people in whose hands their administration lies. . . .

* * *

The large number of executions which took place in the Army during the late war furnishes no evidence that the punishment of death is essential for the enforcement of discipline, the maintenance of efficiency, or the safety of the army. These executions were, in a large proportion of cases, inflicted because the laws governing the army prescribed it specifically under certain articles of war. Had there been no such direction, no suggestion that the death penalty was the one best calculated to bring the speediest and surest correction of disorder, it would not have been so frequently enforced. The Articles of War have, to my personal knowledge, often been consulted before preparing charges and specifications, and the charge of "conduct prejudicial to good order and military discipline" used instead of that naming the specific offense, because the proof to sustain the specification might have supported a graver charge, and carried the sentence of death.

* * *

PRACTICAL OBJECTIONS TO THE DEATH PENALTY

Mr. Speaker, the subject before the House is one to which I have given many years of close study and serious consideration, to which I have brought an experience gained in the field, in the administration of martial law, while serving in all grades from the command of a company to that of a department, administering justice over a large territory at the close of hostilities, without the aid of civil law or its officers, as well as many years in civil life as a legislator and administrator in the enforcement of law, all of which has given me great opportunity to study men, their impulses, and their actions. I have known them in all classes, from prisoners to presidents. I have never found among those blessed with "sound minds in healthy bodies," one absolutely incorrigible, not one in whom might not be found some virtue, which, with proper culture, would grow and enliven and improve his whole being. Nor have I ever seen a man in whose character and qualities there was no improvement to be suggested.

The severe penalties of our laws defeat the ends for which they are enacted. With a penalty which men of humane sentiments can not inflict, and therefore are excused from jury duty, places the administration of our criminal laws in their final determination, in the hands of the stoical and indifferent. Judges say that of men drawn on juries, from one-quarter to three-fourths of the number, generally the most intelligent, are excused because of conscientious scruples against the infliction of the death penalty, and as a consequence the panel is composed of men least qualified to decide the important questions submitted to their determination.

* * *

Legislators have disregarded the demands for a revision of our laws until we have been compelled to enlarge our penitentiaries to receive the dupes of great criminals, while the teachers, through the imperfection of our laws, and not by any means the inefficiency or neglect of the officers of justice, are enabled to escape its penalties. The defeat of the law in its proper enforcement against a single offense tends to its demoralization in every part. Take away irredeemable punishments, so that no man can, by stating his honest convictions or falsely representing his sensibilities, excuse himself from a jury service. . . .

* * *

The dread so many express of permitting the murderer to live so long as the pardoning power is retained has little to justify it. The power to pardon is a provision in the organic law, and can only be reached by constitutional amendment. Those who fear its improper use should know that it is more generally exercised in capital States than it has been or is likely to be in non-capital States. I quite agree with those who desire to see it restricted, and I have the confident opinion that it will be when its promoting cause—capital punishment—for which and only on account of which pardons were first instituted and have since come into general use to thwart and impede justice.

Have man's explorations in the fields of science and philosophy, in his contemplation of natural laws, the gospels, or revelation, yet discovered a standard wherewith accurately to measure the value of a human life? It has been said that the riches of the world are of less value than the salvation of a soul. Are we then, acting within the limits of the great organic law, justified in prescribing a standard and directing its application, on the infallibility of human judgment, if "to shorten a human life puts in jeopardy a human soul?" We are not justified in imitating even in our laws the acts of the vicious; the wise and virtuous will never do it.

* * *

I ask the deliberate judgment of this House on this important principle, that they will without prejudice examine it from every side, and bring to its consideration the facts of history, the experience of States blessed with its beneficent provisions, that we may contribute to the urgent duty of bringing this nation to the side, at least, if not placing her in advance of those we sometimes think less enlightened than our own. Let us enact just laws, whose penalties shall be enforced with certainty against those who violate them, and secure to the orderly and well disposed the opportunity "to enjoy in safety and tranquillity their natural rights and the blessings of life."

14 WILLIAM DEAN HOWELLS

William Dean Howells (1837-1920), one of America's greatest literary figures at the turn of the century, was born in Ohio, where he worked in various newspaper offices from age nine to twenty-three. He had begun to publish some of his work by 1860, when Lincoln's election produced a great change in his life. Howells had written useful campaign material for the newly elected president and received as his reward the post of American consul in Venice. His stay in that city, during the Civil War years, was largely uneventful, but it was an awe-inspiring experience for a young American interested in the arts. Upon his return to the United States, Howells took an editor's job with the influential *Atlantic Monthly* and by 1871 had risen to editor-in-chief. At the same time, he began to produce the realist novels which, in time, were to earn him international fame. In 1881, he resigned his editorial position to spend most of the rest of his life writing novels, poems, and short stories and contributing frequent essays to *Harper's Magazine*.

Howells' views on capital punishment changed radically during his life. In the 1860s he was an advocate of hanging, describing one execution as "the most impressive vindication [of justice] the country ever saw." By 1883, however, he had become opposed to executing all but the cruelest murderers and by 1895 he was of the opinion that "the murder the State does in punishment of killing is the worst murder of all." The present essay employed the biting sarcasm which Howells used to such good effect in several of his other appeals against capital punishment.

State Manslaughter (1904)

When the axe was laid at the root of the good old gallows-tree, whose fruit had nourished Anglo-Saxon civilization in so many climes for so many ages, I had my misgivings whether the electric chair would serve all the philanthropic ends expected of it by its friends. I do not say that I had any prevision of the horrors which have resulted from it in many of the State killings since it was set up in the State shambles, but I could not believe that it would be of such a benign operation as almost to take away the mortal effect of the death penalty. Something like this was what its partisans promised us, with a tender regard equally for the sensibilities of those who wished to have criminals killed painlessly, and for the scruples of those others who believed that the law had no right to the life even of a murderer. What the advocates of the chair, which has so sadly betrayed their confidence, implied if they did not express, was that killing by electricity was almost the same as not killing at all. It would remove with dignity and decorum the offender who had forfeited his life, and not be attended by the depraving incidents inseparable from guillotining, garroting, or even hanging, and of course not by the cruel accidents to which the art of the headsman was subject. They did not forebode and they could not foresee that the mystical element whose agency they had invoked to do the work of the archaic instrumentalities of justice could bungle its sacred mission. The culprit would be carefully seated, somewhat as the subject of photography is, and assuming as cheerful or as submissive an expression as possible, would be thrilled into the other world with the touch of a button, or the turn of a key, by the hand of a scientific gentleman, or at least an educated electrician, on the other side of a wall or screen. No black mask of the headsman here; no show of the halter, or sound of the drop; no binding of the victim on a board like a planked shad; not even the twist of a crank by which the garroter despatched the malefactor from behind.

From William Dean Howells, "State Manslaughter," *Harper's Weekly,* 48 (February 6, 1904), pp. 196-198.

It was not imagined that electricity could fail to kill instantly, much less that the criminal, who had become the State's peculiar care, could be so ineffectually tortured as to froth at the mouth, and strain at his bonds with writhings of agony which almost burst them, or give out the smell of his burning flesh so that the invited guest was often made sick at his stomach by the loathsome and atrocious fact. Yet all this has happened again and again in the execution of the death sentences since the consecration of the electric chair to the hallowed office of the axe, the noose, the screw. It has happened so often that I, at least, had become used to reading of it, and had tranquilly accepted it as of the same necessity as the honored death penalty itself, which our civilization could not get on without, though the civilization of Italy and of Scandinavia seems to do so, not to mention that of our sister republic Switzerland. I generally managed to reconcile myself to the record of the frothing, and burning, and writhing, by learning further that the scientific gentleman, or the educated electrician, on the other side of the wall, had made it all right by discharging another thousand or two thousand volts into the body of his erring brother, and so putting him finally out of his misery.

What was my dismay, then, to read the other morning in the *Sun,* which daily rises over my coffee-cup at breakfast, a letter from so eminent an authority as Dr. Allen McLane Hamilton,[1] which informed me that killing does not kill when done by electricity in the hands of the official homicides. He declared that in the case of a murderer whose life was lately attempted by the appointed agency, six "shocks" so failed of their due effect, that the examining doctor "collapsed from sheer horror when he found that his stethescope still carried the heart beats of the victim to his ear." He alleged three other recent executions as equally "disgraceful," and named one of them in which the electrized man revived, and perished subsequently from the "large quantities of morphine and chloroform" given him. He holds that the "present law provides a method full of all sorts of uncertainties which are recognized by scientific men generally," and he suggests that something like "poisoning with carbonic dioxide" would be "an effective and painless" method, which might be properly substituted for the very fallible means of happy despatch that electricity has been shown to be.

I am afraid that many kind souls who, like myself, had rested in peaceful acceptance of killing by electricity as next to no killing at all, will reconcile themselves with difficulty the substitution of "poisoning by carbonic dioxide," though it sounds like something nearly as merciful as conservative surgery. The question of its employment brings up again the whole question of State homicide, which seemed so gracefully settled by the use of electricity. We have to face again the fact that on humanitarian grounds State homicide seems more barbarous and abominable than any but that most exceptional private murder, since it adds the anguish of foreknowledge to the victim's doom. If one dies by the hand of a private murderer, one mercifully perishes without expectation, as one does in most other circumstances of accident or disease; but if one is to be put to death by the civic authorities, one is warned of it months beforehand, with the date precisely or approximately fixed; or if, as in the more aesthetic conditions of France, the very hour is withheld from one till one is waked to go to the guillotine some morning, still one cannot well lie down to peaceful slumbers with that fate hanging over one. To be sure, it might be said of State homicide that it seems no more excessive than most other criminal sentences, which no one who hears them pronounced in what we so amusingly call our courts of justice, can fail to feel wholly out of proportion to the offences punished by them. For a theft so small that it could only be recognized by the most rigid moralist, a man loses his liberty, and his family loses his labor for two or three months; for a theft a little larger, he loses his liberty and his family loses his labor for as many years. The State, which ought to pay the highest trades-union wages for his work, and daily turn his wages over to his innocent family, pays him nothing, and robs his guiltless wife and hapless children of the living he might have earned for them. But even justice so Asiatic as this does not seem quite so barbarous as the death penalty, whether inflicted by electricity, as now, or by carbonic dioxide poisoning as possibly hereafter, for in Asia we read that the capital offender is often taken from the judge's presence and at once beheaded, or even beheaded in the judge's presence as soon as sentence is pronounced. "He suffers, but he does not suffer long." [2] But under our system he must suffer ages of fear in view of the death that awaits him in such a week, or on such a day and hour.

All this, I hope, is not saying that the death penalty is not a righteous and necessary thing. It is true that several civilized countries, and many of our own States, seem to get on without it, and not to have more murderers in them than the countries and States which cannot get on without it, and which seem equally civilized. In the countries and States which find it essential to the salvation of society, many disciples of One whose teaching superseded the old law of an eye for an eye, and a life for a life, hold it little less than of divine ordinance. It is not, then, for a lay brother to question its inspired origin, and I do not question it. I accept it with all its possible aberrations from justice, in the case of some who perish innocently by it, and in the case of the others who merely die a thousand deaths in view of the death they are doomed to; I accept it because, although other countries and States get on without it, we apparently cannot get on without it. If electricity must go, let not the dear and honored death penalty go with it. If we must have carbonic dioxide, then better carbonic dioxide than the sickly sentimentality which would substitute for State homicide, with its inalienable mental tortures, the imprisonment in which justice can revise its verdicts, if they have erred, or if they are righteous can still keep the guilty soul alive for the penitence and the reform which we cannot refuse to believe possible without denying the faith.

Innumerable affecting memories and associations, summing in themselves a vast share of the poetry and humor of the race, cling about the venerable punishment which we could not deprive ourselves of, without losing a precious part of our heritage from the past. Almost any reader can recall proverbs, verses, jokes, in which its idea is embalmed, and can verify the instances in which these have made him a wiser and a better man. "A thousand names has the Arab for the horse," says Heine,

"the Frenchman a thousand for love, the German a thousand
for drinking, and the Englishman a thousand for hanging."[3] This
saying touches the heart of the fact, and lights it up as by the
introduction of a radioactive flame, so that we see clearly how
impossible, how all but impious, it would be for us to disuse
hanging, or its semi-scientific substitutes. It is true that its beneficent office has been greatly limited with the lapse of time.
People used to be hanged for a shilling's worth; a woman went
to the gallows for stealing a loaf of bread to keep her children
from starving; for imitating too accurately the signature of a
noble lord a doctor of divinity was hanged in the eighteenth
century so righteously that the noble lord could not bring himself to save the forger by his intercession; rape, arson, treason
itself sometimes, which used to bring a man to the scaffold, no
longer do so. But through all these changes the great, vital,
saving principle of the death penalty has remained the same. If
electricity has proved not merely appalling and disgusting, but
ineffective, by all means let us have carbonic dioxide, and if
that fails, too, let us keep on trying till we get the perfect
agency of painless homicide. But let the State never corrupt the
potential private murderer by ceasing to kill with accumulated
terrors such as he never dreamt of.

15 FINLEY PETER DUNNE

Can humor have a place in an appeal against a deadly institution? It can in the hands of Finley Peter Dunne (1867-1936), creator of "Mr. Dooley" and one of the most popular American writers at the turn of the century. Born in Chicago of Irish immigrant parents, Dunne wrote conventional material for several local newspapers until 1892, when he began to compose Irish dialect stories for the *Chicago Evening Post.* One character, Martin Dooley, soon became the central figure in all of Dunne's newspaper columns. A simple, but direct, Irish-American, Mr. Dooley charmed millions of readers with his ability to unmask fraud and pierce hypocrisy. National syndication made him one of the most famous and influential fictional characters in late nineteenth- and early twentieth-century America. Mr. Dooley's fame, in fact, hurt Dunne's career, for the author was never able to break away from writing dialect material for very long and seems to have suffered an eclipse in his ability to write at all in the last fifteen years of his life.

In three decades of writing, Dunne, usually in the voice of Mr. Dooley, attacked many individuals, institutions, and acts he deemed harmful to society. He shared a belief with some "muckraking" friends, like Ray Stannard Baker and Ida Tarbell, that if Americans were told about the evils of their society, the democratic process would work to correct them. It was at the end of an eight-year association with the reformist *American Magazine* that Dunne contributed his only essay on capital punishment, an autobiographical account of events that had turned him against the death penalty thirty years before. Like many of the Mr. Dooley articles, it criticized gently and sarcastically and avoided the strident preaching which is often the only medium of less gifted writers.

156

The Majesty of the Law (1914)

Probably few readers of *The American Magazine* have ever seen a public hanging. At least I hope this is true and believe it must be so since this form of execution of the law has pretty generally ceased to be a free popular entertainment. In certain parts of the country the public is still permitted to enjoy unlicensed performances of the act of public vengeance. The time has gone by in most places, happily, when thousands of men were invited "by courtesy of the Sheriff" to feast their greedy eyes on the spectacle of a fellow human being struggling for air at the end of a hempen rope, although there are still many communities in which this form of private theatricals still thrills those who have an interest with the hangman.

We improve a little in these matters of taste. It is not a long time since public hangings were the amusement of the blackguards of London, when Thackeray wrote his incomparable essay on the subject[1] and Lamb spoke humorously of executions as among the entertainments of the capital.[2] It was not so long before that when little children played at marbles under the wayside gibbets from which the skeletons of criminals tossed in their rags in the wind, and a girl was hanged in London for picking up a bolt of cloth which she afterward replaced on the counter of the shop. And this in a century when the Wesleys were preaching and writing hymns, and Burke was declaiming against the iniquity of the French in guillotining their King. So the world does move a little. We laugh at the ugly figure of the hangman in "Barnaby Rudge," who hated the Government because it had cut down the number of crimes for which men could be hanged and so reduced the importance of his "Protestant, Conservative, and British" office.[3] But aren't we laughing a little early? It took a good many years for "mawkish sentimentality" to soften this particular official manifestation of the passion for revenge and the enjoyment of the sufferings of others which still lurks in the hearts of men.

From Finley Peter Dunne, "The Majesty of the Law," *American Magazine*, 77 (February 1914), pp. 12-16.

But this article was not intended as a sermon, merely as a plain narrative of the impressions of one who was most unfortunately privileged to look upon an exhibition by the Avenging Law in its most tragic rôle. The eyes which saw it were the eyes of a boy of seventeen who by chance had been thrown into the business of daily journalism, in which romantic pursuit he saw the terrors of the world and reported them faithfully and understood them no more than he had the science of trigonometry, from which he had but recently escaped.

In those days the newspapers made more of hangings than they do now. The papers, like the rest of the world, are better than they were—a little. But at that time an execution was a prime piece of news. The most minute details of the preliminary horrors were published. The public, supposed to be starving for such morsels, was fed freely upon accounts of the acts and sayings of the condemned man, the visits of his family, and appeals to the governor in his behalf, and the bill of fare (usually enormous) with which he regaled himself at meals. There was much guessing on the identity of Jack Ketch,[4] a modest hero who preferred with a good taste which might well be followed to conceal his blushes within a little wooden box on the platform of the gallows.

Finally, on the day of the execution, the early editions of the afternoon papers favored their readers with exact accounts of the "last night on earth" of the unfortunate, the presses waited until word came over the telephone that the drop had fallen, and in the pleasant evening, under the cheerful lamplight, with the family gathered around the table, every comfortable citizen could amuse himself by reading an ambitious description of the last dreadful hours of a wretched convict.

Hence our youth felt deeply honored when he was told by his city editor that he must go to the county jail and stay "till the drop fell," for this was no ordinary hanging. For the first time in the memory of the police department of the town three men were to be hanged at one time on the same scaffold.[5]

It was an occasion to stir all his literary and journalistic aspirations. And if he gave all his thought to the occasion as a chance for the exercise of his own skill and none at all to the dreary fact that necks like his own were to be twisted, and hearts like his own stopped, pray reflect that youth doesn't understand or appreciate the meaning of death. It sees persons of all ages fall without taking the lesson to itself. It feels pity or even contempt for the weak mortality that has been overtaken by so unpleasant a mischance. Itself is immortal.

The murder for which the Majesty of the Law was about to exert so opulent a punishment was not in any sense picturesque. In fact it was about as mean and cowardly a crime as could be imagined. Three young Italian laborers, inflamed with the well known and popular passion of avarice, desired to possess themselves of the money which one of their mates had saved up. If they had been more ingenious they might have robbed him at cards; if they had been better trained in the methods of predatory finance they might have created a copper mine and sold it to him. But they were lightly endowed with brains and they chose a more direct method. Having won his confidence they proceeded to strangle him with a piece of clothes line. Then they bought a trunk and shipped the remains of their victim to a cherished friend in a near-by city.

Naturally the case with all its ramifications baffled the police. Their first theory was that the victim had committed suicide. But as this did not bear all the tests of criticism, they advanced various other hypotheses; as, that he had died of heart disease, that he had blown out the gas, and, finally, that he had been killed by burglars—"a long and a short man." For several days it was unsafe for two men of unequal height to be seen in the neighborhood of the house.

When the constabulary were at their wits' end, which was not very far from their beginning, a reporter thought of going to Pittsburgh and examining the trunk. He found the name of the dealer stenciled on the bottom, looked up the man, took him and the freight clerk to the house where the murder was committed, secured a complete identification of the three roommates of the deceased, and then, after his paper had gone to press, gave the information to the police.

They acted with commendable energy, arrested the culprits, beat them on the way to the station and there subjected them to one of the many forms of the "third degree." In this case the exquisite device was practiced of telling each of the cowering wretches that the others had confessed and put the blame on him. The consequence was, of course, that all three confessed at practically the same moment. Discovering that they had been tricked, all three recanted with one voice.

But it was too late. The men were indicted that day and tried the following week. In order to hasten the march of justice and insure a conviction the judge appointed a lady lawyer to defend them. The jury having returned a verdict in accordance with the evidence and the charge of the judge, which was to the effect that the jury were absolutely judge of the fact and the law, but the fact was that the men were guilty and the law was they must be hanged. His Honor put on a black skullcap. After denouncing the iniquity of the crime and the low moral character of the culprits (in a language which they didn't understand) he directed that on a certain Friday (selected because of the tender religious associations of the day), at a certain hour, they should be taken from their cells and hanged by the neck until they were dead, adding the purely formal hope that the Lord, who is presumably of less inflexible character than human judges, might have mercy on their souls.

The Boy's heart beat fast as he crossed the dark jail yard at midnight and was admitted to the jail office. He found other reporters there and a few half-drunken loungers who were sitting up with a temporary night jailer to keep him company. The turnkey was far advanced, but was still more rapidly advancing toward a state of complete inebriety. He was at first genial and with his companions sang interminably, as it seemed, a German song with a chorus beginning, "Hilee, hilo," or something like that. But as the night wore on and his excursions to the cupboard continued he became truculent, suspicious of everyone, entertained delusions of grandeur and of pursuit—in short developed one of these acute cases of temporary paranoia which are often as marked in drunken men as they are in the insane.

A giant of a man, in his shirt sleeves, with a huge revolver sticking out of his hip pocket and a bunch of massive keys hanging from his arm, he was a menacing figure. Once during the night one of the reporters, an old man, got it into his head that the jailer was giving some precious information about the prisoners to another reporter, and said so. The drunkard went into a frenzy of rage, threatened first to lock the old man up and then to shoot him, and seemed to be making ready to carry both threats into action at once when he was seized by his cronies who, with the assistance of watchmen from the cell house, took away his revolver and keys and carried him to an easy-chair.

The jail was, of course, overcrowded; of course it was not ventilated, and it smelled like a thousand New York subways compressed into a small space. From the cell house came the sounds of broken sleep, moans, sobbing, an occasional sharp cry. While the jailer was wrangling, a kind and patient priest sat in the jail library, and to him were brought at various times through the office the three condemned murderers.

The fear of death, that emissary more terrible than itself which death sends to make its own appearance welcome, was heavy on them. It had squeezed the blood out of their hearts and turned their bones to water. Pale beyond all conception of pallor in life, with bowed knees, quaking from heel to head, they looked fitter for the hospital than the jail or the gallows. One by one they went into the library. One by one they were led back to their cells and there, whether from the benefit of the ghostly consolation or from the extreme fatigue,—who can tell?—they fell sound asleep and were still sleeping when their breakfasts were brought to their cells in the morning.

The Boy looked on all the sordid happenings of this night of horror with open, curious eyes and with a degree of fearlessness or indifference which seems wonderful to look back upon. Just before daybreak he wrote his "story" for the early edition and went to sleep on a desk. He was awakened by the bustle of the day guard relieving the night men and by the outcries of the prisoners, who seemed to take an insane delight in yelling at the top of their lungs as soon as they woke up. The jailer aroused himself and, having delivered his keys to the day warden, who grinned appreciatively at his appearance, stumbled out.

The prisoners kept up their noise, singing or yelling foul

names at each other. Two carpenters went through with their kits of tools to put the "finishing touches" to the structure in the north corridor. The ropes were already in place. They had been tested with sand bags the day before and found worthy of the important duty which the Law called on them to perform.

The sheriff arrived an hour later. He was a nervous, vain little man, one of those professional Civil War veterans who were so numerous and so worthless in public offices at that time. He bustled about giving useless orders, visited the dying men and afflicted them with impertinent questions, examined the scaffold and generally was very important and very much of a nuisance.

In a little while the first of the spectators arrived, and soon after the corridors resounded with the tramp of many feet. Most of the early guests stopped to thank the sheriff for his kindness in affording them the opportunity to see the spectacle. Among certain classes an invitation to a hanging was considered a great honor. "If I had granted all the applications," said the sheriff with a magnificent sweep of the hand, "I could have filled the corridor ten times over." He spoke of this as an evidence of his own popularity and merit regardless of the claims of the principal tragedians in the little cells near-by. The cards of invitation were engraved. They were signed "with the compliments" of the sheriff, and so eager was the demand for them that they were sold for ten or twenty dollars apiece by holders whose cupidity was greater than their bloodthirst.

After a while the Boy made his way to the corridor and to his seat at the press tables where groups of seasoned reporters were already gathered, joking and laughing, recounting tales of other hangings they had seen or debating the immediate physical effect of hanging.

The gallows stood at one end of the corridor. It was a platform, with three trap doors, about eight feet above the floor. A heavy beam upon two uprights was set above it. From this beam hung three yellow ropes. At a corner of the platform stood a small box, like a sentry box, in which the hangman had been sitting for several hours, watching through a peephole the crowd coming in, and perhaps wondering what he would buy for the "old woman" with the fifty dollars which was to be his fee. The Boy found out his name and talked with him afterward. He was a gentle sort of ruffian, a Swede, a minor employee of the sheriff's office, and not at all the Ketch of literary commerce. His only explanation of his sad avocation was that it was a good "yob" and "it had to be done by somebody."

The corridor filled rapidly and the cell galleries were crowded until fully one thousand men and one woman—the gentle advocate of the trial—were packed into the space. Most of the men were minor politicians, office holders, saloon-keepers, and the like, although there were representatives of other classes in the community, lawyers, doctors, and "men-about-town." Nothing could have been more cheerful than their demeanor. They were infinitely gayer than an audience at a successful comedy.

They told stories, laughed, bawled songs, and called out humorously to each other: "Say Bill, how did you get in?" "I know one of the stars. He give me a pass." The lady advocate came in for a great share of the banter. "I tell you what, Lizzie, any time I want to be scragged I'll get you for me lawyer sure," called a man in the crowd. "You'll not need my help, young fellow," said Portia. This pleasant repartee amused the crowd immensely. The lady went away before the bitter end. She did not possess the same courage as Lady Hamilton, who witnessed with her beautiful eyes the removal of the Neapolitan prince whom Nelson killed.[6]

Nearly all the men were smoking, and the reek from their cigars further polluted the obscene atmosphere of the jail and thickened it so that objects were seen dimly as in a fog. In the back of the room two politicians fell into an altercation over some question of state and pounded each other with their fists until they were separated. The crowd grew impatient, and the impresario and his troupe failed to appear. They whistled and stamped and yelled.

The only person who was satisfied with the delay was the reporter who sat next to the Boy. He had been writing industriously during the disturbance, never raising his head from his copy paper. "I'm an hour ahead of the proceedings now," he said while he was sharpening his pencil. "If they hold off a little longer I'll have my story finished down to the sheriff's jury's verdict by the time the drop falls, and then I'll have the whole afternoon off and can take my girl for a drive. It's going to be a great afternoon out of town."

Just then a man near the hall leading to the gallows cried, "Here they come!" and the dread procession entered. The sheriff led, with an air of importance, then came the three prisoners, pinioned, and then the priest who through the night had listened to their cries for mercy. The men were sinewy, rather good-looking Italians, under twenty-five. They were led to their appointed trap doors, where they stood, looking out on the unsympathetic crowd with terror-haunted eyes.

The mob in the corridor was quieter now but it was still in holiday mood. There was a steady hum of friendly conversation, a persistent shuffling of feet. Now and then a coarse laugh broke out as the bailiff, who had charge of the vestments for the culprits,—the wardrobe man of this awful show,—went awkwardly about his work. The fumes of a thousand cigars continued to ascend. Heavy-jowled men passed flasks of whisky from hand to hand and drank healths. The figures on the scaffold remained motionless except for the white lips which gabbled incoherent prayers.

The clumsy bailiff managed to open his bundles after much expenditure of useless effort and proceeded to attire the pereformers for their final act. On each of them he first placed a long white sleeveless robe which he tied around the neck and ankles. Over their heads he drew a cone-shaped white cotton hood, and so transformed what was a figure of pity into one of horrible offensive comedy. You could weep for or you could hate the trembling men. But these grotesquely robed and hooded figures were not tragic. The Majesty of the Law jested with these victims at the end, added indignity to death and sent the poor devils as masked clowns to their doom.

The valet pursued his work methodically, carefully attiring one criminal before he touched the next one. As he placed the white hood on the first man and adjusted the rope, the priest stepped forward and in the level voice prescribed by the custom of the Church began to read the most awful of human supplications for divine mercy, "The Litany for the Dying." He read it in Latin. Italian men of the present day are not noted for their piety, but these unfortunates recalled vaguely, through a mist of sin and irreligion, words which they had heard in their child-hood, and they interrupted the prayer with cries of "Ora pro nobis." They knew no more.

Omnes sancti Apostoli et Evangelistae, . . .

"Ora pro nobis," from the ashen lips of the uncovered felons.

"Ora pro nobis," in muffled tones through the hood.

The bailiff had dressed the second man and was at work on the third. The heartrending prayer went on.

A mala morte, . . .

"Ora pro nobis," clearly from the one wretch.

"Ora pro nobis," thickly from the hoods of the two others.

In die judicii, . . .

"Ora pro nobis,"

The voices were all cut off now·by the hoods and the "Ora pro nobis" sounded as if it came from a great distance. The half smothered voices grew more rapid, more eager, more insistent, running the words together: "Orapro nobisora pronobisorapro-nobisora—"

Qui cum Patre et Spiritu sancto, vivis et regnas in saecula saeculorum.

The priest closed his book and stepped back. His fine face was white from pity and horror.

"Ora pro nobis."

The sheriff waved his hand toward the little box in the corner.

The sound of a sharp blow came from the hangman's box, the trap doors swung back with a great clatter, the slack ropes ran taut, and down through the platform shot the three clown-ish figures, recoiled, fell again, twisted for a second, swayed, and then hung still on a level with the eyes of the spectator. But no, not all of them were still. Two only were put out of their agony instantly.

A voice rang out from the crowd: "God ha' mercy, the big fellow is not dead!" It was true. The clumsy mechanics of the operation had failed. For fully five minutes the base crowd watched the awful spectacle with frank enjoyment. Then they tumbled out and discussed the unusual debauch at the neighboring bars.

The Majesty of the Law had been vindicated. Justice was triumphant. Right was made plain to the blindest and a splendid example of punishment put before the eyes of intending sinners.

N. B.—There were just as many capital crimes in the year following the infliction of this notably exemplary punishment as in the year before.

16 CLARENCE DARROW

Some of America's great criminal lawyers have become especially effective opponents of capital punishment because of their fame, their experience in argument and persuasion, and their familiarity with the criminal mind. Few have been more influential than Clarence Seward Darrow (1857-1938). Darrow's fame began to grow when, at age thirty, he moved his practice from his native Ohio to Chicago. He rose to national prominence as a result of the men he defended, Eugene V. Debs and other union officials in 1895, William D. Haywood in 1907, Nathan Leopold and Richard Loeb in 1924, and John Scopes in 1925, to name only a few.

Throughout his career Darrow was a bitter opponent of the death penalty and as a defense attorney for a long string of accused capital offenders, he had frequent opportunity to voice his beliefs in the courtroom. For the public at large, he condemned capital punishment at length in his autobiography of 1935 and in various lectures. In 1925, he helped found the American League to Abolish Capital Punishment.

Darrow's most characteristic public attack on the death penalty came in his debate with Judge Alfred J. Talley in 1924, for there he was in something like the courtroom situation in which he performed best. Talley, a New York City jurist, had attacked Darrow and his views on capital punishment shortly after the lawyer had convinced a Chicago judge to spare the lives of convicted child-murderers Leopold and Loeb. New York's League for Public Discussion arranged for the two men to debate on the subject "Is Capital Punishment a Wise Policy?" at the Metropolitan Opera House on September 23, 1924. On that evening a capacity crowd heard Judge Talley lead off with a thirty-five minute address in which he claimed that the state had the right to execute criminals and that it was necessary that it do so. Then, Darrow moved to the podium. His speech, materialistic and bitter, was far from a forensic masterpiece. But the gruff attorney's almost exclusively utilitarian arguments, spiced with humor, won repeated applause and laughter from the audience.

It is Too Horrible a Thing for a State to Undertake (1924)

NEGATIVE (MR. DARROW)

I had this stand moved up so I could get next to the audience. I hope I will not be obliged to spend too much time on my friend's address. I don't think I shall need to.

First, I deny his statement that every man's heart tells him it is wrong to kill. I think every man's heart desires killing. Personally, I never killed anybody that I know of. But I have had a great deal of satisfaction now and then reading obituary notices, and I used to delight, with the rest of my hundred-per-cent patriotic friends, when I saw ten or fifteen thousand Germans being killed in a day.

Everybody loves killing. Some of them think it is too messy for them. Every human being that believes in capital punishment loves killing, and the only reason they believe in capital punishment is because they get a kick out of it. Nobody kills anyone for love, unless they get over it temporarily or otherwise. But they kill the one they hate. And before you can get a trial to hang somebody or electrocute him, you must first hate him and then get a satisfaction over his death.

There is no emotion in any human being that is not in every

From Clarence Darrow, *Debate Resolved: That Capital Punishment is a Wise Public Policy* (New York: League for Public Discussion, 1924), pp. 29-41, 57-62.

single human being. The degree is different, that is all. And the degree is not always different in different people. It depends likewise on circumstances, on time and on place.

I shall not follow my friend into the labyrinth of statistics. Statistics are a pleasant indoor sport—not so good as crossword puzzles—and they prove nothing to any sensible person who is familiar with statistics.

I might just observe, in passing, that in all of these states where the mortality by homicide is great, they have capital punishment and always have had it. A logical man, when he found out that the death rate increased under capital punishment, would suggest some other way of dealing with it.

I undertake to say—and you can look them up yourselves, for I haven't time to bother with it (and there is nothing that lies like statistics)—I will guarantee to take any set of statistics and take a little time to it and prove they mean directly the opposite of what is claimed. But I will undertake to say that you can show by statistics that the states in which there was no capital punishment have a very much smaller percentage of homicides.

I know it is true. That doesn't prove anything, because, as a rule, they are states with a less diverse population, without as many large cities, without as much mixture of all sorts of elements which go to add to the general gaiety—and homicide is a product of that. There is no sort of question but what those states in the United States where there is no capital punishment have a lower percentage than the others. But that doesn't prove the question. It is a question that cannot be proven one way or the other by statistics. It rests upon things, upon feelings and emotions and arguments, much deeper than statistics.

The death rate from homicide in Memphis and in some other Southern cities is high. Why? Well, it is an afternoon's pleasure to kill a Negro—that is about all. Everybody knows it.

The death rate recently in the United States and all over the world has increased. Why? The same thing has happened that has happened in every country in the world since time began. A great war always increases death rates.

We teach people to kill, and the State is the one that teaches them. If the State wishes that its citizens respect human life, then the State should stop killing. It can be done in no other way, and it will perhaps not be fully done that way. There are infinite reasons for killing. There are infinite circumstances under which there are more or less deaths. It never did depend and never can depend upon the severity of the punishment.

* * *

But let's see what there is in this argument. He says, "Everybody who kills, dreads hanging." Well, he has had experience as a lawyer on both sides. I have had experience on one side. I know that everybody who is taken into court on a murder charge desires to live, and they do not want to be hanged or electrocuted. Even a thing as alluring as being cooked with electricity doesn't appeal to them.

But that hasn't anything to do with it. What was the state of mind when the homicide was committed? The state of mind is one thing when a homicide is committed and another thing weeks or months afterward, when every reason for committing it is gone. There is no comparison between them. There never can be any comparison between them.

We might ask why people kill. I don't want to dispute with him about the right of the State to kill people. Of course, they have got a right to kill them. That is about all we do. The great industry of the world for four long years was killing. They have got a right to kill, of course, that is, they have got the power. And you have got a right to do what you get away with. The words power and right, so far as this is concerned, mean exactly the same thing. So nobody who has any knowledge of philosophy would pretend to say that the State had not the right to kill.

But why not do a good job of it? If you want to get rid of killings by hanging people or electrocuting them because these are so terrible, why not make a punishment that is terrible? This isn't so much. It lasts but a short time. There is no physical torture in it. Why not boil them in oil, as they used to do? Why not burn them at the stake? Why not sew them into a bag with serpents and throw them out to sea? Why not take them out on the sand and let them be eaten by ants? Why not break every bone in their body on the rack, as has been done for such serious offenses as heresy and witchcraft?

Those were the good old days in which the Judge should have held court. Glorious days, when you could kill them by the millions because they worshipped God in a different way from that which the State provided, or when you could kill old women for witchcraft! There might be some sense in it if you could kill young ones, but not old ones. Those were the glorious days of capital punishment. And there wasn't a judge or a preacher who didn't think that the life of the State depended upon their right to hang old women for witchcraft and to persecute others for worshiping God in the wrong way.

Why, our capital punishment isn't worth talking about, so far as its being a preventive is concerned. It isn't worth discussing. Why not call back from the dead and barbarous past the hundred and sixty- or seventy-odd crimes that were punishable by death in England? Why not once more re-enact the Blue Laws of our own country and kill people right? Why not resort to all the tortures that the world has always resorted to to keep men in the straight and narrow path? Why reduce it to a paltry question of murder?

Everybody in this world has some pet aversion to something, and on account of that pet aversion they would like to hang somebody. If the prohibitionists made the law, they would be in favor of hanging you for taking a drink, or certainly for bootlegging, because to them that is the most heinous crime there is.

Some men slay or murder. Why? As a matter of fact, murder as murder is very rare; and the people who commit it, as a rule, are of a much higher type than others. You may go to any penitentiary and, as a rule, those who have been convicted of murder become the trusties; whereas, if you are punishing somebody as a sneak thief or a counterfeiter or a confidence man, they never get over it—never.

Now, I don't know how injustice is administered in New York. I just know about Chicago. But I am glad to learn from the gentleman that if a man is so poor in New York that he can't hire a lawyer, that he has a first-class lawyer appointed to defend him. Don't take a chance and go out and kill anybody on the statement made by my friend.

I suppose anybody can go out and kill somebody and ask to have my friend, Sam Untermeyer, appointed.¹ There never was such a thing. Here and there, a good lawyer may have defended people for nothing. But no court ever interferes with a good lawyer's business by calling him in and compelling him to give his time. They have been lawyers too recently themselves to ever work a trick like that on a lawyer. As a rule, it is the poor and the weak and the friendless who furnish the victims of the law.

Let me take another statement of my friend. He said, "Oh, we don't hang anybody if they kill when they are angry; it is only when they act premeditatedly." Yes, I have been in courts and heard judges instruct people on this premeditated act. It is only when they act under their judgment and with due consideration. He would also say that if a man is moved by anger, but if he doesn't strike the deadly blow until such time as reason and judgment have a chance to possess him, even if it is a second—how many times have I heard judges say, "Even if it is a second?" What does any judge know about premeditation? What does anybody know about it? How many people are there in this world that can premeditate on anything? I will strike out the "pre" and say how many people are there that can meditate?

How long does it take the angry man for his passions to cool when he is in the presence of the thing that angers him? There never was a premeditated murder in any sense of psychology or science. There are planned murders—planned, yes—but back of every murder and back of every human act are sufficient causes that move the human machine beyond their control.

The other view is an outworn, outlawed, unscientific theory of the metaphysicians. Does anybody ever act in this world without a motive? Did they ever act without a sufficient motive? And who am I to say that John Smith premeditated? I might premeditate a good deal quicker than John Smith did. My judgment might have a chance to act quicker than John Smith's judgment had a chance to act.

We have heard talk of justice. Is there anybody who knows what justice is? No one on earth can measure out justice. Can you look at any man and say what he deserves—whether he deserves hanging by the neck until dead or life in prison or thirty days in prison or a medal? The human mind is blind to all who seek to look in at it and to most of us that look out from it. Justice is something that man knows little about. He may know something about charity and understanding and mercy, and he should cling to these as far as he can.

* * *

There is just one thing in all this question. It is a question of how you feel, that is all. It is all inside of you. If you love the thought of somebody being killed, why, you are for it. If you hate the thought of somebody being killed, you are against it.

Let me just take a little brief review of what has happened in this world. They used to hang people on the crossways and on a high hill, so that everybody would be awed into goodness by the sight. They have tortured them in every way that the brain of man could conceive. They have provided every torture known or that could be imagined for one who believed differently from his fellow-man—and still the belief persisted. They have maimed and scarred and starved and killed human beings since man began penning his fellow-man. Why? Because we hate him. And what has added to it is that they have done it under the false ideal of self-righteousness.

I have heard parents punish their children and tell their children it hurt the parents more than it did the child. I don't believe it. I have tried it both ways, and I don't believe it. I know better.

Gradually, the world has been lopping off these punishments. Why? Because we have grown a little more sensitive, a little more imaginative, a little kindlier, that is all.

Why not re-enact the code of Blackstone's day? Why, the judges were all for it—every one of them—and the only way we got rid of these laws was because juries were too humane to obey the courts.

That is the only way we got rid of punishing old women, of hanging old women in New England—because, in spite of all the courts, the juries would no longer convict them for a crime that never existed. And in that way they have cut down the crimes in England for punishment by death from one hundred and seventy to two. What is going to happen if we get rid of them? Is the world coming to an end? The earth has been here ages and ages before man came. It will be here ages and ages after he disappears, and the amount of people you hang won't make the slightest difference with it.

Now, why am I opposed to capital punishment? It is too horrible a thing for a State to undertake. We are told by my friend, "Oh, the killer does it; why shouldn't the State?" I would hate to live in a State that I didn't think was better than a murderer.

But I told you the real reason. The people of the State kill a man because he killed someone else—that is all—without the slightest logic, without the slightest application to life, simply from anger, nothing else!

I am against it because I believe it is inhuman, because I believe that as the hearts of men have softened they have gradually gotten rid of brutal punishment, because I believe that it will only be a few years until it will be banished forever from every civilized country—even New York; because I believe that it has no effect whatever to stop murder.

Now let's make that simple and see. Where do the murders come from? I would say the second largest class of what we call murders grow out of domestic relations. They follow those deep and profound feelings that are at the basis of life—and the feelings which give the greatest joy are susceptible of the greatest pain when they go a-riot.

Can you imagine a woman following a man around with a pistol to kill him that would stop if you said, "Oh, you will be hanged!" Nothing doing—not if the world was coming to an end! Can you imagine a man doing it? Not at all. They think of it afterward, but not before.

They come from acts like burglary and robbery. A man goes out to rob or to burglarize. Somebody catches him or stops him or recognizes him, and he kills to save himself. Do you suppose there was ever a burglar or robber since the world began who would not kill to save himself? Is there anybody who wouldn't? It doesn't make any difference who. Wouldn't he take a chance shooting? Anyone would do it. Why, my friend himself said he would kill in self-defense. That is what they do. If you are going to stop them, you ought to hang them for robbery—which would be a good plan—and then, of course, if one started out to rob, he would kill the victim before he robbed him.

There isn't, I submit, a single admissible argument in favor of capital punishment. Nature loves life. We believe that life should be protected and preserved. The thing that keeps one from killing is the emotion they have against it; and the greater the sanctity that the State pays to life, the greater the feeling of sanctity the individual has for life.

There is nothing in the history of the world that ever cheapened human life like our great war; next to that, the indiscriminate killing of men by the States.

My friend says a man must be proven guilty first. Does anybody know whether anybody is guilty? There is a great deal implied in that. For me to do something or for you to do something is one thing; for some other man to do something quite another. To know what one deserves requires infinite study, which no one can give to it. No one can determine the condition of the brain that did the act. It is out of the question.

All people are products of two things, and two things only— their heredity and their environment. And they act in exact accord with the heredity which they took from all the past, and for which they are in no wise responsible, and the environment, which reaches out to the farthest limit of all life that can influence them. We all act from the same way. And it ought to teach us to be charitable and kindly and understanding of our fellow-man.

* * *

[At this point, Darrow's time was up and he yielded the stand for Judge Talley's affirmative refutation. The jurist, in a twenty-minute address, attacked the "mawkish sentimentality" which fretted over the fate of murderers while ignoring the victims and their families. He ridiculed Darrow's claim that poverty caused crime, citing wealthy and educated criminals throughout the centuries. The cause of crime, Talley said, was not environmental factors, but men of free will who chose to do evil. To mitigate punishment at a time of unprecedented lawlessness and disrespect for authority, the judge concluded, would mark the beginning of America's decay.

Darrow was also challenged at this juncture by Hon. Louis Marshall, chairman of the debate, who took exception to two of Darrow's claims, that first-rate lawyers were virtually never assigned to defend murderers and that English judges had made no efforts to reduce the number of capital offenses in that country. When Darrow rose to give his negative rebuttal, he was obliged to respond to both men.]

NEGATIVE REBUTTAL (MR. DARROW)

Fifteen minutes in which to answer my friend and the chairman is, perhaps, a little short; but still I can do it.

I want to say, in spite of the chairman having the added dignity of a chairman, that every single statement that I made is true as to the judges and the people. The long list of one hundred and seventy crimes was abolished in England because juries would not convict, until here and there, as Mr. Marshall says, some decent judges circumvented the law. For God's sake, Mr. Marshall, a great lawyer like you talking about judges circumventing the law!

Now, there is no use of mincing matters over this. There isn't any human being who ever investigated this subject that doesn't know it. Every step in humanity, in the administration of the law, has been against courts and by the people—every step. It is all right for judges to write essays about it after it has happened. But over and over again, as in New England, they instructed juries to hang old women for witchcraft, and they refused. And every clergyman stood there, urging it. But they refused, and the old women were not hanged—and that was abolished in New England.

Neither am I making a misstatement when I say that good lawyers are not appointed to defend poor clients. Now, look that up. There may be, here and there, some conspicuous case, but the run of poor clients in a court is without the help of lawyers who are fit to do it. And I will guarantee that every man waiting for death in Sing Sing is there without the aid of a good lawyer.

Now, look that up. I know about these good lawyers. They don't do it. Do you suppose you can get a member of the Bar Association to give his time for nothing? No, he leaves it to us criminal lawyers. Nothing doing—they are taking care of the wealth of corporations. That is what they are doing.

A Voice: How about you?

Mr. Darrow: You want to know about me? I have defended more than half of my clients for nothing. Ever since I began the practice of law, I have given more than a third of the time of every man in my office for nothing. If you want to know about me, that is the truth.

A Voice: Was it by appointment?

Mr. Darrow: No, I never was appointed in my life—never. No judge would take my time by appointing me, any more than they do any lawyer when he wants to get paid for his services.

Now, I am going to finish this debate.

* * *

I did not say that every case in prison was that of a poor person. I said that almost all of them were. My friend said that, probably, to make the utterly absurd statement about a terrible crime—the most terrible, he said—because he read it in the newspapers. He doesn't know anything about it—but it is common for a judge to pass judgment upon things he is not acquainted with.

I said that the great mass of people in prison are the poor. Am I right or am I wrong?

Where do you live that you don't know it? I want to get you to look into this question. And you can't do it in a minute. You can sing hosannas when some poor devil is sent to Kingdom Come, but you can't understand without thought and study.

And, contrary to my friend, everybody doesn't think. He says everybody born has free will. Have they? Everybody born has free will—what do you think of that?

Now, am I right in my statement that it is the poor who fill prisons and who go to the scaffold and who are prosecuted and persecuted? Nobody who knows anything about it believes that the rich are the ones, or any considerable fraction of the rich.

He hasn't given me time to shed tears over the victims of the murderers. I am as sorry for them as he is, because I hate cruelty; no matter who suffers, I hate it. I don't love it and get pleasure out of it when it is done by hanging somebody by the neck until dead—no.

But, now, let me tell you. You can find out. I will guarantee that you can go through the Tombs[2] and you won't find one out of a thousand that isn't poor. You may go to Sing Sing and you will not find one out of a thousand who isn't poor. Since the world began, a procession of the weak and the poor and the helpless has been going to our jails and our prisons and to their deaths. They have been judged as if they were strong and rich and intelligent. They have been victims, whether punishable by death for one crime or one hundred and seventy crimes.

And, we say, this is no time to soften the human heart. Isn't it? Whenever it is the hardest, that is the best time to get at it. When is the time? If he is right, why not re-enact the penal codes of the past? What do you suppose the American Bar Association knows about this subject:

A Voice: More than you.

Mr. Darrow: Do you think so? Then you don't know what you are talking about. Their members are too busy defending corporations. There isn't a criminologist in the world that hasn't said what I have said. And you may read any history or any philosophy and they each and every one point out that after every great war in the world, wherever it was, crimes of violence increased. Do I need to prove it?

Let me ask you this: Do you think man, in any sense, is a creature of environment? Do you think you people could, day by day, wish and hope and pray for the slaughter of thousands of Germans because they were your enemies, and not become callous to suffering? Do you think that children of our schools and our Sunday schools could be taught killing and be as kindly and as tender after it as before? Do you think man does not feel every emotion that comes to him, no matter from what source it comes? Do you think this war did not brutalize the hearts of millions of people in this world? And are you going to cure it by brutalizing it still more by capital punishment?

If capital punishment would cure these dire evils that he tells us about, why in the world should there be any more killing? We have had it always. We have had it long enough. It should have been abolished long ago.

In the end, this question is simply one of the humane feelings against the brutal feelings. One who likes to see suffering, out of what he thinks is a righteous indignation, or any other, will hold fast to capital punishment. One who has sympathy, imagination, kindness and understanding, will hate it and detest it as he hates and detests death.

17 KATHLEEN NORRIS

Prolific author and militant feminist Kathleen Norris (1880-1966) was born in San Francisco, where she began to write for newspapers after the death of her parents in 1899. Following Norris' marriage in 1909, she moved to New York. There she wrote prodigiously—short stories, newspaper articles, and the first of eighty romantic novels. Though her work received little critical acclaim, it had an enormous appeal to the general public, and especially women.

Norris was active in a number of causes, including women's rights, prohibition, disarmament, and abolition of the death penalty. In the 1920s she was affiliated with the American League to Abolish Capital Punishment, on whose behalf she delivered several public addresses, suggesting in one that women should band together to end this punishment devised and administered by men. Yet her *Collier's* article of 1927 made no attempt to divide the sexes on the issue. It voiced familiar arguments intelligently and appealingly packaged for a wide audience of ordinary readers.

Our Jungle Passions (1927)

The daring innovations of one generation are the commonplaces of the next. We gasp dutifully at the mere idea of them. Press and pulpit receive them with whirlwinds of protest. And

From Kathleen Norris, "Our Jungle Passions," *Collier's,* 80 (October 8, 1927), pp. 8-9, 46.

then they are quietly accepted, assimilated. They become part of our everyday lives.

Some special survival of stupidity is suddenly perceived among a mass of prejudices, conventions and inconsistencies. It is exploited, made ridiculous, smoothed away. And, having triumphantly abolished one small error, we move on serenely among a thousand others, sure that we have made everything sane and secure once and for all, and that wisdom will perish with us.

* * *

Every situation in our civilization has its neat little conversational stopper. And especially pious and satisfied are the speakers when the suffering, sin, disease and general misery of the less fortunate are up for consideration.

"But think of the hideous things, the plaques and cushions and celluloid, they would buy if they *did* have the money!" said a rich woman to me once, of frightful poverty in her own city. "It keeps the children busy, and you know how mischievous idle children are!" blandly observed the wife of a mill owner who used a great deal of child labor. "We mustn't go against God's decree," said the authoritative voices of 1840, when a little mitigation of the inevitable pains of childbirth was suggested by the discoverers of anaesthetics and opiates.

WHAT'S BEHIND HANGING?

And so for capital punishment. "Would you fill the world with murderers?" the complacent voices ask triumphantly. And usually the word "hysterical" is introduced.

Strangely enough, this primitive attitude has at last made clear to me the truth regarding the Spanish Inquisition, the burning alive or hanging of innocent old "witches" in Scotland and Massachusetts, the fate of Jeanne the Maid, and all the other cruelties formally enacted in the name of Him who said, "Judge not."

These things went on, under the eyes of pious and God-fearing communities, exactly as they are going on under our self-satisfied eyes today. Virtuous Spanish wives and mothers, reading of Torquemada's achievements and activities, probably sighed in much our twentieth-century fashion and turned from the daily news sheet, or the daily gossip, to the more important matter of the children's meals and schooling and teeth. Doubtless our own exact phrases were on their lips.

"Poor souls, it seems terrible! But why, then, do they do it? They know they will be punished, and they go right on! Nobody WANTS to tear open their breasts with hot pincers, or throw them into boiling oil, but they literally force the authorities—Concha, put that down, dear, Mother doesn't want you to break it. Now, let me see about dinner, Dolores, the señor won't be here, and so the polenta will do nicely—"

And so on, comfortably irresponsible, even as you and I.

Those of us whose loyalty to the Christian ideal has made the history of religious persecutions hard to understand need search no further. It is all explained fully by the exactly similar condition that exists today: the great public unseeing and unhearing, the great machinery of stupid punishment moving almost automatically, and the occasional fanatic—Nero, Torquemada, Jeffries[1] —gladly seizing upon the two for a more than ordinarily atrocious abuse of power.

But, incidentally, cruelty is inherent in human nature, and these things have nothing to do with religion, fundamentally. Too many latter-day essayists and commentators fall into the error of thinking the two things are allied. They love to remember the old story of the shipwrecked mariner who, staggering exhausted upon an unknown shore, beheld a gibbet, with a corpse swinging from it in the wind, and gasped fervently: "Thank God, I'm in a Christian country, at least!"

They forget that had this survivor seen a school, a hospital, a cottage surrounded by flowers, a shelf of great books, or a scientist bending concernedly over the twisted spine of a pauper baby, a bakery or kiddie-car or hurdy-gurdy, he would have been equally sure of his surroundings. And they forget that the naked tribes of the jungles have always had their punitive measures, the Sioux burying their victims up to the neck in hot sand, the Asiatics confining political prisoners for life in coffin-sized boxes, and piling them like cordwood in dark cellars, and even the most civilized of Oriental races practicing girl-murder, the chopping off of hands or feet and the skillfully delicate slicing of human flesh so that the wretched life may be as long as possible preserved within it.

"I'll tell you a story of a big snake and a tiger," says one of the characters in Joseph Vance to a small child. "An' wiz is to eat wiz?" asks the little girl, with rapturous anticipation, perfectly expressing Mr. Schopenhauer's sinister views as to human enjoyment.

There is nothing really amazing about prisons, gibbets, racks and stakes and balls and chains, solitary dungeons and stocks.

What is amazing, what may well give all our pain-sickened souls a little hope, is the occasional flicker of pure goodness, the timid upshooting of real charity and service here and there, the courageous struggle made at long intervals for less suffering, for more kindness, for an attempt at least to understand the strange, unnatural doctrine of loving one's neighbor, forgiving one's enemies.

Indeed, if politics, cupidity, cruelty, love of wealth and power had not made all rulers and leaders at times mere engines of hate and power, we should have been supermen and superwomen, walking a stainless and a painless earth, nineteen hundred years ago.

If, among the first great followers of a Great Leader there had not been poor human greed for prestige, for jewels and land, for power abused far more often than used wisely, what a world we might have had! If education, medicine, government were not so honey-combed by graft and untruth, enmities and prejudices, how different life would be for every one of us! If the eager beginner, ready to dedicate his life to his country, to education, to religion, were not stopped, appalled, on the very threshold by the discovery of cruelty and lies and hypocrisy, even in the very holy of holies, then you and I would have no problems to solve today.

Knowing all this, we have to look through the scummy films and fogs of weakness and selfishness, and discover here and there, as best we may, the glowing jewel of the truth. We have to question unceasingly men's flippant and easy standards in their treatment of other men, less powerful men, asking ourselves continually whether indeed the Inquisition does not still exist—whether this very morning they are not hanging witches on Salem Hill?

And when we come to this point it is to discover in our criminal code a survival of cruelties so barbaric, of tortures so primitive in their jungle nature as to make us believe, as a modern scientist has said, that we are truly but one jump ahead of the cave men of old.

To this day we take one murderer out of every seventeen— not the most cruel or deliberate or fiendishly dangerous of the seventeen by any means, but usually the most obscure and poor and friendless—and subject him to an experience that might well make Joan of Arc look upon her pyre with satisfaction and affection.

For Joan, and all the other company of religious and political martyrs of medieval times, at least was handled quickly. Only a few hours elapsed between the sentence and the stake for them; the poor wretches were out of their troubles almost as soon as they were fairly into them.

But today there is no such merciful swiftness. The assassin— perhaps he is no more than sixteen—is subjected to an elaborately long-drawn-out punishment that sometimes extends over months. In certain cases he fluctuates between the decrees of life and death for years. His hopes are raised and dashed, and raised and dashed with a measure of cruelty that sickens even the most casual reader of breakfast-table headlines, and that, in the condemned boy's family, frequently causes actual madness.

Why do we do it? Statistics have proved, and experience has proved, that capital punishment does not check crime. The famous illustration of this is in the fact that at a time when pickpockets, in batches of ten and twenty, were summarily dispatched, on the gallows, the occasion of a public execution was always the scene of lively thieving, and especial pains had to be taken by the police to warn the witnesses of a pickpocket's hanging that other pickpockets were still alive.

In England in those days there were 160 crimes punishable

by death. In certain less civilized countries death punished all crimes, the degree of their seriousness determining merely the type of cruel death permitted. Mothers of small, penniless families were sent to the gallows for the offense of stealing as little as three yards of cloth, and the families of criminals—in what may have seemed a quite natural sequence to the complacent breakfast-eating matrons of the day, but what seems to us an incredible excess of spite—the families of criminals were split brutally into units, the wretched mother being sent alone to a prison colony, the infants to an asylum, and the older children apprenticed in damp cellars or lonely farms.

Gradually the senseless violence faded. Even the gibbet withdrew into decent obscurity; we don't make public holidays of executions now.

CODDLING HIM WITH CANNIBAL CARE

We kill, indeed, for two offenses: high treason and deliberate murder. And it is an astonishing thing that thousands of persons who regard the stake and the rack, prison floggings, brandings, slavery and galleys, tortures and banishment as the barbarism they are, still feel strongly that the only punishment for the killer is to kill him in turn.

It is hard to follow their line of reasoning. They would not punish theft by stealing from the thief, or set fire to the incendiary's house. They would not bite the man convicted of mayhem, or force infidelity upon the outraged wife. This revenge in kind is worthy only of the Mikado himself, with his decree that the "punishment fit the crime."[2] Why preserve this cruel old law, when we have modified all the others?

Not that our law executes all murderers. No, many of them, if they have influence enough, never come to trial at all, and many others walk free of even the shadow of the prison.

We all remember the recent case of a woman who threatened to kill her husband, loaded a pistol, traveled some fifty miles, went up to his dressing-room, shot him through the heart, and not only walked scot-free from the courtroom a few weeks later, but presently made an excellent second marriage. And we all remember the case of two degenerate boys who killed an innocent child for mere brutal amusement, and to whom clemency and life were granted as a matter of course.[3] About seventeen convicted murderers escape death for every one we punish with scaffold or chair.

Dangerous, these acquitted assassins? A menace to the community? We know better. The last man in the world to try a second murder is the man who has escaped from the consequences of a first. Besides, we are satisfied to pore over the agonies of the one we have marked down, and feed our own minds and the developing minds of our children upon the horrible details of his murder.

For murder it is, far more deliberate and revengeful on our parts than anything he ever did. We actually gloat over it. He is tracked. He is followed down. He is caught in a tumble of dust and pistol shots. He is dragged into court. He is brazen or crushed as his nature dictates, and in either case we are glad to hear about it. He is guilty, and to be duly executed—let's see, this is October, well, some time after January 1st. He pleads desperately with the court. He has to be supported from the room. His mother and sisters have an interview with him. He is lodged at last in Death Row.

At this point, perhaps, the poor, terrified, half-educated, bewildered creature tries to kill himself, or perhaps disturbed nature actually does supply him with pneumonia or acute appendicitis. And then all the machinery of mercy moves blandly to his aid. He is placed in the prison hospital. Nurses administer an anaesthetic. He is watched and made comfortable. Broth and milk are given him. He is made well, and so is ready for death once more.

And when the last rites begin, how blasphemously is the tradition of charity and mercy intermingled with the frightful machinery of annihilation! The trouser-leg of the condemned man is slit. His head is shaved for the more secure passage of the fearful current. His pulse and respiration are carefully taken, in love and concern, as they take those of infants and of our nearest and dearest who lie ill.

His jailers will do anything for him. He may eat and smoke

and read and write what he likes, in those long frightful nights before his execution. Only he must remember that at six o'clock on Monday morning the life and youth and vitality, the hopes and fears, and memories and loves of all his days are to be jarred brutally from the flesh and blood envelope that contains them, and that the strong, tall boy who walked to the chair will be lifted from it, uncaring, a cooling, inert mass of dead clay.

To this cause—the cause of the abolition of capital punishment in America—it is hardly necessary to make converts. It is necessary only to organize and recognize the very strong feeling that already exists on the subject. In every mass meeting, and there have been many of late, there are a few objectors, a few old-fashioned folk who still think it is dangerous not to kill murderers, that public safety demands it, and that, as a witty Frenchman said, the real executioner is Monsieur the Assassin.

But these are a dozen times outnumbered by the more modern thinkers who see in this survival of medieval stupidity only a bit of outgrown machinery still clogging our modern scheme. And it is to these that I am speaking after all, to the men and women who will give this matter a little study, take it up in club or business or political meetings, and hasten the inevitable day when capital punishment shall be no more.

Remember that we never catch the greatest criminals; rich men never go to the chair, nor the sons of rich men. A clever and expensive lawyer can do wonders with even the most flagrant offender, as is proved by the positiveness with which, in the cases of wealthy murderers, we all say comfortably, "But don't worry. He'll never hang!"

Remember that wholesale murderers, the men who kill children in mills, who burn women to death in fire-trap factories, who put poisoned meat into army tins and worthless reeds into life-preservers, the men who sell poisoned liquors and drug cheap foods with formaldehyde don't go to the chair. They never even spend a night in the fetid odors of a jail.

No, we execute only a few hundred criminals a year, and those few are often psychological or pathological cases. One warden told me once of a gangster who was executed in his regime. "He was mentally a swaggering, intelligent, eager-to-be-admired child of eight," he said. "I think more than being killed he minded not being made a hero for what he had done."

"But why keep these dangerous and useless men on, as an expense to the government?" certain women reason anxiously. "They've proved that they're not fit to live. Why not put them out of the way, quickly and painlessly, if you like, so as to rid the commonwealth of the burden once and for all?"

Well, there are two objections to that doctrine. In the first place, we can no longer execute our malefactors quickly and quietly and painlessly. The vagaries and loopholes and potentialities of the law are too complex now. By hurrying their torments you may rob them of their chance. And in the second place, to be able to destroy life merely because it is undesirable is a dangerous power.

Logically, we should have to kill all our hopelessly and criminally insane then, all persons who are without means of support and incurably diseased, the crippled pauper, blind and maimed, the indigent aged, and children born defective. And which of us would feel sure of celebrating another birthday under such laws as these? The temptations to bribe doctors and alienists and judges would spring up on all sides. The heir would mysteriously disappear quietly, quickly and painlessly deprived of a life that stood between somebody else and the fortune. A casual tantrum on Aunt Lizzie's part would convince us all that she was going crazy, like Grandmother White, and the quiet, quick and painless formula would settle poor Aunt Lizzie once and for all.

One of the few arguments that the opponents of the abolition of capital punishment have formulated, up to this point, is that several states in America have abolished it, only to note, or fancy they noted, an increase of crime attributable to its cessation, and that they have therefore returned to it.

But this tidal fluctuation has marked all our national movements: equal suffrage, prohibition, even—long ago—public schooling. The Bourbons came back to France—but not for long. Until 1802 or 1803, and perhaps later, there was a very lively organization for the restoration of monarchical power in the trembling little new-born United States. And within a very few years there was an association opposed to suffrage for women.

The point for us to consider, after all, is whether the execution of an occasional murderer is really in accordance with our modern interpretation of the unchanged divine law.

We no longer beat or exile or imprison children, as our forefathers did. Even the most hopeless case of juvenile degeneracy is handled with common kindness.

And before they have a chance to become criminals the girls and boys of our big cities are the objects of a paternal government care in these good days. Thousands of cases of youthful delinquency, we know now, have been caused in the past by hunger, cold, neglected tonsils and adenoids and blood conditions, immoral parents, improper influences generally.

Schools are beginning to take an interest in a child's actual, as well as his mental, foods. "He needs phosphates, he needs milk, he needs vitamins," say the authoritative voices kindly when, sniveling and convicted, he cowers before them. No mention is made of the once-indispensable whip.

Fathers can't beat children into imbecility in America, and even when the boy or girl is taken away from undesirable guardianship it is not any longer to a great gray asylum, with a cold, gray, mechanical life within. Nowadays each child is placed individually, with a woman chosen for her motherliness and gentleness.

My daily rounds in a certain great city used to take me weekly past an enormous institution where five hundred gray-clad children used to be massed together like lead pencils or stalks of asparagus. It has been emptied now, and the children all scattered into sunshine and fresh air, and the building is used for a school—and so more glory to America, just a little nearer the day when the Kingdom shall come.

Criminals, say those who have studied criminals, are more often than not simply children, with the limitations of children's hates and likes, passions and despairs, animating the big bodies and controlling the arrested minds. The murderer acts with a child's cunning, cruelty and stupidity.

The entire case against capital punishment sums itself into

the simple statement that, in this day and generation, it is out of key. It does not accord with our other attitudes.

It is becoming more and more difficult to impanel a jury that will even consider the decree of death, and more than one warden has admitted that the deliberate murderer counts on this prejudice, and prefers to take his chance of entire escape rather than face a definite life sentence of punishment.

FOR OUR CHILDREN'S SAKE

In England a body of most respectable and responsible bankers requested the abolishment of the death penalty for burglary. They pleaded that the burglar was so sure of escape from sentence that robbery was increasing on all sides. They asked for a severe jail term instead, as having a far more preventive value.

Far from being an object of horrified example to his peers, the condemned murderer is often a sort of hero in Death Row, and his execution merely adds the martyr's laurels to his brow.

There is nothing romantic about a twenty-five-year sentence; and it and its victim are soon forgotten.

Nobody ever heard of a sentimental subscription in behalf of a mere life-termer, unless the circumstances were unusual. The veiled mysterious woman, the discarded wife, the "sweet-pea girl," and the "telephone voice" all center only about the man who may be killed.

Capital punishment is one of the surviving fragments of our jungle passions. Our children would grow into a better and more balanced world without it.

18 LEWIS E. LAWES

The most active advocate of abolition in the 1920s had witnessed or supervised the electrocution of hundreds of criminals. He was Lewis E. Lawes (1883-1947), a native of Elmira, New York, who spent thirty-five years of his life working in prisons, twenty as warden of Sing Sing. An enlightened penologist, Lawes introduced a number of humanitarian reforms at Sing Sing and sought in six books and numerous articles and speeches to bring the public around to his views.

When Lawes was appointed warden of Sing Sing in 1920, he favored capital punishment. Yet, pressed by his new duty of overseeing executions, Lawes soon began to question it seriously. By 1923, he had collected statistics proving to his satisfaction that the death penalty was not a deterrent. At this point his opposition to the punishment was so strong, and he felt so close to its victims, that he resolved to campaign for its abolition. Lawes' first book on the subject, *Man's Judgment of Death,* appeared in 1923; in 1925 he helped organize, then became chairman of, the American League to Abolish Capital Punishment. For years thereafter, he was one of the country's most energetic and renowned opponents of the death penalty.

Lawes' *Life and Death in Sing Sing* (1928) contained the reformer's best attack on capital punishment. Whereas *Man's Judgment of Death* showed great reliance on statistics, sometimes treated with little sophistication, here Lawes combined some statistical data with his unique insights about criminals. It was an effective argument when it was written and it remains so today.

Why I Changed My Mind (1928)

On March 1, 1904, after having served three years in the Regular Army of the United States, I was appointed a guard at Clinton Prison, located in the Adirondack Mountains at Dannemora.

Since that time, I have held positions at Auburn Prison, the New York State Reformatory at Elmira, and the New York City Reformatory. I was superintendent of the latter at Hart's Island and then supervised the removal of the institution and its prisoners to a farm colony at New Hampton, Orange County, N.Y. This background can hardly be considered a fertile soil for the development of a real "sob sister."

During all this time I was a firm believer in the social necessity of capital punishment.

On January 1, 1920, I was appointed warden at Sing Sing, undoubtedly a most difficult prison for an executive officer. I still believed in capital punishment, and realized that, under the laws of the State of New York, it would be necessary for me to assume charge of legal executions.

If you, the reader, were directed by name and official title to kill a designated human being, even though the man was a convicted murderer, it would make you pause—and think. It was my duty to determine the day, in fact the exact hour and minute, death should occur. This gruesome task caused me to seek all obtainable facts relating to capital punishment; not only in America, but in all civilized countries of Europe. No vital problem in the world has been considered with so little accurate knowledge.

I had read, with interest, that, in the Canadian Arctic, 600 miles from Dawson City, two Eskimos were hanged on the gallows by Canadian Mounted Police, pursuant to a sentence of death duly and legally pronounced according to the law of the Dominion Government. The men who were executed had been

From Lewis E. Lawes, *Life and Death in Sing Sing* (Garden City, N.Y.: Garden City Publ. Co., 1928), pp. 137-157. Reprinted by permission of William McGehee, Ann Houston McGehee, and Hazel Chisholm.

themselves the executioners, according to due tribal form and ceremony (to them as legal and binding as any white man's laws), of an Eskimo murderer.[1] But because their assumption of the function of executioners was sanctioned only by tribal law, not by the Dominion law, they paid the identical penalty which a few months before they had meted out.

I had also read the story which comes from French Guinea, of Hespel, who was assigned as executioner of the colony. When convicts were to be put to death, his was the duty of guillotining them. It would seem that he, of all men, should have felt the deterrent effect, if any existed. Yet he himself committed murder and was tried and convicted.[2]

I realize that the most horrible crime that can be committed is the killing of a human being, and, likewise, the most horrible punishment that can be imposed is the killing of a human being; the first the community could not prevent; the second is accomplished with premeditation and deliberation.

Ignorance never rightly settled any question, and it is much easier to be critical than to be correct.

Most of us who take sides on the question of capital punishment do so instinctively, without ever questioning ourselves as to the reasons for our feeling as we do. We form an opinion early in life, and we cling to it, never obligating ourselves to reëxamine our reasons for our belief.

Why is there so much interest in capital punishment at present? It is due to the awakening of the public to danger in the growing murder rate.

Three things that will always arouse interest in this subject are the execution of an innocent man, the commission of an unusually atrocious murder, and the threat to the safety of life in general by sudden social disorder or crimes of violence. The cause at present is the alarming increase of homicide in America.

The death penalty originated among primitive savages by whom it was used to eliminate their unfit; that is, the deformed, crippled, insane, aged, and others, including the overfat, who hampered the family or tribe in its activities.

The fundamental theory of punishment is that it is used for

deterrence, for retribution, and for reformation, and in the case of capital punishment there is a further basis urged for its retention—the need of eliminating those who menace the life and security of society.

Reformation, obviously, cannot be accomplished by the death penalty.

The argument that capital punishment is necessary as a process of elimination is faulty; it is unscientific in its application.

The idea of punishment of any type solely as retribution is gradually disappearing. History condemns capital punishment. It must not be forgotten that the death penalty has been tried before on a colossal scale, judged, and found wanting. There is no place for sentiment either of hate or sympathy in dealing with capital punishment, any more than there is in business life. What is needed is common sense and understanding.

Death fades into insignificance when compared with life imprisonment. To spend each night in jail, day after day, year after year, gazing at the bars and longing for freedom, is indeed expiation.

Executions, like war, brutalize men; the more that take place, the greater the number of people there are to execute. The man about to die becomes a hero.

The executed man passes quickly from the mind, while the criminal in life imprisonment remains as a living symbol of the awful consequences of an awful act.

The United States is a nation that leads the world in scientific progress, that boasts achievement in the adjustment of industrial relations and in dealing with complex social and welfare problems, yet hangs its head in shame at 11,000 homicidal deaths each year. In the face of this, why do we cling blindly to capital punishment? In spite of many signs that point to its positive failure as a deterrent, why do we retain our faith in its efficacy? Why do we believe that a punishment applied to one of every eighty homicidal crimes will deter others? It is an actual fact that where the murders are numbered by the thousands, those who go to the chair or the scaffold are numbered by the tens. Even in England statistics show that less than 5 per cent. of homicidal crimes result in imposition of the death penalty. People say that capital punishment might deter if it were enforced. The point is that until the characteristics of mankind change, crime can never be overcome or eradicated. That is why, as a punishment, the death penalty will always remain a failure. The causes of crime are economic and sociological with roots far deeper than mere punishment can hope to affect. We find that whatever deterrence there is in punishment lies in its certainty, not in its severity. If the solution of the crime problem is severity, we are illogical if we stop short of its limits.

I am not asking that we abandon a scheme of punishment that is in successful operation. We have capital punishment and have had it for generations, yet we have a high homicidal rate in shameful contrast to the rest of the civilized world. We are just as far to-day from successful solution of the homicide problem as we have ever been.

* * *

Why do states which have the most legal executions also have the greatest number of homicides in proportion to population?

Why do those states where lynchings are most frequent also have the greatest number of murderers?

If the fear of death is a deterrent, why is it that a man will commit murder in prison, where the chances of escaping detection are one in 10,000?

What explanation is there of the fact that several counties in New York State had no murder convictions for a number of years, some of them for long periods, yet when the first conviction for murder occurred with the subsequent execution of the murderer at Sing Sing, it was immediately followed by a number of murders?

I ask that others will bring to this problem an open and unbiased mind, will ask themselves these questions and answer them without prejudice. I find that those who have given real study to the subject usually favour the abolition of the death penalty.

To have been retained so long in our system of penology, capital punishment must have or appear to have some justification. Let us see whether it is really necessary, whether it has ever had any measure of success in dealing with capital crime.

In the first place, is death necessary in order to balance the debt of the individual to society for the wrong that has been done? This conception of punishment is based on the old belief of retaliation, on the Mosaic Law of "an eye for an eye"—and if we are to follow this old Mosaic Law, why not, with equal logic, follow the Biblical injunction, "Thou shalt not kill"? This theory of retaliation is not used in fixing punishment for other crimes. The state should not stoop to the ethics of the common murderer. The balancing of that debt is a matter between the man and his Creator. The light of modern penology is beginning to demonstrate that capital punishment is not a solution but an avoidance of the real problem; that many crimes, even capital crimes, are the results of maladjustment of the person and not an evil that is inborn and which cannot be cured but must perish with the individual. As a general proposition, I do not subscribe to the theory that all moral evil is the result of physical evil.

Let us consider for a moment the types of individuals who commit these 11,000 capital crimes each year. Many murders occur under the stress of violent emotions, others are the result of a sudden flash of anger. Where is the man that has not at some moment in his life had the overwhelming impulse to kill? Sometimes the difference between the penalty of death and that of a brief period in prison is but the space of a few inches measured on the victim's body, a difference due to the slightest failure of coördination between the mind and the muscular reaction of the man wielding the gun or knife. The impulse to kill is the same. The one possessing coördination and skill succeeds. Still, other murders are committed because of trifling causes, a desire for revenge or some fancied grievance. Of those who commit these crimes not a few are medically, if not legally, insane. These are border-line cases, men who, if they had not committed the particular crime, would sooner or later have given evidence of insanity. After commutation from death, many have gone insane; that is, have been declared legally insane. Where was the line of demarcation? Would they not have been just as insane at the time of execution if they had not been commuted? Not a few murderers of the abnormal category have a mentality as low as a six- or eight-year-old child. There are very few who murder coldly, deliberately, remorselessly. What few there are present the same problem as the dangerous insane and must be controlled in the same manner. We do not advocate killing the insane because they are dangerous or difficult to handle.

Is the death of the murderer necessary as a measure of public safety? Must we admit that we kill because we can devise no better way? that it is the easiest solution of the dilemma? Contrary to public belief, life imprisonment is not an uncertain punishment. Since 1889, when electrocution for murder was legally established in New York State, 431 men and 6 women have been committed to Sing Sing Prison for execution. Of these, 266, including two women, were electrocuted. Before the date set for electrocution, 2 died natural deaths, 3 committed suicide, 2 drowned while escaping, and 11 were pronounced insane and transferred to Dannemora State Hospital; 13 are now in the death house, making a total of 297 who are dead, insane, or awaiting execution.

The convictions of 54 men and 2 women were reversed by the Court of Appeals. Of these 31 were acquitted; 5 were reconvicted and executed; one was reconvicted and his sentence commuted to natural life; 14 were convicted of murder, second degree; 3 of manslaughter, first degree; 1 of manslaughter, second degree, and 1 is awaiting execution. One woman was acquitted and the other was convicted of murder in the second degree. The sentences of 72 men and 2 women were commuted to imprisonment for natural life, and of these only 3 have later been pardoned and only 7 discharged by special commutation; the remainder are now in prison, in the hospital for the criminal insane, or have died in prison.

In the same period (1889-1927), there were 639 commitments for murder, second degree, and 2,112 for manslaughter, first degree. This gives a total of 3,188 commitments for what is popularly known as murder. Thus the death penalty has been exacted in 63 per cent. of the total commitments for murder, first degree, and for 8.3 per cent. of all commitments for murder.

The fact that 31 persons were acquitted and 19 others convicted in a lower degree after having been convicted of a capital crime causes one to wonder how many of the 261 who were executed might not have received new trials and have been acquitted or convicted on a charge which did not exact the death penalty if they too had had money or friends to engage the most able legal counsel.

One man, who fortunately received a commutation to natural life only a few minutes before he was to be strapped in the chair, was later proved positively to have been innocent. Perhaps there were other such cases.

If juries and judges can err in one proved case, is it not possible that there may have been other errors which cannot now be corrected because the unfortunate man is dead? As a matter of fact, the juries and judges erred in 13 per cent. of the original commitments for murder, first degree; and 51 per cent.—more than half—of these persons were acquitted on re-trial as not guilty. Is not the percentage of probable error entirely too high to warrant a penalty that is irrevocable?"

In view of the relatively large number of cases in which the higher court has reversed the lower courts, the number of commutations to life imprisonment is not large. If the lower courts can err in 13 per cent. of the cases, it is within the realm of possibility that a mistake is made in an additional 18 per cent. of the total cases.

IT WILL BE NOTED THAT ONLY THREE PARDONS AND SEVEN SPECIAL COMMUTATIONS HAVE BEEN GRANTED. THIS FACT ANSWERS THE FREQUENTLY HEARD CHARGE THAT LIFE IMPRISONMENT DOES NOT REALLY MEAN LIFE IMPRISONMENT AND IT IS NOT, THEREFORE, A PROPER PENALTY FOR MURDER IN THE FIRST DEGREE.

The further assumption that the murderer is a dangerous criminal from whom society must be protected is flatly disproved by the figures which show that 90 per cent. of the men and women committed for murder, first degree, had no previous felony record. Nor is there a single instance in which a prisoner pardoned or specially commuted for murder, first degree, returned to Sing Sing Prison because of a second homicide.

A study of Sing Sing's records running back to 1850 shows

only slight variations in commitments for homicide. The percentage at no time runs above 8 per cent.; commitments for murder, first degree, average about 1 per cent.

This study also shows that 51 per cent. of the cases of murder, first and second degree, have been committed by foreigners, in comparison with a rate of 26 per cent. for all other crimes committed by foreigners.

From 1850 to 1870 the foreign-born Irish led in the number of commitments for murder, and from 1870 to 1889 the native-born of Irish stock led, with foreign-born Germans second and foreign-born Italians third. Between 1890 and 1919 the foreign-born Italians took the lead, the Irish second; Negro, third; English-Scotch, fourth; German, fifth. From 1920 to the present time, the foreign-born Italians have led, with the Negro in second place; the Irish stock, third; and English-Scotch fourth.

From 1890 to 1927 those of Italian stock (91 per cent. foreign-born) lead with 28 per cent. of all commitments for murder; Irish stock (20 per cent. foreign-born), second with 19 per cent.; Negro (9 per cent. foreign-born), third with 14 per cent.; English-Scotch stock (foreign-born 19 per cent.) and German stock (foreign-born 46 per cent.), fourth with 10 per cent. each; miscellaneous stock (foreign-born 50 per cent.), 19 per cent.

In other words, the typical murderer of any given period comes from that race which is making a place for itself in a new environment. The Irish led for a long period following their immigration and the Germans were a close second following their immigration period. The Italians then took first place, and now the Negro, who is migrating from the South, is rapidly forging toward the lead.

One often hears of the low murder rate in England and other foreign countries, and we are told that this condition is due to more stringent laws, and so on. In the light of these figures, it seems likely that England's favourable record is due to the homogeneity of her population. Murder, in its final analysis, is due to extrinsic conditions rather than to an inherent instinct for killing. Is society justified in taking a life for a crime which is a result of conditions for which it is largely responsible and in exacting a death penalty where the percentage of probable error has been proved to be so large? Would not life imprisonment answer the purpose as well and with greater justice to all?

Life imprisonment does not present a real difficulty in the control of the murderer. If it did, we would expect to see it reflected in the homicide rates in those states and countries where the death penalty is abolished; in the eight states of the United States and in Holland, Rumania, Italy, Portugal, Belgium, and half of Switzerland. We should expect them to have higher rates, whereas, in fact, usually they have lower rates.

Many actual slayers and potential murderers are confined in the Matteawan and Dannemora state hospitals for the criminal insane and there can be no capital punishment for an inmate of either institution who commits murder.

The institutional officials, from the records, seem to be as safe as in the prison where capital punishment may be enforced. Prison wardens of the states where capital punishment has been abolished are nearly all of one mind in agreeing that it is unnecessary as a protection to prison officials. I quote below opinions that are based on experience and actuality, not theory:

Warden Buker[3] of the State Prison of Maine writes me as follows:

With reference to your letter of Nov. 28th to ex-Warden Eaton, concerning capital punishment, etc., will say that as I have been warden at this institution for a period of only six months, I am not able to express a general opinion in the matter.

As near as I can determine from past records and conversations with older exployees of the institution, for over a period of fifty years there has never been an employee of this institution killed. Many years ago before that time, a warden was killed here by an inmate, and the inmate was afterwards hanged in the prison, capital punishment at that time being the law in this state.[4]

We have very few assaults here by the inmates upon our guards in any way. Speaking for myself, I do not consider that capital punishment is necessary at this institution to protect the lives of guards and officers.

Warden Linscott[5] of the State Prison of Rhode Island has written me as follows:

In giving my opinion as to whether or not capital punishment is necessary in order to protect the lives of prison guards and officers, I do not hesitate to say that it is not necessary.

In this state there has been no murder of prison guards in the past ten years and I am reasonably sure that such has not occurred since the institution was established.

Warden Jackson[6] of the State Prison at Jackson, Mich., has written me as follows:

I wish to say that we have inspected our records and although we did not go back over a great period of years, we were unable to find that any guards have been killed by inmates at this institution in the past ten years.

Referring to the law that is suggested, providing that capital punishment should be inflicted when guards and officers are killed in service, I do not know as this would be any more essential than if citizens were killed by persons in commission of crime, and I am doubtful that a law of this kind would be any more effective than our present law which does not provide such a penalty.

Warden Jameson[7] of the South Dakota Penitentiary, Sioux Falls, S.D., writes as follows:

I wish to advise that there has not been any. (Killings or assaults.)

Since the State of South Dakota abolished the capital punishment law, we have had but one serious outbreak at this institution and at that time one officer was stabbed, but not seriously. I do not think that capital punishment would act as a deterrent if a man saw an opportunity to escape from prison. He would attempt it whether or not he was faced with the fact that he could be tried and put to death if he took the life of another.

Warden Mackey[8] of the State Penitentiary, Lansing, Kans., has written me:

I have been acquainted with this institution more or less intimately since 1890, and have made inquiry of present employees who have been employed as long as that or longer, and I am positive there never has been a prison employee killed in this prison.

Capital punishment never has been inflicted here. The prison was established in 1861, and officers on duty in the yard are not allowed to carry guns or clubs, excepting at night, when yard patrolmen are permitted to carry clubs. An officer here is not allowed to strike an inmate unless in self-defence—his remedy is to report the inmate to the deputy warden's office—and I firmly believe the fact that guns are not allowed in the enclosure and that officers are not allowed to strike inmates excepting under great provocation has a great deal to do with our lack of fatalities.

The murderer is not a criminal in his nature as we ordinarily understand the term. During twenty-three years I have known many men who have been commuted from death, and, invariably, they have been quiet, dependable, and trustworthy. I have placed them in posts of responsibility, and they have measured up to the trust. Have you ever heard of a murder committed by a released murderer? When we examine the records of men convicted of murder, we become impressed by the preponderance of those who are "one-crime men." Most of those who come into Sing Sing death house have committed the crime as a first offence. The record of 180 men convicted of various degrees of homicide and paroled from Sing Sing during a period of five years disclosed only three brought back for violation of parole. Those who are commuted from the Death House in prison often exercise great influence for good. Where would society have profited if it had killed these men? It might have satisfied a momentary craving for revenge, but that is all.

Finally, is it necessary as an example to others to kill the murderer? If it is, why surround the act with so much secrecy? It is surely not a deterrent example to perform an act furtively. If the state really believes that execution is necessary to deter others, it should execute openly and unashamed. Does not this furtiveness carry the suggestive thought that the spectacle of legalized killing by the state breeds on the part of the unthinking masses a hardened outlook toward murder which is harmful rather than effective as a deterrent?

It is also very true that the thought of the penalty is rarely in the mind of the person who commits murder. Few crimes of murder are of sufficient premeditation to permit any regard to the consequences in the mind of the perpetrator. The thought of death is far from a powerful deterrent; its very remote threat is of little weight as compared to the temptation of some desperate exigency or to the passion aroused by some overwhelming impulse.

How is it possible to suppose that any penalty that is inflicted so spasmodically can be a deterrent? Statistics show that everywhere it is a punishment it is conspicuous by the infrequency of its application. It may, with truth, be said that the only certain thing about capital punishment is the uncertainty with which it is inflicted. We cannot avoid the conclusion that the sureness of detection reflected in the number of prosecutions in proportion to crimes, the certainty of punishment reflected in the number of convictions, the celerity and accuracy of punishment reflected in the few appeals, are the determining factors in a low proportion of homicidal and other crimes, rather than the severity of the punishment which is meted out. The deterrent effect of a law seems not to depend on the ugliness of its threat, but rather on the certainty and celerity with which the threatening gesture reaches home.

* * *

Definite figures show that capital punishment cannot be justified. We find, in general, fewer homicidal crimes in states which have abolished the death penalty than in those, comparable in character, where it is retained.

Not only does capital punishment fail in its justification, but no punishment could be invented with so many inherent defects. It is an unequal punishment in the way it is applied to the rich and to the poor. The defendant of wealth and position never goes to the electric chair or to the gallows. Juries do not intentionally favour the rich, the law is theoretically impartial, but the defendant with ample means is able to have his case presented with every favourable aspect, while the poor defendant often has a lawyer assigned by the court. Sometimes such assignment is considered part of political patronage; usually the lawyer assigned has had no experience whatever in a capital case. Even after death, distinction prevails. Where there are relatives who can afford to do so, the body may be claimed and taken away. The law states that the unclaimed body shall be buried on prison ground and in quicklime.

It is a punishment, too, that falls most severely on the family of the defendant; for the murderer himself, his suffering is soon over. The wives, the mothers, the children are the ones who suffer. I yield to no one in acknowledging the duty we owe to the family of the murderer's victim, but I have very grave doubt whether society is right in inflicting this terrible burden on the innocent family of the murderer, believing, as I do, that the punishment serves no purpose other than to get rid of the murderer.

It is for a punishment of absolute finality; there is no opportunity for the correction of mistakes. For that very reason, some juries will not inflict a punishment so irrevocable. I have known several men who have been very close to the chair, and who, afterward, were found to be innocent. Still other men have been commuted to life imprisonment in almost the last moments of their lives. If they deserved commutation, they did not deserve death, and yet they were within a few moments of it. Finally, it has so many legal safeguards that it is slow in operation and so arbitrary that it cannot be made to fit all of the varying degrees of even first-degree murder. By reason of all these defects, it remains a useless punishment too seldom applied by judge and jury to be a warning.

Capital punishment has never been and never can be anything but an uncertainty. It is a punishment for revenge, for retaliation, not for protection. We can have a punishment that is possible of application with both certainty and celerity, that presents an opportunity for individualization of treatment, and that is in accord with modern criminological methods. Can we not have the vision to see the possibilities of the future, the courage and faith to progress toward those possibilities?

19 ROBERT G. ELLIOTT

An otherwise undistinguished appeal against capital punishment can have considerable effect when its author is the official executioner for six states. Robert G. Elliott (1874-1939), a native New Yorker, grew up with a fascination for the new science of electricity. After working for private electrical companies for several years, in 1898 he was appointed assistant engineer at Clinton Prison. Once, in an emergency, Elliott threw the switch to electrocute a criminal and it was this experience which suggested his name to Lewis E. Lawes and other officials looking for a new state executioner in 1926. Eventually, New Jersey, Pennsylvania, Massachusetts, Connecticut, and Vermont also contracted for his services. In the next thirteen years he electrocuted almost four hundred felons, including Bruno Hauptmann, kidnapper and murderer of the Lindbergh baby, Nicola Sacco, and Bartolomeo Vanzetti.

Elliott always opposed the death penalty, but he felt that he was a mere functionary in an immoral process created and sustained by others. He explained his feelings on the subject and cast the loathing usually accorded executioners back upon the public in a series of articles which appeared in *Collier's* magazine in 1938.

It is Assumed that I am in Favor of the Death Penalty (1938)

The happiest day I'll ever experience, if I live that long, will be the day that capital punishment is wiped from the statute

From Robert G. Elliott, "I Am Against Capital Punishment," *Collier's,* 102 (October 22, 1938), pp. 28, 31-33.

books, leaving me without any more business, a man out of a job.

Ever since this series of articles began to appear, my friends have asked me, "Do you believe capital punishment is necessary and should be inflicted in this country?"

My answer is "No."

I do not think the death penalty is necessary to protect society and I do not believe it should be inflicted. I firmly believe that the time is coming when death by law will become only a grisly memory throughout the United States, as it already has become in seven states—Maine, Michigan, Minnesota, North Dakota, Rhode Island, South Dakota and Wisconsin.

When that will be, of course, no man knows. We will have capital punishment until a majority of citizens decide that the ancient law of "an eye for an eye and a tooth for a tooth" has been outmoded in the light of present-day intelligence and ethics.

Until that day, I believe it would be wholly just to require that the judge and the jury who demand the death sentence be present in the death chamber as witnesses at the always awful moment that the spark of life is crushed from the man or woman over whom they have sat in judgment. Thus would the real consequence of the verdict and the repugnant horror of the legal slaying be impressed upon them.

I was called for jury duty once, a few years ago, in Queens County, New York. I reported to the office of the clerk, presented the notice and explained in a few words who I was and the position I held as state executioner. I was told, in effect, to get out and not to come back.

"We'll have no further need of you, Mr. Elliott," said the court officer.

I said, "Thank you," and departed. That was all right with me. I should hate, more than anything else I can think of, to be charged with the duty of deciding whether a man is to live or die. Because I don't happen to believe it necessary that any man die for the safety of the rest of us. And I don't believe that man should be permitted to take away the one thing that cannot be restored—life.

Warden Lewis E. Lawes of Sing Sing, who appointed me, is

one of the outstanding articulate foes of capital punishment. No one in the death chamber at Sing Sing is more grave and more deeply affected during an execution than Warden Lawes. I have never seen him look up after the condemned man was strapped in the chair. Usually he bows his head and stands immobile, turned slightly away from the chair. If capital punishment finally is abolished, the name of Lawes will occupy close to the No. 1 position in the list of those to whom humanity owes a debt.

Self-appointed analysts, amateur sociologists, persons who would become evangelists in the fight against capital punishment are the authors of a large part of the mail that comes to me, some of it addressed to my home in Richmond Hill, much of it to the various prisons in which I perform executions. Many of the letters, of course, are bitter. It is assumed by most of the writers that, being an executioner, I am in favor of capital punishment. I have never replied to the letters, nor to the frequent invitations received from well-meaning bodies to speak on various phases of capital punishment. These articles have constituted my first written or spoken views on the subject.

Most of the letters blame society, our failure to guide the young man in his formative years by the provision of proper social, recreational and vocational training. With these, of course, I am in substantial agreement.

Only a few weeks ago I talked with a young New York newspaperman, outstandingly successful in his field. He told me that one of the murderers whom I executed at Sing Sing a couple of years ago had been a member of his boyhood "gang" in Brooklyn.

"As boys in knee pants, we were all alike," he told me. "We played pranks, hooked apples from fruit stands, outran the cops and did the things that any city kid does. But Joe's parents drifted apart. No one kept after him to see that he stayed in school or that he held a job. He went from bad to worse, finally decided that the world owed him a living, and at last found himself in a spot where he had to shoot his way out of trouble. So you got him. I was luckier. I had somebody to keep an eye on me."

I think that's true enough. And yet, as this newspaperman spoke, my mind went back to the night in January, 1936, when four smooth-cheeked, intelligent-looking youths, two of them twenty-one, two of them only twenty, came to the chair at Sing Sing in one of the most harrowing experiences I can recall.[1] It was the first time in many years that the bleak, bare walls of that brightly lighted chamber had seen as many as four men die within a few minutes. And never had four men so young died together. To me there is something especially poignant, and always has been, in the execution of a young man to whom life's best things should still be beckoning.

The four boys were to die for the murder of a New York policeman who had surprised them in the act of burglarizing a New York shop twelve months earlier.

One was the son of a minister in a Southern city. He had had every advantage of a home in which good breeding, good books, religious influences, had pervaded the family circle. He was the first to go. As they lifted his limp body from the chair to the white wheel-table to trundle it into the autopsy room, his heartbroken mother was outside the prison gate in an automobile. Unable to leave her son in his last hour but unable, of course, to watch him die, she had fainted away in complete collapse as the moment approached that, she knew, would end his life.

Here, certainly, was a case in which lack of training, lack of guidance, lack of parental devotion, could not be blamed for the fact that a boy had walked "the last mile."

The second youth who was led into the death chamber that night, on the contrary, was one who had had fewer advantages. But the third had been a high-school athlete, a boy who had enjoyed what we imagine is the valuable training of athletic sports. The fourth, again, was a product of circumstances that should have been conducive to a useful, honest life.

Never, I believe, not even excepting the night that Ruth Snyder and Judd Gray died in that same chair,[2] have I seen witnesses so moved by the sight of death in the electric chair. One witness collapsed and had to be taken from the room. Others covered their eyes with their hands or with handkerchiefs. It was little wonder. I, who could not do that, wished that I could. Never has the work of manning the lethal switch been more repugnant.

But why were they there? Superficially, the reason was that they had come under the baleful influence of a man who, formerly a respected citizen, had become a criminal and had taught them the ways of crime. But considering the influences that had surrounded at least three of them, there was every reason why they should have been launching successful lives.

What is the answer? I'm sure I don't know. But I do know that man becomes more humane in his punishment. For instance, crimes of theft, which in the grim justice of only two or three centuries ago brought the death penalty do so no longer. Where we still demand the death penalty for murder, we seek more humane methods. And, so far as I have been able to discover, the states of our own country and the nations in other parts of the world that have outlawed the death penalty entirely have been visited by no blight of murder.

Slowly but surely the public's attitude toward the legal taking of a life is changing. I may not live to see it but I hope my children and my grandchildren will live to see the day when legal slayings, whether by electrocution, hanging, lethal gas or any other method, are outlawed in all the United States.

20 HERBERT EHRMANN

Herbert Ehrmann (1891-1970), lawyer and philanthropist, was born in Louisville, Kentucky, but lived most of his life in Massachusetts. A graduate of Harvard College and Harvard Law School, Ehrmann began a long affiliation with the Boston law firm of Goulston and Storrs in 1921. It was this association which involved him, in 1925, with the Sacco—Vanzetti case. The trial, the appeals, and the eventual execution of his clients made an indelible impression on the young lawyer, as it did on many others connected with the case. Ehrmann wrote two books on the subject, *The Untried Case* (in 1933) and *The Case That Will Not Die—Commonwealth vs. Sacco and Vanzetti* (in 1969).

Throughout his long legal career, Ehrmann had ample opportunity to observe how capital punishment operated within the criminal justice system. He drew on this rich experience in the scholarly article he wrote for the *Annals of the American Academy of Political and Social Science* in 1952. This article, excerpted here, was as convincing and complete an argument as could be devised with the data available in that year.

The Death Penalty and the Administration of Justice (1952)

Armchair criminology is among the least reliable of the social sciences. It is, however, one of the most popular. To qualify as

From Herbert Ehrmann, "The Death Penalty and the Administration of Justice," *Annals of the American Academy of Political and Social Science,* 284 (November 1952), pp. 73-84.

an expert on crime one needs only to be a legislator, a lawyer, a prosecutor, or a judge. Such persons may actually be authorities in the field. Generally, however, they have had no scholastic preparation and no special experience beyond a few sporadic episodes. All too often the opinions of individuals in such positions are accorded a factitious authority merely because of the office which they hold. Unfortunately, the public does not understand the meagerness of experience and inadequacy of data on which such views are so frequently based.

IRRATIONAL VIEWS

Discussions concerning the death penalty have been especially confused by the voices of unqualified "authorities." For nearly a century and a half change has been delayed and the acquisition of real knowledge hampered by sonorous pronouncements of the eminent, but uninformed. When in 1810 Sir Samuel Romilly introduced a bill in Parliament to abolish capital punishment for stealing five shillings or more from a shop, it was unsupported by a single judge or magistrate.[1] Speaking for the unanimous opposition to the bill by his judicial colleagues in the House of Lords, Lord Ellenborough, Chief Justice of the King's Bench, predicted that the repeal of this law would lead to abolition of the death penalty for stealing five shillings from a dwelling house, in which case no man could "trust himself for an hour without the most alarming apprehensions that, on his return, every vestige of his property will be swept away by the hardened robber."[2]

These and similar laws were eventually repealed without any increase in the number of offenders in the particular class of crime. In fact, the absolute number of such offenders diminished.[3] As lawyer and judge, Lord Ellenborough was no fool. Although inclined to be harsh in criminal cases, he did much to bring the civil law into harmony with mercantile practice. He was a profound legal scholar. He knew the value of evidence. Yet, when it came to the death penalty, he felt qualified to pronounce an authoritative judgment without the aid of any evidence whatsoever other than his own emotional reflexes. His contemporaries accorded his words the respect due his high position; but history has proved that the great Lord Ellenborough, in discussing capital punishment, was talking nonsense.

The efforts to remove or modify the death penalty for the crime of murder have run a similar course. Fortunately, there has now been enough experience with abolition and curtailment to establish as a fact that the repeal of capital punishment is not followed by an increase in the number of murders, nor does its restoration result in a diminution. Whatever other purpose the death penalty may serve, it is now obvious that, in a settled community, it is not needed to protect society from murderers.

Nevertheless, even in this narrow area where data are abundant and easy to obtain, pronouncements of the Ellenborough variety continue to confuse the public. As late as 1950, the legislative halls of Massachusetts still rang with dire predictions that the passage of a bill to give juries a chance to designate life imprisonment as a penalty for murder in the first degree would result in loosing upon the people of the Commonwealth a horde of savage murderers. This was at a time when 38 other states and the federal government already had some form of the alternate penalty and 6 states had abolished capital punishment!

ALTERNATE AND MANDATORY AREAS COMPARED

A similar disregard of experience frequently marks discussion of the effect of the death penalty on the administration of justice. For instance, it was claimed that the giving of the power to impose the alternate penalty of life imprisonment would result in the complete disuse of capital punishment. Those making the claim seemed to think that this would be very bad indeed. In 1948 the then governor of Massachusetts vetoed the proposed bill granting juries the right to choose life imprisonment instead of death on conviction in murder cases, stating in his veto message that such a law would abolish capital punishment by "indirection"; that it pays "lip service to capital punishment" and then "effectively proceeds to destroy it."

Coming from the governor, the veto message was treated with

respect;[4] but it was only another example of armchair criminology. For the ten years ending with 1946, Massachusetts, under a law making death a mandatory punishment for first degree murder, had 12 executions. For the same period, alternate-penalty states had the following record: New Jersey, with a slightly smaller population, 16 executions; Pennsylvania, with something more than twice the population, 50 executions; and New York, with about three times the population, 118 executions. For the same period, North Carolina, a mandatory state, had 118 executions, and its neighbor, Georgia, somewhat smaller in population, under the alternate penalty, had 102.

There are too many variables—such as homicide rates, population characteristics, police efficiency, prosecution standards, jury attitudes, executive clemency—for any quantitative comparison of states within these groups, but the figures indicate clearly that capital punishment continues to flourish in states which provide the alternate penalty.

On the other hand, the residents in certain areas have, in practice, virtually abolished capital punishment in both mandatory and alternative penalty jurisdictions. Vermont, a mandatory state, has had only 2 executions in 28 years; New Hampshire, an alternate state, has had only 1 execution in 28 years; South Dakota, an alternate state, has had only 1 in the 10 years since it restored the death penalty; Nebraska, an alternate state, has had only 2 in 28 years.[5] In Massachusetts during a period of 50 years under the mandatory penalty, Worcester County, with a half-million population, had only 2 executions; Bristol, a sizable county, only 1; Berkshire County, of moderate size, none; and some of the smaller counties, none. . . .

* * *

DEATH PENALTY AND ACQUITTALS

A closely related problem is presented by the claim that the mandatory sentence of death upon a finding of guilty of murder in the first degree results in more acquittals. Some of those who express this opinion are extremely well informed penologists.[6] The reason given is that the infliction of death is so repugnant to most people that juries tend to avoid a conviction if possible. Curiously enough, proponents of the death penalty seem to confirm this tendency in a backhanded sort of way. In arguing that the danger of a miscarriage of justice is slight in a capital case, they frequently urge that the evidence must be overwhelming before a jury would vote to consign a fellow being to his death.

Convincing data on this subject are not available. We may, however, accept the reasoning and observations that the reluctance of jurymen to convict, where death is the penalty, leads, in some cases, to acquittal. Nevertheless, one may well question the conclusion that the net over-all result is a larger percentage of acquittals. There are complicating factors working in the opposite direction. For instance, numbers of prospective jurors are frequently excused from serving in capital cases because of opposition to the death penalty. Sometimes the numbers are so great that the judges assail the veniremen for "jury dodging," and these denunciations reach the newspaper headlines.[7]

This process of weeding out jurors who will not serve because of the death penalty tends to produce an unbalanced jury. Those most likely to lean emotionally toward the defendant are eliminated. No doubt the great majority of those who remain view the death penalty with considerable distaste, but their emotional attitude is likely to be negative. Inevitably, however, on some juries there will be those who favor the use of the death penalty. These people are occasionally forcefully articulate and capable of swaying jurors with less positive attitudes. They are not counterbalanced by those most reluctant to inflict death. Thus hostility toward the death penalty may actually, in some cases, produce juries which are most likely to convict the accused.[8]

EMOTION AND PREJUDICE

There are other factors which work for conviction rather than acquittal in a capital case. Of all crimes, murder is most likely to produce a violent emotional public reaction, a demand for vengeance, a feeling that the perpetrator "deserves" to be

put to death. Jurymen cannot help sharing this feeling. The idea
that a jury "weighs" the evidence in a criminal case to decide
whether the accused is guilty beyond a reasonable doubt, conveys a wrong picture of the process. In many cases it is merely a
question of what evidence the jury chooses to believe. If the
government's case rests largely on identification testimony and
the defense is an alibi, the jury does not "weigh" one against
the other. If it believes the identification testimony, the alibi is
thrown out of the scales of justice entirely, and vice versa.
Where there is conflict of testimony, people tend to believe that
which they would like to believe. The emotional drive to punish
someone for an atrocious murder frequently plays an important
part in conditioning a jury for believing the evidence which
proves the guilt of the accused.

In a recent Massachusetts case the only issue was the criminal
responsibility of the defendant, who had killed his wife. According to the opinion of the Supreme Judicial Court, the evidence portrayed "the sudden destruction, while in apparent
good health, of one member of a harmonious and cultured
household by the only other member, in a series of acts paradoxically done, it is confessed, solely in kindness to benefit the
victim, yet revoltingly achieved in the grossest barbarity with
the crudest of weapons."[9] Two eminent psychiatrists testified
that the defendant was not criminally responsible at the time of
the killing. There was no medical testimony that he was responsible. Nevertheless, the jury returned a verdict of guilty.
The conclusion that the accused was sane beyond a reasonable
doubt can be explained only on the ground of emotion aroused
by the sheer horror of the deed itself. Although there was no
error of law, the Supreme Judicial Court ordered a new trial
under a statute passed in 1939 for the review of capital cases.[10]
The defendant was tried a second time, found insane, and committed to a mental institution.

When prejudice is added to the emotional reactions induced
by a slaying, the jury finds even greater difficulty in believing
evidence offered for the accused.[11] If the jury is composed of
the dominant or "in-group" and the defendant and his witnesses
belong to an "out-group"—as they frequently do—the defen-

dant's evidence is often discounted to zero. The jury tends to believe that foreigners, Negroes, or members of any minority group will lie for one another and "stick together" under all circumstances.

The United States Supreme Court has recognized this human failing, in holding that the exclusion of Negroes from a jury trying a Negro is a denial of equal protection of the laws.[12] Massachusetts had a case where a Chinese, arrested and tried with others for a tong killing was convicted of murder although no witness identified him or implicated him in the affair.[13] In Kentucky it used to be said that if a Negro killed a white man it was murder, if a white man killed a Negro it was unfortunate, but if a white man killed a white man it was self-defense, unless the affray was over a woman, in which case the cause of death was apoplexy.

PUBLIC HOSTILITY

If to a brutal killing and prejudice there is added the element of public hostility against the accused, the jury listens to the defendant's evidence with ears that are stone-deaf. This is the combination which produces most of our *causes celebres* subsequently believed by many to be miscarriages of justice, such as the cases of Leo Frank, Tom Mooney, and Sacco and Vanzetti. In the last-named case, the jury, after thirty-five days of trial, received the case in the afternoon and returned a verdict of guilty in the evening. According to one of the jurymen, his colleagues were ready to vote a guilty verdict immediately at the close of the case, but he forced an hour's discussion because he thought such precipitate action was improper.

Regardless of the eventual verdict, the jury could not possibly have considered the mass of testimony in favor of the defendants or weighed the improbabilities in the government's case in so brief a time. Even without the benefit of the subsequent revelations which threw new doubt on the defendants' guilt, a relaxed and unprejudiced jury would have debated at great length the validity of the fleeting and even silly identifications and would not have lightly assumed that a large number of reputable Italian alibi witnesses were perjurers.

Strip the case of the then current antiradical hysteria, change the defendants into Massachusetts veterans of World War I, the identifying witnesses into Italians, and the alibi witnesses into native New Englanders, and it becomes inconceivable that the weaknesses of the prosecution and the massive evidence for the defense would have received such brief consideration by the jury.

DEATH PENALTY AND SECOND DEGREE CONVICTIONS

Whether or not the mandatory death penalty results in more acquittals, there seem to be some general data indicating that it produces a smaller proportion of convictions for first degree murder and a larger proportion for second degree murder.[14] Opponents of capital punishment claim that this is due to the fact that juries shy away from the infliction of death; proponents allege that the possibility of the extreme penalty produces more pleas of guilty to murder in the second degree, for which the sentence is imprisonment. Without further and more precise research, it is impossible to draw any general conclusions. People and conditions differ. Doubtless both theories are valid, but it is not known to what extent.

* * *

DEATH PENALTY AND NUMBER OF TRIALS

Again, it is claimed that fewer trials are required in abolition states because obviously guilty defendants are more likely to plead guilty where they do not have to battle for their lives. There are, indeed, some instances where this appears to be the fact. On the other hand, there are those who claim that it is harder to secure pleas of guilty in abolition states because the prosecutor has less inducement to offer the guilty defendant. The answer necessarily depends upon the attitude of prosecutors in a death penalty state. If, for instance, the prosecutor insists on first degree with death as the penalty, the accused has nothing to lose by trial; if the prosecutor is willing to trade for a plea of guilty in the second degree, the defendant has much to gain by not risking a trial. How do we know, however, what prosecutors will do?

The application of armchair psychology to forecast the conduct of prosecutors—or any other public authority—is no easier than the Ellenborough method of predicting the reaction of criminals. For instance, as early as 1900, Hosea M. Knowlton, then attorney general of Massachusetts, recommended the commutation of the death sentence of a seventeen-year-old murderer whose crime was particularly vicious, on the ground that Massachusetts public sentiment would not tolerate the execution of so young a boy.

In 1942, after forty years' development in the field of handling juvenile delinquency, another Massachusetts prosecutor insisted on the death penalty for a seventeen-year-old offender despite the suggestion of the judge that the case was a proper one for a plea of guilty to murder in the second degree. The boy's previous record had been good, and there was a conflict of medical testimony as to whether the cause of the victim's death was the wound or a heart ailment, since the victim lived for seven weeks and his injuries had apparently healed. Nevertheless, the lad was allowed by the governor to be electrocuted, with the assent of the parole board acting in an advisory capacity.

A few years later, in another case involving a seventeen-year-old boy, another Massachusetts judge took the initiative and accepted a plea of guilty to second degree on the ground that no Massachusetts governor would ever allow so youthful an offender to be electrocuted!

A very conscientious district attorney will sometimes secure a conviction which the facts require, in the belief that the governor will take care of mitigation. Such a case was *Commonwealth v. Desatnick*,[15] where the father of an illegitimate child, plagued by accusing parents and a religious sense of guilt, murdered the infant. Instead of commuting, however, the governor sent for clerics of the defendant's faith and asked them whether illegitimacy was a more serious offense than murder. On the basis of the obvious answer, the young man was electrocuted.

Within a short time, however, another Massachusetts district attorney, regarded by many as more hard-boiled than the one who prosecuted Desatnick, nol-prossed the case of a mother who had abandoned her illegitimate child to die, on the ground that, although the crime would ordinarily be murder, "society needs no penalty for this, unfortunate as it is."

These instances are sufficient to indicate the futility of generalizing on insufficient data. Research alone, in a wide area and covering a period of years, could establish what prosecutors tend to do in the death penalty states by way of accepting pleas of guilty to second degree murder.

DEGREES OF MURDER

Degrees of murder present such a confusing problem that they create a further obstacle to predictability in the administration of criminal justice. In states where capital punishment has been abolished, the situation is not too serious. An intelligent parole board may ultimately adjust any gross errors in the jury's verdict or in the pleas. But where the penalty is death, a confused jury may eternalize its mistakes.

The principal variety of "first degree" murder is generally defined as including "malice aforethought," and involves "premeditation" and "deliberation." However, judicially defined "malice" does not necessarily involve malice against the victim in the ordinary dictionary sense. Moreover, the courts have explained "deliberation" and "premeditation" in such a way that these words also have lost their usual meaning. Under judicial definition, "premeditation" and "deliberation" can both occur within a few seconds of the killing itself. In the now rather celebrated case of *Fisher v. United States*,[16] a Negro of low-grade intelligence, suddenly feeling that he was insulted by his victim, struck her, and then killed her "to stop her from hollering." The jury by its verdict found deliberation and premeditation, essential to first degree murder.

Mr. Justice Frankfurter, in his dissenting opinion in the United States Supreme Court, referred to the judge's charge on the subject as the "dark emptiness of legal jargon." According to

Mr. Justice Frankfurter, the insult "pulled the trigger of Fisher's emotions." We shall never know how many defendants have been hanged or electrocuted for a "deliberate" and "premeditated" killing where some unexpected incident "pulled the trigger" of the accused's emotions.

"Is it possible," asked Sir Ernest Gowers of Mr. Justice Frankfurter at hearings held by the Royal Commission on Capital Punishment in 1950, "to express premeditation clearly and logically without mumbo-jumbo entering into it?" Mr. Justice Frankfurter thought that it was possible, but conceded that "the charges given by trial judges in the United States are often not very helpful." The Royal Commission appeared to think this observation to be an understatement.[17]

Another type of first degree murder is usually defined as a homicide occuring in the act of committing a serious felony. Here again the situation may be far from clear. If the jury believes that the accused, at the time of the killing, had given up all intention of committing the felony, and killed the victim because of fear for his own safety, the crime is not first degree murder. In a close case, how is the jury to read the defendant's mind in order to apply the instructions of the judge?

It would be unfair, however, to blame the judges for their inability to explain clearly the different degrees of murder. The fact that so many do not succeed suggests that the real blame rests with the rather fanciful distinctions between first degree and second degree murder. Mr. Justice Cardozo himself found it difficult, if not impossible, to draw a satisfactory line:

> I think the distinction is much too vague to be continued in our law.... The statute is framed along the lines of a defective and unreal psychology.... The present distinction is so obscure that no jury hearing it for the first time can fairly be expected to assimilate and understand it. I am not at all sure that I understand it myself after trying to apply it for many years and after diligent study of what has been written in the books. Upon the basis of this fine distinction with its mystifying psychology, scores of men have gone to their deaths.[18]

Degrees of murder were introduced into the law originally in order to give juries an opportunity to mitigate the harshness of the death penalty. No doubt in many cases they have accomplished their purpose. Some juries find second degree despite the facts and the judge's instructions; other juries, more conscientious than merciful, find first degree where warranted; still others muddle through the "mystifying psychology" to a bewildered finish. In conjunction with the death penalty, these degrees of murder have created a combination which tends to produce a most haphazard application of the criminal law in capital cases. Once the death penalty has been abolished, however, the criminal law may safely drop such metaphysical distinctions and relate the period of imprisonment to modern penology for the protection of society and the rehabilitation of the convicted.

MENTAL RESPONSIBILITY

Another cause for the haphazard application of the death penalty is the submission of the issue of mental responsibility to juries under legal definitions of insanity which are completely at variance with medical science. Most jurisdictions still apply the century-old rule in M'Naghten's case, namely: Did the defendant know that his act was morally and legally wrong? The rule has been somewhat qualified by such exceptions as the "irresistible impulse" test, but on the whole, M'Naghten still dominates judicial charges and decisions.

Under this definition of insanity, the lowest-grade morons and the most disturbed psychopaths are repeatedly convicted because they "knew the difference between right and wrong." It has also provided astute defense counsel with a handy means of getting guilty clients off without any penalty whatever, through a verdict of "not guilty by reason of insanity," and a subsequent speedy cure of a nonexistent mental disease.

In Massachusetts, under the Briggs law, the issue of insanity in capital cases is now usually decided before trial by the report of two impartial psychiatrists. In most states, however, the juries must continue to choose between contending alienists who are paid for their opinions by the side which calls them to the stand. Since there can be no reconciliation between the legal test for insanity and a conscientious psychiatrist's ideas about mental disease, the expert testimony from the witness stand is given under conditions which often confuse rather than assist a jury in reaching a verdict.

If imprisonment or confinement were the result in any event, then a finding of either sanity or insanity would provide opportunity for further study and possible treatment. Under the present system, a mistaken finding of guilty or not guilty where insanity is pleaded may result in irrevocable error. It is the presence of the death penalty that hinders a new approach to the entire question of mental responsibility.

DEATH PENALTY AND COST OF TRIAL

Whether there is actually a larger proportion of pleas of guilty without trial where capital punishment has been abolished is also largely unexplored territory. The trial of murder cases is an expensive process. The ordinary murder trial may cost the county thousands of dollars, and some of the more bitterly contested cases may run high up in five figures. In Massachusetts, the trial of the Millen brothers and Abraham Faber in 1934 for murder in the commission of robberies ran for nearly eight weeks at very great cost to the county. These criminals and their lawyers knew that the government's case was overwhelmingly strong and that public feeling ran high against them. Slim as their chances were, however, they went to trial because no prosecutor in a mandatory death penalty state, on the facts of their outrageous crimes, would have accepted a plea of second degree. Under the same conditions in an abolition state, would the accused have pleaded guilty? [19]

California was put to a great expense in the trial of the sensational Hickman case involving the fiendish sex killing of a child. Would the defendant have pleaded guilty in an abolition state? Shortly after the Hickman trial, Michigan had a murder case almost exactly the same in its gruesome details, apparently induced by the lurid press treatment of the California crime. The accused, one Hoteling, promptly pleaded guilty, thereby sparing the state much expense and the public a recital of the macabre details.

The money spent on the trial of capital cases would pay the

salaries of a substantial number of additional parole officers, badly needed in a constructive effort to reduce crime. It might repay any state to investigate the probability of saving the cost of these expensive murder trials through repeal of the death penalty.[20]

Whether or not capital punishment increases the expense of administering justice by forcing to trial a greater number of murder cases, there can be no doubt that the cost of cases actually tried is greatly increased because of the reluctance of jurors to serve where they may feel compelled to decree death to the accused. This is a universally observed phenomenon. Where the cases are notorious, the delay in securing a jury may be fantastic. In the trial for the murder of "King" Solomon in Boston, only one of 90 veniremen failed to disqualify himself on the ground that he was opposed to capital punishment. After 160 had been interrogated, there still were not enough to make up a jury.[21] In the case of Sacco and Vanzetti, four days were consumed in impaneling a jury.[22] These instances may be extreme, but they underscore a fact which should properly be considered in any evaluation of the death penalty in the administration of justice.

DEATH PENALTY AND SENSATIONALISM

Expert observers also agree that the trial of murder cases where death may be the penalty tends to be more sensational than where imprisonment is the only punishment. The spectacle of a human being fighting for his life is stirring drama inside and outside of the courtroom. Frequently, in order to sway a jury toward the fatal verdict—and possibly to reassure his own conscience—a prosecutor will inflame the jurors against the accused by playing upon every prejudice and ghastly detail. It is generally recognized that some prosecutors, because of political ambition or simple vanity, are not above deliberately seeking the headlines.

Of course, noncapital cases may also tend toward sensationalism; but where this occurs, it is because of reasons other than the penalty involved. Generally speaking, the trial of cases where the penalty may be death is surcharged with an emotional tension not present in other prosecutions. Defense counsel, witnesses, judges, and even prosecutors have been visibly affected by the strain. This atmosphere, created by invoking the specter of death to destroy the life in the dock, is hardly a help to calm consideration of the evidence.

DEATH PENALTY DISTORTS
ADMINISTRATION OF JUSTICE

Indeed, the one conclusion on which practically all criminologists agree is that the death penalty tends to distort the course of the criminal law. In the phrase of Professor Sheldon Glueck, it "bedevils the administration of justice."" Data may indicate that in some instances it may result in acquittals or findings not merited by the accused; in others, in convictions and executions not justified by an unemotional consideration of the evidence. In either case, the normal is deflected. The penalty is erratically inflicted at different times in different places. It retards progress in the criminal law by maintaining concepts which should have little to do with the process of ascertaining guilt, innocence, or responsibility.

Just as the death penalty is a paradoxical block in a modern system of penology, so does the fear of its finality hinder reform in the administration of criminal justice. Professor Sam Bass Warner, then on the faculty of the Harvard Law School, declared to the Joint Judiciary Committee of the Massachusetts Legislature in 1935 that "the existence of the death penalty for first degree murder is one of the principal reasons, if not the main reason, why it is extremely difficult to get judges and legislators to remove procedural barnacles from our law."

It may be said that all human processes are imperfect, and that those of justice are no different; but the fact of human fallibility is not a good reason for increasing it. If to err is human, then it becomes all the more important to reduce the probability of errors—especially fatal ones. On the massive evidence now available dealing with the use and disuse of the death penalty, there would seem to be no sufficient compensating advantage in retaining it. Its disappearance could only improve the administration of justice.

21 CARYL CHESSMAN

One of America's most poignant appeals against the death penalty was also one of the briefest. Its effect was achieved not by clever argumentation but in the reader's knowledge of the circumstances of its composition. For its author, the talented writer Caryl Chessman (1921-1960), was himself about to die at the hands of an executioner.

Chessman was born in Michigan but lived most of his life in California, where he repeatedly ran afoul of the law. His experiences in reform schools and county jails did not deter him from further criminal activity and his twentieth birthday found him serving a sixteen-year to life sentence in San Quentin for robbery, assault, and attempted murder. Paroled in December 1947, he was arrested again in January 1948, this time for kidnapping, a crime which Chessman insisted he did not commit. A jury found him guilty, however, and on May 22, 1948, he was sentenced to death. Complicated legal maneuvering over the next twelve years postponed Chessman's execution again and again, leaving the convict time to develop and give expression to his considerable writing talents. His first book, *Cell 2455, Death Row*, was published in 1954 and won him national attention. It was soon followed by *Trial by Ordeal* (1955) and *The Face of Justice* (1957). In all three, Chessman criticized the American prison system as a dehumanizing school for crime, and capital punishment as a useless act of vengeance.

Literary renown could heighten support and build a defense fund for Chessman, but it could not save his life. After many reprieves, his execution was set for May 2, 1960. His lawyers and friends fought literally to the last minute to win another delay, but failed. In the last hours of his life, Chessman wrote the following letter to lawyer George T. Davis of San Francisco, a long-time battler against capital punishment.

Now My Long Struggle is Over (1960)

May 2, 1960

Dear George,

Now my long struggle is over. Yours isn't. This barbarous, senseless practice, capital punishment, will continue. In our society other men will go on taking that last walk to death until . . . when? Until the citizens of this State and this land are made aware of its futility. Until they realize that retributive justice is not justice at all.

I die with the burning hope that my case and my death will contribute to this awareness, this realization. I know that you will personally do all in your power, as citizen and lawyer, to convince your fellows that justice is not served, but confounded, by vengeance and executioners.

Good luck.

My best,
Caryl

From Brad Williams, *Due Process: The Fabulous Story of Criminal Lawyer George T. Davis and His Thirty-Year Battle Against Capital Punishment* (New York: William Morrow, 1960), p. 330.

22 THORSTEN SELLIN

Thorsten Sellin (1896-   ), is one of the outstanding criminologists of the twentieth century and the dean of America's scholarly opponents of capital punishment. Born in Sweden, Sellin received his college education in the United States and began his long association with the University of Pennsylvania in 1916. There he received his Ph.D. in sociology in 1922, and there he taught for most of the next half century. Through his teaching and his scholarly articles and books, Sellin's impact on his discipline has been enormous, and he has received a host of honors in testament to his work.

Sellin's contribution to the campaign against capital punishment has been professional, unemotional, and enormously effective. In 1951, he was a consultant to the British Royal Commission on Capital Punishment and influenced that body's negative conclusions about the penalty. In 1959, he wrote a report on the death penalty to accompany the American Law Institute's Model Penal Code. He has become a fixture at legislative hearings on the subject in this country and abroad, and his presentations have claimed the attention and respect of some of the reform's bitterest opponents. The article reprinted here is, with its foundation in solid research, one of the most convincing arguments ever written against the death penalty.

Capital Punishment (1961)

Last year 57 men were executed in the United States. Five states—Arkansas, California, Georgia, New York, and Texas—

From Thorsten Sellen, "Capital Punishment," *Federal Probation,* 25 (September 1961), pp. 3-11. Reprinted by permission.

accounted for 37 of the executions. Two of them were for kidnaping—one in California (the Chessman case) and one in Oklahoma. There was 1 execution in Georgia for robbery, 1 in California for aggravated assault by a life prisoner, and 8 for rape—3 in Texas and 1 in each of the states of Florida, Georgia, Mississippi, South Carolina, and Tennessee. The remaining 45 executions were for murder in the first degree.[1]

Although there have been during the 31-year period 1930 to 1960 11 executions for burglary, 23 for armed robbery, and 434 for rape, all in the Southern states, as well as 5 executions in California for aggravated assault by a life prisoner, 8 for espionage, and 18 for kidnaping, it is the 3,186 executions for murder that have evoked most discussion. The literature on the death penalty in the United States can be said to deal almost exclusively with this crime. Because of the dearth of data concerning the use of capital punishment for other crimes than murder, I shall therefore focus this article on the murder problem.

It is evident from the figures given above that the death penalty is the rarest of all punishments. To an objective observer of the social scene, it is therefore amazing to note the emotional fervor that animates any discussion about it. Numerically insignificant as it is in practice, attitudes toward it are rooted deep in the sentiments of people and arouse powerful emotions whenever its justification is questioned. So long as the status quo is undisturbed nothing happens, but the moment it is attacked, either by abolitionists who want to eliminate the death penalty from the law or by retentionists who want to maintain or reinstate it, the debate begins. The antagonists bombard each other with "facts." Beliefs and opinions, often based on spurious or anecdotal evidence, are offered in support of the one or the other viewpoint, the Bible is liberally quoted by both sides, and each side mocks at the views of the other. In the heat engendered by the debate, epithets are flung. The abolitionists are called "maudlin" or "misguided do-gooders," and the retentionists backward, out-of-tune with the times, and at the worst, "sadists." It is only fair to say that in abusive name-calling the abolitionists lag far behind their opponents.

PURPOSE OF THE DEATH PENALTY

Although it is sometimes said that the death penalty serves a eugenic purpose, this argument is absurd since so few are executed and since their sterilization would just as effectively prevent them from having offspring. It has also been claimed that it is an economical way of disposing of criminals who, otherwise, would have to be supported at public expense—perhaps for the rest of their lives. Those who employ this cynical argument may be ignorant of the sometimes mountainous costs of the administration of justice in capital cases and they certainly have no knowledge of the realities of prison administration. It is no doubt true that some prisoners, including some lifers, do not make adequate returns to the state—measured in dollars and cents—for some of them are mentally or physically incapable of doing so. But most lifers work in prison. They perform domestic services, they work in prison shops, they do clerical work. If they were paid a wage commensurate with their services, they would be able to pay the costs of their maintenance, but since they are paid little or nothing, it is easy to forget that they are a source of financial profit to the institution in one way or another. Any prison warden will testify to the fact that it is from the group of lifers that he draws a considerable number of trusted inmate employees.

In the last analysis there are only two purposes of the death penalty that are worthy of attention, for the fate of this punishment hangs on them alone. One of these purposes might be called "the protection of the community." Those who embrace this aim say that the death penalty is needed as a threat or warning to deter potential murderers, and that murderers are too dangerous, once they have committed the crime, to be kept alive, since they may kill fellow prisoners or prison personnel and may escape or be ultimately released on parole or pardon, in which case they would again become a menace to the community. Hence, it would be too risky to substitute life imprisonment, so called, for the death penalty.

The other purpose is of a different kind. Those who support it simply feel that someone who murders another, perhaps under certain circumstances, for certain motives, or by certain means, has forfeited his life. In such cases they see the death penalty as the only just punishment, its aim being retribution.

It would be difficult to classify retentionists into those who support the one and those who support the other purpose mentioned. Although these purposes are distinct, from a conceptual point of view, it is by no means certain that they are mutually exclusive in people's minds. I suspect—and the reading of many debates on capital punishment gives support to that suspicion—that many find it possible somehow to cherish both of them.

Are the purposes of social protection and retribution achieved by capital punishment and achieved better than by the use of some other sanction? For someone who is interested in the death penalty as a social institution and curious about its survival in the criminal law, it is natural to wonder how one might be able to find an answer to this question.

DOES THE DEATH PENALTY GIVE
MAXIMUM SOCIAL PROTECTION?

I stated above that there are two separate problems that confront us in the study of this matter. First, does the existence of the death penalty instill such fear in men's hearts that the thought of it keeps them from committing murder? Second, if a murderer is not executed for his crime, does he remain a constant danger to the prison community, if he is given a prison sentence, and to the larger community, if he is granted a later release?

The Problem of General Deterrence

In an article published in the June 1961, issue of the *FBI Law Enforcement Bulletin*,[2] Mr. J. Edgar Hoover writes: "No one, unless he can probe the mind of every potential killer, can say with any authority whatsoever that capital punishment is not a deterrent. As one police officer has asked, how can these 'authorities' possibly know how many people are not on death row because of the deterrent effect of executions." This statement contains a tacit assumption that the death penalty is a deterrent, but no one can state with any authority whatsoever that capital punishment *is* a deterrent. So we have reached an impasse. If no one can say either Yes or No on this point, it means either that the question is unanswerable or that no one has tried to find an answer.

Now, I am not unaware of the fact that police officers, prison wardens, or judges now and then claim to know cases where a given individual refused, for instance, to carry a firearm when participating in a burglary or robbery or refused to participate at all if any member of the group was so armed, and that this is assumed to prove that fear of the death penalty dictated this conduct. It is not impossible that some of these instances may be true. But the stories as printed have never clearly indicated whether it was the fear of capital punishment rather than the fear of taking or participating in taking a human life—regardless of the consequences—that motivated the refusal. Furthermore, the information seems in many cases to have been secured or given under circumstances that would make it suspect. Even if it were accepted as fact, there is just as good evidence that the availability of instruments used to inflict the punishment of death has induced people of unbalanced mind to seek that punishment as a devious means of suicide. When we place these contradictory "facts" in a balance it would be rash for any one to claim with assurance that the one outweighs the other.

Even if we recognize that the fear of punishment may have some deterrent effect and helps to prevent the commission of some crimes, there is good reason to think that it does not or cannot be operative in preventing murders. Life is generally regarded as man's most valued and even sacred possession, and the protection of life by the avoidance of doing deliberate harm to others or to ourselves is taught to us from childhood in many ways and by many means. When in spite of this general social aversion to murder, killings occur, it means that the perpetrators have either not been properly taught to respect human life or that they find themselves in a situation where hatred, desire, anger, greed, necessity, or the mores of a group to which the offender belongs acquire such dominance that all else is ignored or forgotten, including the possible punishment. The person who carefully plans his crime so as to avoid detection has no fear of consequences since he is certain he will never suffer any. Discounting war and revolution, all but very few people, even most murderers, consider the taking of life as a terrible moral wrong. It is this feeling that ultimately is the great deterrent.

If we were to take the ultracynical view that people obey the law only because they want to avoid the consequences of disobedience and not because they live according to a moral code which also finds its expression in legal prohibitions, we would have to assume that potential offenders fear the consequences somewhat in proportion to the risk of suffering them. But, statistics tell us that the risk of being executed for murder is small. It is extremely small for gangsters who, according to the supporters of the death penalty, are among those who should be made to fear it most. According to the last annual report of the Chicago Crime Commission there were 947 gang murders in Chicago since 1919. I suppose it is not an overestimate to assume that at least two persons, the actual killer and the one who ordered the killing, participated in these murders. In that case, there were a minimum of 1,900 murderers involved. Of these 17 were convicted but several of them were later freed by the Supreme Court on appeal.[3] There is nothing new in this story, for it has its counterpart in all cities where organized crime is found.

If the risk of execution is regarded as the important element in deterring persons from committing murder we are therefore leaning on a mighty weak reed. That risk is so much smaller than the risk of the potential murderer being killed by his intended victim, by the police, or by some bystander during or after the crime.

During the period 1934-1954 (in Chicago), for instance, policemen killed 69 and private citizens 261 criminals or suspects involved in homicide, or a total of 331. During the same period there were 45 persons executed for murder in the Cook County Jail. In other words, there were nearly 8 times as many homicidal offenders killed unofficially, so to speak, as were those electrocuted. There were 5,132 murders and nonnegligent manslaughters known to the police during those years. In connection with 6.45 percent of these homicides, a criminal or suspect met his death at the hands of police or citizens, while 0.88 percent were put to death in the electric chair. [4]

Judging from the number of murders and nonnegligent manslaughters known to the police and published in *Uniform Crime Reports* for the year 1959, and taking into account a slight increase in 1960, there were a minimum of 8,400 murders and nonnegligent manslaughters last year (1960) in the states that still have the death penalty, and of these offenses the number punishable by death would probably be at least 1,260, or 15 percent of the total. This is a most conservative estimate. It would be equally conservative to say that at least 1,300 persons were guilty of these murders and that 1,250 of these will never be executed.

If fear of being executed for murder played the great deterrent role claimed by retentionists, it would be reasonable to assume that when this fear is not experienced, as in states that have abolished capital punishment, or is suddenly removed, when a state abolishes this penalty, the result would in the first case mean that murder rates would be higher than in states that have retained the punishment, and in the second case that these rates would show an increase, which could be stopped or even reduced by the simple device of reinstating the penalty. When statistics appear to give support to such assumptions, retentionists are quick to seize upon them to illustrate the soundness of their views, but when the statistics fail them they are wont to claim that statistics demonstrate nothing.

The only way of testing the correctness of the above assumptions, however, is by the use of statistics. We have to admit that the data available for use are far from perfect for the purpose of counting the exact number of capital murders that occur during any given period of time in any jurisdiction, small or large. There are no reliable statistics of *capital* murders. Such murders are of two types. The first includes premeditated malicious killings and especially those committed by certain methods, such as arson or ambush. The second includes killings that occur in connection with the commission of crimes, such as burglary, robbery, rape, kidnaping, etc. Although no count of capital murders has so far been made by any official agency on a state-wide basis, it would probably be possible to get a rather accurate count of the so-called felony murders, i.e., the second class mentioned above, but the premeditated murders defy any accurate enumeration, since their qualification depends so greatly on the state of mind of the offender, who is often undetected or unknown. Therefore we have to use other kinds of statistics in an attempt to arrive at conclusions.

For many years we have had statewide statistics of deaths due to willful homicides. They are based on an analysis of death certificates submitted to the Bureau of Vital Statistics of the Federal Government from all the states of the Union. These certificates do not contain any information that would make it possible to segregate capital murders from other kinds of willful killings. They do make it possible to compute rates of deaths due to willful homicide and it is these death rates which are generally assumed to be usable as an index to capital murders, on the assumption that the *proportion* of capital murders, hidden among these homicides, remains constant from year to year. An increase or a decrease in the total homicide death rate in a state, from one year to another, is then assumed to reflect a proportionate increase or decrease in the number of capital murders in that state. Experts in various countries who have made a study of this problem have concluded that this assumption is valid. Until it has been disproved we have to accept that judgment.

Abolitionists are frequently guilty of making assertions that the states that have retained the death penalty have much higher homicide crime rates than the states that have abolished it. They arrive at that conclusion by simply comparing the rates of the two classes of states. This is a reprehensible practice. The conclusion is accurate but the inference is false. Except for Delaware and Rhode Island, the abolition states on our continent all border on Canada, and all the northern states have fairly low rates of homicide compared with the South, where no state has dropped capital punishment. The only fair comparison is one that takes into account regional differences and therefore compares the homicide rates of an abolitionist state with that of its neighbor states.

The diagrams shown [below] are based on such comparisons. They show both the annual size of the homicide death rate per 100,000 population for the period 1920-1958 and the general trend of the rate for each set of states compared. Diagram I compares the abolitionist state of Maine with the states of New Hampshire and Vermont. Diagram II shows rates for Rhode Island (an abolition state), Massachusetts, and Connecticut. Diagram III contains two abolition states, Minnesota and Wisconsin, compared with Iowa. Diagram IV compares Michigan, which has no death penalty for murder, with Ohio and Indiana. [5]

The striking thing about these diagrams is that within each set of states the rates are so nearly the same annually and the trends so closely alike that if the lines were not identified with each specific state, no one would dare to guess which lines represented the abolition states. Generally speaking, all the states involved showed a decline in homicide deaths during the 39 years examined. The decline was slight in New England and much more pronounced in the middle west, but then the New England rates were also generally much lower to begin with.

It is proper to conclude that states which are similar in the character of their population, their urban and industrial development, and their mores have similar homicide rates, whether or not they have the death penalty. In other words, the presence of the death penalty for murder in a state appears to have no more influence on its homicide rates than the absence of the penalty in a comparable state has on the rates of that state. And, if our basic assumption is correct, what holds true for the homicide rates would hold true for the capital murder rates, were they obtainable.

When it once becomes generally understood that the amount and the trends of murder depend on demographic, social, economic, and political conditions, one would realize that the explanation for rises or falls in the statistics of this crime must be sought through a study of these conditions, and that through such study alone could any possible remedy be found. To hope that this remedy could be found in the application of the death penalty or in its introduction is to grasp at a straw.

We have had some experience in this country with such vain efforts.[6] Several states have temporarily abolished the death

penalty and have then reintroduced it. In some of them abolition was followed by a rise in homicides, in others by a fall.
And when the death penalty was reintroduced the rates usually
rose. For the reasons already stated, the law of murder had
apparently nothing to do with these variations.

The Dangers of Life Imprisonment

But if we do not execute murderers, they will remain a menace to all within the walls of prisons, it is said, and if they are
ever released the community will again be threatened by them.
We should, therefore, attempt to discover how capital murderers who have been imprisoned for life—which is the usual punishment when the death penalty is not applied—behave while in
prison and after release.

The experience of prison administrators is, broadly speaking,
that lifers are among the best behaved prisoners in an institution. They obviously may become disciplinary problems at
some time or other, as do other prisoners, but their conduct
record is on the whole very good. There have been instances
where such prisoners have committed a homicide in an attempt
to escape or as a result of conflicts with other inmates or the
prison staff, but almost all killings committed inside prisons are
done by prisoners serving sentences for other crimes than homicide. Are such events more common in abolition states than in
death-penalty states? No one knows, since no study has been
made of this matter.[7]

The paroled lifer has had an enviable record of good behavior
so far as we can gather from available information. I have given
elsewhere[8] some data which demonstrate this fact. Within the
last few months the Ohio Legislative Service Commission has
furnished additional information on this point. In a staff research report, published in January, we learn that since Ohio's
present parole law became effective in 1945, there have been
169 first degree murderers paroled in that State, as of October
1, 1960. These 169 parolees "have compiled the highest parole
success ratio of any offense group among the more than 6,000
paroled convicts now administered by the Ohio Bureau of Probation and Parole. Only two of the 169 have been returned to

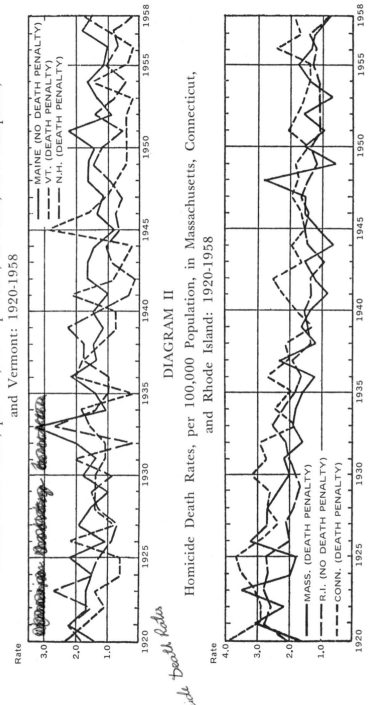

DIAGRAM I

Homicide Death Rates, per 100,000 Population, in Maine, New Hampshire, and Vermont: 1920-1958

MAINE (NO DEATH PENALTY)
VT. (DEATH PENALTY)
N.H. (DEATH PENALTY)

DIAGRAM II

Homicide Death Rates, per 100,000 Population, in Massachusetts, Connecticut, and Rhode Island: 1920-1958

MASS. (DEATH PENALTY)
R.I. (NO DEATH PENALTY)
CONN. (DEATH PENALTY)

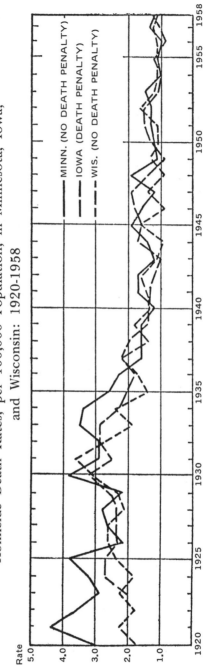

DIAGRAM III

Homicide Death Rates, per 100,000 Population, in Minnesota, Iowa, and Wisconsin: 1920-1958

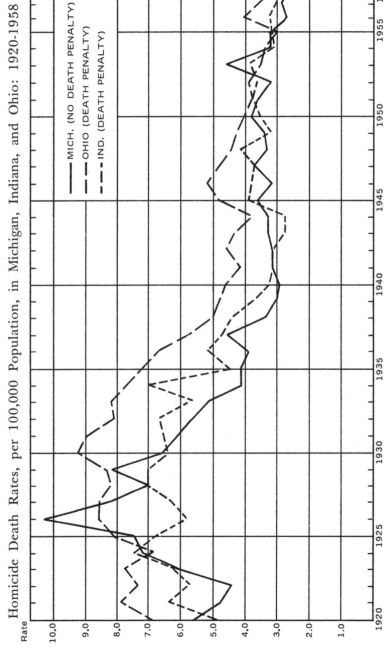

DIAGRAM IV

Homicide Death Rates, per 100,000 Population, in Michigan, Indiana, and Ohio: 1920-1958

MICH. (NO DEATH PENALTY)
OHIO (DEATH PENALTY)
IND. (DEATH PENALTY)

penal institutions for the commission of new felonies. One of these was returned after committing armed robbery while on parole, and the other for assault with intent to commit a felony. Eight more paroled first degree murderers have been returned to penal institutions for technical violations of parole rules and regulations or because of general failure to adjust satisfactorily to life outside the penitentiary."[9] The report suggests that the explanation may be found in the facts that a large proportion of first degree murderers are highly reformable, that those paroled —in Ohio at least—were 30 years old on the average when they were committed to serve life sentences, but 53 years old on the average when they were paroled, and finally that those who were not good parole risks serve their life sentences in full. In 1957, for instance, when one prisoner was executed in Ohio, 11 prisoners, who were serving definite life sentences, died.[10]

Police Safety

Among those who wish the death penalty retained there are, of course, people from all walks of life, but certain occupational groups or professions appear to contain a particularly high or at least vocal proportion of them. This is particularly true of the police who rather consistently—except in the states that have abolished capital punishment—individually or through their professional organizations or unions make known their views, that if the fear of the death penalty is removed by the abolition of this punishment, the policeman's vocation would become more hazardous. It is assumed that persons engaging in crime would, then, be more likely to kill police officers who are pursuing, questioning, or arresting them. This belief, as well as the belief that the death penalty acts generally as a unique deterrent, has even led the Federal Bureau of Investigation to express its support of capital punishment, in spite of its avowed policy of neutrality. Last year, Mr. J. Edgar Hoover stated that policy in clear terms. "The F.B.I. . . . is strictly a fact-gathering agency. It does not make recommendations or evaluations . . . or pass opinion relative to information gathered. . . . Certainly, it is not the function of an agency, which collects the facts in a given situation to also pass judgment on them."[11] In fairness to Mr.

Hoover, I must say that he was discussing facts gathered in the *investigation* of crime, but the FBI also gathers facts about the state of crime in the country, publishes these facts in its annual *Uniform Crime Reports* and has no hesitation about evaluating them. In the report published in 1960, covering the year 1959, a perfectly amazing page is devoted to a defense of capital punishment. Its last two paragraphs read as follows:

> Some who propose the abolishment of capital punishment select statistics that "prove" their point and ignore those that point the other way. Comparisons of murder rates between the nine states which abolished the death penalty or qualified its use and the forty-one states which have retained it, either individually, before or after abolition, or by group are completely inconclusive.
>
> The professional law-enforcement officer is convinced from experience that the hardened criminal has been and is deterred from killing based on the prospect of the death penalty. It is possible that the deterrent effect of capital punishment is greater in states with a high murder rate if the conditions which contribute to the act of murder develop more frequently in those states. For the law-enforcement officer the time-proven deterrents to crime are sure detection, swift apprehension, and proper punishment. Each is a necessary ingredient.[12]

And, in the "Summary" that precedes the text of the report we find the sentence, "Proponents of abolition of capital punishment cannot find support for their cause in study of state murder rates, since results are inconclusive."[13]

Having read these statements, one would assume that the report contained some facts about capital punishment that might explain and justify the statements even though the "fact-gathering agency" is not supposed to "make recommendations or evaluations." Not so. The statements are gratuitously introduced into an official governmental report that offers nothing to support them. They are mentioned here only to show the length to which police authorities are willing to go in defense of the death penalty, even though they have never been willing to make any scientific attempt to test the validity of their opinions.

The only more extensive inquiry to discover if policemen are better protected in states that have capital punishment was made in 1955 by the author for the Joint Committee of the Senate and the House of Commons on Capital Punishment of the Canadian Parliament.[14] In a recent report it is summarized as follows:

> It was based on a questionnaire sent to all police departments in cities with more than 10,000 inhabitants, according to the 1950 census, in the six states that had no death penalty in 1955 and the eleven states that bordered on them. Information was requested on the number of policemen killed by lethal weapons in the hands of criminals or suspects each year beginning with 1919 and ending with 1954. Full reports were returned by 266 cities, representing 55 percent of the cities in the abolition states and 41 percent of those in the capital punishment states.
>
> Several interesting facts appeared from an analysis of the responses to the questionnaire. First, when comparing groups of cities in the two types of states, according to the size of the cities, it was found that there was no difference in the rates of policemen killed in the cities of the capital punishment states and in those of the abolition states. Second, it was found that in both types of states in the northeast part of the country, the killing of policemen was less frequent than in the middle west. Third, it was found that the decade of 1920-30 had been most hazardous to the police of both types of states and that the number of police killed had declined regularly, whether the state had or did not have the death penalty.... It is, therefore, impossible to conclude that the existence of this punishment in law or practice affords any special protection to the police that would not be afforded by the threat of life imprisonment.[15]

This conclusion can be extended. The belief that the death penalty is a unique instrument for the protection of society against murder and superior to life imprisonment in this respect is not supported by any credible evidence now available to us.

IS RETRIBUTION EFFECTIVE?

There is no denying that many persons feel that a person who takes another's life under circumstances that qualify the crime as murder in the first degree should, in all justice, forfeit his life. Some of them are quite willing to agree that so far as the protection of society is concerned life imprisonment would be just as effective, but they feel that the grievous wrong done to the family of the victim, the robbing of the victim of his chance to enjoy perhaps a long life of usefulness, and the display of recklessness and of perhaps a wicked or depraved character on the part of the murderer, fully merit his execution.

This view of justice must be reckoned with. Its nature is such that if logic prevailed those who hold it would maintain it even if it were proved that the use of the death penalty had socially undesirable by-products. Opponents of the view are equally strong in their feelings that to take a life deliberately by the state is just as reprehensible as murder and is morally wrong.

I do not propose to enter into any debate on this issue. Its resolution lies entirely within the sphere of moral philosophy. It is in such debates that capital punishment is discussed, not from point of view of its effectiveness in protecting society but from the point of view of its inherent rightness or wrongness. However, if I were an adherent of the view of retributive justice, I might—if my emotions did not deprive me of my reason—wish to find out if retributive justice is efficiently and properly administered.

One might begin with some basic assumptions. The first is that every person who commits first degree murder should lose his life. Since this poses a dilemma, not all such murderers being discovered, at least every person convicted of this kind of murder should be executed. A second assumption is only a logical consequence of the first, namely, that since all such persons should be executed, there could be no discrimination. All murderers would be equally dealt with.

The gap between what should happen, if these assumptions are correct, and the realities of the administration of capital justice is enormous. It begins to develop in the courtroom, where the skilled defense lawyer may stave off a first-degree murder conviction and where juries may inequitably determine a verdict or a sentence, depending on their attitudes toward a defendant or the feelings of the community rather than the strict nature of the crime. It is well known that the number of women murderers sentenced to death is disproportionately low compared with the proportion of male murderers so sentenced. In Ohio, during 1955-1958, 31 percent of the males and 8 percent of the females charged with murder in the first degree were found guilty of that crime.[16] And it has been observed that in many states, racial attitudes hinder the equal application of justice.

But if a sentence of death is finally imposed there is still the matter of commutation by boards of pardons or governors. Whether or not a death sentence will actually be executed depends, in the last resort, on these authorities. At times the policy of commutation depends on the particular attitude toward the death penalty held by them. One governor, opposed to this punishment, may commute every sentence; another who holds the opposite view may commute few of them. Bias or adventitious circumstances may also exert an influence. In Ohio, of the persons under death sentence in the prisons during 1950-1959, not counting 7 cases yet to be disposed of by November 1960, 78 percent of the Negroes and but 51 percent of the whites were put to death. This discrepancy may in part reflect economic as well as racial inequalities, for commutations were received in 44.4 percent of the cases where the defendant was able to afford private counsel, but only in 31 percent of the cases where he was served by a court appointed one.[17] A Pennsylvania study of 439 persons sentenced to death and placed on death row between 1914 and 1958 showed that Negro felony-murderers received commutation in only 6 percent of the cases while white felony-murderers did so in over 17 percent of the cases.[18]

There is no need to multiply these or similar data. If only about 4 percent of those who actually commit murders in the first degree, a figure based on what we conservatively estimate to be the number of capital murders committed annually in the United States and the accurate knowledge we have of the number of executions, it is obvious that, whatever the elements may be that produce the attrition, retribution is but rarely achieved and in no equitable manner. Therefore, just as the death penalty has proved to fail as a special means of social protection, so it has failed as an instrument of retributive justice. It is vain to hope for an improvement, because the spirit of the times is unfavorable to it. To prove that this is so, we need only to take a glance at history and especially at the history of abolition.

THE ABOLITION MOVEMENT

Speaking of the abolition movement there are two aspects of it that are interesting. First of all, of course, is the extent to which the death penalty, at least in peace times, has disappeared from the criminal law of nations and states. In Western Europe, only France, the United Kingdom, Spain, and Eire have retained it, and most countries of Central and South America, including Brazil, Argentina, and most of Mexico, have abolished it. In the United States, four states abolished it during the last century (Michigan, Wisconsin, Maine, and Rhode Island). During the present century five states have done so without restoring it again, namely, Minnesota, North Dakota, Delaware, Alaska, and Hawaii, the last three joining the others within the last half decade. It does not exist in Puerto Rico nor in the Virgin Islands.

This is, however, but a part of the story. The last century and a half has seen changes which explain the decline of the death penalty in states that have kept it in the law. We have seen a general trend toward the reduction of the number of offenses punishable by death, despite occasional minor reversals. We have gradually eliminated public executions, for while desiring to make the penalty as frightening as possible—that is, as a deterrent—we have also become more and more averse to such unesthetic and revolting spectacles. Moved by sentiment, we have sought for more and more quick and painless methods of killing murderers, as witness the spread first of the electric chair, and now of the gas chamber, in replacement of the traditional gallows. Finally, we have removed the mandatory death sentence and left in the hands of the jury or the judge, the choice of an alternative—life imprisonment.

The combined result of these policies has caused capital punishment to become an anachronism in many states. If we add the changing attitudes toward punishment in general as reflected in the establishment of juvenile courts, the introduction of parole and probation, and the rise of a correctional philosophy which stresses rehabilitation, it is not difficult to explain the rapid downward trend in the number of executions annually from a high of 199 in 1935 to 57 in 1960. And this trend is likely to continue, barring unforeseen social crises, until executions will become a much greater rarity than today and will ultimately be abandoned.

23 WILLIAM STYRON

Anti-capital punishment appeals are sometimes weakened because they attack an abstraction. Not many advocates of the reform have sought to remedy this problem by concentrating their arguments on an individual victim or potential victim of the executioner. The success of such a tactic, in the right hands, has been brilliantly demonstrated by novelist William Styron (1925-   ).

Born in Virginia, Styron graduated from Duke University in 1947 and settled in the North, first in New York City, then on a farm in Connecticut. His first novel, *Lie Down in Darkness* (1951), received considerable acclaim and won the Prix de Rome; two more books followed in 1955 and 1960. In 1967, he published *The Confessions of Nat Turner,* which was grandly successful but which met with a storm of protest from black critics.

It was during the planning stages of *The Confessions* that Styron, fascinated with the image of the captured slave, alone in his cell, awaiting execution, learned of another condemned black man much closer to home. The resulting article, "The Death-In-Life of Benjamin Reid," published in *Esquire* in 1962, achieved its immediate goal. It aroused enough interest, especially among the faculty and students of Hartford's Trinity College, to encourage a plea for clemency to the Connecticut State Board of Pardons. That body granted Reid a last minute commutation to life imprisonment with the possibility of parole. More generally, Styron's article remains effective even after Reid's life has been saved, for it forces readers to confront a man—unglamorous, unintelligent, but a man—as they consider the abstract arguments about capital punishment.

The Death-in-Life of Benjamin Reid (1962)

The Connecticut State Prison at Wethersfield is a huge, gloomy Victorian structure whose very appearance seems calculated to implant in the mind of the onlooker the idea of justice in its most retributive sense. It is one of the oldest prisons in America. Uncompromisingly somber, the penitentiary suggests not only that crime does not pay but that whosoever is a wrongdoer is quite conceivably beyond redemption. On Death Row, the condemned cells were built for an epoch when, after a man was told he must die, the supreme penalty was administered far more swiftly than in these present days of interminable legal postponements. Each cell still measures only seven by seven feet, implying momentary residence. A strong electric light shines in the face of the condemned all night and all day. The condemned are not allowed to communicate with one another and, until very recently, were denied even the solace of an earphone radio. To live on Death Row at Wethersfield is in effect to dwell in solitary confinement until the day of one's execution. As I write these words (mid-October, 1961), the state of Connecticut is preparing to kill a twenty-four-year-old felon named Benjamin Reid. Reid is no Caryl Chessman; as a matter of fact, he is subliterate, and possesses an intelligence which, if not so low as to be called defective, can only be described as marginal. The condemned at Wethersfield are allowed to read and to write letters, but it is doubtful that Ben Reid has availed himself much of these privileges; and this is a circumstance which must have made his confinement all the more forsaken, because Reid has lived in the presence of the electric chair for four years and three months.

On a bitterly cold night in Hartford in January of 1957, Ben Reid, who was nineteen at the time, waylaid a middle-aged woman in a parking lot and beat her to death with a hammer. His avowed and premeditated motive was profit (the woman

From William Styron, "The Death-in-Life of Benjamin Reid," *Esquire*, 57 (February 1962), pp. 114, 141-145. Copyright 1962 by William Styron. Reprinted by permission of the Harold Matson Co., Inc.

was a friend of his mother's, and had been known to carry large sums of money with her), but this aspect of his crime he so ruinously botched that he got nothing. Over two thousand dollars was discovered on the woman's frozen body, which Reid in his final panic had jammed into a car. It would appear that Reid scarcely bothered to conceal his tracks, fleeing to the home of a relative in New Haven where he was found in short order by the police. He seemed rather relieved to be caught. He made several confessions and, in the summer of that same year, was brought to trial by jury in the Superior Court at Hartford. The trial was a fairly brief one, as murder trials go. On June 27, 1957, Reid was sentenced to die by electrocution. He was taken to Wethersfield (a suburb of Hartford and, except for the eyesore of its prison and several small factories, a lovely elm-lined New England town) and there in a cell seven feet by seven feet, brightly illuminated night and day, he has been for more than four years, awaiting what must be, for him, the ever-present but always undiscoverable moment of his death.

There is, of course, no such thing as absolute justice, but even advocates of capital punishment will grant that, when a human's life is at stake, there should be the closest approximation of absolute justice the law can attain. In terms of absolute justice, to make evident the reasonableness of Ben Reid's execution for murder it would have to be proved that his crime was morally more reprehensible than a similar crime, for which some other murderer received a lesser sentence. There have been, and still are, murderers whose crimes repel us by their violence and brutality quite as strongly as does Ben Reid's. Some of these criminals have been put to death as creatures past salvation; more frequently sparing their lives, the State has sentenced them to serve a life term, with the possibility of parole, or a number of years, and by this relative leniency has granted, at least theoretically, the rather more lucid assumption that some men's crimes are not so depraved as to place them forever beyond redemption. But the logic of this random choice is as fearful as it is mysterious. The wickedness, the inherent immorality, of any crime is a quality which it is beyond the power of any of us to weigh or measure. Ben Reid's crime, however, has been weighed, and Reid himself has been found completely and irrevocably wanting. Neither absolute justice nor any kind of justice, so far as the eye can see, has been served. It might be interesting to learn something about this young man, and perhaps discover why the State has judged him irredeemable, past hope of recovery.

Warden Lewis E. Lawes of Sing Sing,[1] an expert foe of the death penalty, once said that in order to be executed in America a person had to be three things: poor, a man, and black. He was speaking of the North as well as the South. He was also admittedly generalizing, if not being somewhat facetious, for a great many white men and a few woman of both races have, of course, been executed and, on exquisitely rare occasions, the State has taken the life of a criminal of wealth. But the implication of his remark, it is safe to say, is borne out by the statistics —North and South—and Ben Reid fills the bill: he is a poor black man. To read of his background and career is to read not only of poverty and neglect and a mire of futile, petty crime and despair, but, in the end, of a kind of wretched archetype: the Totally Damned American. If one wished to make a composite portrait of the representative criminal upon whom the State enacts its legal vengeance, one's result would be a man who looked very much like Ben Reid. Like his victim, who was also a Negro, he was born in a dilapidated slum area on the north side of Hartford. When he was two his father died, leaving his mother virtually destitute and with several children to support besides Ben. These years toward the end of the Depression were bleak enough for a large number of Americans; for people in the situation of Ben Reid and his family the times were catastrophic, and left ineradicable scars. When Reid was almost eight his mother got into a shooting scrape and was grievously wounded; she was left crippled for life and partially paralyzed. At this point Reid was forced to enter the Hartford County Home, and there he remained for eight years. He was not alone among his family to become a ward of the People; during the time he was at the county home his twin brother was committed to the state hospital for the insane at Norwich, while an older sister, adjudged to be mentally deficient, was sent to the

Mansfield State Training School. Most children are released from the county home at the age of fifteen, but since no one wanted Reid he received the dispensation granted, in special cases, to the totally unwanted, and was privileged to stay an extra year. One pauses to speculate, hesitates, goes on, feeling presumptuous (there is no other word) as one tries to imagine Ben Reid's thoughts during this weary, bedraggled era. He was never too bright, so probably—unlike other adolescents somewhat more richly endowed in mind as well as circumstance—he entertained no Deep Thoughts about life at all. To Reid, coming out of oblivion into this existence which, so far as one can tell, had seemed to guarantee the unfulfillment and frustration of every ordinary childish yearning, life must have begun to appear simply and demonstrably lacking in significance. Lacking in significance, it must necessarily have lacked any values whatever, and it is not at all surprising that Reid, soon after he was sent away from the county home, began feloniously and emptyheadedly to trifle with those values in life which society so highly regards.

When the county home finally discharged him, the nation was experiencing a time of prosperity such as no country has ever seen, but very little of this abundance rubbed off on Ben Reid. For a year or so he was shunted from one foster home to another; he went hungry again from time to time, and there were occasions when he was reduced to foraging from garbage cans on the back streets of Hartford. It was during this period that Reid has his first brush with the law, in an involvement which has come to seem numbingly typical of his age and background: he was caught acting as a runner for a narcotics peddler, and for his offense was placed on probation. A few months later he tried to rob a store, hopelessly bungled the endeavor, and was sentenced to serve a term in the state reformatory at Cheshire. It is apparent that he was in no way reformed. However, it may be said that, after his release from the reformatory, an episode occurred in Reid's life which tends in some small way to alleviate the harshness and ugliness of his career until then. He met a girl. She was a few years older than he, but they began seeing each other and, presumably fell in love, and they were married in 1956. It might have been an answer to Reid's trouble, but it wasn't. He was unable to get a job. Not long after their marriage, Ben began to brood about money and commenced hitting the wine bottle. His wife apparently did her best to straighten him out, but these efforts led to nothing. She was pregnant, and had just left him, when Reid, thinking about money, went out into the snow that night and committed the crime for which he is now scheduled to die.

Often, it seems, what appears to be justice is merely a shadow-image of justice, determined by queer circumstances which can only be discerned in retrospect. This sinister element in the law might alone be enough to cast final doubts upon the infliction of the death penalty; for only under conditions of absolute justice—a kind of aseptic legal vacuum completely invulnerable to fleeting social panic, hysteria, shifts in public temper—could we presume to condemn a man utterly, and absolute justice nowhere exists. It of course cannot strictly be proven, but it seems at least probable that had Ben Reid not come to trial at the particular time he did, he would not have been condemned to die. The reason for this conjecture is the existence in Hartford at that same time of two particularly viscious criminals: a huge, lantern-jawed ex-con and ex-resident of Death Row named Joseph ("The Chin") Taborsky, and his moronic accomplice, Arthur Culombe. Taborsky, who was a psychopath of fearfully sadistic dimensions, and Culombe, a kind of torpid, blinky-eyed caricature of the dim-witted henchman, had finally been apprehended after a series of hold-up-murders which had terrorized central Connecticut and, quite literally, sent many of the people of Hartford in off the streets. A notable feature of their *modus operandi* was to make their victims kneel down at their feet before shooting them. Taborsky and Culombe had been dubbed by the newspapers, with scant originality though in luminous headlines, "The Mad Dog Killers," and when they came to be tried there can be no doubt that the public, which attended the trial in droves, was in something less than a mood of composure. Ben Reid was tried at the same time and in the same building. His mother, crippled and woefully concerned, was the only spectator on the first day of the trial, when the jurors were sworn in, and except for Reid's wife and one or two interested onlookers, remained the only spectator until the trial's end. The People's interest was in the Mad Dogs, not in Ben Reid. There seems little doubt that the Taborsky-Culombe affair next door, with its public hubbub and its reverberant atmosphere of mass outrage, did nothing to help Ben Reid's case, and in fact subtly contaminated his own courtroom with the odor of vengeance.

The trial, as I have said, lasted only a few days. Reid's defense was almost nonexistent; he had, after all, killed someone with what in the legal sense is surely malice and premeditation. His defense counsel (since Reid had no money, this job fell to the Public Defender) made strenuous efforts in his client's behalf, outlining his squalid background and the nature of his upbringing. But the jury (Respectability in its pure, concentrated essence, disarmingly mild-eyed and benign, like a Norman Rockwell tableau: five Christian housewives and among the rest, as might be anticipated in Hartford, a clutch of insurance adjusters) was not terribly moved. . . .

The jury was asked if it would like to retire and deliberate right away, or if it would like to have lunch first. It replied that it would like to have lunch. After it fed itself it retired and came back with the verdict in a little over an hour. As happens with rather enigmatic frequency in capital trials, the judge flubbed the reading of the death sentence. In setting the date of execution, he said, "the year 1958," instead of "the year 1957," and the entire pronouncement, for the record, had to be read over again. Up until this time, Reid had showed very little emotion during the trial, except for the moment when the prosecutor began to describe his crime in its bloody detail, at which point, in a gesture which can only be described as childlike, he furiously clapped his hands over his ears. Now perhaps he felt that the judge was damning him twice. At any rate, he broke down and wept.

One curious fact which tends to underline the basic senselessness of capital punishment is the way in which we are regularly brought into touch with an evil apart from the nagging, chronic, yet somehow endurable distress which the death penalty itself causes us: this is the almost unendurable incongruity it manifests in its choice of victims. If in Caryl Chessman, for instance, we were confronted with a plucky, dogged, intelligent man (so intelligent, in fact, as to have blurred in the minds of many people the nature of his morality, which was that of a cynical, self-justifying hoodlum; he verged as close to an embodiment of the perfect son of a bitch as the mind can conceive) who possessed the right at least to the possibility of redemption, in Ben Reid we are faced with a man so egregiously lacking in gifts, so totally desolate in circumstance, in quality of mind and spirit, that though he bears an almost antipodean relationship to Chessman as a man, we find ourselves questioning by this very contradistinction his implacable abandonment by society. Of course, the facts of heredity and environment cannot be allowed completely to eliminate responsibility and guilt. Reid's crime was an appalling one—one of such blind ruthlessness that it should have been apparent at the outset that he must be removed from the community until that time when it might reasonably be made certain that he could take his place again among his fellow men. Failing this approximate certainty, it would have to be made sure that he was incarcerated for good. But here we are not speaking of correction. We are not even speaking of that reasonable punishment which might carry with it vitalizing connotations of remorse and contrition. We are speaking of total abandonment. Perhaps not so wise but no less unfortunate than Chessman, Reid too had been judged beyond salvation. It is this abrupt, irrevocable banishment, this pre-emption by the state of the single final judgment which is in the providence of God alone—and the subtle but disastrous effect this act has upon the whole philosophy of crime and punishment—that wrecks the possibility of any lasting, noble concept of justice, and causes the issue of the death penalty to become, not peripheral, but central to an understanding of a moral direction in our time.

Against an awesome contemporary backdrop of domestic trouble and crisis, and the lingering image of concentration camps, and the threat of mass annihilation, the case of Ben Reid might seem an event of such small moment that there is hardly any wonder that it has commanded no one's attention. It is a case little enough known in Hartford, much less in the state of Connecticut or the broad, busy world. If it is true that crime in general, save in its most garish, tabloid aspects, fails to gain our serious regard, it may also be said that the question of capital punishment commands even less interest on the part of thinking people, especially in America. It becomes one of those lofty moral issues relegated to high school debates. To most thinking people, crime is something we read about at breakfast. The infliction of the death penalty, even further removed from our purview, is a ceremony which takes place in the dead of night, enacted, like some unnamable perversion, in shame and secrecy, and reported the next morning, on a back page, with self-conscious and embarrassed brevity. Our feelings are usually mixed; conditioned by two decades of James Cagney movies, and the memory of the jaunty wisecrack when the warden comes and the last mile commences, few of us can escape a shiver of horrid fascination which the account of a man's judicial execution affords us. But the truth is that few of us, at the same time, are left without a sense of queasiness and discomfiture, and indeed there are some—not simply the quixotic or the "bleeding hearts," as Mr. J. Edgar Hoover describes those who abhor the death penalty—who are rendered quite inescapably bereft. "For certain men, more numerous than is supposed," wrote Albert Camus, "knowing what the death penalty really is and being unable to prevent its application is physically insupportable. In their own way, they suffer this penalty, too, and without any justification. If at least we lighten the weight of the hideous images that burden these men, society will lose nothing by our actions." This is not alone an interior, personal viewpoint which would subvert a general evil in the name of delicate feelings; Camus' other arguments against capital punishment are too fierce and telling for that. The fact remains that all of us, to some degree, are spiritually and physically diminished by the doctrine of legal vengeance, even though it manifests itself as nothing more than a chronic, insidious infection beneath the public skin. We need only the occurrence of a sudden Chessman, flaunting his anguish like a maddened carbuncle, to make evident the ultimate concern we have with our own debilitating and corrupting sickness. That we do not discuss this problem until a Chessman appears is only an indication of one of our most ruinous human feelings—our inability to think about any great issue except in the light of the unique, the glamorous, the celebrity. Chessman was indisputably unique as a criminal and as one condemned; it is not to demean that uniqueness to declare that we shall never resolve the issue of the capital punishment until we ponder it in terms, not alone of Chessman, but of Ben Reid.

It is more than likely that apathy about the question is generated by the knowledge that capital punishment is on the decrease. With great pride the commonwealth acknowledges that, on the average, it now exterminates only about fifty people a year—like stars on a flag, one for each sovereign state. A common attitude might be articulated in the words of *Time* Magazine, which said during the Chessman affair: "If opponents of capital punishment were patient enough, they could just sit back and wait for it to fade away—in practice, if not on the statute books. But abolitionists try to hasten that fade-away by argument." Aside from the fact that very few evils have been hastened into extinction without the benefit of incessant argument, such a statement represents a blindness to the profounder truths which seems to seize *Time* at intervals. There is very little patience among men who are waiting to die. "To sit back and wait for it to fade away," is of small consolation to the "160 or so" people (including Ben Reid) which *Time* in the same article stated were awaiting execution on Death Rows all over America at the time of the Chessman affair. I do not know how *Time*'s writer visualized the number 160—if indeed he tried to visualize it at all: larger than fifty maybe? less than a thousand? As for myself, the more I ponder 160 condemned faces the more the number acquires a queerly disproportionate hugeness, and to use any phrase which implies such a gradual, far-off diminution seems to me, quite simply, a triumph of indifference. Moreover, I am not at all sure that capital punishment will in fact fade away, as long as Mr. J. Edgar Hoover, the guardian of our public morals, has any say in the matter.

Mr. Hoover, according to a news item last June in the New York *Herald Tribune,* for the first time in his long career as our premier law-enforcement officer, has allowed himself, in what I suppose must be called a policeman's trade journal, to proclaim his belief in the efficacy of the death penalty.[2] The article went on to describe the particular malfeasance which had impelled Mr. Hoover to take this position. It was a singularly hideous crime. A California woman, who happened incidentally to be pregnant, enticed a little girl of six into a car. There in the woman's presence her thirty-year-old husband raped the "screaming" child, who thereupon was bludgeoned to death by the wife with a tire jack. Apprehended and tried swiftly, the man was sentenced to die in the gas chamber, while his wife received life imprisonment. Past any doubt this was a deed so horrible as to tempt one to view it almost metaphysically, as if it were enacted in a realm beyond even abnormal behavior. All of our emotions are unhinged, displaced, at the contemplation of such a monstrous crime. As Anthony Storr, writing in a recent issue of the *New Statesman,* remarks: "To rape and murder a little girl is the most revolting of crimes. It is easy to sympathize with those who feel that a man who could do such a thing should be flogged or executed. . . . We think of our own young daughters and we shudder. The child rapist has alienated himself from our society, and we want to eliminate him, to suppress him, to forget that he ever existed."

Yet as one thinks about the *Herald Tribune* article and the crime and, more particularly, Mr. Hoover's attitude toward it, it seems evident that, in lending his great prestige to the further-ance of capital punishment and, moreover, in using this partic-ular case as an example of its presumed "efficacy," Mr. Hoover (who after all is not a law-giver, but a law-enforcement officer) is committing a two-fold error. Because where one might say, *purely for the sake of argument,* that the death penalty was effective in preventing such crafty and meticulously deliberate crimes as kidnaping for ransom, or treason, or even the hijack-ing of airplanes, one would be almost obliged to admit, if he had any understanding of criminal behavior, that its value in a crime of this type was nil. For the two wretched people who perpetrated this outrage were not, in any sense of the word, rational, and clearly not susceptible to rational controls. To believe that by taking away the life of even one of these sickening perverts we shall deter others from similarly mad acts is demonstrably a false belief: only one conceivable end is served, and that is vengeance, an emotion which—instinctive as it may be—society can no longer afford. As Anthony Storr goes on to say: "It is also important that we should not simply recoil in horror, but that when we catch the child rapist we should study him and the conditions which produced him. In that way only may we be able to . . . offer help to those who are driven by similar desires. . . . You and I may imagine that we could never rape a child and then murder it: but, if we are honest with ourselves, we have to admit that even this potentiality exists within us. We do not know what internal pressures drive the rapist, nor what conditions determine his dreadful acts. But he cannot be regarded as a different kind of animal with different instincts; for he is also human, and subject to the same laws and the same forces which determine the desires of every one of us. It is tempting to treat him as something utterly foreign from ourselves and so avoid looking into our own depths. . . . To condemn him as inhuman is to fall into the trap of treating him as he treated his victims: as a thing, not a person, a thing on whom we can let loose our own sadistic impulses, not a fellow creature who might, even yet, be redeemed."

At this juncture, whether we are viewing a child rapist or Ben Reid, we are admittedly faced with problems which do not lend themselves to ready solutions. For one thing, there is the familiar question: "Wouldn't Ben Reid, when all is said and done, be better off dead if he had to serve a life sentence in prison?" This, or something like it, is a commonly heard sentiment, often uttered by people who are compassionate and well-meaning. But in the end it only emphasizes a corollary evil of capital punishment—the equally vengeful notion that there is no alternative to the death penalty save a sentence of perpetual incarceration. Significantly, if it is true that a life term with no hope of parole is worse than death (and one cannot help but agree that it may be worse), it becomes necessary to ask why we do not sentence our most villainous offenders to life, reserving the death penalty for lesser criminals. But more importantly, to assume that, short of killing a man, we must doom him to a lifetime behind prison walls is to succumb to the doctrine of retaliation in its most hateful sense; and it is the practice of capital punishment more than any other single factor which tends to blight our administration of justice and to cast over our prisons the shadow of interminable revenge and retribution. Now it would appear that some criminals are hopelessly incorrigible. Taborsky would seem to be mad or half-mad, or, though sane within the legal sense of the word, seemingly devoid of any kind of understanding of right or wrong; from these people it would certainly be clear that we must protect ourselves by keeping them behind high walls forever. At the very least, as Anthony Storr points out, we can study them, and learn why they and their kind behave as they do. A majority of criminals, however—including those whose deeds have been quite as ugly as Ben Reid's—are amenable to correction, and many of them can be, and have been, returned to society. As for Ben Reid, in arbitrarily inflicting upon him the sentence of death, in denying him even the chance of rehabilitation we have just as arbitrarily granted others, we have committed a manifest injustice; and the death penalty, once again, reveals its ignoble logic.

It has been argued that opponents of capital punishment are swayed by emotion, that they are sentimental. To the degree that sentimentality may be considered a state of mind relying more upon emotion than reason, it would seem plain that it was the defenders of the death penalty who are the sentimentalists. If for example, it could be proved that capital punishment was an effective deterrent to crime, even the most emotionally vulnerable, die-hard humanitarian would be forced to capitulate in favor of it. But, unable to fend off the statistical proof that it is no deterrent at all, proponents of capital punishment find themselves backed into a corner, espousing emotional, last-ditch arguments. In the present instance, its lack of deterrent effect may be shown in the fact that it did not deter Ben Reid. Even more strikingly it is true in the case of the terrible Taborsky, finally executed, who had barely escaped electrocution for mur-

der once (he was released from Death Row on a judicial error
and freed from prison), whereupon he committed the series of
brutal slayings I have mentioned. If it is evident that Taborsky
should never have been released into society, it seems almost as
clear that he is a case in point of that theory, proposed by a
number of serious observers, that the death penalty in significant and not-too-rare instances actually exerts a fatal lure,
impelling certain unbalanced people to crimes which ordinarily
they would not commit. (In a recent English case, one Frederick Cross of Stockport, near Manchester, said in testimony:
"When I saw the man in his car I got the idea that if I was to kill
him I would be hanged. . . . I don't wish to be defended at all. I
killed him so that I would be hanged." The victim was a complete stranger. Cross achieved his desire: he was hanged.) Finally, in order to make reasonable the argument that capital punishment is a deterrent, why is it that the public is not incessant-
ly exposed to its horrible finality, forced to witness the barbarous rite itself, and thereby made to reflect on the gruesome fate
awaiting malefactors? But it remains a secret, shameful ceremony and, except for the most celebrated cases, it is even in-
differently reported in the press. Until by legislative mandate all
executions are carried on the television networks of the states
involved (they could be sponsored by the gas and electric companies), in a dramatic fashion which will enable the entire population—men, women, and all children over the age of five—to
watch the final agonies of those condemned, even the suggestion that we inflict the death penalty to deter people from
crime is a farcical one.

Shorn of all rational, practical arguments, those who favor
the death penalty must confront those who would eliminate it
upon the solitary grounds of vengeance, and it is here upon
these grounds, and these grounds alone, that the issue will have
to be resolved. There is no doubt that the urge for revenge is a
strong human emotion. But whether this is an emotion to be
encouraged by the State is a different matter. As for Ben Reid,
how much actual vengeance society still harbors toward him can
only be a matter of conjecture. It would be a disgrace to all of
us to say that it could be much. Having dwelt in his seven by

seven cell on Death Row, as I have said, for over four years, he would seem to have endured such a torture of bewilderment, anxiety and terror as to make the question of vengeance academic. Since that day in June, 1957, when he entered his cell on Death Row, there have been numberless writs, reprieves, reversals, stays for execution, all carried out in that admirable spirit of Fair Play which marks American justice but which, like a pseudo-smile masking implacable fury, must seem to a condemned man pitiless and sadistic beyond any death sentence. A year-and-a-half ago, indeed, it appeared that Ben Reid would have his opportunity for redemption; the judge of the U.S. District Court vacated his conviction on the grounds that his trial had been "fundamentally unfair," because the police had exacted his confessions without informing him of his rights to counsel or, for that matter, of any of his rights. At this point, Reid's attorney told him the good news: it looked as if he was going to live. This past September, however, the U.S. Circuit Court of Appeals in New York took a different view: since counsel had not brought up the point of illegal confessions at the trial, Ben had in effect "waived his rights." Thus the lower court was overruled—not without, however, a vigorous dissenting opinion by one of the justices, Judge Charles E. Clark, one-time dean of the Yale Law School, who said that the view that Reid waived his rights "borders on the fantastic in any human or practical or, indeed, legal sense." Reid has just recently been granted a reprieve, until April 30, 1962, in order that his case may be argued before the U.S. Supreme Court. Especially in the light of Judge Clark's angry dissent, it seems likely that Reid's case will at least be accepted for review. Whether by these nine old metaphysicians, as Mencken called them, the legal point will be resolved in Reid's favor remains, as usual, a mystery. In any event, for Reid it has been a splendid ordeal. His present lawyer (who incidentally is also a Negro) has protested to the State, asking his removal from the tiny cell. After four years there, he contends, Ben's mind has badly deteriorated. Nowhere else on earth is a man dragged by such demoralizing extremes to the very edge of the abyss.

"The little man, despite the pratings of Democracy," Judge

Curtis Bok has written of the death penalty, "is still the scapegoat." And he added this observation: "Someday we will look
back upon our criminal and penal processes with the same horrified wonder as we now look back upon the Spanish inquisition." Should the U.S. Supreme Court turn down his appeal, I
am told that there is an outside chance at least that Ben Reid—
due to those considerations of environment and mentality
which his lawyer initially argued for in vain—may have his sentence commuted by the State Board of Pardons. This is highly
unlikely: the Board of Pardons has never yet commuted a death
sentence of a man convicted under the same Connecticut law.
But there is a chance. If this comes to pass and Reid is allowed
to live, he will gain, aside from the fragments of his life, an
ironic kind of victory: nothing could demonstrate more cruelly
the travesty of justice which is capital punishment than this
shabby and belated mercy, predicated upon the identical arguments which were advanced in his favor in a court of law nearly
five years before. On the other hand, should the fact if not the
spirit of justice be served, and Ben Reid goes to the electric
chair one night this spring, it may be said that the soul which is
taken will have been already so diminished by our own inhumanity that what shall be lost is hardly a soul at all, and that
the death penalty, having divested a man not alone of his life
but of that dignity with which even the humblest of men must
be allowed to face death itself, has achieved its ultimate corrup-
tion. *Or when saw we Thee sick, or in prison, and came unto
Thee?* It is perhaps a late date in history to summon up the
gospel in behalf of a derelict Negro boy; having abandoned him,
it does not become a Christian society to waste a shred of its
jealously guarded piety upon him whom it has cast out into
darkness. Only the condemned can truly know the heaviness of
guilt; it settles upon their spirits like the weight of all the universe, and the quality of their bereavement is solitary and
unique among humankind. To attempt to soothe this bereavement through Christian homilies would seem to be, like that
final promenade with the chaplain whispering from Holy Writ,
an act of outrageous hypocrisy. Yet somehow, try as we might
to evade the verdict, we find ourselves being measured: *Inas-*

much as ye have done it unto one of the least of these My brethren, ye have done it unto Me. Until, searching our hearts, we can reconcile these words with the murder we inflict, in the name of justice, upon Ben Reid, and his fellows likewise outcast and condemned, we stand ourselves utterly condemned.

24 ATTORNEYS FOR THE NAACP LEGAL DEFENSE AND EDUCATIONAL FUND

One of the most original and effective arguments ever made against capital punishment in America was written in 1971 and presented to the United States Supreme Court as the brief for the petitioner in *Aikens* v. *California, dismissed as moot,* 406 U.S. 813 (1972). For it sought to prove not that capital punishment was immoral or inefficacious but that it was illegal, that it was a cruel and unusual punishment forbidden by the Eighth Amendment to the Constitution.

The attorneys who devised the strategy of the *Aikens* brief operated under the aegis of the NAACP Legal Defense and Educational Fund, Inc., a corporation established in 1939 to provide legal aid to the poor and to support litigation in the interests of equality for black Americans. The Fund's lawyers were already handling a great many civil rights cases in the early 1960s when some of their number began to consider challenging the death penalty—so often meted out to blacks—on constitutional grounds. Soon, with the approval of Fund Director Jack Greenberg and the extraordinarily able and energetic assistance of consultant Anthony G. Amsterdam, professor of law at the University of Pennsylvania, later at Stanford University, the most successful abolition campaign in American history was underway.

This campaign culminated on January 17, 1972, when Amsterdam presented oral argument before the Supreme Court in support of the *Aikens* brief. The Court's decision, handed down on June 29, 1972, under the title of *Furman* v. *Georgia* (Aikens' death sentence having been vacated as a result of the California Supreme Court's decision, in *People* v. *Anderson*), was far from tidy. Its nine separate opinions confused many readers and left the future of capital punishment in doubt (see selection 26). It was certain that two justices, Brennan and Marshall, accepted the *Aikens* argument that all capital punishment violated the Eighth Amendment. The three other members of the majority, Justice Douglas, Stewart, and White, agreed that capital punishment was unconstitutionally cruel and unusual in its arbitrary and capricious selection of victims. Whether the decision left room for new constitutional death penalty statutes was unclear. There was no doubt, however, that *Furman* saved the lives of over six hundred men and women awaiting execution in June 1972. No other reform argument had accomplished so much.

A Cruel and Unusual Punishment (1971)

I. INTRODUCTION

This case presents the question whether the infliction of the penalty of death for the crime of murder, in the form in which the death penalty is administered in California and throughout the United States in this third quarter of the twentieth century, is a cruel and unusual punishment forbidden by the Eighth and Fourteenth Amendments. That question is, we think, an open one, uncontrolled by any prior decision of this Court. For while the Court has several times assumed, and expressed in *dicta*, that "the mere extinguishment of life"[1] is not a constitutionally prohibited cruel and unusual punishment, it has never focused squarely upon that issue or given it the consideration warranted by a major question arising under the Bill of Rights, particularly a question upon which hundreds of human lives depend.

We make this point at the outset for two reasons. It is, of

From Brief for the Petitioner in *Aikens* v. *California*, O. T. 1971, No. 68-5027 (prepared by attorneys for the NAACP Legal Defense and Educational Fund, Inc.), pp. 7-63.

course, important that our Eighth Amendment contention against the death penalty does not ask the Court to "depart from . . . firmly established principle," *Abbate v. United States,* 359 U.S. 187, 195 (1959), or to overturn any "deliberately decided rule of Constitutional law," *Mapp v. Ohio,* 367 U.S. 643, 677 (1961) (Mr. Justice Harlan, dissenting). To the contrary, the way is perfectly clear for the Court to hold that the death penalty is a cruel and unusual punishment consistently with the proper application of principles of *stare decisis* in constitutional adjudication. But the matter goes further than that. In a very practical as well as a jurisprudential sense, the Eighth Amendment question raised requires a judgment of first impression from this Court.

In saying so, we do not naively suggest that the Court's prior opinions treat the constitutionality of capital punishment as debatable. Obviously, the Court has long and firmly supposed its constitutionality; and if the question had been appropriately posed in *Wilkerson*[2] or *Kemmler,*[3] capital punishment plainly would have been sustained. The same may be true as late as *Francis,*[4] or even *Trop,*[5] although it is difficult to speculate what the Court would have concluded if a square presentation of the Eighth Amendment question had directed its attention to the enormous and constitutionally significant changes which the institution of capital punishment had already undergone between the late nineteenth century and 1947 or 1958. Still further changes have occurred since 1958; and the issue of the constitutionality of capital punishment today is an altogether different issue than its validity a century ago. Because the Court has not directly confronted the issue during this century, it has not had occasion to consider the constitutional consequences of the century's changes; and it is for this reason that the Eighth Amendment question presented in 1971 must fairly be viewed afresh, unconstrained by assumptions of the death penalty's validity which the Court first made in 1879 and continued to make—without examination—twenty or a dozen years ago.

What has happened, during the century, is an overwhelming, accelerating, nation-wide and world-wide abandonment of death as a punishment for civilian crime. We shall shortly discuss the precise constitutional implications of that evolution; but, upon any view, it is relevant to, and will ultimately be decisive of, the constitutionality of capital punishment under the Eighth Amendment. Capital punishment has largely gone the way of flogging and banishment, progressively excluded by this Nation and by the civilized nations of men from the register of legitimate penal sanctions. Like flogging and banishment, capital punishment is condemned by history and will sooner or later be condemned by this Court under the Constitution. The question is whether that condemnation should come sooner or later. It is whether the evolution of civility that is inexorably rendering the death penalty intolerable has so far advanced as to make the Eighth Amendment take hold upon this doomed, deadly institution; or whether the United States—following a period of more than four years since June 2, 1967 without an execution—must now relapse into killing some or all of the more than 660 men on its death rows before that evolution reaches the stage at which their killings are established to be unconstitutional.

We put the issue in this way not because we enjoy the presumptuous exercise of predicting history and the future outcome of this Court's decisions but because, inescapably, that *is* the issue. No one can dispute, we believe, either the fact of the evolution we describe or the legal consequence that, at some point in its development, that evolution must call into play the Cruel and Unusual Punishment Clause of the Eighth Amendment. It must, for the same reasons that a similar evolution has brought flogging and banishment under the Eighth Amendment's ban. The questions then arise: What principles should this Court use to determine the course of historical development, and the point upon that course, which mark a progressively repudiated punishment as cruel and unusual for Eighth Amendment purposes? And with regard to capital punishment, has that course been followed and that point been reached?

These questions are not without difficulty because, as has frequently been noted, the Eighth Amendment itself is not without difficulty. The Court's decisions have not undertaken to define in comprehensive terms the concept of "cruel and unusual punishments." Different approaches to that concept are available which would bring the death penalty within its prohibition. The approach taken in this brief is narrower than others that have been persuasively argued. Our approach concentrates upon the particular characteristic of capital punishment that it shares with only a very few other punishments, notably flogging and banishment which have already been constitutionally forbidden.

That characteristic is extreme contemporary rarity resulting from a demonstrable historical movement which can only be interpreted fairly as a mounting and today virtually universal repudiation. Today, "[d]eath is the rarest of all punishments for crime."[6] So far has its repudiation advanced that, if the United States were in fact to execute its 660 condemned men in 1971, it would thereby become uncontestably the greatest killer of human beings by judicial process in the world—probably, the killer of more men than all other non-communist nations of the world combined. This observation speaks strongly to the question whether death is a cruel and unusual punishment within the meaning of the Constitution of a Nation which aspires to be one of the world's more enlightened peoples.

But our approach to the Eighth Amendment concentrates primarily upon the evolution of the death penalty in the United States itself. Properly viewed, that evolution has brought this country to a stage at which the relevant constitutional indicators of a cruel and unusual punishment have abundantly matured. America has had its time of "experimentation" with the killing of men; the experiment has led to one inexorable conclusion; and further development can only make more manifest—at a terrible cost—what is already manifest and manifestly fitting as a basis for judicial application of the Constitution. To demonstrate why this is so, we first discuss the nature of the Eighth Amendment's concern against cruel and unusual punishments, and then proceed to test the death penalty in light of that concern.

II. THE RELEVANT EIGHTH AMENDMENT STANDARD

At the heart of the Eighth Amendment lurks an extraordinary dilemma whose resolution is, we think, the key to decision of this case. The dilemma arises from the confrontation of three basic principles.

First, in the context of American government, the Eighth Amendment's proscription of cruel and unusual punishments forbids the legislative enactment of such punishments as well as the judicial imposition of them. This has always been accepted. *Weems v. United States*, 217 U.S. 349, 366, 378-379, 382 (1910); *Trop v. Dulles*, 356 U.S. 86, 103-104 (1958) (plurality opinion of Chief Justice Warren); *Robinson v. California*, 370 U.S. 660 (1962); and see *Wilkerson v. Utah*, 99 U.S. 130, 133, 136-137 (1879) (dictum); *In re Kemmler*, 136 U.S. 436, 446-447 (1890) (dictum).

Second, the force of the Amendment is not limited to the prohibition of those atrocities that would have turned the stomachs of the Framers in the Eighteenth Century. This conclusion is compelled by both authority and reason. "[I]t is a constitution we are expounding,"[7] and the Constitution "states or ought to state not rules for the passing hour, but principles for an expanding future."[8] Thus, *Trop v. Dulles*, 356 U.S. 86 (1958), outlawed the hoary penalty of banishment with the observations that the scope of the Cruel and Unusual Punishment Clause "is not static," and that the "Amendment must draw its meaning from the evolving standards of decency that mark the progress of a maturing society." (*Id.*, at 101 (plurality opinion of Chief Justice Warren).) See also *Robinson v. California*, 370 U.S. 660, 666 (1962) (referring to "the light of contemporary human knowledge"); *Jackson v. Bishop*, 404 F.2d 571, 578-580 (8th Cir. 1968); *Goss v. Bomar*, 337 F.2d 341, 342-343 (6th Cir. 1964) (*dictum*). Such a conception of evolving standards is a constitutional commonplace and is firmly entrenched in the jurisprudence of the Eighth Amendment in particular. The Cruel and Unusual Punishment Clause "may be therefore progressive, and is not fastened to the obsolete but may acquire meaning as public opinion becomes enlightened by a humane justice." *Weems v. United States*, 217 U.S. 349, 378 (1910).

To deny this dynamic character to the Eighth Amendment would produce inconceivable results. . . . If 1791 is indeed the constitutional benchmark and if the Constitution does not forbid capital punishment today upon the theory that it was

widely allowed by law and practice in 1791, then the Eighth
Amendment also does not forbid today and will never forbid—
the stocks and the pillory, public flogging, lashing and whipping
on the bare body, branding of cheeks and forehead with a hot
iron, and the slitting, cropping, nailing and cutting off of ears.
Further discussion of a "static" theory of the Eighth Amendment seems unnecessary.

Third, in applying the Eighth Amendment to advancing and
changing times, the courts are to be guided by the touchstone
of "contemporary human knowledge,"[9] "public opinion . . . enlightened by a humane justice,"[10] and "the evolving standards
of decency that mark the progress of a maturing society."[11]
What other standards, after all, could possibly be used? Surely it
was not the purpose of the Eighth Amendment that succeeding
generations of judges should mirror in it their own individual
philosophies of the criminal sanction. So, if the obsolete and
eldritch customs of 1791 are not to be perpetually controlling,
where else may judges look but to enlightened public opinion
for conception of the "cruel and unusual punishments" which
the Constitution forbids?

And there stands the dilemma. Quite perceptibly, an extreme
difficulty must attend any process of constitutional adjudication by which this Court subjects legislation to the test of "enlightened public opinion," and adjudges the validity of a legislature's product according to society's "standards of decency."
For, both in constitutional contemplation and in fact, it is the
legislature, not the Court, which responds to public opinion and
immediately reflects the society's standards of decency. If the
question asked by the Eighth Amendment really be whether our
democratic society can tolerate the existence of any particular
penal law that is on the books, the Eighth Amendment's answer
will always be that it can—and for the simple reason that the
law is on the books of a democratic society. The conclusion
therefore seems to be required either that the Eighth Amendment is *not* a judicially enforceable restriction upon legislation,
or that the *Weems-Trop* test referring to contemporary public
standards of decency is not a usable measure of the Amendment; or else that the question which we have just posed is not

the proper question to which the Amendment and the *Weems-Trop* test respond.

As this way of putting the matter suggests, we think that the question—whether the maintenance of a particular harsh penalty on the statute books is consistent with prevailing standards of decency—is the wrong question. We suggest what we think is the right one below. For we cannot believe that the Eighth Amendment is not a restriction upon cruel and unusual penal legislation rightly enforceable by this Court. Nor can we believe that the Amendment's prohibition is restricted to live disembowelment and similar long-gone butcheries—nor, on the other hand, that it invokes the unassisted penological impressions of particular Justices. The *Weems-Trop* test *is*, we submit, the proper one. Common standards of decency in our contemporary society *do* set the limits of punishment allowable under the Eighth Amendment. The problem is how those standards are to be ascertained, and with regard to what specific question.

We begin with the specific question. When a man such as Earnest Aikens comes before the Court claiming that the law under which he was sentenced provides for an unconstitutional cruel and unusual punishment, the question is not: will contemporary standards of decency allow the existence of such a general law on the books? The question is, rather: will contemporary standards of decency allow the general application of the law's penalty *in fact*? The distinction which we draw here lies between what public conscience will allow the law to *say* and what it will allow the law to *do*—between what public decency will permit a penal statute to threaten and what it will allow the law to carry out—between what common revulsion will forbid a government to put upon its statute books as the extreme, dire terror of the State (not to be ordinarily, regularly or in other than a few rare cases enforced), and what public revulsion would forbid a government to do to its citizens if the penalty of the law were generally, even-handedly, non-arbitrarily enforced in all of the cases to which it applied.

This last point—regarding general, even-handed, non-arbitrary application is critical. For in it lies, we think, a large part of the need to have a Cruel and Unusual Punishment Clause in the

Constitution, and of the need to have courts enforce it. The government envisaged for this country by the Constitution is a democratic one, and in a democracy there is little reason to fear that penal laws will be placed upon the books which, in their general application, would affront the public conscience. The real danger concerning cruel and inhuman laws is that they will be enacted in a form such that they can be applied sparsely and spottily to unhappy minorities, whose numbers are so few, whose plight so invisible, and whose persons so unpopular, that society can readily bear to see them suffer torments which would not for a moment be accepted as penalties of general application to the populace.

Herein is found the difference between the judgment which the legislator makes, responding *politically* to public conscience, and the judgment which a court must make under the obligation that the Eighth Amendment imposes upon it to respond *rationally* to public conscience. A legislator may not scruple to put a law on the books (still less, to maintain an old law on the books) whose general, even-handed, non-arbitrary application the public would abhor—precisely because both he and the public know that it will not be enforced generally, even-handedly, non-arbitrarily. But a court cannot sustain such a law under the Eighth Amendment. It cannot do so because both the Amendment itself and our most fundamental principles of due process and equal protection forbid American governments the devices of arbitrariness and irregularity, even as a sop to public conscience.

To put the matter another way, there is nothing in the political process by which public opinion manifests itself in legislated laws that protects the isolated individual from being cruelly treated by the state. Public conscience often will support laws enabling him to be so mistreated, provided that arbitrary selection can be made in such a fashion as to keep his numbers small and the horror of his condition mute. Legislators neither must nor do take account of such individuals. But it is the precise business of courts to take account of them, and to disallow under the Eighth Amendment the application to them of penalties so harsh that public conscience would be appalled by their less arbitrary application.

We shall develop this theme more fully, in the pages that follow, with regard to the death penalty. But we have said enough, at this point, to enable us to state our major submission on behalf of Earnest Aikens. His sentence of death for the crime of first-degree murder is an unconstitutional cruel and unusual punishment because it affronts contemporary standards of decency, universally felt, that would condemn the use of death as a penalty for that crime if such a penalty were uniformly, regularly, and even-handedly applied either to all first-degree murderers or to any reasonable proportion of those eligible for the penalty under California law.

We use the term "reasonable proportion" in order to exclude the sort of tolerance which a law may obtain through rare—or, in the constitutional sense, "unusual"—application. We do so for the reasons which we have just stated: that it, because we believe that the Cruel and Unusual Punishment Clause is designed precisely to condemn any penalty so oppressive that it can command public acceptance only by virtue of extremely infrequent and sporadic enforcement. Laws are written to be enforced with practicable generality in the cases to which they apply; and so it is a fair measure of a law's acceptability to imagine its general enforcement. Let us do so with regard to capital punishment for first-degree murder.

Let us take a very modest standard of generality and assume that the United States were to execute 184 first-degree murderers this year. We have chosen that figure—in the absence of any obtainable information concerning the number of first-degree murder convictions annually—because it represents the largest number of murderers executed in the country since reliable counts began to be kept in 1930. During the year 1935, 184 men and women were put to death for murder in the United States. Of course, it is absurd to suppose that as few first-degree murder convictions are returned yearly in the 1970's as in the 1930's; and even in the 1930's such knowledgeable observers as Warden Lewis E. Lawes of Sing Sing recognized that the death penalty was not being generally enforced.[12] Nonetheless, let us take the 1935 national high-water mark of 184 first-degree murderers as a measure of some generality of enforcement of the death penalty for murder.

Imagine now 184 electrocutions and gassings in the United States in 1971. That is four times the number of human beings executed during any of the past ten years, and exceeds by 50 the total number of executions for the ten-year period. If, in fact, 184 murderers were to be executed in this year 1971, we submit it is palpable that the public conscience of the Nation would be profoundly and fundamentally revolted, and that the death penalty for murder would be abolished forthwith as the atavistic horror that it is. Our detailed reasons for this submission follow. First, we pause for one additional paragraph to make our legal point clear.

We disagree not at all with the reasoning process, but we dispute the factual premise—unexamined then and now demonstrably incorrect—of the *dictum* announced by this Court thirteen years ago in *Trop v. Dulles,* 356 U.S. 86 (1958):

> ". . . Whatever the arguments may be against capital punishment, both on moral grounds and in terms of accomplishing the purposes of punishment—and they are forceful—the death penalty has been employed throughout our history, and, *in a day when it is still widely accepted,* it cannot be said to violate the constitutional concept of cruelty." (*Id.* at 99 (plurality opinion of Chief Justice Warren; emphasis added).)

We think that it is simply not correct that the death penalty is today "still widely accepted." We speak, for the reasons that we have already stated, not of its acceptance on the pages of the statute books, but of its acceptance in actual usage—and of such acceptance as it does not illegitimately obtain by being irregularly and arbitrarily applied. Far from being "widely accepted", the death penalty today is with rare public unanimity rejected and repudiated. We proceed next to demonstrate this point and to develop its constitutional implications.

III. THE PENALTY OF DEATH

The acceptance which a punishment is given by contemporary society, and its acceptability under that society's prevailing standards of decency, may be measured by objective indicators.

In the case of the death penalty today, numerous indicators point in a single direction. Language requires that we state them one by one; but it is their plain convergence that, we think, marks the punishment of death as unacceptable, cruel and unusual.

(1) All informed observers of the death penalty agree in describing a world-wide trend toward its disuse that is nothing short of drastic. This has been a relatively constant long-term development, despite expectable short-term swings. Whereas Jeremy Bentham wrote in 1831 that "on the part of rulers—general custom—general at least, not to say universal—delivers its testimony in favour of this punishment,"[13] it is now the case that most of the nations of Western Europe and the Western Hemisphere have legally abolished capital punishment as a penalty for civilian crime. The majority of nations in the world retain the death penalty on the books but use it relatively infrequently. Estimates of the total number of executions in the world today must necessarily remain speculative, but the figure probably does not much exceed the 560 executions estimated to have occurred in London and Middlesex alone each year during the mid-sixteenth century. These figures are assuredly very crude, but in general terms they mark the magnitude of the trend toward *de facto* abolition. So far has this trend progressed that the Secretary-General of the United Nations recently reported to the Economic and Social Council that: "Those countries retaining the death penalty report that in practice it is only exceptionally applied and frequently the persons condemned are later pardoned by executive authority."[14] And, notwithstanding its habitual cautiousness and deference to national sovereignty in domestic matters, the United Nations Economic and Social Council recently adopted a resolution affirming "that the main objective to be pursued is that of progressively restricting the number of offences for which capital punishment might be imposed with a view to the desirability of abolishing this punishment in all countries so that the right to life, provided for in Article 3 of the Universal Declaration of Human Rights may be fully guaranteed."[15]

(2) This historical development has not been a mere collec-

tion of happenings unanimated by a theme. Capital punishment has not simply atrophied or gone out of fad in the world, but has been progressively rejected in the course of an ideological and moral debate resonant with concerns that are intimately connected with the "principle of civilized treatment" and "the dignity of man." *Trop v. Dulles,* 356 U.S. 86, 99, 100 (1958) (plurality opinion of Chief Justice Warren). Any sampling of the literature of this debate makes manifest that although there are entirely convincing practical reasons for putting an end to the death penalty—the principal arguments urged to support its abolition have always been humanistic, and concerned with fundamental human decency. . . .

It is for this reason, of course, that capital punishment, uniquely among secular penal institutions, has become the subject of intense concern by religious groups. For the same reason, the long-enduring struggle for legal abolition has been waged with the fervor of a crusade. The same reason brought Albert Camus to call the abolition of the death penalty "a great civilizing step";[16] it brought former Attorney General Ramsey Clark to call abolition "a major milestone in the long road up from barbarism;"[17] and it brought the Archbishop of Canterbury to conclude, following the abolition of capital punishment for murder in Great Britain in 1969, that:

> "Abolition of capital punishment, once and for all, will help create a more civilized society in which to continue the search for the causes of crime . . . I am certain it will redound in very many ways to the advantage and honor of the nation."[18]

We set forth these expressions not for the purpose of convincing the Court that Albert Camus, or Ramsey Clark, or Michael Ramsey, is correct, as a moral matter. The point is simply that the terms they use are archetypal reflections of the terms in which the capital punishment controversy has been fought during the years in which world history has progressively, and now quite thoroughly, abandoned the death penalty. Opposition to capital punishment has invariably been asserted on the basis of "fundamental moral and social values in our civilization and in our society."[19] For this reason, the present marked attrition of the use of capital punishment throughout the world must be seen as something more than a sort of aimless obsolescence. It can only fairly be seen, in the light of the forceful struggle waged around the penalty of death, as a repudiation.

(3) One further point connected with the ideological history of this repudiation of the death penalty bears emphasis. The values which have been most consistently opposed to capital punishment, and which have largely extirpated it in the western world over the course of the last two centuries, lie very close to the root of the Anglo-American conception of a free and civilized society. Sellin has written that:

> ". . . the struggle about this punishment has been one between ancient and deeply rooted beliefs in retribution, atonement or vengeance on the one hand, and, on the other, beliefs in the personal value and dignity of the common man that were born of the democratic movement of the eighteenth century, as well as beliefs in the scientific approach to an understanding of the motive forces of human conduct, which are the result of the growth of the sciences of behavior during the nineteenth and twentieth centuries."[20]

This is not to say, of course, that no one does or can approve the death penalty for other reasons than belief in retribution, atonement or vengeance; but it is significant that those beliefs have been historically the mainstays of support for the institution of capital punishment, while the movement for abolition has been spearheaded by concerns derived from conceptions of the worth and dignity of the individual. The ultimate premise and lesson of capital punishment is " 'that a man's life ceases to be sacred when it is thought useful to kill him.' "[21] Little wonder that the nations of the world most closely allied with our own in traditions, and sharing our heritage and aspirations of respect for the citizen, have now overwhelmingly rejected the death penalty.

(4) So has the United States. In this country, the decreasing trend of executions has been consistent and dramatic. The National Crime Commission recently noted that:

> "The most salient characteristic of capital punishment is that it is infrequently applied. . . . [A]ll available data indicate that judges,

juries and governors are becoming increasingly reluctant to impose or authorize the carrying out of a death sentence." (PRESIDENT'S COMMISSION ON LAW ENFORCEMENT AND ADMINISTRA- TION OF JUSTICE. REPORT (THE CHALLENGE OF CRIME IN A FREE SOCIETY) (1967), 143.)

The extent to which this is true appears upon inspection of the highly reliable figures on executions maintained by the Federal Bureau of Prisons since 1930. Its latest cumulative report shows that 3,859 persons were executed under civil authority in the United States between 1930 and 1968. UNITED STATES DE- PARTMENT OF JUSTICE, BUREAU OF PRISONS, NA- TIONAL PRISONER STATISTICS. Bulletin No. 45, *Capital Punishment 1930-1968* (August 1969) [hereafter cited as NPS (1968)], p. 7. Of these 3,859 men and women, only 191 were executed during the decade of the 1960's, only 25 since the end of 1963, and no one has been executed in the United States during more than four years since June 2, 1967. The trend is adequately shown by setting out the figures for the number of executions during each of the following representative years:

Total Number of Executions
in the United States

1930	155	1963	21
1935	199	1964	15
1940	124	1965	7
1945	117	1966	1
1950	82	1967	2
1955	76	1968	0
1960	56	1969	0
1961	42	1970	0
1962	47		

Although forty-one States, the federal government and the District of Columbia authorize the death penalty by law for at least one offense, fourteen of these forty-three jurisdictions have carried out no executions since 1960. Nineteen have car- ried out no executions since 1961. Twenty-four have carried out no executions since 1962. Thirty have carried out no executions since 1963. Thirty-five have carried out no executions since 1964.

It is interesting to note the regional distribution of the executions. (We shall return later to the racial figures.) Of the 3,859 persons killed since 1930, 33 were executed by the federal government; 608 by nine northeastern States; 403 by twelve north-central States; 509 by thirteen western States; and 2,306 by sixteen southern States and the District of Columbia. Since 1960, the corresponding figures for 191 executions are as follows: federal—1; northeastern States—17; north-central States—21; western States—48; southern States and D.C.—104. As of December 31, 1968, there were 479 men on death row throughout the entire country. One of these was a federal prisoner; 62 were in the northeastern States; 67 were in the north-central States; 114 were in the western States; and 235 were in the southern States and D.C.

(5) We summarize our conclusions from the preceding paragraphs as follows: Actual use of the death penalty throughout the world has declined precipitously against the background of a strong ideological controversy in which the increasingly prevailing forces of abolition have staked their case primarily upon the inhumanity and indecency of the penalty. They have prevailed virtually universally—and most notably in countries sharing our western humanist traditions—to the extent that today, the execution of a capital sentence is an almost indescribably uncommon event. Within the United States, it is plainly the most uncommon of all punishments for crime. In this country, executions vary as a function of geography and are preponderately a southern phenomenon; but, since 1958 at the least, executions in all regions of the United States for any crime have been rare. Since 1963 they have been freakishly rare.

(6) What do these almost incredible rarities in the use of capital punishment imply for the constitutional issue before the Court? In the first place, they obviously imply—in the language of *Trop v. Dulles, supra* that capital punishment is *not* "still widely accepted" in contemporary America. Recently, this Court cited public opinion polls indicating that about half the American people say they believe in the death penalty.

Witherspoon v. Illinois, 391 U.S. 510, 519-520 (1968). While it seems to us unthinkable that human life should be taken in the name of an institution that is so equivocally and marginally received—even in theory—as this, we do not rely upon the polls. For the value of such polls is very slight as a gauge of the standards of decency to which the Eighth Amendment bids this Court look.

This is so because opinions tapped in this fashion are notoriously fickle and particularly unreliable after several years without an execution. But it is so primarily because the citizen who deals with a poll-taker—like the legislator who puts or maintains a capital statute on the books—can have his cake and eat it too. He can afford to approve the principle of killing because in practice the persons selected to die will be so few as to go unnoticed. The real measure of American moral attitudes about the death penalty is reflected in what this Nation of 200 million people does. What it has done, in the years 1965-1970 inclusive, is to execute only ten people.

Of course, stays of execution and state and federal post-conviction proceedings on behalf of condemned men affect these figures, but not very much. In May of 1971, there were only 648 men on death row, notwithstanding the near cessation of executions since the end of 1964. And even this figure conveys an inflated image of the number of men destined to be killed. Plainly, the processes of American justice through which the conscience of a people may be glimpsed are sending very, very few men onto death row, and taking most of them off again before execution day. What American acceptance of the death penalty now boils down to is that America can stomach a few legal killings a year.

(7) One may look at these figures from another direction as well. No one knows or can estimate accurately how many convictions of capital crimes are returned in the United States yearly. But we do know that thirty-six States, the District of Columbia, and the federal jurisdiction all retain on their books statutes of general applicability punishing one or more offenses with death. In some States, half a dozen or more crimes may be so punishable. Yet, with all this capital armament in the arsenal

of a Nation of enormous and burgeoning population, with a growing crime rate and a going crime scare, only a few rare men are sentenced to death and fewer executed. This phenomenon reflects, we suggest, an overwhelming national repulsion against actual use of the penalty of death. Such a repulsion is all the more striking when one takes into account: (a) that for the past several years the country has undergone one of the most intense of its recurring periods of public agitation about and fear of crime; (b) that for a number of years there have been so few executions as to provide almost no focus for the mobilization of public sentiments against the death penalty; (c) that during these years, and many more before them, American executions have been conducted in secret, their most horrible aspects carefully concealed from public view; (d) that the death penalty is sponsored by the State, publicly approved by State officials, and supported by claims prevalent in law-enforcement quarters (although quite without basis in fact) that the penalty has unique penological values, particularly as a deterrent. It strongly appears, we think, that even under the most favorable conditions for capital punishment—with the vices of the death penalty concealed and its virtues inaccurately extolled—the American conscience has repudiated it hands down.

(8) The concealment, the secrecy, with which we hide away our executions, is doubly significant. First, it gravely inhibits the opportunity for contemporary society to make a clear-sighted and fully informed judgment upon the acceptability of what is really being perpetrated in its name. We assume that—whatever may be the measure of enlightened public opinion—the constitutional standard does not refer to opinion which is kept in the dark by suppression of the relevant facts. Of course, there are perfectly good and humane reasons for forbidding public executions, as every American jurisdiction now does—reasons which (as we shall shortly see) themselves bespeak eloquently the barbarity of capital punishment in any form. But suppression is nonetheless suppression because inspired by good intentions; and, particularly in determining what is a cruel and unusual punishment within the Eighth Amendment, it can hardly be supposed that the conscience-calming effects of sup-

pression are to be discounted on account of their humanity. Nor can it be supposed that a punishment is entitled to claim acceptability, as a demonstration of its conformance with enlightened standards of decency, *because* it is so repellant that it forces society to look away and not examine it too closely. In Camus' phrase: "The man who enjoys his coffee while reading that justice has been done would spit it out at the least detail."[22] This is not acceptance, but its opposite.

(9) That leads us to our second point concerning the uniform contemporary practice of secret executions: their concealment itself shows their repugnance of present-day standards of decency. Repugnance is the only answer to Justice Bok's trenchant question: "Why is the State so ashamed of its process that it must kill at dead of night, in an isolated place, and on an unnamed day?" BOK, STAR WORMWOOD (1959), 197. Notwithstanding that virtually the only argument still made in the twentieth century to support the death penalty is its supposed efficacy as a general deterrent, the men killed for deterrence's sake today are killed clandestinely, out of public view. Camus' forthright analysis of all that this implies is unavoidable:

> "As an example and for the sake of security, it would be wiser, instead of hiding the execution, to hold up the severed head in front of all who are shaving in the morning. . . .
>
> "Indeed, one must kill publicly or confess that one does not feel authorized to kill. If society justifies the death penalty by the necessity of the example, it must justify itself by making the publicity necessary. It must show the executioner's hands each time and force everyone to look at them—the over-delicate citizens and all those who had any responsibility in bringing the executioner into being. Otherwise, society admits that it kills without knowing what it is saying or doing. Or else it admits that such revolting ceremonies can only excite crime or completely upset opinion."[23]

It should be noted that Camus and others who have made the same point are not indulging in the sort of simplistic argument that is sometimes attributed to them. They are not naive enough to assert, and their point does not rest upon the assertion, that a punishment must be publicly exhibited in order to deter. Nor do they deny that there can be degrees of deterrence, and that society may rationally choose the diminished degree that is involved in private infliction of a punishment whose public exhibition would have untoward effects. Allowing the legitimacy of that choice, they ask only what the choice made by our modern society in regard to capital punishment indicates.

Plainly the decision to use capital punishment at all today indicates both the belief that it is a superior deterrent to even life imprisonment, and the desire to maximize the deterrent power of the law in regard to the offenses for which the extreme penalty is prescribed. From a deterrent point of view, the fact "[t]hat capital punishment is horrible and cruel is the reason for its existence."[24] A society which uses a punishment of that sort with the aim of maximizing deterrence can scarcely be expected to depreciate its deterrent force by hiding it—particularly in light of its centuries-old tradition of public executions—unless there is some very strong countervailing force. What then is that force? Can there be any doubt at all that it is the force of decency?

We hide our executions because we are disgusted to look at them, because the view of them would make men sick. We hide them because their public display would render them unacceptable and flout the dignity of man. Could this Court today sustain a *public* execution as consistent with the Eighth Amendment? No consideration that is urged to support closeted executions would be lacking in the case of a public one; and to the condemned man it would make relatively little difference. The one way of killing a human being is not more cruel to him than the other, although it is intolerably more cruel to us. This surely is because

"if people were to witness the decay of the waiting man, to hear his cries and watch his final struggles, they would be affronted in their consciences, and in their standards of humanity and of human dignity and decency. Our systematic concealment of executions creates a strong inference that capital punishment now falls under our expanded definition of 'cruelty,' particularly when we contrast this present custom of secrecy with the one-time public display of executions."[25]

(10) We have said that secret executions both demonstrate
the general unacceptability of killing as a penalty for crime in
contemporary America and provide the necessary basis for such
slight and uninformed acceptance as it has. The same is true of
the rarity of executions. We have already discussed the first of
these two aspects of the virtual cessation of American executions during the past several decades (pp. 39-43, *supra*); and we
return now to the second.

Almost forty years ago, Warden Lawes made the point that
the maintenance of capital legislation on the statute books depends upon its unenforcement.[26] It is, of course, a matter of
history, recognized by this Court in *McGautha v. California*,
402 U.S. 183 (1971), that public acceptability of the death
penalty in this country in this century has been secured only by
replacing mandatory capital penalties with statutes allowing
jury and court discretion in capital sentencing. These statutes,
combined with the prosecutorial discretion at the outset of a
capital case and the executive's commutative power at the end
of it, allow a "small and capricious selection of offenders [to
be] . . . put to death."[27] "Public awareness diminishes as the
frequency of imposing the penalty decreases, and legislative action is not likely to be prompted when the consequences befall
only a few prisoners." *Ralph v. Warden*, 438 F.2d 786, 792 (4th
Cir. 1970).

(11) It is important also to note the identity of the prisoners
upon whom the consequences fall. *Whose* killings today does
society accept, when it accepts any? Former Governor Michael
DiSalle of Ohio has answered this question.

". . . Generally they have one thing in common, they are penniless,
of low mental capacity, with little or no education, and have few
friends. The fact that they have no money is of particular import in
their being condemned to death. . . . It is the poor, the illiterate, the
underprivileged, the member of the minority group who is usually
sacrificed by society's lack of concern."[28]

The same point has been made repeatedly by knowledgeable
observers. Those who are selected to die are the poor and pow-
erless, personally ugly and socially unacceptable. In dispropor-

tionate percentages, they are also black. Racial discrimination is strongly suggested by the national execution figures; it has been borne out in a number of discrete and limited but carefully done studies, and it has seemed apparent to responsible commissions and individuals studying the administration of the death penalty in this country. Assuredly, the proof of discrimination is stronger in rape than in murder cases; and, in any case, an irrefutable statistical showing that a particular State has violated the Equal Protection of the Laws by consistent racial inequality in the administration of the death penalty is difficult to establish. This is so principally because the total number of death sentences is so exceedingly small in comparison to the number of factors which prosecuting officials, sentencing judges and juries, correctional officials and physicians, and commutative authorities may consider in the exercise of the many selective judgments which finally determine who shall live or die.

Where the occurrence of any phenomenon is rare and the factors that may cause it to occur are unlimited, neither statistics nor any other analytical tool can provide a sure-fire test for the detection of racial bias among those factors. Thus, a State can discriminate racially and not get caught at it if it kills men only sporadically, not too often, by being arbitrary in selecting the victims of discrimination. Or, to put the matter another way, if a State invokes a particular penalty sufficiently rarely so that no regular pattern of its use develops, the State *may* be acting discriminatorily; it *likely will* be acting in a fashion such that the penalty falls most harshly on the poor and disadvantaged; but it *surely will* be acting in a way that escapes the safeguards of the Constitution, unless the Eighth Amendment forbids. Equal Protection and Due Process provide no judicially usable devices to protect the individual from the arbitrariness of the freakishly rare, harsh penalty. This is all the more reason, we believe, for application of the constitutional guarantee against cruel and unusual punishments.

(12) But there are other consequences, as well, of the freakishly rare use of a harsh criminal penalty. We have pointed out above that such use escapes not only meaningful control under the constitutional guarantees of Equal Protection and Due Pro-

cess; it escapes also the fair scrutiny of public conscience, with its attendant pressure to keep the legislature acting decently. A public can easily bear the rare, random occurrence of a punishment which, if applied regularly, would make the common gorge rise. It seems to us that this is just the kind of penalty at which a prohibition of cruel and unusual punishments must aim. Whether it happen by accident or design that penalties of this sort fall most furiously upon the poor and friendless and upon racial minorities, the supposed "acceptance" of the penalty is nonetheless a product of the outcast nature of those who bear the brunt of it. As rarely as we tolerate the infliction of the death penalty today, we still more rarely tolerate its infliction upon *us*.

That the death penalty is rare and unusual permits public and political acceptance of its cruelty, but, for that very reason, requires judicial condemnation under the Eighth Amendment. Rare and uneven usage which evades the public conscience politically demands the supervision by the public conscience, speaking through the courts, which the Eighth Amendment promises. This is the more true because, we think such usage itself affronts "the dignity of man," *Trop v. Dulles, supra,* and those cherished principles of fair and regular, nonarbitrary treatment of the citizen which the Eighth Amendment, no less than the Fourteenth, supposes.

> "[T]he issue . . . is not . . . whether it is fair or just that one who takes another person's life should lose his own. Whatever you think about that proposition it is clear that we do not and cannot act upon it generally in the administration of the penal law. The problem rather is whether a small and highly random sample of people who commit murder or other comparably serious offenses ought to be despatched, while most of those convicted of such crimes are dealt with by imprisonment." [29]

(13) The reasons why our society is no longer willing generally to act upon the penal principle of a life for a life are, in part, pragmatic. The primary pragmatic consideration of this sort is, of course, our modern development of large-scale penal and correctional institutions which we must maintain whether

or not we use them for "capital" criminals, and into which we can now also place our "capital" criminals if we choose. But it is not the mere availability of this alternative to the penalty of death that has made our society choose overwhelmingly to use it and to reject capital punishment. It is the profound appreciation that, once we have developed an alternative, it would be intolerably cruel not to use it.

We have focused our argument in this brief upon the word "unusual" in the Eighth Amendment rather than upon the word "cruel." That is because, as we read this Court's prior decisions, they have not denied the cruelty of the death penalty, but have assumed its constitutionality as not "unusual." Plainly, the death penalty is cruel. Even if it involved no more than the calculated and deliberate extermination of a human life it would be cruel. "The killing of a helpless captive is a brutally degrading experience. If those alone who have participated in an execution could vote on the death penalty, it would be abolished tomorrow."[30] But more is involved. Uniquely among punishments, a death sentence inflicts upon the condemned man "a fate of ever-increasing fear and distress."[31] "The devastating, degrading fear that is imposed on the condemned for months or years is a punishment more terrible than death. . . ."[32]

(14) It is important, finally, that such rare and unusual use as American society makes of the death penalty today deprives it of any functional place in the rational scheme of a state's penal law. Harsh punishments used in this manner cease to be instruments of public justice or of reasoned penal policy, and hence cease to have any claim to legitimacy that might be set off against the commands of the Eighth Amendment. Capital punishment generally can be shown to have no particular efficacy, in achieving the legitimate aims of the criminal law, that less harsh penalties do not have. But whatever claims of penological efficacy might be made for the death penalty if it were generally, regularly, fairly and even-handedly applied as a punishment for crime, surely vanish when it is applied as the United States now applies it rarely, irregularly, unfairly and unevenly— to execute a few stray men out of a "capital" criminal population of thousands.

(15) The conclusion is inescapable, we think, that this rare penalty, inflicted upon the smallest handful of murderers, is no part of the regular criminal-law machinery of California or of any other State. It is a freakish aberration, a random extreme act of violence, visibly arbitrary and discriminatory—a penalty reserved for unusual application because, if it were usually used, it would affront universally shared standards of public decency. Such a penalty—not Law, but Terror—has no place in a democratic government. It is a cruel and unusual punishment, forbidden by the Eighth Amendment.

CONCLUSION

Trop v. Dulles said in 1958 that the death penalty could not be constitutionally condemned "in a day when it is still widely accepted."[33] In the same year, Justice Barry wrote:

> "The time when nations will cease to execute spies and traitors will not be seen while wars, hot or cold, inflame national passions and create a climate of fear and hatred. But plainly the distaste for death as a punishment for crimes that affect the individual and only indirectly the State is growing more general, and the complete abandonment of capital punishment as a feature of the criminal law is not far distant."[34]

The time foreseen by Justice Barry, and to which this Court in *Trop* deferred, has come. The Court should now reverse Earnest Aikens' sentence of death.

25 LOUIS J. WEST

Psychiatrist Louis J. West (1924-) was born in New York City and attended college and medical school at the University of Minnesota. He has practiced or taught medicine at Cornell University, Lakeland Air Force Base Hospital, and the University of Oklahoma School of Medicine. In 1969, he assumed his present position as head. of the Department of Psychiatry at UCLA and Psychiatrist-in-Chief of the UCLA hospital and clinics.

West was, in his words, "perfectly content" with capital punishment until 1952 when he acted as medical examiner at a hanging in Iowa. After the drop, he listened to the victim's heart beat for over twelve minutes before it finally stopped. Appalled, he began to study the death penalty and soon had learned enough to become an advocate of its abolition.

In his capacity as a reformer, Dr. West has testified at legislative hearings, debated on television, and campaigned within his profession. In 1969, he helped convince his colleagues on the American Psychiatric Association's Board of Trustees to adopt a resolution condemning capital punishment and to file an *amicus curiae* brief against the penalty in *Maxwell* v. *Bishop,* argued before the United States Supreme Court in October of that year. In 1972, he headed the Committee of Psychiatrists for Evaluation of the Death Penalty, which presented a similar brief in *Aikens* v. *California* (see selection 24).

Dr. West's unique arguments against the death penalty are most ably arrayed in a paper he presented at a meeting of the American Orthopsychiatric Association in 1974, a slightly revised version of which is excerpted here. A complete text of Dr.

West's paper is reproduced in the July 1975 issue of the *American Journal of Orthopsychiatry.*

Psychiatric Reflections on the Death Penalty (1974)

[T]here are some complexities of the problem of the death penalty that are particularly significant to psychiatrists like myself. . . .

The psychiatrist is a physician, and the physician is sworn to preserve life. There have been ironic occasions when physicians have worked long and hard to keep a man alive for the hangman. The technical rationale for this lies in the possibility of last-minute clemency, but a deeper meaning is expressed in the determination to prevent the prisoner from "cheating the hangman"—and with the hangman, society—of its rightful ceremonial revenge. The doctor lives closer to the issue of life and death than most people. He knows from personal experience how remarkable is the investment of cold flesh and bones with the vital spark; to preserve this spark he has taken an oath. Thus his role in relation to executions borders on the bizarre. As Dr. Karl Menninger has put it: "To a physician discussing the wiser treatment of our fellow men it seems hardly necessary to add that under no circumstances should we kill them. It was never considered right for doctors to kill their patients, no matter how hopeless their condition. . . .[1]

* * *

If the physician happens to be a psychiatrist, he learns that the death penalty tends even further to pervert his professional identity. The employment of psychiatrists in trials at law has gone far beyond what society expects from any other type of expert witness. This is manifest primarily in trials where the death penalty is involved. Here we find the anomaly of a physi-

From Louis J. West, "Psychiatric Reflections on the Death Penalty," *American Journal of Orthopsychiatry* (July 1975). Copyright 1975, the American Orthopsychiatric Association, Inc. Reproduced by permission.

cian, sworn to devote himself to the preservation of human life, dealing out opinions whereby the survival or destruction of another human being hinges on the turn of a word. Many psychiatrists refuse any longer to serve as expert witnesses in capital cases, only to find themselves consequently criticized for lack of social responsibility.

After the sentence of death is passed, we discover a phenomenon to make any physician shudder. Death sentences create a grisly reservoir of condemned men living under unbelievable stress in a situation commonly called Death Row. As a student of experimental psychopathology I have become aware of many laboratory methods for inducing changes in the mood, thoughts, or behavior of normal subjects. In the scientist's laboratory such undertakings are always approached with the utmost caution and handled with many safeguards for the mental well-being of the research subject. But in Death Row, organized and controlled in grim caricature of a laboratory, the condemned prisoner's personality is subjected to incredible stress for prolonged periods of time.[2]

Often prisoners deteriorate rapidly following the imposition of the death sentence. I examined Jack Ruby a number of times from April 28, 1964 (some weeks after his trial, conviction, and death sentence for the murder of Lee Harvey Oswald) until his death. By every objective medical criterion, Ruby became grossly psychotic soon after being sentenced to die, and never recovered his sanity. There are many other cases less well known. Actually, in some ways perhaps, the stress upon Ruby was less than that experienced by many condemned individuals who, over the course of many years, approach scheduled death down to the last month, or week, or minute; then live through a breath-taking reprieve, only to face another horrible countdown.

Slovenko[3] pointed out how, while executions decreased in number during the 1950s and 1960s, the numbers on Death Row grew. At the end of 1962, there were 275 prisoners under sentence of death. During 1963, 21 were executed and 91 were sentenced to die, leaving a new total of 345 awaiting extermination. Eventually, there were more than 600 individuals living on

Death Row until the Supreme Court decision brought relief. Today the population of Death Row is steadily rising again.

A good many of these doomed men end up in the hands of the psychiatrist. The strain of existence on Death Row is very likely to produce behavioral aberrations ranging from malingering to acute psychotic breaks. In most states the warden will transfer such a person to the psychiatric unit of the prison or the security area of a mental hospital. Here the prisoner is not unlikely to pass the rest of his days as a member of that vaguely defined population, "the criminally insane."

What is the psychiatrist to do with such a patient if and when he improves? Specify him as ready for death? In practice this almost never happens. The psychiatrist is not likely to choose to serve as the executioner's assistant. Ironically, the ward personnel may employ the threat of sending the prisoner back to the penitentiary for execution as a powerful restraining influence upon his behavior, thus making of him a model patient. Then, paradoxically, a situation may develop in which the patient who recovers his sanity and cooperates fully with the staff is allowed to stay in hospital indefinitely, while the more disturbed patient who becomes a chronic nuisance is sent back to the executioner.

Of course the question of the nonexecutability of the condemned man who becomes mentally ill points to the heart of the capital punishment issue. Why should the madman not be executed? Wouldn't it protect society as well? Wouldn't it deter others just as well? True, the psychotic prisoner is less likely to produce new evidence or to participate knowledgeably in a last-minute appeal; but it could just as logically be said of a sane man that, no matter how long the execution had been postponed, he should be kept alive because eventually he might be able to devise a better defense, or help his attorneys to develop new appeals, or benefit from new evidence. Whatever the rationalizations, there is probably a deeper and basically shameful reason for postponing execution of the condemned maniac. It is that he must not be executed unless or until he is in full possession of his mental faculties so that he can appreciate what is being done to him. This reflects the most basic motive for most executions—revenge.

Of all the arguments against the death penalty, however, there is one that is perhaps both least understood and most paradoxical. It is this: *Capital punishment breeds murder.*

Philosophers and social scientists have long contended that the legal extermination of human beings in any society generates a profound tendency among the citizens to accept killing as a solution to human problems.[4] In fact there are convincing data cited elsewhere to show that around the time and place of a well-publicized execution the murder rate is quite likely to go up (paradoxically) rather than down (as would be expected if there were actually a deterrent effect).[5] No matter how ultimate the death penalty as a solution may seem, or how rarely it is employed, its official existence or acceptance in the law symbolizes the fact that it is permissible—even desirable—to resolve issues by murder; it is only necessary to define the criteria for justification. The late Albert Camus steadfastly held that it would be necessary for mankind to eliminate the death penalty before we could ever hope to eliminate war.[6] He took pains to point out that no nation which had wholly and permanently abolished capital punishment ever started a war.

But I am convinced that there is an even more specific way in which the death penalty breeds murder. It becomes more than a symbol. It becomes a promise, a contract, a covenant between society and certain (by no means rare) warped mentalities who are moved to kill as part of a self-destructive urge. These murders are discovered by the psychiatric examiner to be, consciously or unconsciously, an attempt to commit suicide by committing homicide. It only works if the perpetrator believes he will be executed for his crime. I believe this to be a significant reason for the tendency to find proportionally more homicides in death penalty states than in those without it.[7] I even know of cases where the murderer left an abolitionist state deliberately to commit a meaningless murder in an executionist state, in the hope thereby of forcing society to destroy him. But there are many instances far less elaborate, and quite obvious not only to the psychiatrist but to any sensible observer.

For example, in 1965 an Oklahoma truck driver parked to have lunch in a Texas roadside cafe. A total stranger—a farmer from nearby—walked through the door and blew him in half with a shotgun. When the police finally disarmed the farmer and asked why he had murdered the trucker, he replied, "I was just tired of living."

In 1964 Howard Otis Lowery, a life-term convict in an Oklahoma prison, formally requested a judge to send him to the electric chair after a District Court jury found him sane following a prison escape and a spree of violence. He said that if he could not get the death penalty from one jury he would get it from another, and complained that officials had failed to live up to an agreement to give him death in the electric chair when he pleaded guilty to a previous murder charge in 1961.

Another murderer, James French, asked for the death penalty after he wantonly killed a motorist who gave him a ride while French was hitchhiking through Oklahoma in 1958. However, French was foiled by his court-appointed public defense attorney who made a deal with the prosecutor, pleaded his client guilty, and got him a life sentence instead of the requested execution. French was outraged. He thought the guilty plea would bring certain execution. Repeated letters to the governor demanding execution or a new trial were ignored. Finally, three years later, in the State Penitentiary at McAlester, French strangled his cell mate. This was a deliberate, premeditated slaying, without any known motive except to get himself executed. This was the motive given by French himself. For this crime French was convicted three times. (There were two successful appeals by public defenders for new trials on technical grounds, much to French's irritation.) He was declared legally sane and sentenced to death each time. This sentence he deliberately invited in well-organized, literate epistles to the courts and in provocative, taunting challenges to judges and jurors. During a psychiatric examination in 1965 French admitted to me that he had seriously attempted suicide several times in the past but always "chickened out" at the last minute. His basic (and obviously abnormal) motive in murdering his inoffensive cell mate was to force the State to deliver to him the electrocution to which he felt entitled and which he deeply desired. French was the only man who was executed in the United States during 1966. He had successfully forced the State of Oklahoma to fulfill its contract to reward murder with murder.

Many other examples may be found in which the promise of the death penalty consciously or unconsciously invites violence. Sellin reviewed a number of them.[8] Wertham's analysis of Robert Irwin, who attempted suicide by murder, is a classic.[9] Some who seek execution even confess to somebody else's murder. For example, in 1966 Joseph Shay in Miami admitted that he had falsely confessed to an unsolved murder "because I wanted to die" (cited in various local and national news reports). The intimate connection between murder and suicide has been discussed by Alexander,[10] Menninger,[11] Zilboorg,[12] and other psychiatrists. In a recent book, West[13] noted that in England nearly half of all murders are followed by serious suicidal attempts, of which two-thirds succeed. In other words, about one-third of all murderers in England die by suicide. In Denmark, where there has been no death penalty for generations (and where, of course, the murder rate is far lower than ours), 40 per cent of all murderers subsequently commit suicide.

That the death penalty is a failure as a deterrent to murder has been demonstrated in many ways. That it is a success as an incentive to murder, either generally (through its influence as a symbolic representation of the acceptability of killing) or specifically in cases like those described above, is increasingly clear. It makes it easier to understand why, for example, in the year following the widely publicized reestablishment of capital punishment in formerly abolitionist Oregon in 1920, that State's homicide rate nearly doubled.[14]

Why, in light of the general trend toward abolition of capital punishment in the Western World, and of the successful experience of Michigan (abolitionist since 1847), and of a dozen other states for many years, is there still such great desire among the American people to see the death penalty restored? Some of the current pressure undoubtedly comes from the steadily rising rate of violent crime which has accompanied the population explosion, the acute problems of urbanization, and the easy availability of handguns. A number of unusually horrible and highly publicized murders, like those by Charles Manson and his followers, has also been cited as causative. Of course pressure is also due to the reiteration by prominent public figures (some of whom should know better) that capital punishment is a successful deterrent to violent crime and is needed to protect the community. But many people are remarkably quick to accept such arguments, and peculiarly resistant to any arguments to the contrary.

Thus it seems to me that the psychodynamics of *resistance* to abolition of the death penalty deserve special scrutiny. In discussing the death penalty with colleagues, students, and the public for many years, my own experience suggests that various seemingly cognitive factors (e.g., ignorance, inertia, misinformation, rationalization, etc.) are less important in this resistance than are emotional factors. Sometimes these emotions are conscious, and frankly expressed (e.g., outrage at the crime, vengefulness, fear that the dangerous criminal may be released to strike again). These feelings are natural enough and to be expected, more or less, in any society. As the society becomes more enlightened, the death penalty is increasingly likely to be abolished—as it has been in most of the Western democracies. But why is it that enlightenment . . . should be growing so slowly? Exploring this question one discovers a trio of resistances to enlightenment, in which unconscious factors may play a significant role. These might be labeled: "The Scapegoat," "The Sacrificial Lamb," and "The Secret Self-Deterrent."

The "Scapegoat" phenomenon has been considered elsewhere at some length.[15] The true scapegoat is of course a nonhuman substitute for a human offender. In the present context the scapegoat is a person whose misdeeds are discovered and punished by death. He serves through his death to expiate the guilt engendered by the crimes of all. The primitive, magical, primary process thinking that has perpetuated scapegoating through the ages is probably still a significant factor in modern man, especially in times of national turbulence and anxiety.

The "Sacrificial Lamb" is rather different. The purpose of

the sacrifice is to ward off the powers of evil, or the dangers present in an uncertain universe. Society uses its occasional legal victim of the gas, the rope, or the electric chair, as a lightning rod to focus upon the chosen one divine vengeance against general human sinfulness, while at the same time magically insinuating the survivors into the good graces of the gods by the blood sacrifice. Logical arguments related to the unevenness of justice by penalty of death in this country will obviously have little effect upon such psychological forces, especially if they are not openly or consciously realized. As Shirley Jackson's classic story, "The Lottery," so well reminds us, these requirements are just as well fulfilled randomly, or by lot, as by reason.[16]

The dynamic forces involved in the "Secret Self-Deterrent" are related to the foregoing but have a structure of their own. Each civilized individual must develop defenses against his own secret violent and destructive impulses. Into the effort he is likely to throw all of the resources that his culture provides. Developmentally, fear of punishment or retaliation plays a certain part. The average citizen senses, and strives to defend himself against, his basic instinctual kinship to the violent criminal. Thus the citizen whispers to himself, "Perhaps all that restrains *me* from an act of violence is fear of the talionic destruction I would bring upon myself. This must be all that restrains many others like myself. I become anxious at the prospect of eliminating the death penalty because it means I—not to mention everyone else—will be forced to rely more upon my own internal controls and less upon the fear of punishment."

But in this the citizen fails to comprehend the significance of his own much healthier ego structure. (Most violent criminals are psychologically severely impaired.) In fact it is not fear of retaliation ("a death for a death") that keeps most normal people from murder. Rather it is a healthy appreciation for the value of human life, the capacity for empathy with others, and the sense of belonging to a society in which persons have meaning. It should be no surprise to find that those states and countries which have long since abolished the death penalty have in their statutes also reflected many other humane considerations.

This may also contribute to the persistent finding that such states and nations have no more capital crimes, even without the death penalty, than do comparable neighbors that have retained capital punishment, and that indeed the abolitionist society is likely to be somewhat less violent than the executionist one.

Obviously, these three more-or-less preconscious or unconscious factors will affect different individuals in different ways. From them may arise ambivalent feelings leading to all kinds of behavioral paradoxes. Thus we find, on the one hand, the passionate believer in capital punishment who readily admits he would never throw the switch himself and who shudders at the prospect of watching an execution. On the other hand, there is the highly vocal humanitarian who deplores the horrors of legalized murder but is strangely apathetic when it comes to taking part in any organized action that might bring about the desired end.

What can be done to ensure the permanent abolition of the death penalty in America? Certainly continuing public information is vital. However, the importance of individual leadership by prominent persons is particularly great in this area of social progress, because of the role that fear plays in resistance to abolition of capital punishment. The increased sense of security that large groups of people may feel when ministers, judges, and great public figures take a positive stand can help to swing the balance toward abolition. Men like Governors DiSalle and Brown—both Senior and Junior—strike important blows against the death penalty, even though at times it may be hard to discern the results.

But resistances are stubborn. Dr. Karl Menninger has been a colossus on the scene of American psychiatry for half a century, yet his stirring appeals were never sufficient to move the people of Kansas to reform on this issue while he moved them successfully on so many others. (In 1965 there were four executions in Kansas.[17]) Nor have voices like Menninger's inspired notable action within the medical profession. This is particularly regrettable because of the general respect in which physicians are held (and hence the influence they could exercise) and also because of the profound ethical implications in the physician's commitment to the preservation of human life. . . .

* * *

There is hope that today the medical profession as a whole will follow psychiatry's lead. A powerful step would be a national medical declaration that henceforth it would be considered professionally unethical for a physician to lend his presence to an execution, even as an official examiner to certify the fact and time of death. Since nearly every American executionist jurisdiction in the recent past has required such participation by one or more physicians, a doctor's boycott of executions could have a powerful effect.

The struggle to eliminate the penalty of death is a continuing one. The forces of progress are at work, not only in medicine, but in other professions as well. Working together, the many professional organizations and learned societies of the United States could do much to secure the final and permanent abolition of the death penalty in our country. This would be a signal victory in the never-ending struggle to create progress through the exercise of reason.

26 HUGO ADAM BEDAU

Hugo Adam Bedau (1926-), professor of philosophy and chairman of the philosophy department at Tufts University since 1966, is one of today's leading proponents of the abolition of capital punishment. Bedau's interest in the reform began in 1957 while he was on the faculty of Princeton University. His interest turned to action during the following years; he testified before New Jersey legislative committees, wrote articles, debated the issue on television, and rallied sympathetic citizens to the cause. When he moved to a new teaching position at Reed College in 1962, Bedau bolstered the reform in Oregon in similar fashion. There he served as research director of the Oregon Council to Abolish the Death Penalty and was one of the leaders of the referendum campaign which led to abolition in 1964. Soon after his move to Tufts in 1966, Bedau became research director of the Massachusetts Council to Abolish the Death Penalty and president of the American League to Abolish Capital Punishment. In 1968, he began an informal association with attorneys of the NAACP Legal Defense and Educational Fund, to whom he contributed several memoranda for use in preparation of the *Aikens* brief (see selection 24). After the *Furman* victory, Bedau, with the aid of a Russell Sage Foundation grant, undertook to stimulate and coordinate legally relevant social science research on capital punishment. He returned to full-time teaching in the fall of 1973, but continues to work with researchers in an informal capacity.

Bedau has written many articles on capital punishment and, in 1964, published an anthology, *The Death Penalty in America,* an outstanding collection of articles and statistics on the subject. In 1972, the American Civil Liberties Union invited him to write a pamphlet outlining the post-*Furman* reform position. His broad-ranging yet succinct statement, slightly revised and with a postscript reflecting events to January 1975, is reproduced here in its entirety.

The Case Against the Death Penalty (1973, 1975)

The Supreme Court has, in effect, outlawed capital punishment in the United States by its decision in *Furman v. Georgia.* Because of *Furman,* by the end of 1972, nearly two dozen states had overturned their death penalty statutes and ordered resentencing of persons awaiting execution. The ACLU, with the NAACP Legal Defense and Educational Fund, Inc., and other civil liberties and civil rights organizations, has properly pointed to the *Furman* decision as the watershed in its long struggle against capital punishment.

In the immediate aftermath of the Court's decision, many commentators made much of the narrowness of the victory and the lack of firm consensus among the five-man majority on the Court. This is understandable—but misleading. It obscures several major points of agreement:

• The majority agreed that the death penalty is a cruel and unusual punishment because it is imposed infrequently and under no clear standards.

• The majority agreed that the purpose of the death penalty, whether it be retribution or deterrence, cannot be achieved when it is so rarely and unpredictably used.

• The majority agreed that one purpose of the Eighth and Fourteenth Amendments is to bar legislatures from imposing punishments like the death penalty which, because of the way they are administered, serve no valid social purpose.

• All the Court, with the exception of Justice Rehnquist,

From Hugo A. Bedau, *The Case Against Capital Punishment* (New York: American Civil Liberties Union, 1973; rev. 1975).

indicated personal opposition to capital punishment.

• All the Court, again excepting Justice Rehnquist, indicated substantial belief that capital sentencing is arbitrary and substantial disbelief that it is uniquely effective in deterring crime.

The ACLU's opposition to the death penalty has been based on several grounds, including those which the Court found compelling:

• Capital punishment is cruel and unusual, in violation of the Eighth Amendment of the U.S. Constitution. It is a relic of the earliest days of penology, when slavery, branding and other corporal punishments were commonplace; like these other barbaric practices, it has no place in civilized society.

• Executions in prison gave the unmistakeable message to all society that life ceases to be sacred when it is thought useful to take it and that violence is legitimate so long as it is thought justified by pragmatic concerns that appeal to those having power to kill.

• Capital punishment denies due process of law. Its imposition is arbitrary, and it forever deprives an individual of the benefits of new law or new evidence that might affect his conviction.

• The worst and most dangerous criminals are rarely the ones executed. The death penalty is applied randomly at best and discriminatorily at worst. It violates the constitutional guarantee of the equal protection of the laws because it is imposed almost exclusively against racial minorities, the poor, the uneducated—persons who are victims of overt discrimination in the sentencing process or who are unable to afford expert and dedicated legal counsel.

• Reliance on the death penalty obscures the true causes of crime and distracts attention from the effective resources of society to control it.

• Capital punishment is wasteful of resources, demanding a disproportionate expenditure of time and energy by courts, prosecuting attorneys, defense attorneys, juries, courtroom and correctional personnel; it burdens the system of criminal justice, and it is counter-productive as an instrument for society's control of violent crime. It uniquely epitomizes the tragic ineffi-

cacy and brutality of a resort to violence rather tha/
the solution of difficult social problems.

Two facts—plainly recognized by the majority of u.
preme Court in *Furman*—buttress our entire case: *capital punishment does not deter crime,* and *the administration of the death penalty has been provably unfair.*

DETERRENCE

The argument against the deterrent efficacy of the death penalty takes three mutually supportive forms.

(1) Any punishment can be an effective deterrent only if it is consistently and promptly employed. Capital punishment does not meet those conditions. Only a small proportion of first degree murderers are sentenced to death, and even fewer are executed. Between 1930 and 1960, there was one execution for every 70 homicides. During the decade 1951-1960, nine out of ten persons convicted of first degree murder did not get executed;[1] and in the decade of the '60's executions became still rarer. The delay in carrying out the death sentence has become notorious. Between 1961 and 1970, the average time spent under death sentence rose from 14.4 months to 32.6 months.[2] The sobering lesson is that we must either abolish the death penalty or try to enhance its deterrent efficacy by abandoning the procedural safeguards and constitutional rights of suspects, defendants and convicts in order to reduce delay (with the attendant high risk of executing innocent persons). The former alternative is surely the only tolerable one: Repeal the death penalty entirely in favor of a more efficiently administrable mode of punishment.

(2) Persons who commit murder and other crimes of personal violence either premeditate them or they do not. If they do not, then the requisite *mens rea* (criminal intent) of a capital crime is missing; and it is impossible to imagine how in such cases any punishment could deter. In cases where the crime is premeditated, the criminal ordinarily expects to escape detection, arrest and conviction. It is impossible to see how the threat of a severe punishment can deter an individual who does not expect to get

caught. Gangland killings, air piracy, kidnapping for ransom are among the more obvious categories of capitally punishable crimes which continue to occur because some think they are too clever to get caught.

(3) Experience over the past three decades tends to establish that the death penalty as currently administered is no more effective than imprisonment in deterring crime and that it may even be an incitement to criminal violence:

(A) Use of the death penalty in a given state does not decrease the subsequent rate of criminal homicide in that state.[3]

(B) Use of the death penalty in a given state may increase the subsequent rate of criminal homicide in that state.[4]

(C) Death penalty states as a group do not have lower rates of criminal homicide than non-death penalty states.[5]

(D) States that abolish the death penalty do not show an increased rate of criminal homicide after abolition.[6]

(E) States that have reinstituted the death penalty after abolishing it have not shown a decreased rate of criminal homicide.[7]

(F) In two neighboring states—one with the death penalty and the other without it—the one with the death penalty does not show any consistently lower rate of criminal homicide.[8]

(G) Police officers on duty do not suffer a higher rate of criminal assault and homicide in states that have abolished the death penalty than they do in death penalty states.[9]

(H) Prisoners and prison personnel do not suffer a higher rate of criminal assault and homicide from prisoners in abolition states than they do in death penalty states.[10]

Actual experience establishes these conclusions beyond reasonable doubt. No comparable body of evidence contradicts these views.

In addition, an increasing number of cases have been clinically documented where the death penalty actually incited the capital crimes that it was supposed to deter. These included cases of the so-called suicide-murder syndrome—persons who wanted but feared to take their own lives, and committed murder so that society would kill them—and the so-called executioner syndrome—persons who became the self-appointed ministers of death and used the ultimate weapon legitimated by society's acceptance of capital punishment to avenge real or fancied wrongs. Indeed, the more that is known about the mind of murderers, the more obvious it becomes that the picture of a rational and calculated decision to kill upon which the supposed deterrent efficacy of capital punishment entirely depends is almost never encountered in actual life.

UNFAIRNESS

Constitutional due process as well as elementary justice require that the judicial functions of trial and sentencing, especially where the irreversible sanction of the death penalty is involved, be conducted with fundamental fairness. In both rape and murder cases (since 1930, 99 per cent of all executions have been for these crimes), there has been substantial evidence to show that courts have been arbitrary, racially biased and unfair in the way in which they have tried and sentenced some persons to prison and others to death.

Nearly thirty years ago, Gunnar Myrdal, in his classic *An American Dilemma* (1944), reported that "the South makes the widest application of the death penalty, and Negro criminals come in for much more than their share of the executions." Statistics confirm this discrimination, only it is not confined to the South. Since 1930, 3,859 persons have been executed in the United States. Of these, 2,066, or 54 per cent, were black. For the crime of murder, 3,334 have been executed; 1,630, or 49 per cent, were black. During these years blacks were about one-eleventh of the population. For rape, punishable by death in 1972 in only sixteen states and by the federal government, a total of 455 have been executed, all but two in the South; 405, or 90 per cent, were black.[11]

More exact statistical studies show that the higher rate of executions of blacks for rape and homicide cannot be explained by any factor except the race of the defendant. In Pennsylvania, for example, it has been shown that only the defendant's race explains the fact that among individuals convicted of felony murder and sentenced to death a lower percentage of blacks than whites eventually have their sentences commuted to imprisonment.[12]

In New Jersey, it was shown that juries tended to bring in the death sentence for blacks convicted of felony murder more readily than they did for whites convicted of the same offense.[13]

Such statistically significant evidence of racial discrimination at both the trial and commutation phases of death penalty proceedings has not been shown in every state. Moreover, in some, e.g., California, studies have revealed no evidence of race discrimination.[14] The California study did, however, show discrimination against the poor; and in our society racial minorities are, of course, disproportionately poor. Racial bias inevitably shows up in application of the death penalty.

No doubt the most thorough statistical proof of racial bias in capital punishment has been provided in connection with rape. In 1965, 3,000 rape convictions in 250 counties in 11 Southern states were carefully studied. The results consistently pointed to the race of the defendant (and the victim) as the decisive factor in how the courts would dispose of the case.

One analyst noted: "Negroes convicted of rape are disproportionately frequently sentenced to death compared with whites, and . . . Negroes convicted of raping white victims, particularly, are disproportionately frequently sentenced to death." Moreover, "of over two dozen possible aggravating non-racial variables that could account for the higher proportion of Negroes sentenced to death upon conviction of rape, not one of these non-racial factors has withstood the tests of statistical significance. . . . We are now prepared to assert that a significantly higher proportion of blacks are sentenced to death upon conviction of rape . . . because they are black . . . and the victims were white."[15]

Race is not the only morally and legally invidious factor which in practice plays a role in determining who gets executed and who does not. A defendant's poverty, lack of firm social roots in the community, inadequate legal representation at trial or on appeal—all these have in the past been common factors among "Death Row" populations. Race, however, has proved to be the most influential of them all. There is no reason to believe that were capital punishment once again permitted, it would prove to be less discriminatory in the future than it has been in the past.

PUBLIC OPINION

Despite the decision of the Supreme Court in the *Furman* case, and the widespread acceptance of our arguments on deterrence and unfairness, it is premature to conclude that the death penalty has been forever eliminated from our criminal law.

"Public support for capital punishment is currently at its highest point in nearly two decades."[16] The Gallup Poll reported that 57 per cent of all adults said they favored the death penalty for convicted murderers; 32 per cent said they opposed it; 11 per cent were undecided. This represents a loss of 15 per cent since 1966 among those declaring opposition to the death penalty. Influential public spokesmen, such as President Nixon, Attorney General Kleindienst, California Governor Ronald Reagan and Philadelphia Mayor Frank Rizzo all have openly endorsed capital punishment, and their endorsements may help to account for the resurgence of popular support for execution.

Public referenda on the death penalty in recent years have failed to abolish it (except in Oregon, in 1964). Last year in California, after the State Supreme Court ruled that the death penalty violated the state constitutional prohibitions against "cruel or unusual punishments," an initiative was devised by the State Attorney General to defy this ruling. Last November, by a vote of 2 to 1, the California electorate passed a measure to restore the death penalty as the mandatory punishment for several crimes and to deny the courts any review of the constitutionality of this action.

There is some colorable legal ground for attempts to preserve the death penalty in the wake of *Furman*, *Furman* left several crucial questions about the death penalty undecided. Therefore, some believe that "correctly" framed death penalty statutes may be found acceptable by the Supreme Court. Three kinds of statutes are being proposed: those that spell out explicit standards the jury must follow in choosing between death and imprisonment; those that allow the jury to impose the death penalty at its discretion but only for a crime well-defined by a narrowly drawn statute; and statutes making the death penalty mandatory for certain crimes. ,

The first two kinds of statutes are not especially threatening.

The issues were canvassed in some detail by the Supreme Court during the 1970 term, and the problems in framing acceptable statutes seem to be substantial, perhaps insurmountable. Justice Harlan, writing for the Court in 1971, noted: ". . . the history of capital punishment for homicides . . . reveals continual efforts, uniformly unsuccessful, to identify before the fact those homicides for which the slayer should die. . . . Those who have come to grips with the hard task of actually attempting to draft means of channeling capital sentencing discretion have confirmed the lesson taught by history. . . . To identify before the fact those characteristics of criminal homicides and their perpetrators which call for the death penalty, and to express these characteristics in language which can be fairly understood and applied by the sentencing authority, appear to be tasks which are beyond present human ability." (*McGautha v. California,* 402 U.S. 183, 1971)

Chief Justice Burger, in his dissent from the majority in the *Furman* case, singled out these very words of Justice Harlan to express his own skepticism over the possibility of drawing up suitable standards to guide juries or of drafting capital statutes sufficiently narrowly.

MANDATORY DEATH

Mandatory death penalty statutes present a larger problem. *Furman* did not explicitly establish the unconstitutionality of any of the many mandatory death penalty statutes in force around the nation. Hence, in Delaware, for instance, the State Supreme Court last November, instead of nullifying Delaware's capital statute in response to the mandate of the U. S. Supreme Court in *Furman,* chose to retain the death penalty and did so by eliminating the provision for the jury's sentencing discretion (*State v. Dickerson*). The California initiative, a resolution by the National Association of Attorneys General to seek "appropriate legislation for the death penalty" and the avowed purpose of the Nixon administration to ask Congress to reinstate capital punishment for kidnapping, assassination, bombing of a public building, aircraft hijacking, and killing a prison guard—all these are efforts to reinstitute or extend the mandatory death penalty for selected categories of crime. One may expect such efforts to grow rather than to abate in the near future.

There is a strong practical case to be made against the mandatory death penalty. The history of capital punishment clearly shows that jury sentencing discretion was introduced over the past century in every jurisdiction in the United States in order to avoid hung juries and acquittals (or convictions of lesser included offenses) in the face of plain guilt. As often as not, it was prosecutors themselves who sought to give juries sentencing discretion so they could get convictions. There is no evidence that juries will respond differently in the future from the way they did during the past century.

Furthermore, mandatory death penalties do not eliminate discretion. They shift it from the trial jury to the prosecutor's office. Instead of leaving it up to the jury whether to sentence to death or to prison, mandatory death penalties allow the prosecutor to decide whether to indict for a capital crime or for a lesser offense, in order to reduce the risk of the jury's refusal to convict. There is no reason to believe that such discretion would be exercised without bias, especially in death penalty cases, where aroused community sentiment and possible political advantage are involved. It is very unlikely that the Supreme Court would allow such discretion to prosecutors when it has denied comparable discretion to juries.

The ACLU takes the position that the moral and legal principles and the array of factual evidence that persuaded the majority of the Supreme Court in 1972 to rule against the death penalty as currently administered destroy the basis for reintroduction of the death penalty in *any* form for *any* crime. The death penalty, we believe, continues to be the symbolic representation of everything that is brutal and futile in our present system of criminal justice. We cannot rest until it is thoroughly uprooted and eliminated from our law.

POSTSCRIPT

In the two-and-one-half years since the Supreme Court's decision in *Furman,* the forces to restore capital punishment in the states and federal criminal code have not been inactive. Thirty states across the nation have enacted new death penalty statutes. Almost two hundred persons in nineteen states have been sentenced to death under these new laws. Although the *de facto* moratorium on capital punishment continues (there has been no execution anywhere in the United States since June, 1967), it is clear that we are still a long way from having totally abolished the death penalty.

The new legislation restoring the death penalty has taken two main forms: a "mandatory" death penalty, or a sentence of life or death based on the court's "guided discretion." Idaho's new law of March, 1973, is typical of the former. It decrees simply that "Every person guilty of murder in the first degree shall suffer death." First degree murder is redefined as premeditated murder, murder of an on-duty law officer, or murder by anyone already convicted of murder. Typical of the second category is the new Connecticut statute. It imposes the death penalty for either of two crimes (five kinds of murder, and death from illegal sale of narcotic drugs by a non-addict). After the court has convicted the defendant of one of these crimes, he is sentenced to death only if the court also finds that the crime was accompanied by one or more "aggravating" circumstances (the statute lists six, e.g., the crime was committed in an especially heinous, cruel or depraved manner), and that no "mitigating" circumstances apply (the statute lists five, e.g., the defendant was under the age of 18 at the time of the crime, he could not have reasonably foreseen that his conduct would cause grave risk of death to others). Of the two types of death penalty statutes, most legislatures seem to prefer the latter type. The pending death penalty legislation in Congress is on this pattern, and if enacted, may well have considerable influence.

How are these statutes working out in practice? The great majority of those currently under death sentence were convicted of first degree murder. However, several were sentenced to death for rape, and some for such offenses as burglary, armed robbery, and kidnapping. The racial breakdown of those under sentence of death is specially revealing. When *Furman* was decided, 42.3% of those on death row were white, 57.7% nonwhite. Two-and-one-half years later, the percentages were unchanged. What these data suggest is that although capital punishment today is being administered under new statutes designed to avoid the constitutional flaws in the pre-*Furman* statutes, with their arbitrary and unguided sentencing discretion, the results today are essentially the same.

In the past two years, none of these new statutes has been tested before the Supreme Court. Meanwhile, in the state appellate courts, a remarkable divergence of meaning has been extracted from the *Furman* ruling itself. At one extreme is the decision in North Carolina, (*State v. Waddell*), which declared that the import of *Furman* was to leave intact all state death penalty statutes, so long as the jury discretion feature of these statutes was nullified. Under this interpretation, pre-*Furman* death penalty statutes can be cured of their unconstitutionality by judicial revision of them into mandatory death statutes. In late 1974, there were over sixty persons on death row in North Carolina, most of whom arrived there as a result of the ruling in *Waddell*.

At the other extreme is a decision of the Massachusetts Supreme Judicial Court (*Commonwealth v. A Juvenile*). In this case, the court held that a mandatory death penalty imposed on a juvenile defendant was invalid under *Furman*, because the trial judge had the unfettered discretion to try the defendant as a juvenile delinquent, rather than as an adult felon, and no death penalty could issue upon a juvenile conviction.

These impressively divergent interpretations show that the scope and impact of *Furman*, as intended by the Supreme Court, remains unclear. This, plus the new death penalty statutes which pose unsettled constitutional questions, assures that the Court will be called upon in the years immediately ahead to give further rulings on the constitutionality of capital punishment.

The gravamen of the objection to capital punishment is that it is unnecessary, ineffective, and degrading. The Supreme Court has already taken a major step toward reading this judgment into our constitutionally protected rights. We may also have reached the point where, although the death penalty is author-

ized by statute in some jurisdictions, public opposition to executions effectively nullifies these provisions. In due course, the
laws themselves will reflect this judgment, and capital
punishment will become a thing of the past.

NOTES

INTRODUCTION

1. *Colonial Laws of New York* (Albany, N.Y.: Lyon, 1894-96), vol. 1 pp. 20-21; Max Farrand, ed., *The Laws and Liberties of Massachusetts* (Cambridge, Mass.: Harvard Univ. Press, 1929), pp. 5-6.

2. James Hill Nutting, "The Poor, the Defective and the Criminal," in Edward Field, ed., *State of Rhode Island and Providence Plantations at the End of the Century: A History* (Boston: Mason, 1902), vol. 3, pp. 432-435.

3. Philip Alexander Bruce, *Institutional History of Virginia in the Seventeenth Century* (New York: G.P. Putnam's Sons, 1910, vol. 1, pp. 473-475; Thomas Jefferson Wertenbaker, *The First Americans, 1607-1690* (New York: Macmillian, 1927), pp. 210-211; O.P. Chitwood, *Justice in Colonial Virginia* (Baltimore: Johns Hopkins University Press, 1905), pp. 16-17.

4. Herbert William Keith Fitzroy, "The Punishment of Crime in Provincial Pennsylvania," *Pennsylvania Magazine of History and Biography* 60 (July 1936), p. 249; Harry B. and Grace Weiss, *An Introduction to Crime and Punishment in Colonial New Jersey* (Trenton, N.J.: Past Times, 1960), p. 11.

5. Leon Radzinowicz, *A History of English Criminal Law* (New York: Macmillian, 1948), vol. 1, pp. 3-5, 153; Philip English Mackey, "Anti-Gallows Activity in New York State, 1776-1861" (Ph.D. dissertation, University of Pennsylvania 1969), pp. 12-16; Albert Post, "Early Efforts to Abolish Capital Punishment in Pennsylvania," *Pennsylvania Magazine of History and Biography* 68 (January 1944), p. 38; *Acts and Laws of His-Majesties Colony of Rhode-Island, and Providence-Plantations in America* (Boston: John Allen, 1719), pp. 4-6; *Acts and Laws of the English Colony of Rhode-Island and Providence-Plantations in New-England in America* (Newport, R.I.: Samuel Hall, 1767), p. 61.

6. Kenneth Scott, "The Slave Insurrection in New York in 1712," *New York Historical Society Quarterly* 45 (January 1961), p. 62; Abner Cheney Goodell, Jr., *The Trial and Execution for Petit Treason of Mark and Phillis, Slaves of Capt. John Codman* (Cambridge, Mass.: J. Wilson, 1883), pp. 29-30; Hugh F. Rankin, *Criminal Trial Proceedings in*

the General Court of Colonial Virginia (Williamsburg: University Press of Virginia, 1965), pp. 133, 225.

7. For discussions of leniency see Fitzroy, "Punishment," pp. 255-258; Hugh F. Rankin, "Criminal Trial Proceedings in the General Court of Colonial Virginia," *Virginia Magazine of History and Biography* 72 (April 1964), pp. 68-69, 73; Weiss and Weiss, *Introduction*, pp. 18-19; Julius Goebel and T. Raymond Naughton, *Law Enforcement in Colonial New York* (New York: Commonwealth Fund, 1944), pp. 704-705.

8. Julian Boyd, ed., *The Papers of Thomas Jefferson* (Princeton, N.J.: Princeton Univ. Press, 1950-), vol. 2, pp. 313, 492-507.

9. *Capital Punishment in North Carolina* (Raleigh, State of North Carolina, Board of Charities and Public Welfare, 1929), p. 12; chaps. 40, 42, 66, Massachusetts Acts of 1784, Mackey, "Anti-Gallows Activity," p. 41.

10. For maiming and stealing from a church, see chap. 37, New York Laws of 1788; for actual executions for particular crimes see Mackey, "Anti-Gallows Activity," p. 42.

11. Cesare Beccaria, *An Essay on Crime and Punishments* (London: J. Almon, 1767); Bernard Bailyn, *Ideological Origins of the American Revolution* (Cambridge: Harvard Univ. Press, 1967), pp. 27-29; Marcello Maestro, "A Pioneer for the Abolition of Capital Punishment," *Journal of the History of Ideas* 34 (July-September 1973), pp. 463-468; Post, "Early Efforts," pp. 38-39; Fitzroy, "Punishment," pp. 244-245. Bellers' opposition to capital punishment antedated that of the more famous Beccaria by sixty-five years; see A. Ruth Fry, *John Bellers, 1654-1725: Quaker Economist and Social Reformer* (London: Cassell, 1935), pp. 23, 75-78.

12. Post, "Early Efforts," pp. 39-40; for a complete history of the Philadelphia society see Negley K. Teeters, *They Were in Prison* (Philadelphia: John C. Winston, 1937).

13. Post, "Early Efforts," pp. 41-42; David Freeman Hawke, *Benjamin Rush: Revolutionary Gadfly* (Indianapolis: Bobbs-Merrill, 1971), pp. 363-366.

14. Post, "Early Efforts," pp. 40-41; William Bradford, *An Enquiry* (Philadelphia: Dobson, 1793).

15. *Statutes at Large of Pennsylvania, 1786-1809* (Harrisburg, Pa.: C.E. Aughinbaugh, 1906-15), vol. 15, pp. 174-181. A series of earlier laws, in 1788, 1789, 1790, and 1791, had produced successive ameliorations of Pennsylvania's capital code.

16. Mackey, "Anti-Gallows Activity," pp. 63-65.

17. Mackey, "Anti-Gallows Activity," pp. 65-70; *Laws of the State of New York* [1777-1801] (Albany, N.Y.: Weed, Parsons, 1886-87), vol. 3, pp. 669-676.

18. Adolph Paul Gratiot, "Criminal Justice on the Kentucky Frontier" (Ph.D. dissertation, University of Pennsylvania, 1952), pp. 414-417, 433-436; *Laws of the State of Vermont, 1797* (Rutland, Vt.: Josiah Fay, 1798), pp. 155-164; *Report of the Committee on Capital Punishment to*

the Legislative Council of Maryland (Baltimore: State of Maryland, 1962), p. 6; chap. 41, New Hampshire Laws of 1812; Salmon P. Chase, ed., The Statutes of Ohio . . . 1788 to 1833 Inclusive (Cincinnati, Ohio: Covey and Fairbank, 1833-35), vol 2, pp. 856-857.

19. Robert J. Turnbull, A Visit to the Philadelphia Prison (Philadelphia: Budd and Bartram, 1796); Public Laws of the State of Rhode Island and Providence Plantations (Providence: Carter and Wilkinson, 1798), pp. 584-586; Fourth Annual Report of the Prison Discipline Society (Boston: Perkins and Marvin, 1830), pp. 285-287.

20. Pennsylvania Senate Journal 20 (1809-10), pp. 19, 82; Post, "Early Efforts," pp. 42-43.

21. Charles Z. Lincoln, ed., State of New York. Messages from the Governors (Albany, N.Y.: J. B. Lyon, 1909), vol. 2, pp. 702-703; Mackey, "Anti-Gallows Activity," pp. 93-94.

22. Evening Fire-Side, June 22, 1805; "Philanthropos," Essays on Capital Punishments (Philadelphia: Brown and Merritt, 1811); John Edwards, Serious Thoughts on the Subject of Taking the Lives of our Fellow Creatures (New York: n.p., 1811); [Samuel Whelpley], Letters Addressed to Caleb Strong, Esq., 3rd ed. (Philadelphia: B. & T. Kite, 1818); Albert Post, "The Anti-Gallows Movement in Ohio," Ohio State Archaeological and Historical Quarterly 54 (April-June 1945), pp. 105-106; G. F. H. Crockett, An Address to the Legislature of Kentucky (Georgetown, Ky.: N. L. Finnell, 1823). For the views of the clergymen, see [Whelpley], Letters; Abel Charles Thomas, A Lecture on Capital Punishment (Philadelphia: n.p., 1830); Charles Spear, Essays on the Punishment of Death (Boston: Spear, 1844).

23. The Complete Works of Edward Livingston on Criminal Jurisprudence (New York: National Prison Assn., 1873), vol. 1, pp. 35-59, 194-224; Edward Livingston, A System of Penal Law for the United States of America (Washington, D.C.: Gales and Seaton, 1828). On Livingston's life see William B. Hatcher, Edward Livingston: Jeffersonian Republican and Jacksonian Democrat (University: Louisiana State Univ. Press, 1940); for Livingston's reform activity and his influence on later reform see Philip English Mackey, "Edward Livingston and the Origin of the Movement to Abolish Capital Punishment in America," Louisiana History 16 (Spring 1975), pp. 145-166.

24. New York Assembly Document 187 of 1832; An Argument Against Capital Punishments (Nashville: State of Tennessee, 1832); Massachusetts House Document 2 of 1832; Edward Livingston, Introductory Report to the Code of Prison Discipline (Philadelphia: Carey, Lea & Carey, 1827); Pennsylvania House Journal (1828-29), p. 812.

25. Descriptions of public executions may be found in Thomas M. McDade, The Annals of Murder (Norman: Univ. of Oklahoma Press, 1961), p. xxxi and passim; Negley K. Teeters, Hang by the Neck (Springfield, Ill.: Charles C. Thomas, 1967), pp. 19-46 and passim.

26. *Albany Evening Journal*, March 10, 1834; *Albany Argus*, March 11, 1834; *Prisoner's Friend*, n.s. I (March 1849), p. 317. In some cases, executions remained semi-public in spite of the new laws, as hundreds of spectators obtained passes from sheriffs or found elevations from which to watch a prison yard hanging. See selection 15 for one such case.

27. *New Yorker*, June 12, 1836.

28. *Portland Daily Advertiser*, January 5, 1835; Maine House Document 25 of 1835, pp. 22-23; Maine *House Journal* (1835), p. 27.

29. Maine House Document 37 of 1836; Tobias Purrington, *Report on Capital Punishment Made to the Maine Legislature*, 3rd ed. (Washington, D.C.: n.p., 1852), p. 19; chap. 292, Maine Laws of 1837.

30. David M. Ludlum, *Social Ferment in Vermont, 1791-1850* (Montpelier: Vermont Historical Society, 1948), p. 214; Post, "Early Efforts," p. 44; Massachusetts House Documents 36 of 1835, 32 of 1836, 43 of 1837, and 6 of 1838; Philip English Mackey, " 'The Result May Be Glorious': Anti-Gallows Movement in Rhode Island, 1838-1852," *Rhode Island History* 33 (February 1974), pp. 19-23; Erwin L. Feiertag, "Capital Punishment in New Jersey, 1664-1950" (master's thesis, Columbia University, 1951), p. 59; Post, "Ohio," pp. 106-107; Harold M. Dorr, ed., *The Michigan Constitutional Conventions of 1835-36; Debates and Proceedings* (Ann Arbor: University of Michigan Press, 1940), p. 350.

31. *Hangman*, December 10, 1845; Amory Dwight Mayo, *The Death Penalty: A Sermon* (Cleveland, Ohio: n.p., 1855), p. 4. For Cheever's career see Philip English Mackey, "Reverend George B. Cheever: Yankee Reformer as Champion of the Gallows," *Proceedings of the American Antiquarian Society* 82 (October 1972), pp. 323-342.

32. *Punishment By Death*, pp. 13-58, 93-101, 102, 108-111, 119-124, 131-132, 135, 147.

33. Post, "Early Efforts," p. 48; *Prisoner's Friend*, May 27, 1846; *First Annual Report of the Massachusetts Society for the Abolition of Capital Punishment* ([Boston: Spear], 1846), p. 2; Post, "Ohio," pp. 108-109; *New York Weekly Tribune*, April 18, 1844; May 17, November 22, 1845; *Prisoner's Friend*, May 27, 1846; *Brooklyn Eagle*, February 3, 1846; "Captial Punishment," *United States Magazine and Democratic Review* 14 (June 1844), pp. 657-659.

34. James H. Titus, "Third Annual Report of the New York State Society for the Abolition of Capital Punishment," in *Reports and Addresses of James H. Titus upon the Subject of Capital Punishment* (New York: n.p., 1848), p. 10.

35. Chap. 5, Vermont Laws of 1842, chap. 27, Vermont Laws of 1844; "Capital Punishment," *New Englander* 1 (January 1843), p. 28; David Brion Davis, "Murder in New Hampshire," *New England Quarterly* 28 (June 1955), p. 161.

36. Post, "Michigan Abolishes Capital Punishment," *Michigan History Magazine* 29 (January 1945), pp. 44-50.

37. Post, "Ohio," pp. 110-111; *New York Tribune*, February 26, 1851; Connecticut *Senate Journal* (1853), pp. 269-270; Chap. 855, New Hampshire Laws of 1849; chaps. 259, 274, Massachusetts Laws of 1852.

38. Mackey, "Rhode Island," pp. 19-27.

39. Carrie Cropley, "The Case of John McCaffary," *Wisconsin Magazine of History* 35 (Summer 1952), pp. 286-288; Wisconsin Legislative Reference Library, "Capital Punishment in the States with Special Reference to Wisconsin," Information Bulletin 210 (Madison, Wis., 1962), p. 2; Maynard Shipley, "Does Capital Punishment Prevent Convictions?" *American Law Review* 43 (May-June 1909), p. 324.

40. *Brooklyn Daily Times*, May 22, 1858.

41. For the Massachusetts hearings of 1854 see Philip English Mackey, "An All-Star Debate on Capital Punishment: Boston, 1854," *Essex Institute Historical Collections* 110 (July 1974) pp. 181-199.

42. Marvin H. Bovee, *Christ and the Gallows* (New York: Masonic Publishing Co., 1869); Bovee to Wendell Phillips, Whitewater, Wisconsin, January 5, 1882, Boston Public Library Manuscript Collection; Mackey, "Anti-Gallows Activity," pp. 294-300; *Appletons' Cyclopaedia of American Biography* (New York: D. Appleton, 1888-1931), vol. 7, p. 31; *New York Times*, May 31, 1868, p. 4, col. 4; Edmund c. Stedman, "The Gallows in America," *Putnam's Magazine* 13 (February 1869), pp. 233-234.

43. Philip English Mackey, "The Inutility of Mandatory Capital Punishment: An Historical Note," *Boston University Law Review* 54 (January 1974), pp. 32-35; Bovee to Phillips, January 5, 1882.

44. James A. Saathoff, "Capital Punishment in Iowa" (master's thesis, University of Iowa,1927), pp. 7-12; Albert H. Horton, "The Death Penalty in Kansas," *Proceedings of the Bar Association of the State of Kansas* (Topeka, Kans., 1887), pp. 13-15.

45. *Acts and Resolves of the 62d Legislature of the State of Maine* (Augusta, Maine, 1885), p. 295; chap. 55, Maine Laws of 1875; chap. 114, Maine Laws of 1876; chap. 205, Maine Laws of 1883; chap. 133, Maine Laws of 1887; *Nation* 24 (May 3, 1877), p. 263.

46. *New York Times*, May 31, 1868, p. 4, col. 4; January 17, 1888, p. 4, col. 4; Theodore Bernstein, "A Grand Success . . . ," *IEEE Spectrum* (February 1973), pp. 54-58.

47. Bernstein, "Success," p. 58; *General Curtis on the Death Penalty* [London, 1891], p. 4; Medical Society of the State of New York, *Report on Capital Punishment* [New York, 1892]; "The Death Penalty," *Public Opinion* 13 (April 16, 1892), pp. 33-34; "Legalized Corporate Murder," *The Nationalist* 3 (September 1890), p. 95.

48. Chap. 29 of 1897, 54th Congress, 2d Sess.; Norman S. Hayner and John R. Cranor, "The Death Penalty in Washington State," *Annals* 284 (November 1952), p. 101; "Capital Punishment in Colorado," *Charities* 2 (February 1, 1902), p. 103; J. E. Cutler, "Capital Punishment and Lynching," *Annals* 29 (May 1907), pp. 622-625.

49. Florence Spooner, *Prison Reform and Abolition of the Death Penalty Movement in Massachusetts* (Boston, n.p., 1900), pp. 24-26; *New York Times,* January 14, 1900, p. 2, col. 4; January 6, 1901, p. 4, col. 1; Leonard D. Savitz, "A Brief History of Capital Punishment Legislation in Pennsylvania," *Prison Journal* 38 (October 1958), p. 58; *New York Times,* August 20, 1905, p. 12, col. 5; Illinois Legislative Council, "Bills to Abolish Death Penalty in Illinois," *Research Memorandum 1:549* (Springfield: State of Illinois, 1951), p. 3; Allan Nevins, ed., *The Letters and Journal of Brand Whitlock* (New York: Appleton-Century, 1936), vol. 1, p. 49; *New York Times,* February 20, 1906, p. 8, col. 5.

50. Raymond Bye, *Capital Punishment in the United States* (Philadelphia: Committee on Philanthropic Labor of Philadelphia Yearly Meeting of Friends, 1919), pp. 8-10; Walter N. Trenerry, *Murder in Minnesota* (St. Paul: Minnesota Historical Society, 1962), pp. 163-167.

51. Ohio Legislative Service Commission, "Capital Punishment," Staff Research Report 46 (Columbus, Ohio, 1961), p. 10. The vote in Ohio was 303,246 to 258,706. The six states in which one house voted for abolition were California, New Jersey, Pennsylvania, New Hampshire, Illinois, and Colorado. The territory was Alaska.

52. *New York Times,* December 26, 1911, p. 6, col. 2; August 27, 1915, p. 3, col. 1; November 20, 1914, p. 1, col. 5; March 4, 1915, p. 7, col. 2-3; *Proceedings of the Eighth Meeting of the Governors of the States of the Union* (Boston, 1915), pp. 130-159; *Proceedings of the Ninth Meeting . . . the Union* (Washington, D.C., 1916), pp. 91-98; Shipley, "Does Capital Punishment," pp. 321-334; Edward Wagenknecht, *William Dean Howells* (New York: Oxford Univ. Press, 1961), pp. 274-275; Samuel Gompers, *Seventy Years of Life and Labor* (New York: E.P. Dutton, 1925), vol. 1, pp. 132-133; *New York Times,* December 3, 1911, p. 2, col. 6; *Law Notes* 29 (January 1926), p. 181.

53. *New York Times,* December 11, 1916, p. 7, col. 3; April 1, 1917, sect. 1, p. 14, col. 5.

54. Massachusetts Civic Alliance, *Abolition of the Death Penalty* (Boston: n.p., 1916), reproduced in Lemar T. Beman, ed., *Selected Articles on Capital Punishment* (New York: H. W. Wilson, 1925), pp. 126-130; Jacob Goldstein, "Shall Capital Punishment Be Abolished?" *Outlook* 116 (May 2, 1917), p. 19.

55. Illinois Legislative Council, "Bills to Abolish," pp. 1, 4; Savitz, "Brief History," p. 59; Goldstein, "Should Capital Punishment," pp. 18-19.

56. Robert H. Dann, "Abolition and Restoration of the Death Penalty in Oregon," *Annals* 284 (November 1952), pp. 110-114; this time the vote in Oregon was 81,756 for capital punishment and 64,589 against. For the Massachusetts vote, see *Survey* 44 (April 10, 1920), p. 88.

57. Harry L. Davis, "Death by Law," *Outlook* 131 (July 26, 1922), pp. 525-528; *New York Times,* December 11, 1921, p. 21, col. 4; February 6,

1923, p. 10, col. 4; September 17, 1923, p. 4, col. 2; *Outlook* 134 (August 15, 1923), pp. 589-591; *New York Times,* February 20, 1924, p. 5, col. 4; March 30, 1924, sect. 2, p. 2, col. 6; April 2, 1924, p. 21, col. 6.

58. *New York Times,* September 19, 1924, p. 22, col. 6; December 26, 1924, p. 14, col. 6.

59. *New York Times,* July 20, 1925, p. 7, col. 1; December 21, 1925, p. 16, col. 2; January 4, 1926, p. 40, col. 1.

60. *New York Times,* March 22, 1926, p. 9, col. 6; July 2, 1928, p. 5, col. 3; February 18, 1929, p. 9, col. 5; Will Durant, *Abolish the Death Penalty* (New York, 1927); Charles Edward Russell, *I Saw a Guiltless Man Hanged* (New York, [1929?]).

61. J. Woodford Howard, Jr., Mr. *Justice Murphy: A Political Biography* (Princeton: Princeton Univ. Press, 1968), pp. 27-29; *Literary Digest* 89 (April 24, 1926), p. 31; *New York Times,* January 18, 1925, sect. 7, p. 5, col. 1-3; February 5, 1927, p. 7, col. 1; March 17, 1929, sect. 2, p. 2, col. 5; March 9, 1948, p. 25, col. 6.

62. The Puerto Rico legislature abolished capital punishment in 1929, after a suspension of executions suggested that they had no deterrent effect; *New York Times,* April 30, 1929, p. 20, col. 4.

63. *New York Times,* February 13, 1927, p. 15, col. 3; July 2, 1928, p. 5, col. 3; March 15, 1931, p. 23, col. 2; March 22, 1931, sect. 3, p. 6, col. 6; April 8, 1931, p. 30, col. 6; December 5, 1933, p. 11, col. 2; March 10, 1935, p. 26, col. 2; *Nation* 124 (March 23, 1927), p. 307; Lee Emerson Deets, "Changes in Captial Punishment Policy Since 1939," *Journal of Criminal Law, Criminology and Police Science* 38 (March-April 1948), pp. 590-591. No one was executed in Kansas until 1944 and then only after the warden of the state penitentiary resigned, rather than supervise the killing; *Survey* 80 (April 1944), p. 139.

64. *New York Times,* March 3, 1932, p. 8, col. 7; *Literary Digest,* 116 (August 12, 1933), p. 6; Hugo A. Bedau, ed., *The Death Penalty in America,* rev. ed. (Chicago: Aldine, 1967), p. 13.

65. *Literary Digest,* 121 (March 7, 1936), p. 18; *New York Times,* February 8, 1936, p. 14, col. 7; January 5, 1937, p. 16, col. 7; June 16, 1938, p. 19, col. 4; Lewis E. Lawes, *A Brief History of Capital Punishment* (New York, 1941); Michael A. Musmanno, *Is It Possible to Execute Innocent Men?* (New York, 1940); Karl Menninger, *Why We Kill* (New York, 1940).

66. *New York Times,* February 12, 1954, p. 8, col. 2.

67. Hazel Erskine, "The Polls: Capital Punishment," *Public Opinion Quarterly* 34 (Summer 1970), p. 291. A similar 62 per cent of the American public had approved of capital punishment in a Gallup poll of 1936.

68. Arthur Koestler, *Reflections on Hanging* (New York: Macmillian, 1957), pp. vii-xx; originally published, London, 1956.

69. *New York Times,* October 27, 1958, p. 55, col. 4.

70. *New York Times,* June 7, 1957, p. 5, col. 4; Herbert L. Cobin,

"Abolition and Restoration of the Death Penalty in Delaware," in Bedau, ed., *Death Penalty in America*, pp. 359-365.

71. *New York Times*, August 29, 1956, p. 15, col. 6; May 10, 1957, p. 53, col. 4; March 26, 1959, p. 23, col. 6; *Nation* 190 (February 20, 1960), pp. 167-169; Hugo A. Bedau, "The Struggle Over Capital Punishment in New Jersey," in Bedau, ed., *Death Penalty in America*, pp. 374-382; Bedau, "Capital Punishment in Oregon, 1903-64," *Oregon Law Review* 45 (December 1965), p. 38.

72. *New York Times*, March 3, 1960, p. 18, col. 4, 6; March 11, 1960, p. 1, col. 8; April 27, 1960, p. 41, col. 3.

73. *New York Times*, April 10, 1960, p. 57, col. 1; *Time*, 75 (March 21, 1960), pp. 16-18.

74. Thorsten Sellin, ed., *Capital Punishment* (New York: Harper and Row, 1967), pp. 121-122; "Statement of Donal E. J. MacNamara," in *Abolition of Capital Punishment*, Hearings of Subcommittee No. 2 on H.R. 870, U.S. House of Representatives, Committee of the Judiciary, 86th Congress, 2d Sess., Serial No. 21: 158-167 (Washington, D.C.: G.P.O., 1960).

75. *New York Times*, March 12, 1961, p. 64, col. 1; February 28, 1965, sect. 4, p. 10, col. 1; Truman Capote, *In Cold Blood* (New York: Random House, 1965).

76. Brad Williams, *Due Process: The Fabulous Story of Criminal Lawyer George T. Davis and His Thirty-Year Battle Against Capital Punishment* (New York: William Morrow, 1960), p. 320; *New York Times*, January 5, 1959, p. 58, col. 7.

77. Cobin, "Abolition," pp. 366-373.

78. Hugo A. Bedau, "The Persistence of the Executioner, *Nation* 194 (March 10, 1962), p. 217; Bedau, "The Death Penalty in America," *Federal Probation* 35 (June, 1971), p. 32.

79. Bedau, "Death Penalty," p. 32.

80. Hugo A. Bedau, "The Abolition of Capital Punishment in Oregon, 1964" (unpublished typescript, 9 pp.).

81. *New York Times*, February 19, 1965, p. 21, col. 1; March 6, 1965, p. 11, col. 2; March 13, 1965, p. 8, col. 8; May 13, 1965, p. 1, col. 5; April 1, 1969, p. 38, col. 2.

82. *New York Times*, May 13, 1965, p. 1, col. 5; Michael Meltsner, *Cruel and Unusual: The Supreme Court and Capital Punishment* (New York: Random House, 1973), pp. 64-65. New York retained capital punishment for murder of a policeman in the line of duty and for murder by a prisoner under a life sentence.

83. Bedau, "Death Penalty," p. 34; Erskine, "The Polls," p. 291. One Gallup sample, in 1966, showed a plurality opposing capital punishment, 47% to 42%. By 1969, however, the situation had reversed and those favoring capital punishment predominated 51% to 40%.

84. Meltsner, *Cruel and Unusual*, pp. 28-44, 86-88. Goldberg's sug-

gestion came in *Snider v. Cunningham,* 375 U.S. 889 (1963). For the first influential attack on the constitutionality of capital punishment, see Gerald Gottlieb, "Testing the Death Penalty," *Southern California Law Review* 34 (Spring 1961), pp. 268-281.

85. Meltsner, *Cruel and Unusual,* pp. 101-110.

86. Meltsner, *Cruel and Unusual,* pp. 110-113.

87. Meltsner, *Cruel and Unusual,* pp. 113-114.

88. Meltsner, *Cruel and Unusual,* pp. 79-86, 149-244, and *passim.*

89. Meltsner, *Cruel and Unusual,* pp. 244-252, 266-279.

90. Meltsner, *Cruel and Unusual,* pp. 281-285.

91. Meltsner, *Cruel and Unusual,* pp. 286-305.

92. *New York Times,* March 15, 1973, p. 24, col. 3; February 3, 1974, sect. 4, p. 14, col. 7; *Time* 104 (December 16, 1974), p. 75.

93. *Facts on File* 33 (July 15-21, 1973), p. 611; *New York Times,* November 8, 1972, p. 28, col. 1; *Congressional Quarterly* 32 (November 9, 1974), p. 3102.

1 BENJAMIN RUSH

1. The "marquis of Beccaria" is more commonly known as Cesare Beccaria (1738-1794), whose *On Crimes and Punishment,* first published in 1764, persuaded Grand Duke Leopold of Tuscany to abolish capital punishment.

2. Dr. John Moore (1729-1802), a Scottish physician and author who had written several volumes about customs and conditions in Italy.

3. Genesis 9.6.

4. Rev. William Turner (1714-1794), an English Dissenting minister.

5. Catherine the Great of Russia (1729-1796), King Gustavus III of Sweden (1746-1792), and Grand Duke Leopold of Tuscany (1747-1792). Of the three, however, only Leopold had actually abolished capital punishment, and Rush could have possessed no proof that murder had been much reduced in any of their realms.

6. Exodus 21.12.

7. Rush, *An Enquiry,* quoted above.

8. Ebenezer Hazard (1744-1817) was an early compiler of American historical documents. His two-volume *Historical Collections* was published in Philadelphia in 1792-94.

9. Rush refers to documents of the American Revolution published in the same issue of the *American Museum* as the original form of this essay.

2 EDWARD LIVINGSTON

1. Livingston overstated the case in his reference to "universal" acknowledgment. Many states in the mid-1820s threatened, and some prac-

ticed, capital punishment for additional crimes. Massachusetts, for example, in 1822 executed two men for robbery.

2. Livingston was to devise elaborate procedures for regulating the lives of prisoners in his "Code of Reform and Prison Discipline" of 1825.

3   ROBERT RANTOUL, Jr.

1. Romans 13.1.

2. Rantoul quotes from Governor Edward Everett's annual message of 1836.

3. The Massachusetts legislature abolished capital punishment for highway robbery and burglary by Chapter 127 of 1839. Arson remained a capital crime until 1852.

4. Massachusetts abolished capital punishment for rape by Chapter 259 of 1852.

5. Massachusetts substituted life imprisonment for the death penalty as punishment for treason by Chapter 259 of 1852.

6. Rantoul again quotes Governor Edward Everett's annual message of 1836.

4   JOHN L. O'SULLIVAN

1. Caleb Lownes, "An Account of the Alteration and Present State of the Penal Laws of Pennsylvania," in William Bradford, *An Enquiry How Far the Punishment of Death is Necessary in Pennsylvania* (Philadelphia: T. Dobson, 1793).

2. O'Sullivan's account of Roman history is somewhat tendentious. Capital punishment for nobles was virtually abandoned in the last three hundred years of the Republic, it is true; see William M. Green, "An Ancient Debate on Capital Punishment," *Classical Journal* 24 (January 1929), pp. 267-275. However, there is no evidence to support O'Sullivan's claim that the prohibition applied to Roman citizens of the inferior orders. Cicero was exiled primarily because he put the conspirators to death *without a trial.* His speech against capital punishment (*Pro Rabirio* 5) should be taken as his means of protecting a client, not as a general statement of Roman sentiment. Indeed, it was later the same year that Cicero ordered the execution of the Catilinarians.

3. In the absence of corroborating Egyptian evidence, these tales of Egyptian "abolition" (Herodotus 2.137 and Diodorus 1.65) are of doubtful reliability. Sabaco or Shabaka (*c.* 712-*c.* 700 B.C.) was the first king of the Twenty-fifth Dynasty.

4. W. F. Reddaway, ed., *Documents of Catherine the Great: The Correspondence with Voltaire and the Instruction of 1767* (Cambridge, England: Cambridge University Press, 1931), p. 249. As in his interpretation of Roman history, O'Sullivan has apparently read Elizabeth's and

Catherine's promises to the nobility as general abolitions of capital punishment. In this case, O'Sullivan may have been deceived by Catherine's Instruction of 1767, the articles of which were not laws, but merely Catherine's ideas about important matters of state.

5. John Howard, *The State of the Prisons in England and Wales* (Warrington, England: Eyres, 1777).

6. James C. Prichard, *A Treatise on Insanity* (London: Sherwood, 1835).

7. James Simpson, *The Necessity of Popular Education* (Boston: Marsh, 1834).

8. O'Sullivan refers to Edward Livingston (see selection 2) and Daniel D. Tompkins (1774-1825), vice-president of the United States from 1817 to 1825, who had proposed abolition while governor of New York in 1812.

6 CHARLES SPEAR

1. George B. Cheever (see pp. 00-00). The quoted material is from Cheever's *Capital Punishment* (New York: Saxton and Miles, 1843), p. 39.

2. Cheever's *Capital Punishment* was a modified version of the arguments he had used in debate with John L. O'Sullivan (see selection 4) in 1843.

3. Genesis 9.2-6.

4. Robert Rantoul, Jr. (see selection 3).

5. John Calvin discussed this passage in his commentary on Genesis, *Ioannis Calvini Opera Quae Supersunt Omnia* (Brunswick, Germany: Schwetschke, 1863-1900), vol. 23, pp. 146-147.

6. Jean Le Clerc (1657-1736), Swiss Protestant theologian and scholar.

7. Thomas C. Upham (1799-1872), Congregationalist minister and professor of philosophy at Bowdoin College.

8. Johann David Michaelis (1717-1791), German Protestant theologian and biblical exegete.

7 CHARLES C. BURLEIGH

1. Frelinghuysen (1787-1862), chancellor of New York University, wrote a pro-hanging introduction to George B. Cheever's *Punishment By Death*, 2d ed. (New York: M.W. Dodd, 1843).

2. Stephen and Jesse Bourne, or Boorn, were sentenced to hang on January 28, 1820, for killing and hiding the remains of Russell Colvin. They were pardoned in December 1819, when Colvin turned up alive.

3. Jonathan Dymond, *Essays on the Principles of Morality* (Philadelphia: Book Committee of the Philadelphia Yearly Meeting of Friends, 1896), p. 362; originally published in London in 1830.

4. La Fayette made this much-quoted remark before the French Chamber of Deputies on August 17, 1830; Charles Lucas, *Recueil des*

débats des assemblées législatives de la France sur la question de la peine de mort (Paris: Béchet, 1831), Part 2, p. 42.

5. A slight misquotation of *Measure for Measure,* act 4, sc. 2, lines 162-165.

10 ELIZABETH CADY STANTON

1. Stanton apparently refers to the execution of convicted murderer Moses Lyons on December 18, 1829, in Johnstown, New York, though she has misstated her age in that year.

2. Many public executions in early nineteenth-century America were preceded by funereal band music, solemn parades, and other pomp designed to impress onlookers.

11 MARVIN H. BOVEE

1. Bovee's mistaken spelling of the name Vanarsdale.

12 EDMUND CLARENCE STEDMAN

1. Sir Walter Raleigh, just before his decapitation in 1618, is said to have felt the headsman's axe and remarked, "This is a sharp medicine, but it is a sure cure for all diseases."

2. Stedman refers to colonial executions for witchcraft.

3. See selection 1, n. 1.

4. Sir Henry Wotton, in his *The Difference and Disparity between the Estates and Conditions of George Duke of Buckingham, and Robert Earl of Essex,* published in 1641, cited Buckingham's belief that "hanging was the worst use man could be put to."

5. Louis XI of France (1423-1483), renowned for his severity, spent the last few years of his life at Plessis-les-Tours in Touraine and gave that castle a reputation for the sort of scene which Stedman portrays.

6. Ralph Waldo Emerson expressed this sentiment of John Brown in a lecture read in Boston on November 8, 1859, shortly before Brown's execution.

7. John Sheppard (1702-1724) and Richard Turpin (1706-1739) were two English thieves who died by hanging. Neither seems to have merited the fame which has attached to his name.

8. Jack Ketch was a common nickname for hangmen in Britain and America; the term derives from the name of an actual executioner in seventeenth-century England.

9. William Calcraft (1800-1879) was hangman for the city of London from 1829 to 1874. Most of his executions were public, many of them just outside London's Newgate Prison.

10. Charles Lynch (1736-1796), Virginia legislator and patriot, presided

over an extralegal court during the American Revolution, thus linking his name with unfair and excessive procedures against criminal defendants.

13 NEWTON M. CURTIS

1. Theologians Augustin Calmet (1672-1757), Jean Frederic Osterwald (1663-1747), John Wycliffe (1330-1384), and Kasper Scio or Scioppius (1576-1649).

2. The *Chicago Tribune* figures showed 1,467 murders as having occurred in 1882, 5,906 in 1891. The number of hangings during that period had not increased. There were 121 hangings and 117 lynchings in 1882, 123 hangings and 195 lynchings in 1891; George P. Upton to Curtis, Chicago, March 6, 1892, in Curtis, *To Define the Crime of Murder* (Washington, D. C.: G.P.O., 1892), p. 13.

14 WILLIAM DEAN HOWELLS

1. Howells has misspelled the first name of Allan McLane Hamilton 1848-1919), grandson of Alexander Hamilton and a prominent physician and a professor of mental diseases at Cornell University Medical College. College.

2. This is a slightly altered version of line 2 of Tennyson's *Will*.

3. Howells paraphrases a passage from Heinrich Heine's essay of 1828, *talien. Reise von München nach Genua* [*Italy. Journey from Munich to Genoa*]. See Heine, *Sämtliche Werke* [*Collected Works*] (Leipzig: Bibliographisches Institut, 1898), vol. 3, p. 223. The editor wishes to thank Professor Helen M. Mustard for her help in locating this passage.

15 FINLEY PETER DUNNE

1. William Thackeray's "Going to See a Man Hanged" first appeared in *raser's Magazine* in August 1840.

2. Charles Lamb, "On the Inconveniences From Being Hanged," in *The Complete Works and Letters of Charles Lamb* (New York: Modern Library, 1935), pp. 385-391.

3. Charles Dickens, *Barnaby Rudge* (London: Chapman and Hall, 849).

4. See selection 12, n. 7.

5. Dunne refers to the executions of Agostino Gelardi, Ignazio Silvestri, and Giovani Azari in Chicago on November 14, 1885; *New York Times*, November 15, 1885, p. 7, col. 2.

6. Horatio Nelson supervised the trial and execution of Francesco aracciolo, Duca di Brienza and commander of the Neapolitan navy, in 799.

16 CLARENCE DARROW

1. Samuel Untermyer (1858-1940) was a brilliant New York City attorney who gained prominence as an opponent of corporate corruption and abuses.

2. Nickname of the New York City Prison, built in 1902 and still in use in the 1970s.

17 KATHLEEN NORRIS

1. Tomás de Torquemada (1420-1498) was the founder and first head of the Spanish Inquisition. George Jeffries (or Jeffreys) (1648-1689) was English Lord Chancellor during the Bloody Assizes following the Duke of Monmouth's rebellion in 1685.

2. The reference is to a line from a chorus in act 2 of Gilbert and Sullivan's *Mikado*.

3. Although the author does not provide enough information to identify the homicidal wife, her second reference is apparently to Nathan Leopold and Richard Loeb, tried and sentenced to life imprisonment in 1924.

18 LEWIS E. LAWES

1. *New York Times*, October 10, 1924, p. 18, col. 5.

2. *New York Times*, October 12, 1923, p. 19, col. 7.

3. George A. Buker was warden of the Maine State Prison from 1927 to 1930.

4. Buker's reference is to Francis Spencer, executed on March 12, 1864.

5. Charles E. Linscott was warden of the Rhode Island State Prison from 1919 to 1930.

6. Harry H. Jackson was warden of Jackson Prison for most of the period 1925-1945.

7. George T. Jameson was warden of the South Dakota State Penitentiary from 1920 to 1933.

8. William H. Mackey was warden of the Kansas State Penitentiary from 1925 to 1929.

19 ROBERT G. ELLIOTT

1. The four victims were Newton Raymond, Jr., Amerigo Angelini, Thomas Gilbride, and Raymond K. Orley, executed on January 9, 1936, for the murder of Patrolman J. M. J. Killian.

2. Elliott had executed the young and attractive Ruth Snyder and her lover, Judd Gray, on January 12, 1928, for the murder of Snyder's husband.

20   HERBERT EHRMANN

1. [*Hansard*, May 1, 1810.] —Ehrmann.

2. [*Ibid.*, May 30, 1810.] —Ehrmann.

3. [Second Report on the Criminal Law by His Majesty's Commissioners, 1836, p. 21.] —Ehrmann.

4. [Not, however, by the dean of the Harvard Law School, who commented on the fact that the message ignored available data.] —Ehrmann.

5. [Data from *Memorandum on Capital Punishment*, prepared by Thorsten Sellin for the Royal Commission on Capital Punishment, 1951, pp. 657-60.] —Ehrmann.

6. [For instance, Lewis E. Lawes, former warden of Sing Sing Prison, *Man's Judgment of Death* (New York: G. P. Putnam's Sons, 1925), p. 58; Austin H. MacCormick, formerly Commissioner of Corrections, New York City, then executive director of the Osborne Association, in *Boston Sunday Herald*, December 11, 1949.] —Ehrmann.

7. [See, for instance, the quoted remarks of Chief Justice Higgins in the *Boston Daily Record*, November 5, 1942; those of Judge Warner in the *Boston Herald*, June 7, 1933; and those of District Attorney Foley in the *Boston Herald*, April 10, 1930.] —Ehrmann.

8. The Supreme Court eventually recognized this argument in *Witherspoon v. Illinois* (1968).

9. [Mr. Justice Wilkins in Commonwealth v. Cox, 1951 A. S. 857; 100 N. E. 2d 14.] —Ehrmann.

10. [Mass. St. 1939, Sec. 341; G. L. (Ter. Ed.) C. 278, Sec. 33E. This case was an unusual one for Massachusetts, where, under the Briggs law, so-called, insanity is usually determined before trial. G. L. (Ter. Ed.) C. 123, Sec 100A.] —Ehrmann.

11. [See Arthur Garfield Hays, *Trial by Prejudice*, New York: Covici Friede, 1933.] —Ehrmann.

12. [Smith v. Texas, 311 U. S. 128, 61 S. Ct. 164, 85 L. Ed. 84 (1940); Pierre v. Louisiana, 306 U. S. 354, 59 S. Ct. 536, 83 L. Ed. 760 (1939); Strauder v. W. Virginia, 100 U. S. 303, 25 L. Ed. 664 (1879).] —Ehrmann.

13. [Related by Wendell Murray, Esq., of the Boston Bar, called in as counsel for Wong Duck after the trial. Three of the defendants were executed, but Wong Duck was among those granted a new trial.] —Ehrmann.

14. [Royal Commission on Capital Punishment. Minutes of Evidence taken before the Royal Commission on Capital Punishment, Thirtieth Day, Thursday, 1st February, 1951. Witness: Professor Thorsten Sellin. [Pp. 647-678] London: H.M. Stationery Office, 1951.] —Ehrmann.

15. [262 Mass. 408 (1928).] —Ehrmann.

16. [328 U. S. 463, 66 S. Ct. 1318, 90 L. Ed. 1382 (1946).] —Ehrmann.

17. [See Testimony of Mr. Justice Frankfurter before the Royal Commission on Capital Punishment, 1950, pp. 580-82.] —Ehrmann.

18. [Benjamin N. Cardozo, *Law and Literature* (New York: Harcourt, Brace & Co., 1931), pp. 99-101.] —Ehrmann.

19. [Cf. *Boston Globe,* October 14, 1930. "Battle Creek, Michigan [an abolition state]. Only a little more than 12 hours following their capture after the killing of a state policeman and the robbery of a bank, Thomas Martin and James Gallagher were sentenced to life imprisonment in Jackson Prison." The Millen-Faber cases are notable for reasons other than great expense. At the time of the arrest of these criminals, two innocent men, Beret and Molway, were being tried for one of the murders committed by the Millen gang. The trial was nearing a conclusion, and eight reputable witnesses, with good opportunity to observe, had identified Beret and Molway as the robbers, when the real criminals were apprehended, bringing confessions and ballistic evidence to the rescue. No one familiar with the Beret-Molway trial has ever doubted that these men would have been convicted—and executed—but for this timely occurrence.] —Ehrmann.

20. [Commenting on the execution of Irene Schroeder by the State of Pennsylvania in 1931, Dr. Harvey M. Watkins, of Reading, a social worker, is quoted in a bulletin issued by the American League to Abolish Capital Punishment as saying: "It cost the State of Pennsylvania $23,658 to prosecute, convict and electrocute Irene Schroeder at the Western Penitentiary. If one twentieth of this sum had been spent 10 years ago by any social workers on that 22-year-old girl, that electrocution would have been prevented."] —Ehrmann.

21. [*Boston Herald,* June 7, 1933.] —Ehrmann.

22. [Record published by Henry Holt & Co., 1928.] —Ehrmann.

23. [Minutes of Faculty Meeting on Capital Punishment, Twentieth Century Club, January 18, 1936.] —Ehrmann.

22 THORSTEN SELLIN

1. [All data concerning executions have come from *National Prisoner Statistics,* No. 26, March 1961: *Executions 1960.* Washington, D.C.: Bureau of Prisons, U. S. Department of Justice.] —Sellin.

2. [Reproduced in *The Philadelphia Inquirer,* June 18, 1961.] —Sellin.

3. [Virgil W. Peterson, *A Report on Chicago Crime for 1960.* Chicago: Chicago Crime Commission, 1960, p. 56.] —Sellin.

4. [Thorsten Sellin, *The Death Penalty.* A Report for the Model Penal Code Project of The American Law Institute. Philadelphia: The American Law Institute, 1959, p. 62.] —Sellin.

5. [These diagrams are reproduced from *Capital Punishment.* Staff Research Report No. 46. Columbus: Ohio Legislative Service Commission, January 1961, pp. 40-42. They were copied from Sellin, *op. cit.,* and brought up to date.] —Sellin.

6. [Cf. Sellin, *op. cit.*, pp. 34-38: *Capital Punishment, op. cit.*, pp. 43-45; General Assembly of Pennsylvania, *Report of the Joint Legislative Committee on Capital Punishment.* Harrisburg: The Committee, June 1961, pp. 24-26.] —Sellin.

7. Sellin has since made an exploratory study of the subject in "Prison Homicides," in his *Capital Punishment* (New York: Harper and Row, 1967), pp. 154-160.

8. [Sellin, *op. cit.*, pp. 76-78.] —Sellin.

9. [*Capital Punishment, op. cit.*, pp. 81-82.] —Sellin.

10. [Communicated by Mr. James McCafferty, Criminologist, Bureau of Prisons, Washington, D.C.] —Sellin.

11. [J. Edgar Hoover, "The Federal Bureau of Investigation: The Protection of Civil Liberties," *American Bar Association Journal,* Vol. 46, August 1960, pp. 836-837.] —Sellin.

12. [*Uniform Crime Reports for the United States . . . 1959.* Washington, D.C.: Federal Bureau of Investigation, September 16, 1960, p. 14.] —Sellin.

13. [*Ibid.*, p. 3.] —Sellin.

14. [Thorsten Sellin, "The Death Penalty and Police Safety," Second Session—Twenty-Second Parliament 1955; *Appendix "F" of the Minutes of Preceedings and Evidence No. 20 of The Joint Committee of the Senate and the House of Commons on Capital and Corporal Punishment and Lotteries.* Ottawa: Queen's Printer, 1955, pp. 718-728.] —Sellin.

15. [General Assembly of Pennsylvania, *Report, op. cit.*, pp. 28-29.] —Sellin.

16. [*Capital Punishment, op. cit.*, p. 61.] —Sellin.

17. [*Ibid.*, pp. 62-63.] —Sellin.

18. [As yet unpublished study on a "Comparison of the Executed and the Commuted Among Admissions to Death Row," by Marvin E. Wolfgang, Arlene Kelly, and Hans C. Nolde.] —Sellin. Since published in *Journal of Criminal Law* 53 (September 1962), pp. 301-311.

23   WILLIAM STYRON

1. See selection 18.

2. Hoover's statement is reprinted in Hugo A. Bedau, *The Death Penalty in America* (Garden City, New York: Doubleday, 1964), pp. 132-134.

24   ATTORNEYS FOR THE NAACP
LEGAL DEFENSE AND EDUCATIONAL FUND

1. [*In re Kemmler,* 136 U.S. 436,447 (1890) (dictum).] —in original.

2. [*Wilkerson v. Utah,* 99 U.S. 130 (1879).] —edited.

3. [*In re Kemmler,* 136 U.S. 436 (1890).] —edited.

4. [*State ex rel. Francis v. Resweber,* 329 U.S. 459 (1947).] —edited.

5. [*Trop v. Dulles,* 356 U.S. 86 (1958).] —edited.

6. [Sellin, *The Inevitable End of Capital Punishment,* in SELLIN, CAPITAL PUNISHMENT (1967), 239.] —edited.

7. [*M'Culloch v. Maryland,* 4 Wheat. 316, 407 (1819).] —in original.

8. [CARDOZO, THE NATURE OF THE JUDICIAL PROCESS (1921), 83.] —in original.

9. [*Robinson v. California,* 370 U.S. 660, 666 (1962).] —in original.

10. [*Weems v. United States,* 217 U.S. 349, 378 (1910).] —in original.

11. [*Trop v. Dulles,* 356 U.S. 86, 100 (1958) (plurality opinion of Chief Justice Warren).] —in original.

12. [LAWES, TWENTY THOUSAND YEARS IN SING SING (1932), 306-307.] —edited.

13. [BENTHAM, TO HIS FELLOW CITIZENS OF FRANCE, ON DEATH PUNISHMENT (1831), 3.] —in original.

14. [UNITED NATIONS, ECONOMIC AND SOCIAL COUNCIL, Note by the Secretary-General, *Capital Punishment* (E/4947) (February 23, 1971), p. 3.] —in original.

15. [UNITED NATIONS, ECONOMIC AND SOCIAL COUNCIL, Resolution 1574(L), *Capital Punishment,* adopted May 20, 1971 (E/RES/1574(L), May 28, 1971).] —in original.

16. Albert Camus, "Reflections on the Guillotine," in Camus, *Resistance, Rebellion and Death* (New York: Knopf, 1961), p. 232.

17. [Statement of Attorney General Ramsey Clark, in *Hearings Before the Subcommittee on Criminal Laws and Procedures of the Senate Committee on the Judiciary, 90th Cong., 2d Sess., on S. 1760,* To Abolish the Death Penalty (March 20-21 and July 2, 1968) (G.P.O. 1970) [hereafter cited as *Hearings*], at 91. See CLARK, CRIME IN AMERICA (1970), 336.] —edited.

18. [*The New York Times,* December 19, 1969, p. 9.] —in original.

19. [Prime Minister Lester E. Pearson, in CANADA, HOUSE OF COMMONS, IV DEBATES, 27th Parl., 2d Sess. (16 Eliz. II), 4370 (Nov. 16, 1967).] —edited.

20. [SELLIN, THE DEATH PENALTY (1959), published as an appendix to AMERICAN LAW INSTITUTE, MODEL PENAL CODE, Tent. Draft No. 9 (May 8, 1959), 15.] —edited.

21. [Francart, quoted in CAMUS 229.] —in original.

22. [CAMUS 187.] —edited.

23. [CAMUS 186-188.] —in original.

24. [Darrow, *A Comment on Capital Punishment,* in LAURENCE, A HISTORY OF CAPITAL PUNISHMENT (1960), xv, xvii.] —edited.

25. [Gottlieb, *Capital Punishment,* 15 CRIME & DELINQUENCY 1, 6 (1969).] —in original.

26. [LAWES, TWENTY THOUSAND YEARS IN SING SING (1932), 306-307.] —edited.

27. [Statement of Attorney General Ramsey Clark, in *Hearings*, at 93.] —edited.

28. [DiSalle, *Trends in the Abolition of Capital Punishment*, 1 U. TOLEDO L. REV. 1, 12-13 (1969).] —edited.

29. [Professor Wechsler, in *Symposium on Capital Punishment*, 7 N.Y.L. FORUM 247, 255 (1961).] —edited.

30. [West, *Medicine and Capital Punishment*, in *Hearings*, at 125.] —edited.

31. [*Trop v. Dulles*, 356 U.S. 86, 102 (1958) (plurality opinion of Chief Justice Warren).] —edited.

32. [CAMUS 200.] —edited.

33. [*Trop v. Dulles* 356 U.S. 86, 99 (1958) (plurality opinion of Chief Justice Warren).] —in original.

34. [Barry, *Hanged by the Neck Until . . .*, 2 SYDNEY L. REV. 401, 411 (1958).] —in original.

25 LOUIS J. WEST

1. [MENNINGER, K. 1959. Verdict guilty—now what? *In* A Psychiatrist's World: The Selected Papers of Karl Menninger, B. H. Hall, ed. Viking Press, New York.] —West.

2. [BLUESTONE, H., and McGAHEE, C. L. 1962. Reactions to extreme stress: Impending death by execution. Amer. J. Psychiat. 119:393-396; Gallemore, J. L., Jr. and Panton, J. H. 1972. Inmate responses to lengthy death row confinement. Amer. J. Psychiat. 129:167-172.] —West.

3. [SLOVENKO, R. 1964. And the penalty is (sometimes) death. Antioch Rev., pp. 351-364.] —West.

4. [KOESTLER, A. 1957. Reflections on Hanging. Macmillan, New York.] —West.

5. [GRAVES, W. F. 1964. The deterrent effect of capital punishment in California. *In* The Death Penalty in America, H. A. Bedau, ed. Doubleday (Anchor Books), New York, pp. 322-332.] —West.

6. [CAMUS, A. 1959. Reflections on the Guillotine. FridtjofKarla Publications, Michigan City, Michigan.] —West.

7. [SCHUESSLER, K. F. 1952. The deterrent influence of the death penalty. The Annals of the Amer. Acad. Pol. Soc. Sci. 284: 54-62.] —West.

8. [SELLIN, T. 1959. The Death Penalty. American Law Institute, Philadelphia.] —West.

9. [WERTHAM, F. 1949. The Show of Violence. Doubleday, New York.] —West.

10. [ALEXANDER, F. and STAUB, H. 1956. The Criminal, the Judge, and the Public. Free Press, Glencoe, Illinois.] —West.

11. [MENNINGER, K. 1968. The Crime of Punishment. Viking Press, New York.] —West.

12. [ZILBOORG, G. 1936. Differential diagnosis of types of suicides. Arch. Neurol. Psychiat. 35:270-291.] —West.

13. [WEST, D. J. 1966. Murder Followed by Suicide. Harvard University Press, Cambridge, Mass.] —West.

14. [SELLIN, T. 1959. The Death Penalty. American Law Institute, Philadelphia.] —West.

15. [DiSALLE, M. V. 1965. The Power of Life or Death. Random House, New York.] —West.

16. [JACKSON, S. 1949. The Lottery and Other Stories. Farrar, New York.] —West.

17. [National Prisoner Statistics. Number 39, June 1966, "Executions 1930-1965."] —West.

26 HUGO A. BEDAU

1. [See Bedau, ed., *The Death Penalty in America* (1967), p. 36.] —Bedau.

2. [See *National Prisoner Statistics* (1969).] —Bedau.

3. [Dann, *The Deterrent Effect of Capital Punishment* (1935); Savitz, in *J. Criminal Law, Criminology & Police Science* (1958).] —Bedau.

4. [Graves, in Bedau, ed., *The Death Penalty in America* (1967).] —Bedau.

5. [Schuessler, in *The Annals* (1952); Reckless, in *Crime & Delinquency* (1969).] —Bedau.

6. [Sellin, *The Death Penalty* (1959); Wolfgang, in "Capital Punishment," *H. R. Hearings* (1972).] —Bedau.

7. [Sellin, *The Death Penalty* (1959); Samuelson in *J. Criminal Law, Criminology & Police Science* (1969).] —Bedau.

8. [Sellin, *The Death Penalty* (1959); Wolfgang, in "Capital Punishment," *H. R. Hearings* (1972).] —Bedau.

9. [Sellin and Campion, in Bedau, ed., *The Death Penalty in America* (1967); also Cardarelli, in *J. Criminal Law, Criminology & Police Science* (1968).] —Bedau.

10. [Sellin, ed., *Capital Punishment* (1967).] —Bedau.

11. [See *National Prisoner Statistics* (1969).] —Bedau.

12. [Wolfgang, Kelly and Nolde, in *J. Criminal Law, Criminology & Police Science* (1962).] —Bedau.

13. [Wolf, in *Rutgers Law Review* (1964).] —Bedau.

14. [*Stanford Law Review* (1969).] —Bedau.

15. [Wolfgang, "Capital Punishment," *H. R. Hearings* (1972), pp. 178, 179; see now Wolfgang and Reidel, *The Annals* (May 1973).] —Bedau.

16. [*New York Times*, Nov. 23, 1972, p. 18.] —Bedau.

SELECT BIBLIOGRAPHY

Bibliographies and Collections

American Journal of Orthopsychiatry. July 1975.

Annals of the American Academy of Political and Social Science. November 1952.

Bedau, Hugo A., ed. *The Death Penalty in America,* rev. ed. Chicago: Aldine, 1967. Bibliography, pp. 565-574.

Beman, Lemar T., ed. *Selected Articles on Capital Punishment.* New York: H. W. Wilson, 1925. Bibliography, pp. xxxi-lxviii.

Congressional Digest. January 1973.

Crime and Delinquency. January 1969.

Editorial Research Reports. January 10, 1973.

Fanning, Clara E., ed. *Selected Articles on Capital Punishment.* Minneapolis: H. W. Wilson, 1913. Bibliography, pp. xiii-xxvi.

Johnsen, Julia E., ed. *Capital Punishment.* New York: H. W. Wilson, 1939. Bibliography, pp. 245-262.

Lyons, Douglas B. "Capital Punishment: A Selected Bibliography." *Criminal Law Bulletin* 8 (November 1972), p. 783.

—— and William J. Bowers, "Selected Bibliography and References on Capital Punishment." In Bowers, *Executions in America.* Lexington, Mass.: D.C. Heath, 1974, pp. 403-452.

McCafferty, James A., ed. *Capital Punishment.* Chicago: Aldine, Atherton, 1972. Bibliography, pp. 262-266.

McClellan, Grant S., ed., *Capital Punishment.* New York: H. W. Wilson, 1961. Bibliography, pp. 176-180.

McDade, Thomas M. *The Annals of Murder: A Bibliography of Books and Pamphlets on American Murders from Colonial Times to 1900.* Norman: Univ. of Oklahoma Press, 1961.

McGehee, Edward G. and William H. Hildebrand, eds. *The Death Penalty: A Literary and Historical Approach.* Boston: D. C. Heath 1964. Bibliography, pp. 152-160.

333

Meyer, Hermann H. B. *Select List of References on Capital Punishment.* Washington, D.C.: G.P.O., 1912.

Prison Journal. October 1932 and October 1958.

Sellin, Thorsten, ed. *Capital Punishment.* New York: Harper and Row, 1967. Bibliography, pp. 275-279.

United States. Library of Congress. Division of Bibliography. "Capital Punishment: A Bibliographical List." Washington, D.C.: G.P.O., 1931. Mimeographed.

Works by and about Authors Represented in this Book*

Bates, Ernest Sutherland. "Edmund Clarence Stedman." In *Dictionary of American Biography.* 21 vols. New York: C. Scribners, 1928-36, vol. 17, pp. 552-553.

Bedau, Hugo A. "A Bibliography on Capital Punishment and Related Topics, 1948-1958." "A Survey of the Debate on Capital Punishment in Canada, England and the United States, 1948-1958." *Prison Journal* 38 (October 1958), pp. 41-45, 35-41.

––––. "Capital Punishment in Oregon, 1903-64." *Oregon Law Review* 35 (May 1963), pp. 410-419.

––––. "Death Sentences in New Jersey, 1907-1960." *Rutgers Law Review* 19 (Fall 1964), pp. 1-64.

––––. "The Struggle Over Capital Punishment in New Jersey." In Hugo A. Bedau, ed., *The Death Penalty in America,* rev. ed. Chicago: Aldine, 1967, pp. 374-395.

––––. "The Death Penalty as a Deterrent: Argument and Evidence." *Ethics* 80 (April 1970), pp. 205-217.

––––. "The Death Penalty in America." *Federal Probation* 35 (June 1971), pp. 32-43.

–––– and Stephen Caswell. "*Trial* Interview: Hugo Adam Bedau." *Trial* 10 (May-June 1974), pp. 49, 51-53.

Bovee, Marvin H. *Reasons for Abolishing Capital Punishment.* Chicago, 1878 (a republication of Bovee's *Christ and the Gallows*)—see selection 11.

Brasher, Thomas L. *Whitman as Editor of the Brooklyn Daily Eagle.* Detroit: Wayne State Univ. Press, 1970.

Bulkley, Robert DeGroff, Jr. "Robert Rantoul, Jr., 1805-1852: Politics and Reform in Antebellum Massachusetts." Ph.D. dissertation, Princeton University, 1971.

*Works exerpted in this book not included.

Curtis, Newton M. *General Curtis on the Death Penalty* [London, 1891].

Darrow, Clarence. *The Story of My Life.* New York: C. Scribners, 1934.

———. "Is Capital Punishment a Wise Policy?" In Arthur Weinberg, ed., *Attorney for the Damned.* New York: Simon and Schuster, 1957.

Dobson, Eleanor Robinette. "Charles C. Burleigh." In *Dictionary of American Biography.* 21 vols. New York: C. Scribners, 1928-36, vol. 3, pp. 284-285.

Elliott, Robert G. *Agent of Death: The Memoirs of an Executioner.* New York: E. P. Dutton, 1940.

Ellis, Elmer. *Mr. Dooley's America: A Life of Finley Peter Dunne.* New York: A. A. Knopf, 1941.

Fanning, Charles F. "Finley Peter Dunne and Mr. Dooley: The Chicago Years." Ph.D. dissertation, University of Pennsylvania, 1972.

Harris, Sheldon H. "The Public Career of John Louis O'Sullivan." Ph.D. dissertation, Columbia University, 1958.

Hawke, David Freeman. *Benjamin Rush: Revolutionary Gadfly.* Indianapolis: Bobbs-Merrill, 1971.

"H. B. Ehrmann, 77, in Famous Trial." *New York Times,* June 19, 1970, p. 37, col. 4.

Howells, William Dean. "Editor's Easy Chair." *Harper's* 130 (March 1915), pp. 634-637.

Kunstler, William M. *Beyond A Reasonable Doubt? The Original Trial of Caryl Chessman.* New York: William Morrow, 1961.

Lawes, Lewis E. *Man's Judgment of Death.* New York: G. P. Putnam's Sons, 1924.

———. *Twenty Thousand Years in Sing Sing.* New York: R. Long and R. R. Smith, 1932.

———. *Meet the Murderer!* New York: Harper & Brothers, 1940.

Lutz, Alma. *Created Equal: A Biography of Elizabeth Cady Stanton, 1815-1902.* New York: John Day, 1940.

Lynn, Kenneth S. *William Dean Howells: An American Life.* New York: Harcourt Brace Jovanovich, 1970.

Machlin, Milton and William Read Woodfield. *Ninth Life* [Caryl Chessman]. New York: G.P. Putnam's Sons, 1961.

Mackey, Philip English. "Edward Livingston and the Origins of the Movement to Abolish Capital Punishment in the United States." *Louisiana History* 16 (Spring 1975), pp. 145-166.

MacLear, Anne B. "Newton Martin Curtis." In *Dictionary of American Biography.* 21 vols. New York: C. Scribners, 1928-36, vol. 4, pp. 618-619.

"Marvin H. Bovee." In *Appletons' Cyclopaedia of American Biography.* 7

vols. New York: D. Appleton, 1887-1900, vol. 7, p. 31.

Meltsner, Michael. *Cruel and Unusual: The Supreme Court and Capital Punishment* [NAACP Legal Defense and Educational Fund]. New York: Random House, 1973.

"Mrs. Kathleen (Thompson) Norris." In *Twentieth Century Authors*. New York: H. W. Wilson, 1942, pp. 1032-33.

[O'Sullivan, John L.] "Capital Punishment." *United States Magazine and Democratic Review* 12 (April 1843), pp. 409-424.

[———.] "The Anti-Gallows Movement." *United States Magazine and Democratic Review* 14 (April 1844), pp. 430-431.

[———.] "Capital Punishment: The Proceedings of the Recent Convention of the Friends of the Abolition of the Punishment of Death." *United States Magazine and Democratic Review* 14 (June 1844), pp. 657-659.

Pratt, Julius W. "John L. O'Sullivan and Manifest Destiny." *New York History* 14 (July 1933), pp. 213-234.

Rantoul, Robert, Jr. *Letters on the Death Penalty*. Boston, 1846.

———. *Memoirs, Speeches and Writings of Robert Rantoul, Jr.*, ed. Luther Hamilton. Boston: J. P. Jewett, 1854.

Ratner, Marc L. *William Styron*. New York: Twayne, 1972.

Sellin, Thorsten. *The Death Penalty*. Tentative Draft No. 9, Model Penal Code Project of the American Law Institute. Philadelphia: American Law Inst., 1959.

———. "Death and Imprisonment as Deterrents to Murder." "Does the Death Penalty Protect Municipal Police?" In Hugo A. Bedau, ed., *The Death Penalty in America*, rev. ed. Chicago: Aldine, 1967, pp. 274-284, 284-301.

———. "The Inevitable End of Capital Punishment." "Prison Homicides." In Thorsten Sellin, ed., *Capital Punishment*. New York: Harper and Row, 1967, pp. 239-253, 154-160.

Spear, Charles. Manuscript Diary, 1841-1849. Boston Public Library.

———, ed. *The Prisoner's Friend*. 1845-1857, 1860-1861.

Stone, Irvin. *Clarence Darrow for the Defense*. Garden City, N.Y.: Garden City Publ. Co., 1943.

Styron, William. "The Aftermath of Benjamin Reid." *Esquire* 58 (November 1962), pp. 79-81, 158-164.

Van Deusen, Glyndon G. *Horace Greeley: Nineteenth-Century Crusader*. Philadelphia: Univ. of Pennsylvania Press, 1953.

Wagenknecht, Edward C. *John Greenleaf Whittier: A Portrait in Paradox*. New York: Oxford Univ. Press, 1967.

———. *William Dean Howells: The Friendly Eye*. New York: Oxford Univ. Press, 1969.

Whitman, Walt. *The Gathering of the Forces.* 2 vols. New York: G. P. Putnam's Sons, 1920, vol. 1, pp. 97-120.

Sources for the History of Capital Punishment, and Efforts to End It, in the United States*

Armstrong, Lebbeus. *The Signs of the Times.* New York: R. Carter, 1848.

[Bacon, Leonard.] "Shall Punishment Be Abolished." *New Englander* 4 (October 1846), pp. 563-588.

Barbour, James J. "Efforts to Abolish the Death Penalty in Illinois." *Journal of Criminal Law* 9 (February 1919), pp. 500-513.

Barnes, Harry Elmer. *The Evolution of Penology in Pennsylvania: A Study in American Social History.* Indianapolis: Bobbs-Merrill, 1927.

Beccaria, Cesare. *On Crimes and Punishment,* trans. Henry Paolucci. Indianapolis: Bobbs-Merrill, 1963 (originally published in 1764).

Beichman, Arnold. "The First Electrocution." *Commentary* 35 (May 1963), pp. 410-419.

Black, Charles L., Jr. *Capital Punishment: The Inevitability of Caprice and Mistake.* New York: W. W. Norton, 1974.

Borchard, Edwin M. *Convicting the Innocent.* New Haven: Oxford Univ. Press, 1932.

Bowers, William J. *Executions in America.* Lexington, Mass.: D.C. Heath, 1974.

Browning, James R. "The New Death Penalty Statues: Perpetuating a Costly Myth." *Gonzaga Law Review* 9 (Spring 1974), pp. 651-705.

Bye, Raymond T. *Capital Punishment in the United States.* Philadelphia: Committee on Philanthropic Labor of Philadelphia Yearly Meeting of Friends, 1919.

"Capital Punishment." *United States Magazine and Democratic Review* 20 (January, March 1847), pp. 71-73, 204-208.

"Capital Punishment in the United States." *Law Reporter* 8 (March 1846), pp. 481-495.

"Capital Punishment in Virginia." *Virginia Law Review* 58 (January 1972), pp. 97-142.

Carver, Leonard D. *Capital Punishment in Maine.* N.p., 1901.

Caswell, Stephen. "Cementing a Fragile Victory." *Trial* 10 (May-June 1974), pp. 47-48, 51-52.

Cheever, George B. *Capital Punishment: The Argument of Rev. George B. Cheever in Reply to J.L. O'Sullivan, Esq.* New York: Saxton and Miles, 1843.

*Works exerpted in this book not included.

[——.] *Punishment by Death: Its Authority and Expediency.* New York: J. Wiley, 1849 (originally published in 1842).

Cheever, George B. and Tayler Lewis. *A Defence of Capital Punishment and An Essay on the Ground and Reason of Punishment, with special reference to the Penalty of Death.* New York: Wiley and Putnam, 1846.

Cheever, George B., Samuel Hand, and Wendell Phillips. "The Death Penalty." *North American Review* 133 (December 1881), pp. 534-559.

Chitwood, Oliver Perry. *Justice in Colonial Virginia.* Baltimore: Johns Hopkins Press, 1905.

Cobin, Herbert L. "Abolition and Restoration of the Death Penalty in Delaware." In Hugo A. Bedau, ed., *The Death Penalty in America*, rev. ed. Chicago: Aldine, 1967, pp. 359-373.

Cogswell, Jonathan. *A Treatise on the Necessity of Capital Punishment.* Hartford, Conn.: E. Geer, 1843.

Cropley, Carrie. "The Case of John McCaffary." *Wisconsin Magazine of History* 35 (Summer 1952), pp. 281-288.

Dalzell, George W. *Benefit of Clergy in America.* Winston-Salem, N.C.: J.F. Blair 1955.

Dana, James. *The Intent of Capital Punishment: A Discourse.* New Haven: T. & S. Green, [1790].

Dann, Robert H. "Capital Punishment in Oregon." *Annals of the American Academy of Political and Social Science* 284 (November 1952), pp. 110-114.

Davis, David Brion. "Murder in New Hampshire." *New England Quarterly* 28 (June 1955), pp. 147-163.

——. "The Movement to Abolish Capital Punishment in America, 1787-1861." *American Historical Review* 63 (October 1957), pp. 23-46.

DiSalle, Michael V. *The Power of Life or Death.* New York: Random House, 1965.

[Dod, Albert Baldwin.] "Capital Punishment." *Biblical Repertory and Princeton Review*, 14 (April 1842), pp. 307-346.

Dole, Benjamin. *An Examination of Mr. Rantoul's Report for Abolishing Capital Punishment in Massachusetts.* Boston, 1837.

[Eddy, Thomas.] *An Account of the State Prison or Penitentiary House, in the City of New-York.* New York: Isaac Collins & Son, 1801.

Edwards, John. *Serious Thoughts on the Subject of Taking the Lives of our Fellow Creatures by way of Punishment for Any Crime Whatsoever.* New York, 1811.

Ehrmann, Sara. "Capital Punishment Today." In Herbert Bloch, ed., *Crime in America.* New York: Philosophical Library, 1961, pp. 78-97.

Ekirch, Arthur A. "Thomas Eddy and the Beginnings of Prison Reform in New York." *New York History* 24 (July 1943), pp. 376-391.

Erskine, Hazel. "The Polls: Capital Punishment." *Public Opinion Quarterly* 34 (Summer 1970), pp. 290-307.

"An Essay on the Ground and Reason of Punishment." *United States Magazine and Democratic Review* 19 (August 1846), pp. 90-103.

An Exercise in Declamation in the Form of a Debate on Capital Punishment. Boston, 1849.

Feiertag, Erwin L. "Capital Punishment in New Jersey, 1664-1950." Master's thesis, Columbia University, 1951.

Filler, Louis. "Movements to Abolish the Death Penalty in the United States." *Annals of the American Academy of Political and Social Science* 284 (November 1952), pp. 124-136.

Fitzroy, Herbert W. K. "The Punishment of Crime in Provincial Pennsylvania." *Pennsylvania Magazine of History and Biography* 60 (July 1936), pp. 242-269.

Geis, Gilbert. "The Death Penalty in Oklahoma." *Proceedings of the Oklahoma Academy of Science* 34 (1953), pp. 191-193.

Goebel, Julius and T. Raymond Naughton. *Law Enforcement in Colonial New York. A Study in Criminal Procedure (1664-1776).* New York: Commonwealth Fund, 1944.

Grayson, W. S. "Capital Punishment." *Southern Literary Messenger* 33 (December 1861), pp. 453-458.

Guillot, Ellen Elizabeth. "Abolition and Restoration of the Death Penalty in Missouri." *Annals of the American Academy of Political and Social Science* 284 (November 1952), pp. 105-109.

[Hall, Edward Brooks.] "The Punishment of Death." *North American Review* 62 (January 1846), pp. 40-70.

Hanged By the Neck Until You Be Dead. Brooklyn, N.Y.: W.C. Wilton, 1877.

Haskins, George L. "The Capitall Laws of New England." *Harvard Law School Bulletin* 7 (February 1956), pp. 10-11.

Hatcher, William B. *Edward Livingston: Jeffersonian Republican and Jacksonian Democrat.* University: Louisiana State University Press, 1940.

Hayner, Norman S. and John R. Cranor. "The Death Penalty in Washington State." *Annals of the American Academy of Political and Social Science* 284 (November 1952), pp. 101-104.

[Hazard, Thomas R.] *Christianity Opposed to the "Death Penalty."* Providence, R.I.: Knowles, Anthony, 1852.

Hochkammer, William O., Jr. "The Capital Punishment Controversy." *Journal of Criminal Law* 60 (September 1969), pp. 360-368.

Horton, Albert H. "The Death Penalty in Kansas." *Proceedings of the Bar Association of the State of Kansas*, Topeka, Kans., 1887, pp. 13-24.

Illinois. Legislative Council. Research Memorandum 1-549, "Bills to Abolish Death Penalty in Illinois." Springfield, 1951.

Keedy, Edwin R. "History of the Pennsylvania Statute Creating Degrees of Murder." *University of Pennsylvania Law Review* 97 (May 1949), pp. 759-777.

Kentucky. Legislative Research Commission. Informational Bulletin No. 40, *Capital Punishment*. Frankfort, 1965.

Kirkpatrick, Clifford. *Capital Punishment*. Philadelphia: Philadelphia Committee on Philanthropic Labor, 1945.

"Legislative History of Capital Punishment in Massachusetts." In *Report and Recommendations of the Special Commission Established for the Purpose of Investigating and Studying the Abolition of the Death Penalty in Capital Cases* (Massachusetts House Doc. No. 2575). Boston: Commonwealth of Massachusetts, 1958, pp. 98-110.

Mackey, Philip English. "Anti-Gallows Activity in New York State, 1776-1861." Ph.D. dissertation, University of Pennsylvania, 1969.

———. "Reverend George B. Cheever: Yankee Reformer as Champion of the Gallows." *Proceedings of the American Antiquarian Society* 82 (October 1972), pp. 323-342.

———. "The Inutility of Mandatory Capital Punishment: An Historical Note." *Boston University Law Review* 54 (January 1974), pp. 31-35.

———. " 'The Result May Be Glorious': Anti-Gallows Movement in Rhode Island, 1838-1852." *Rhode Island History* 33 (February 1974), pp. 19-30.

———. "An All-Star Debate on Capital Punishment, Boston, 1854." *Essex Institute Historical Collections* 110 (July 1974), pp. 181-199.

Maestro, Marcello. *Cesare Beccaria and the Origins of Penal Reform*. Philadelphia: Temple Univ. Press, 1973.

Mason, Charles. *Address of the Hon. Charles Mason Before the Iowa Anti-Capital Punishment and Prison Discipline Society*. New York: New York State Society for the Abolition of Capital Punishment, 1848.

Michigan. Legislative Research Bureau. "History of Capital Punishment in the State of Michigan." [Lansing] 1957.

Murdy, Ralph G. "Brief History of Capital Punishment in Maryland." In *Report of the Committee on Capital Punishment to the Legislative Council of Maryland*. October 3, 1962, pp. 5-8.

Nadal, E. S. "The Rationale of Opposition to Capital Punishment." *North American Review* 116 (January 1873), pp. 138-150.

North Carolina. State Board of Charities and Public Welfare. *Capital Pun-

ishment in North Carolina. Special Bulletin No. 10. Raleigh: State of North Carolina, 1929.

Ohio. Legislative Service Commission. Staff Research Report No. 46, *Capital Punishment.* Columbus, 1961.

Osborne, Thomas Mott. "Thou Shalt Not Kill." *The Forum* 73 (February 1925), pp. 156-161.

Palm, A. J. *The Death Penalty.* New York: G. P. Putnam's Sons, 1891.

Parker, Theodore. *Sermon of the Dangerous Classes in Society.* Boston: Spear, 1847.

Patterson, Henry S. *A Brief Statement of the Argument for the Abolition of the Death Penalty.* Philadelphia, 1844.

[Philanthropos.] *Essays on Capital Punishments, Republished from Poulsen's Daily Advertiser.* Philadelphia: Brown and Merritt, 1811.

Phillips, Wendell. *Speeches Lectures, and Letters,* 2d series. Boston: Lee and Shepard, 1905, pp. 77-109.

Polsby, Daniel D. "The Death of Capital Punishment? *Furman v. Georgia.*" *Supreme Court Review* (1972), pp. 1-40.

Porter, Benjamin F. *Argument of Benjamin F. Porter, in Support of a Bill . . . to Abrogate the Punishment of Death.* Tuscaloosa, Ala., 1846.

Post, Albert. "Early Efforts to Abolish Capital Punishment in Pennsylvania." *Pennsylvania Magazine of History and Biography* 68 (January 1944), pp. 38-53.

———. "Michigan Abolishes Capital Punishment." *Michigan History Magazine* 29 (January 1945), pp. 44-50.

———. "The Anti-Gallows Movement in Ohio." *The Ohio State Archaeological and Historical Quarterly,* 54 (April-June 1945), pp. 104-112.

Powers, Edwin. *Crime and Punishment in Early Massachusetts, 1620-1692.* Boston: Beacon Press, 1966.

Purrington, Tobias. *Report on Capital Punishment Made to the Maine Legislature in 1836,* 3rd ed. Washington, D.C., 1852.

Quaife, M. M. "Capital Punishment in Detroit." *Burton Historical Collection Leaflet* 4 (January 1926), pp. 33-48.

Quinby, G. W. *The Gallows, the Prison and the Poor House.* Cincinnati, Ohio: Quinby, 1856.

Rankin, Hugh F. *Criminal Trial Proceedings in the General Court of Colonial Virginia.* Williamsburg: Univ. Press of Virginia, 1965.

Reed, Henry Clay. "A History of Crime and Punishment in New Jersey." Ph.D. dissertation, Princeton University, 1939.

Report of the Commission to Investigate and Report the Most Humane and Practical Method of Carrying into Effect the Sentence of Death in Capital Cases. Albany, N.Y., 1888.

Saathoff, John A. "Capital Punishment in Iowa." Master's thesis, University of Iowa, 1927.*

Savitz, Leonard D. "A Brief History of Capital Punishment Legislation in Pennsylvania." *The Prison Journal* 38 (October 1958), pp. 50-62.

Scott, Arthur P. *Criminal Law in Colonial Virginia.* Chicago: Univ. of Chicago Press, 1930.

Semmes, Raphael. *Crime and Punishment in Early Maryland.* Baltimore: Johns Hopkins University Press, 1938.

Shipley, Maynard. "Does Capital Punishment Prevent Convictions?" *American Law Review* 43 (May-June 1909), pp. 321-334.

Silver, Isidore. "American Influence on Nineteenth Century English Criminal Law Reform: The Movement to Abolish Capital Punishment." Master's thesis, New York University, 1965.

Skidmore, Rex A. "Penology in Early Utah." *Western Humanities Review* 2 (April 1948), pp. 145-168.

Spooner, Florence. *Prison Reform and Abolition of the Death Penalty Movement in Massachusetts.* Boston, 1900.

Sutton, Charles. *The New York Tombs.* San Francisco: Roman, 1874.

Taylor, Timothy Alden. *The Bible View of the Death Penalty.* Worcester, Mass.: Howland, 1850.

Teeters, Negley K. *Scaffold and Chair: A Compilation of Their Use in Pennsylvania, 1682-1962.* Philadelphia: Pennsylvania Prison Society, 1963.

——. *Hang by the Neck.* Springfield, Ill.: Charles C. Thomas, 1967.

—— and Charles J. Zibulka. "Executions Under State Authority—An Inventory [1864-1966]," In William J. Bowers, *Executions in America.* Lexington, Mass.: D. C. Heath, 1974.

Thomas, Abel Charles. *A Lecture on Capital Punishment.* Philadelphia, 1830.

Titus, James H. *Reports and Addresses of James H. Titus upon the Subject of Capital Punishment.* New York, 1848.

Trenerry, Walter N. *Murder in Minnesota.* St. Paul: Minnesota Historical Society, 1962.

Turnbull, Robert J. *A Visit to the Philadelphia Prison.* Philadelphia: Budd and Bartram, 1796.

Upham, Thomas C. *The Manual of Peace.* New York: Leavitt, Lord, 1836, pp. 217-251.

Van Den Haag, Ernest. "On Deterrence and the Death Penalty." *Journal of Criminal Law* 60 (June 1969), pp. 141-147.

Wahl, Albert. "The Congregational or Progressive Friends in the Pre-Civil-War Reform Movement." Ph.D. dissertation, Temple University, 1951.

Washington Research Project. *The Case Against Capital Punishment.* Washington, D.C.: Washington Research Project, 1971.

Wayland, Francis. "Opening Address of the President." *Journal of Social Science* 18 (May 1884), pp. 1-18.

Weihofen, Henry. *The Urge to Punish.* New York: Farrar, Straus and Cudahy, 1956, pp. 146-170.

Weiss, Harry B. and Grace M. Weiss. *An Introduction to Crime and Punishment in Colonial New Jersey.* Trenton, N.J.: Past Times, 1960.

[Whelpley, Samuel.] *Letters Addressed to Caleb Strong, Esq.*, 3rd ed. Philadelphia: Kite, 1818 (originally published in 1816).

White, J. B. "Capital Punishment." *Southern Literary Journal* 1 (January 1836), pp. 302-310.

Whitlock, Brand. "Thou Shalt Not Kill." *The Reader* 9 (March 1907), pp. 383-392.

Williams, Brad. *Due Process: The Fabulous Story of Criminal Lawyer George T. Davis and His Thirty-Year Battle Against Capital Punishment.* New York: William Morrow, 1960.

[Williams, Elisha.] *Remarks on Capital Punishment: To which are added, Letters of Morris N. B. Hull,* 2d ed. Utica, N.Y.: W. Williams, 1821.

Williams, Jack Kenny. *Vogues in Villainy: Crime and Retribution in Ante-Bellum South Carolina.* Columbia: University of South Carolina Press, 1959.

Wisconsin. Legislative Reference Library. Information Bulletin No. 210, "Capital Punishment in the States with Special Reference to Wisconsin." Madison, 1962.

York, Robert M. *George B. Cheever, Religious and Social Reformer, 1807-1890.* Orono: Maine University Press, 1955.

Zanger, Jules. "Crime and Punishment in Early Massachusetts." *William and Mary Quarterly,* series 3, 22 (July 1965), pp. 471-477.

INDEX

Abbate v. *United States,* 266
Abel (Old Testament), 78
Abraham (Old Testament), 6, 54
Absalom (Old Testament), 144
Adam (Old Testament), 9
Adams, John Quincy (reform supporter), xxii-xxiii
Addams, Jane (reform supporter), xxxiv
Adler, Herman (reform supporter), xxxviii
Aikens, Earnest, 271, 273, 288
Aikens v. *California,* lii, 264-88, 289, 300
Alabama, mandatory capital punishment abolished in, xxx
Alaska, abolition in, xliii, 245
Alexander, F., 295
Alternate penalty. See Capital punishment, Mandatory, abolition of
American Bar Association, 178
American Civil Liberties Union, vii, xliv, xlviii, 301, 302, 309
American Dilemma, An, 305
Americans for Democratic Action, xliv
American Journal of Orthopsychiatry, 290
American Law Institute, Model Penal Code of, 227
American League to Abolish Capital Punishment: leading reform organization, vii, xxxviii-xxxix, xl, xli, xlviii, 167, 180, 191, 300; publications, xxxix, xli; state affiliates, xxxix, xlvi; associated reformers, 167, 180, 191, 300
American Magazine, 156, 157
American Museum, 1, 13
American Prison Association, xxxvii
American Psychiatric Association, 289
American Society for the Abolition of Capital Punishment, xxv
Amsterdam, Anthony G. (reform supporter), l-liii, 264

Anderson, Rufus B., 138
Angelini, Amerigo, 326
Annals of the American Academy of Political and Social Science, xlii, 210
Anthony, Susan B., 120
Anti-Capital Punishment League, xxxiv
Anti-capital punishment movement. See Capital punishment, Movement to abolish or limit
Anti-capital punishment organizations. See Capital punishment, Opposition to
Anti-Capital Punishment Society of America, xxxiv
Anti-communism, effect on reform, xli, xlii
Anti-Death Penalty League, xxxiii
Anti-slavery movement: effect on reform, xxviii, 110, 123; mentioned, 1, 13, 70, 91, 132, 133
Appelbaum, Mischa (reform supporter), xxxiv-xxxv
Ararat, Mount, 144
Argentina, 245
Arizona: abolition in, xxxiii; referendum in, xxxiii; reform activity in, xxxiv; restoration in, xxxvii
Arkansas, incidence of capital punishment in, 227-28
Arson, inappropriateness of capital punishment as punishment for, 48. *See also* Capital Punishment, Crimes punishable by, and Capital punishment, Crimes punished by
Asia, 154, 182-83
Athens, 30
Atlantic Monthly, 150
Auburn Prison (N.Y.), xxxi-xxxii, 192
Austin, Neveda, 138
Azari, Giovani, 325

Baker, George (reform supporter), xxv
Baker, Ray Stannard, 156
"Ballad of Caryl Chessman, The," xlv

345

900 dl
0450